Norihiro Yagi won the 32nd Akatsuka Award for his debut work, *UNDEADMAN*, which appeared in *Monthly Shonen Jump* magazine and produced two sequels. His first serialized manga was his comedy *Angel Densetsu* (Angel Legend), which appeared in *Monthly Shonen Jump* from 1992 to 2000. His epic saga, *Claymore*, is running in *Monthly Jump Square* magazine.

In his spare time, Yagi enjoys things like the Japanese comedic duo Downtown, martial arts, games, driving, and hard rock music, but he doesn't consider these actual hobbies.

CLAYMORE VOL. 13
The SHONEN JUMP ADVANCED Manga Edition

STORY AND ART BY
NORIHIRO YAGI

English Adaptation & Translation/Arashi Productions
Touch-up Art & Lettering/Sabrina Heep
Design/Izumi Evers
Editor/Leyla Aker

Editor in Chief, Books/Alvin Lu
Editor in Chief, Magazines/Marc Weidenbaum
VP, Publishing Licensing/Rika Inouye
VP, Sales & Product Marketing/Gonzalo Ferreyra
VP, Creative/Linda Espinosa
Publisher/Hyoe Narita

Printed in the U.S.A.

Published by VIZ Media, LLC
P.O. Box 77010
San Francisco, CA 94107

SHONEN JUMP ADVANCED Manga Edition
10 9 8 7 6 5 4 3 2 1
First printing, November 2008

THE WORLD'S MOST
CUTTING-EDGE MANGA

www.shonenjump.com

SHONEN JUMP ADVANCED Manga Edition

クレイモア
Claymor

Vol. 13
The Defiant Ones

Story and Art by Norihiro Yagi

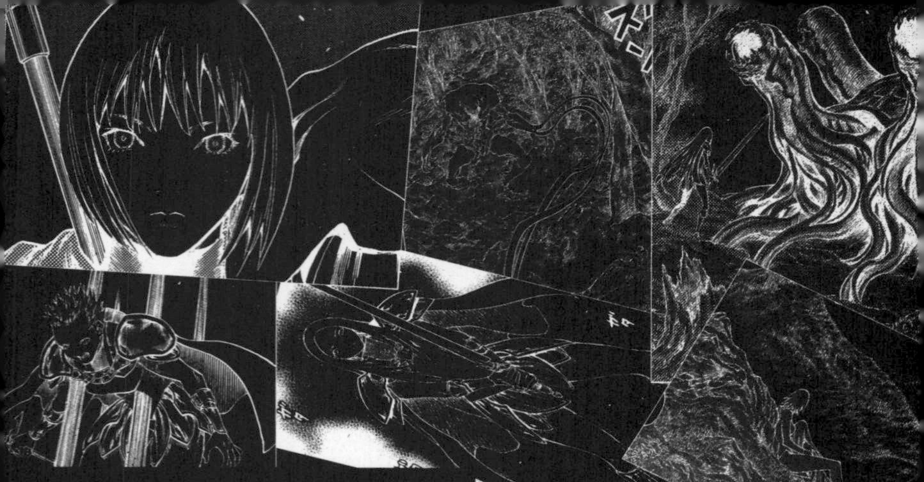

Seven years after the Battle of the North, Clare and her comrades decide to end their isolation. Moving south, they come upon a battle being waged between a new group of warriors and one of the Three Great Awakened Ones. Perceiving that it is Riful of the West, and that the warriors are about to be wiped out, they rush to the scene...

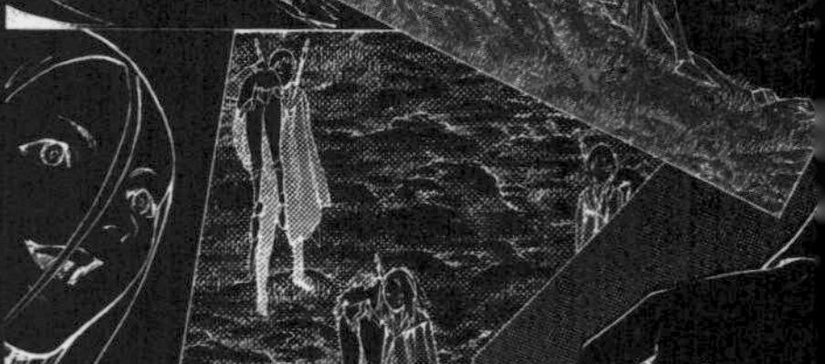

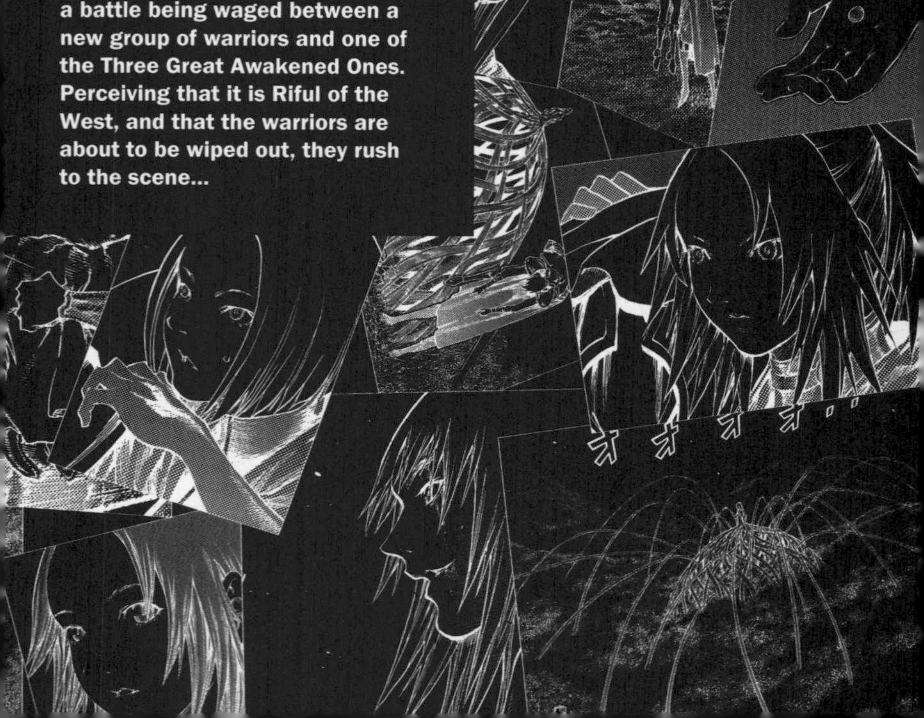

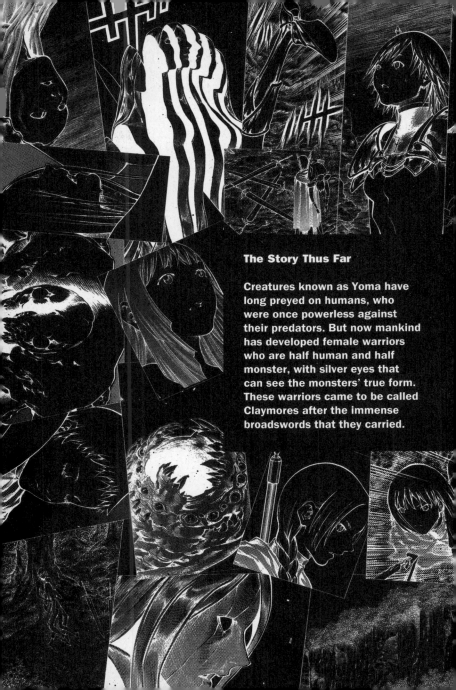

The Story Thus Far

Creatures known as Yoma have long preyed on humans, who were once powerless against their predators. But now mankind has developed female warriors who are half human and half monster, with silver eyes that can see the monsters' true form. These warriors came to be called Claymores after the immense broadswords that they carried.

Claymore
クレイモア

Vol. 13

CONTENTS

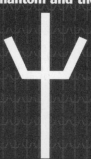

SCENE 70: THE DEFIANT ONES, PART 3

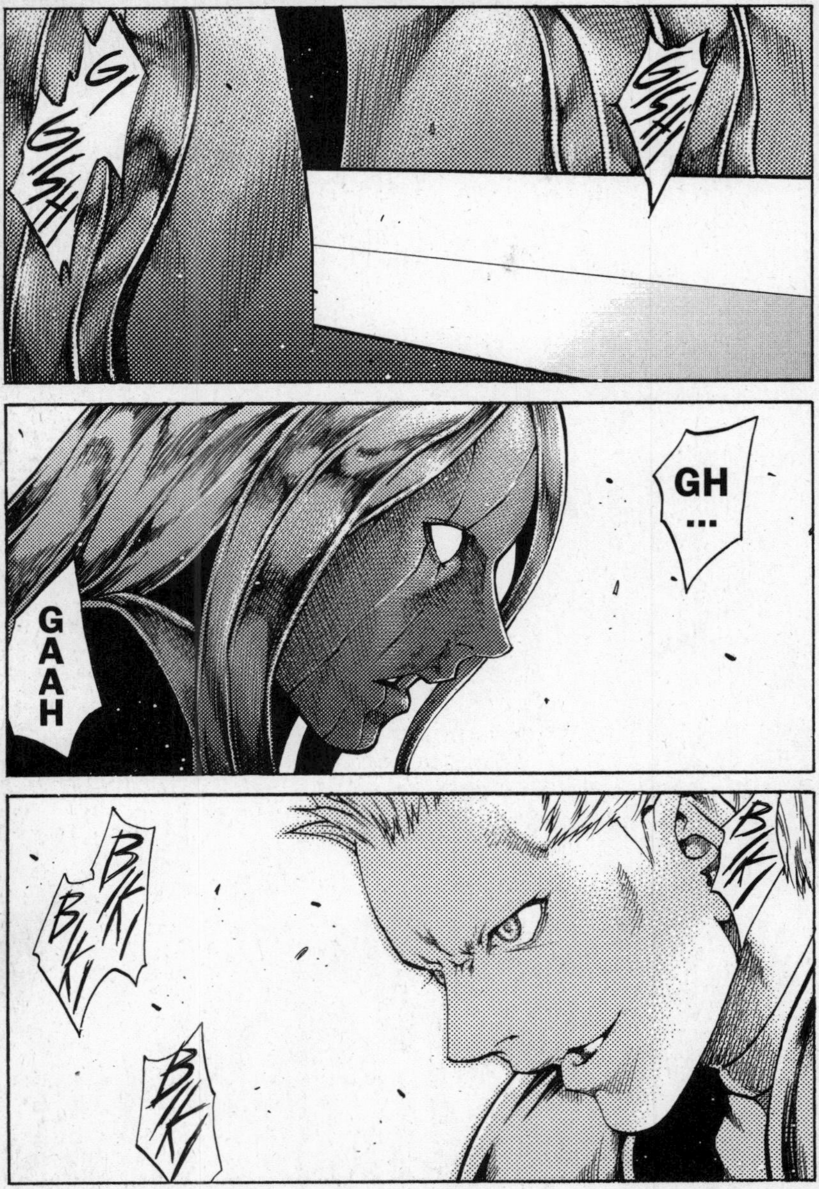
GISH
GI GISH
GH ...
GAAH
BIKI
BIKI BIKI
BIKI

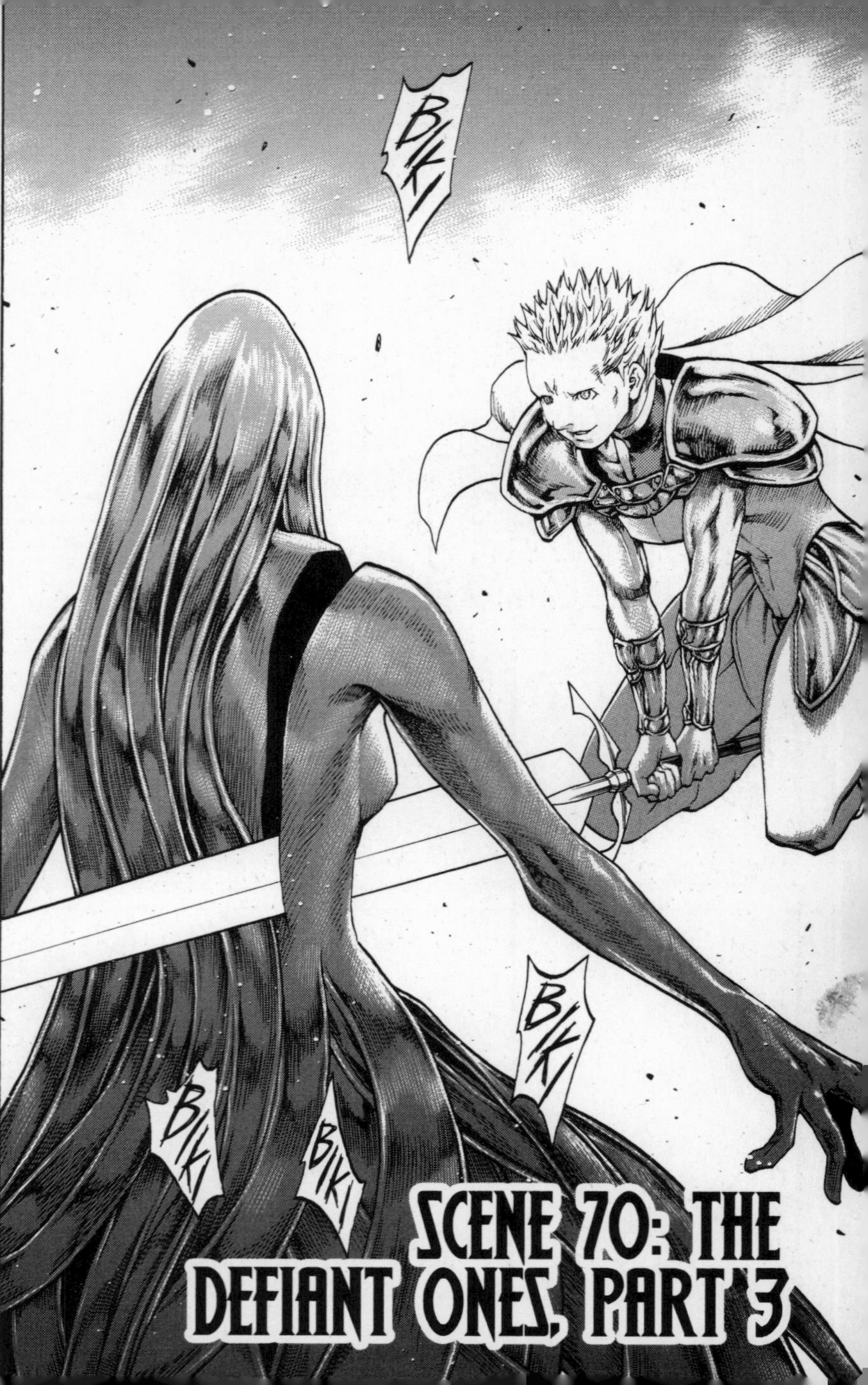
BIKI
BIKI
BIKI
BIKI
SCENE 70: THE DEFIANT ONES, PART 3

READ THIS WAY

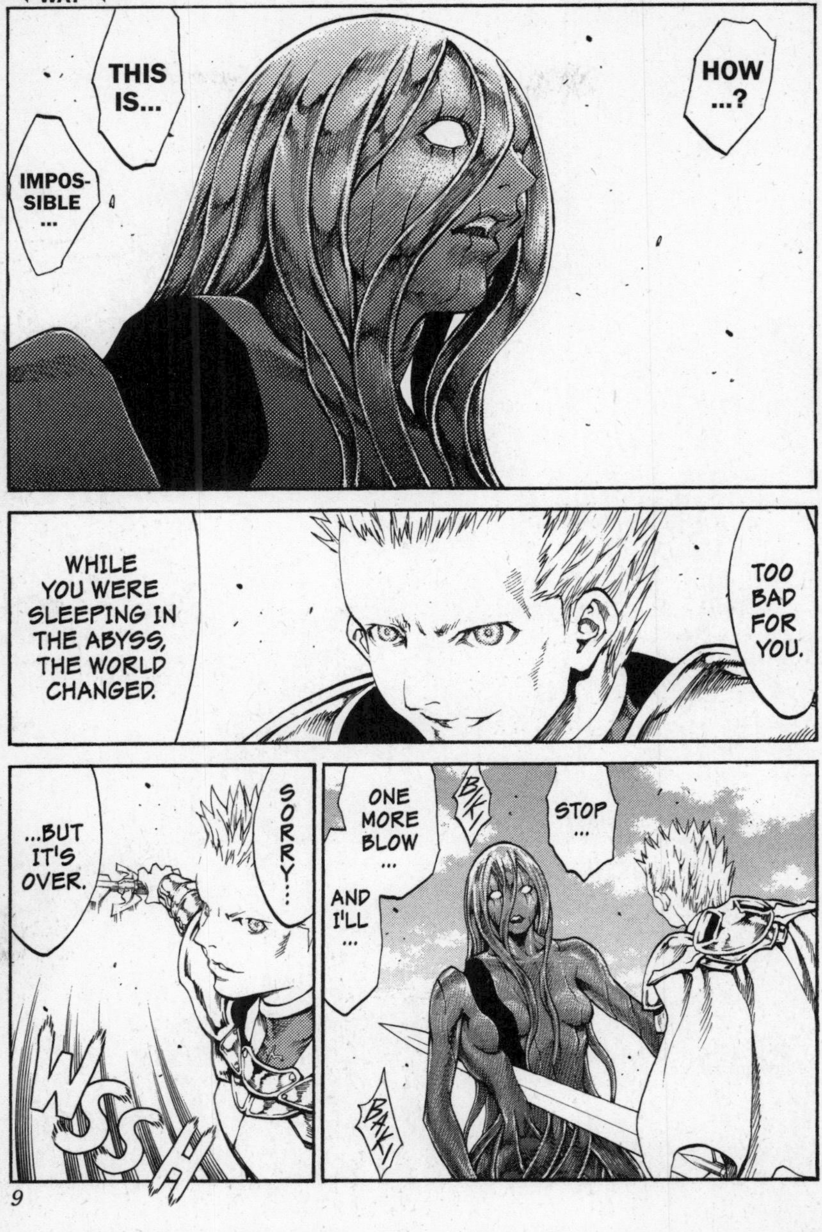
HOW ...?
THIS IS...
IMPOSSIBLE ...
TOO BAD FOR YOU.
WHILE YOU WERE SLEEPING IN THE ABYSS, THE WORLD CHANGED.
STOP ...
BAKI
ONE MORE BLOW ...
AND I'LL ...
BAKI
SORRY...
...BUT IT'S OVER.
WSSH

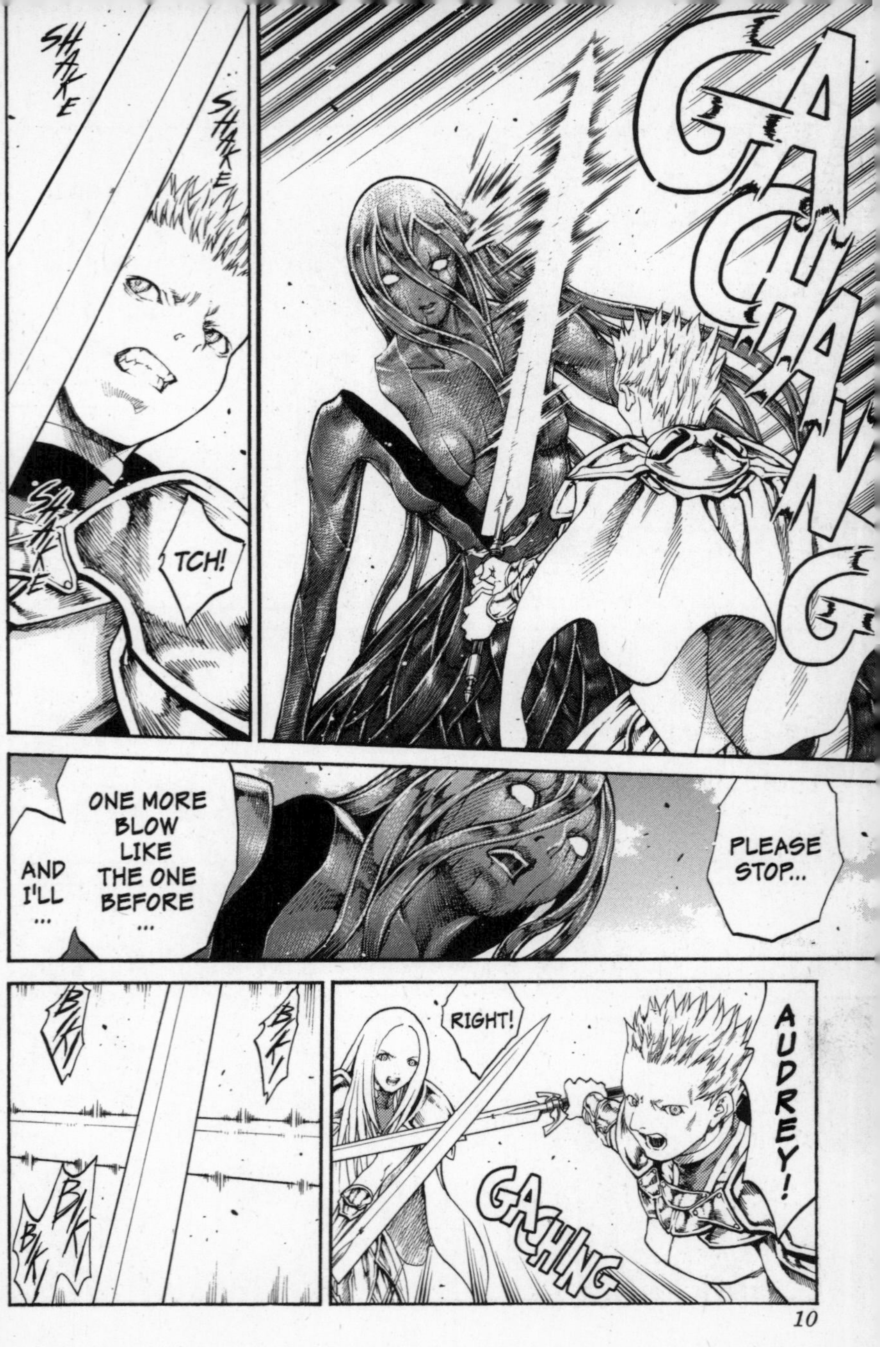
GACHANG
SHAKE
SHAKE
TCH!
SHAKE
PLEASE STOP...
ONE MORE BLOW LIKE THE ONE BEFORE ...
AND I'LL ...
AUDREY!
RIGHT!
GACHING
BIKI
BIKI
BIKI
BIKI

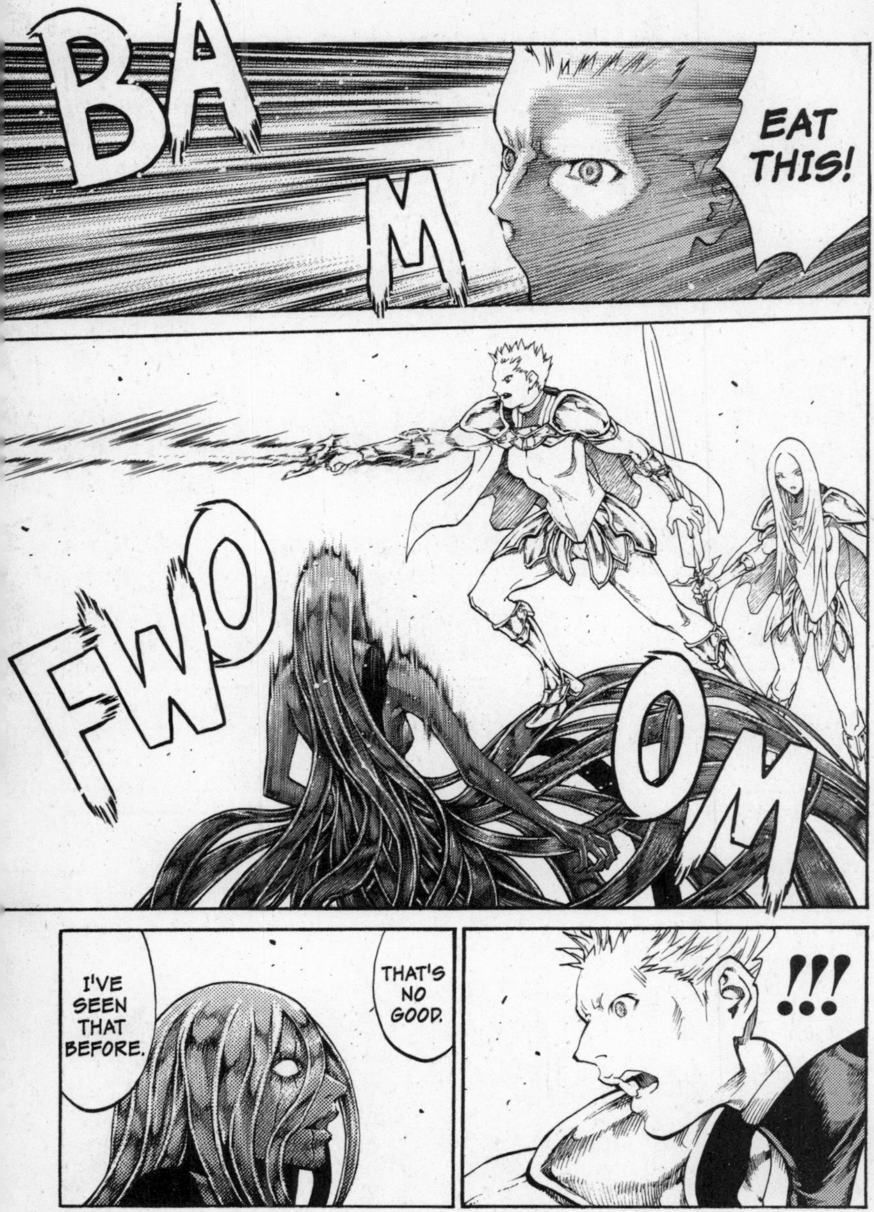
EAT THIS!
BAM
FWOOM
!!!
THAT'S NO GOOD.
I'VE SEEN THAT BEFORE.

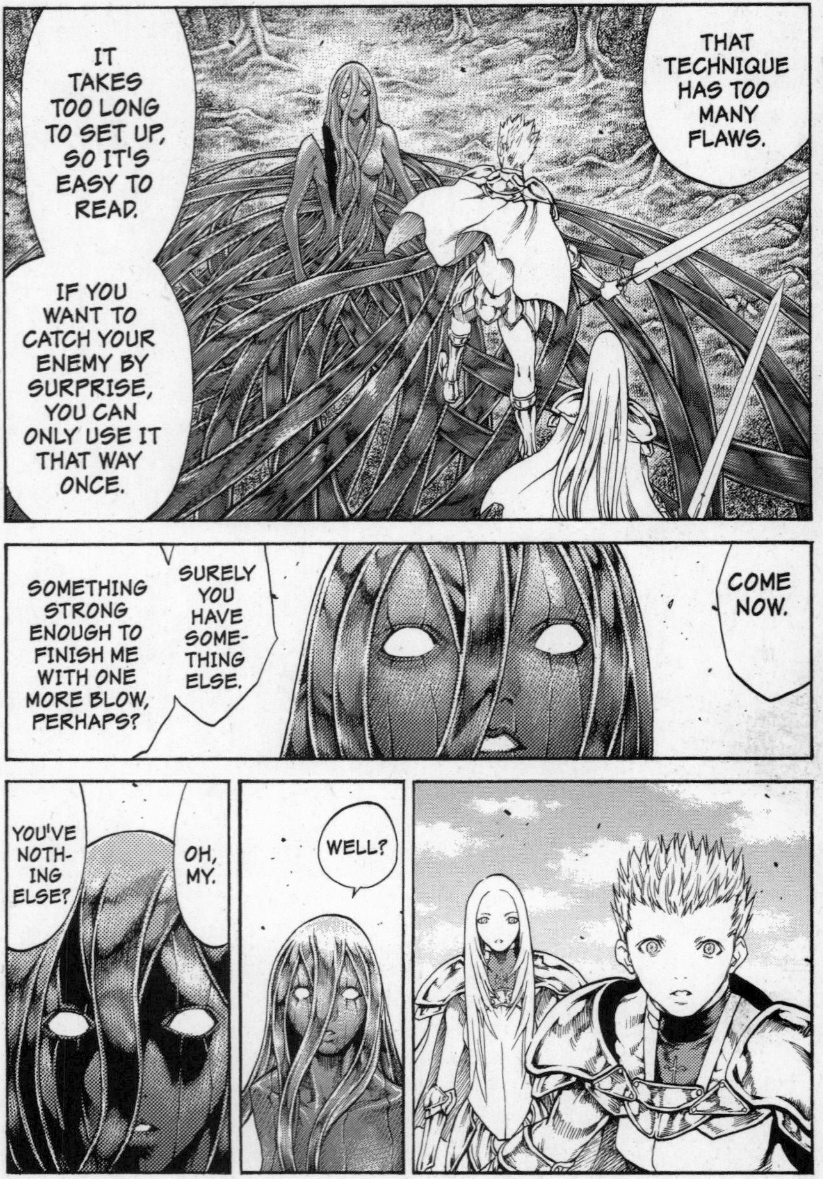
THAT TECHNIQUE HAS TOO MANY FLAWS.
IT TAKES TOO LONG TO SET UP, SO IT'S EASY TO READ.
IF YOU WANT TO CATCH YOUR ENEMY BY SURPRISE, YOU CAN ONLY USE IT THAT WAY ONCE.
COME NOW.
SURELY YOU HAVE SOME-THING ELSE.
SOMETHING STRONG ENOUGH TO FINISH ME WITH ONE MORE BLOW, PERHAPS?
WELL?
OH, MY.
YOU'VE NOTH-ING ELSE?

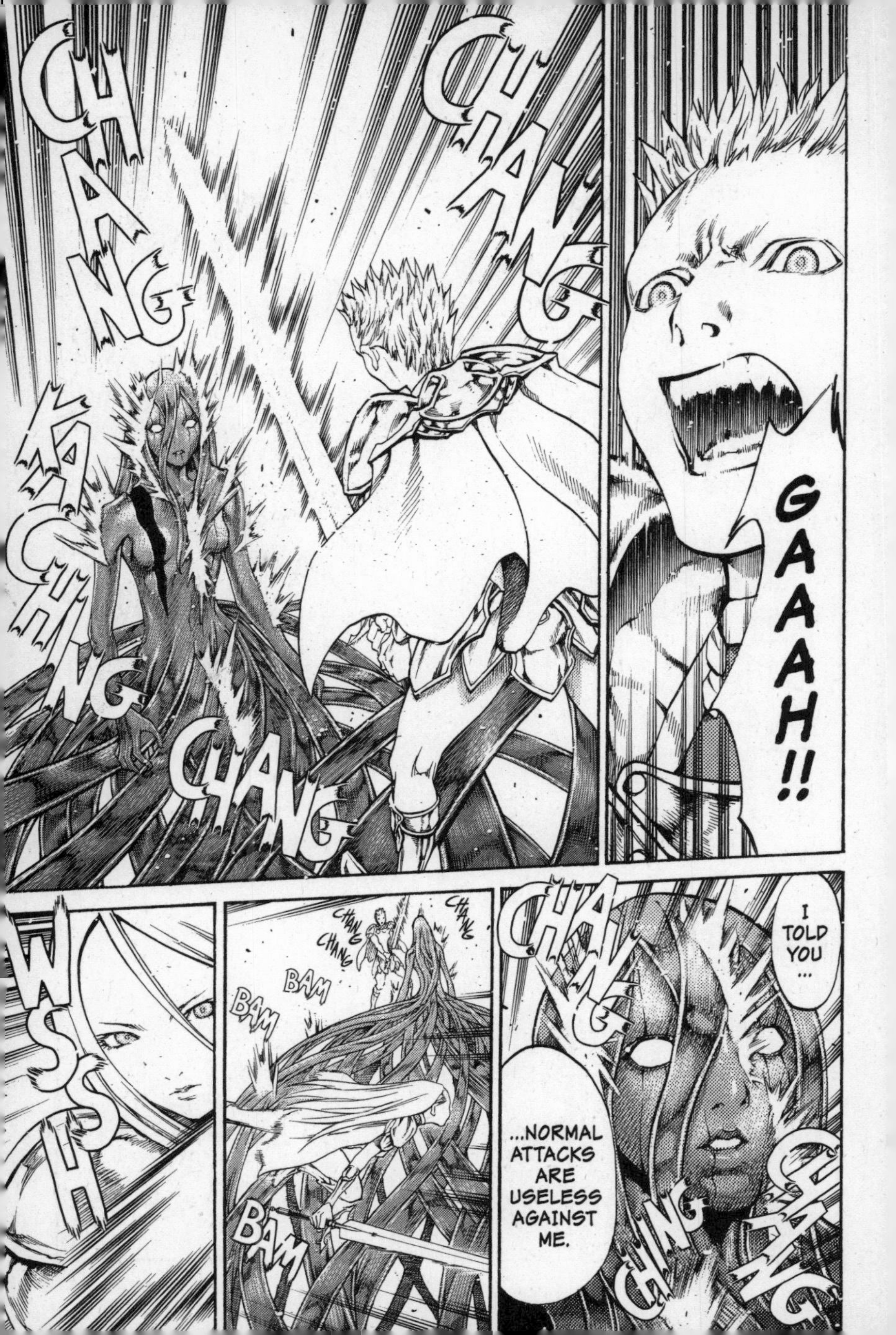
GAAAH!!
CHANG
CHANG
KACHING
CHANG
CHANG
I TOLD YOU ...
...NORMAL ATTACKS ARE USELESS AGAINST ME.
CHING
CHANG
CHANG
CHANG
CHANG
BAM
BAM
BAM
BAM
WSSH

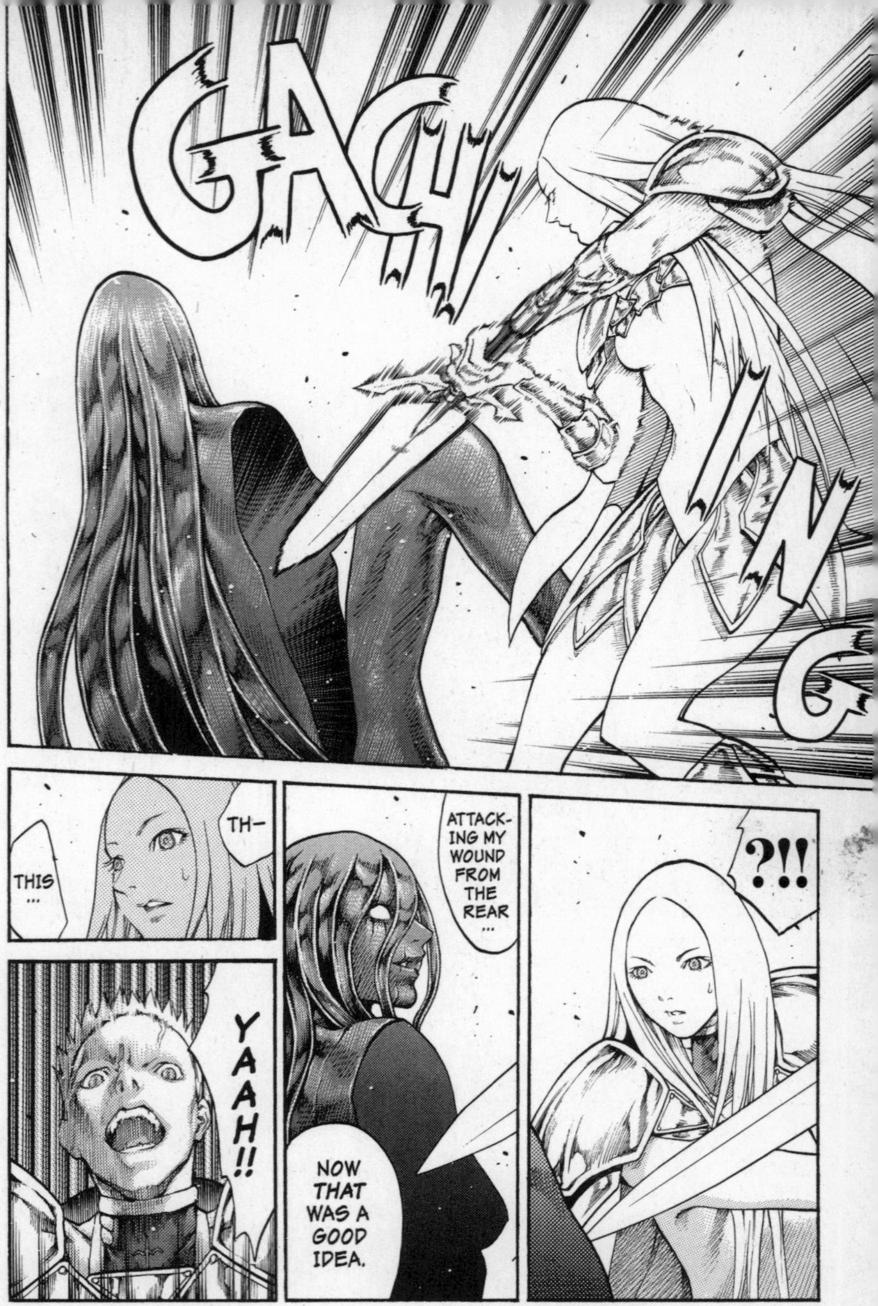
GACHI
ING
?!!
ATTACKING MY WOUND FROM THE REAR ...
NOW THAT WAS A GOOD IDEA.
TH—
THIS ...
YAAH!!

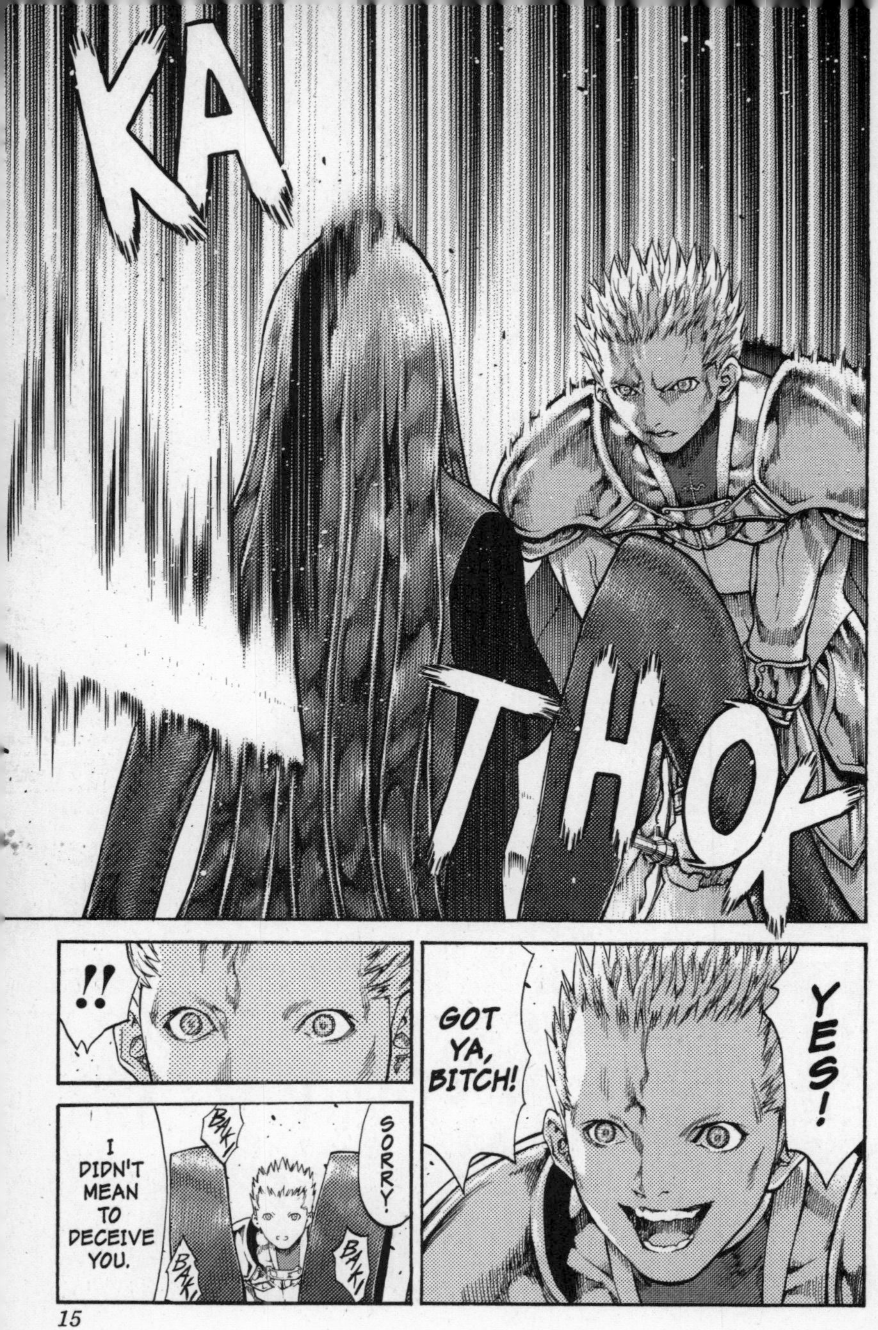
KA
THOK
YES!
GOT YA, BITCH!
!!
SORRY.
BAKI
I DIDN'T MEAN TO DECEIVE YOU.
BAKI
BAKI

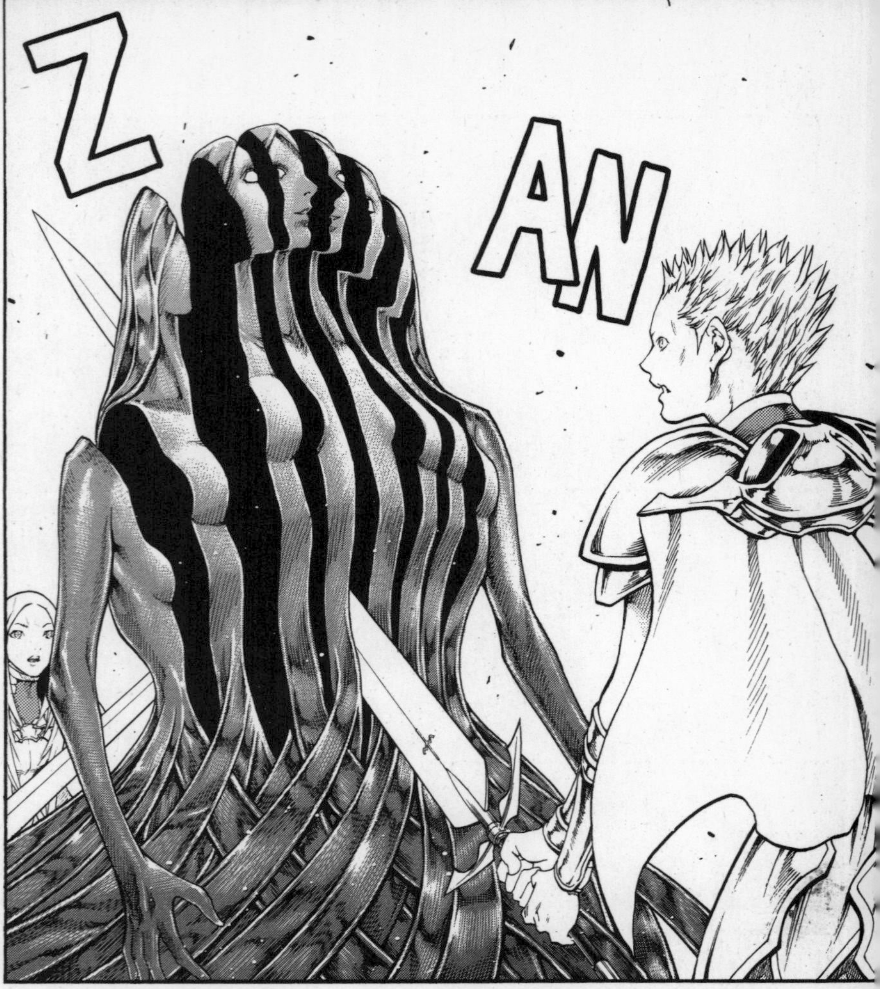
ZAN

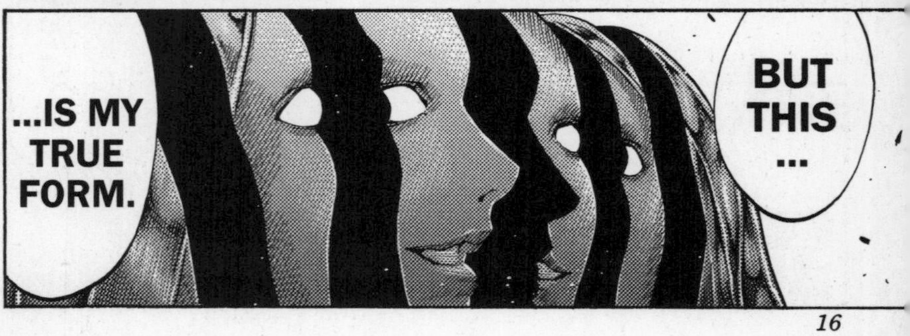
BUT THIS ...
...IS MY TRUE FORM.

READ THIS WAY

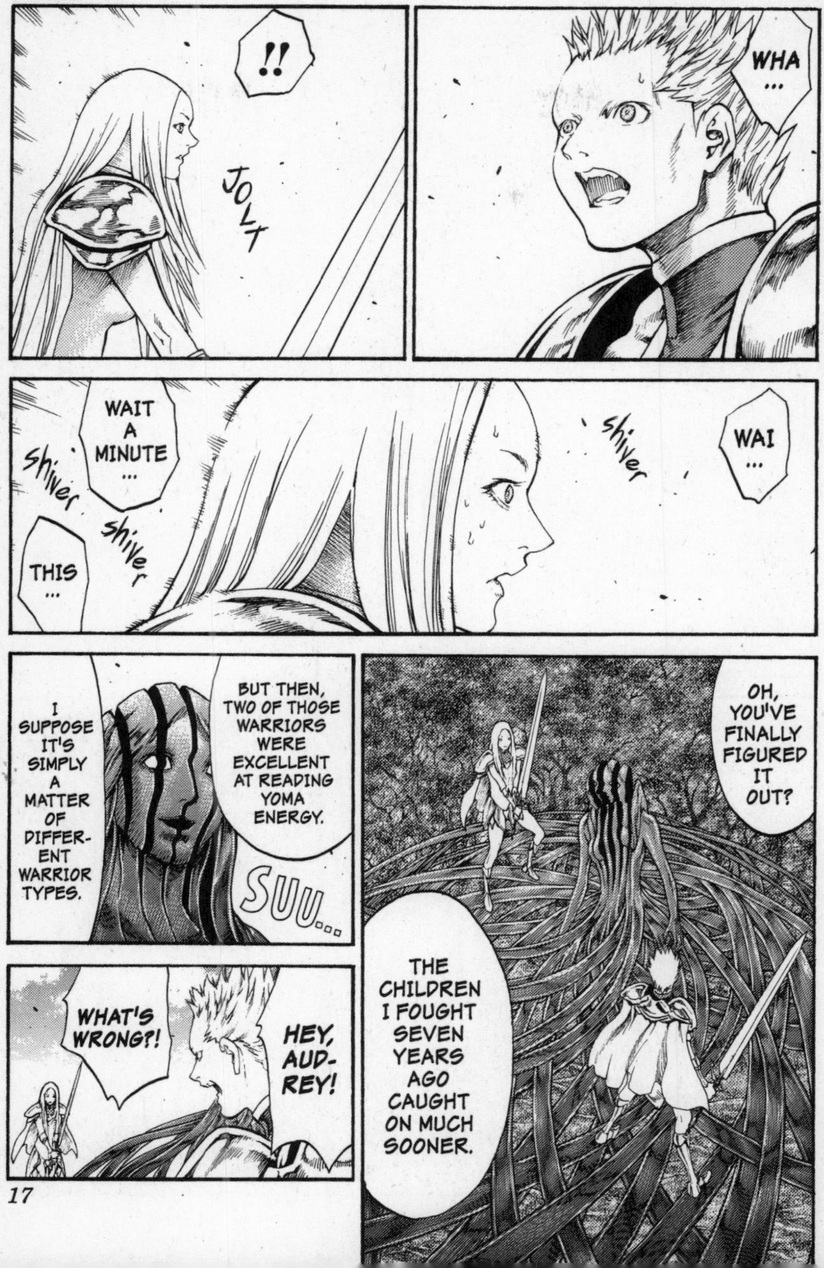

WHA ...
!!
JOLT
WAI ...
shiver
WAIT A MINUTE ...
shiver
shiver
THIS ...
OH, YOU'VE FINALLY FIGURED IT OUT?
THE CHILDREN I FOUGHT SEVEN YEARS AGO CAUGHT ON MUCH SOONER.
BUT THEN, TWO OF THOSE WARRIORS WERE EXCELLENT AT READING YOMA ENERGY.
I SUPPOSE IT'S SIMPLY A MATTER OF DIFFERENT WARRIOR TYPES.
SUU...
HEY, AUD-REY!
WHAT'S WRONG?!

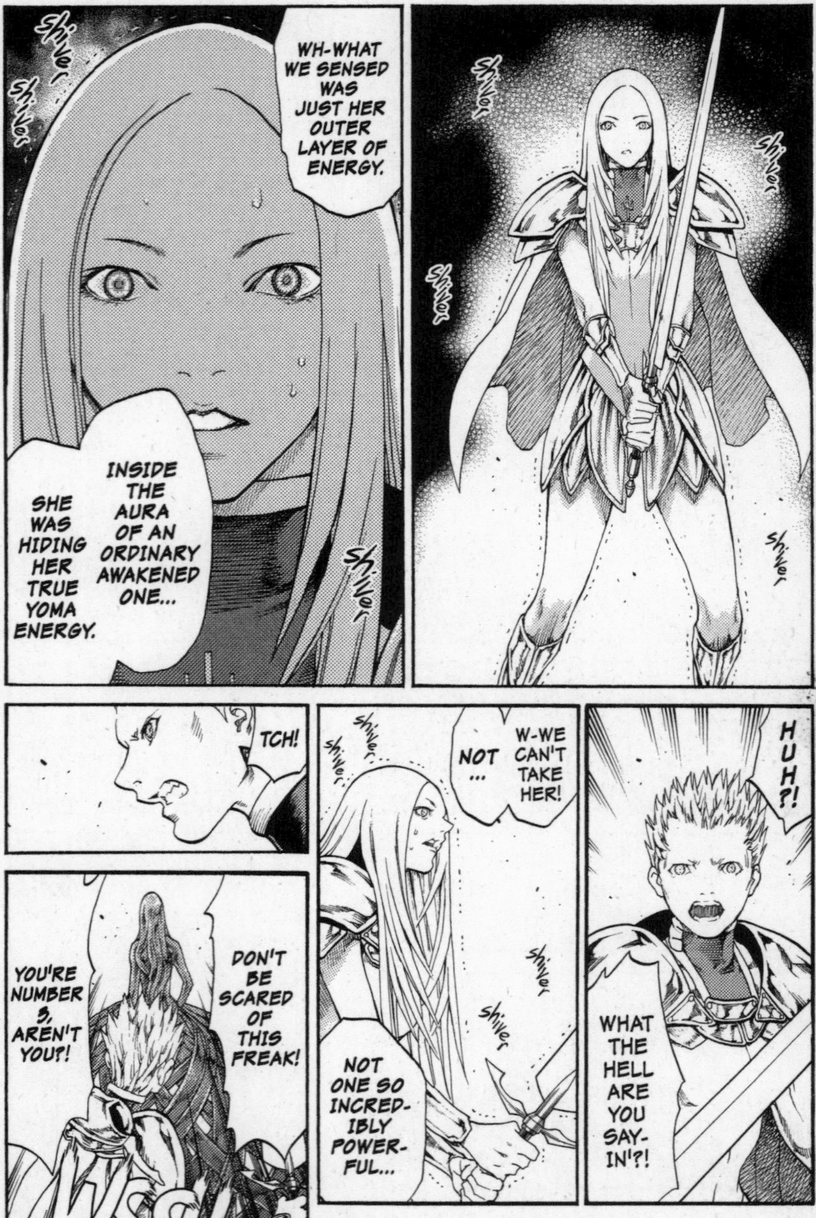
shiver
shiver
shiver
shiver
WH-WHAT WE SENSED WAS JUST HER OUTER LAYER OF ENERGY.
shiver
shiver
INSIDE THE AURA OF AN ORDINARY AWAKENED ONE...
SHE WAS HIDING HER TRUE YOMA ENERGY.
shiver
HUH?!
WHAT THE HELL ARE YOU SAYIN'?!
W-WE CAN'T TAKE HER!
NOT ...
shiver
shiver
shiver
shiver
NOT ONE SO INCREDIBLY POWERFUL...
TCH!
DON'T BE SCARED OF THIS FREAK!
YOU'RE NUMBER 3, AREN'T YOU?!
WSSH

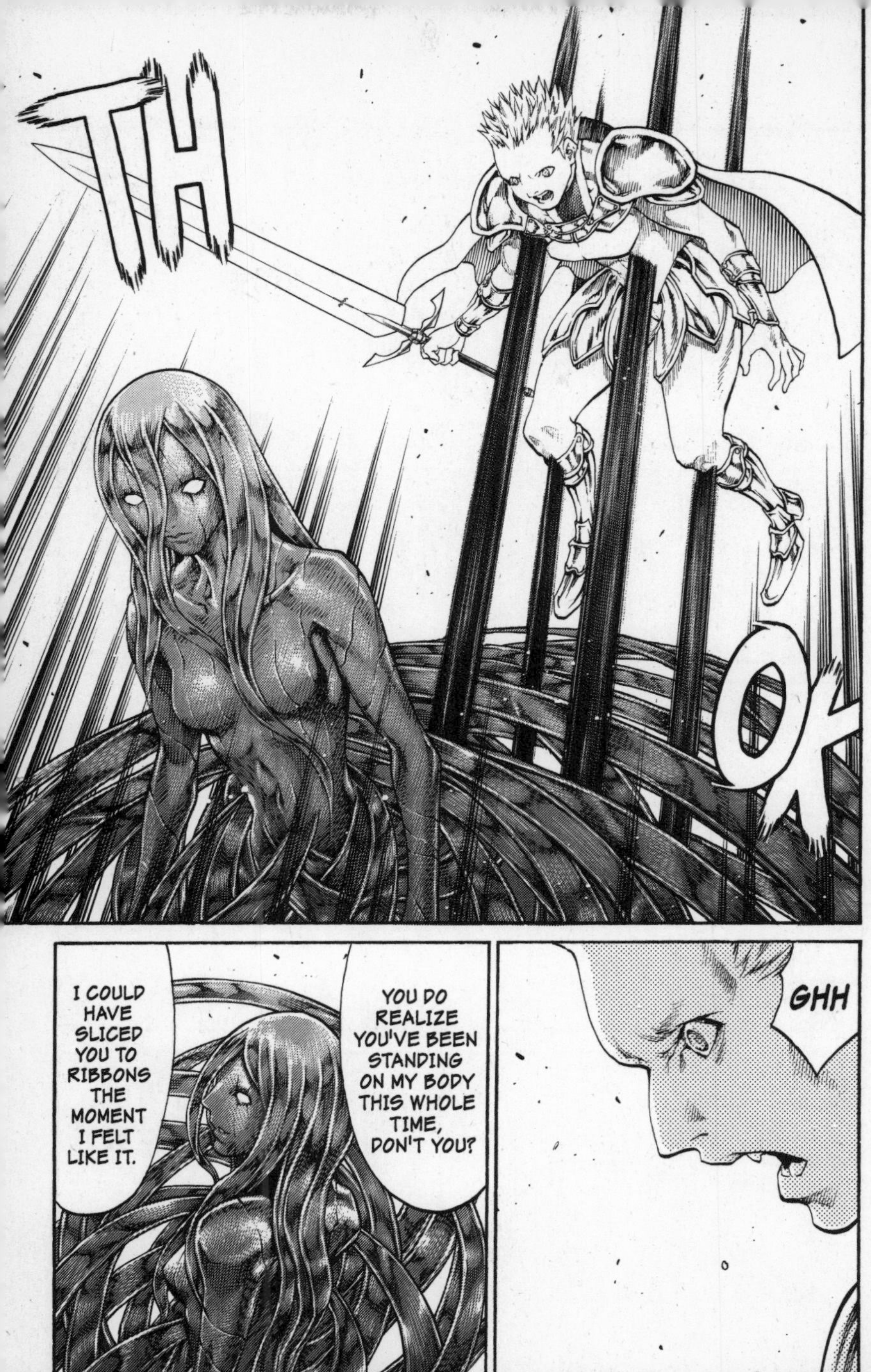
TH
OK
GHH
YOU DO REALIZE YOU'VE BEEN STANDING ON MY BODY THIS WHOLE TIME, DON'T YOU?
I COULD HAVE SLICED YOU TO RIBBONS THE MOMENT I FELT LIKE IT.

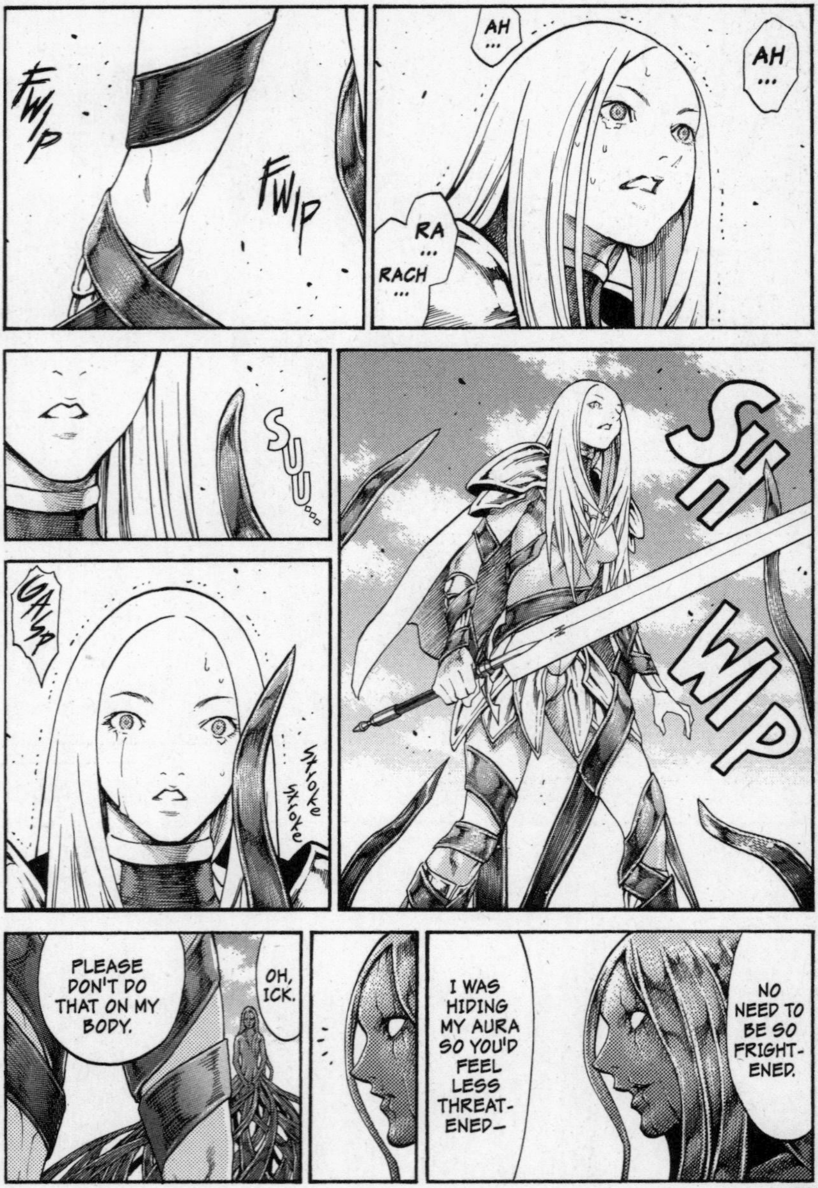
AH ...
AH ...
RA ... RACH ...
FWIP
FWIP
SHWIP
SUUU...
GASP
stroke stroke
NO NEED TO BE SO FRIGHT-ENED.
I WAS HIDING MY AURA SO YOU'D FEEL LESS THREAT-ENED—
OH, ICK.
PLEASE DON'T DO THAT ON MY BODY.

READ THIS WAY

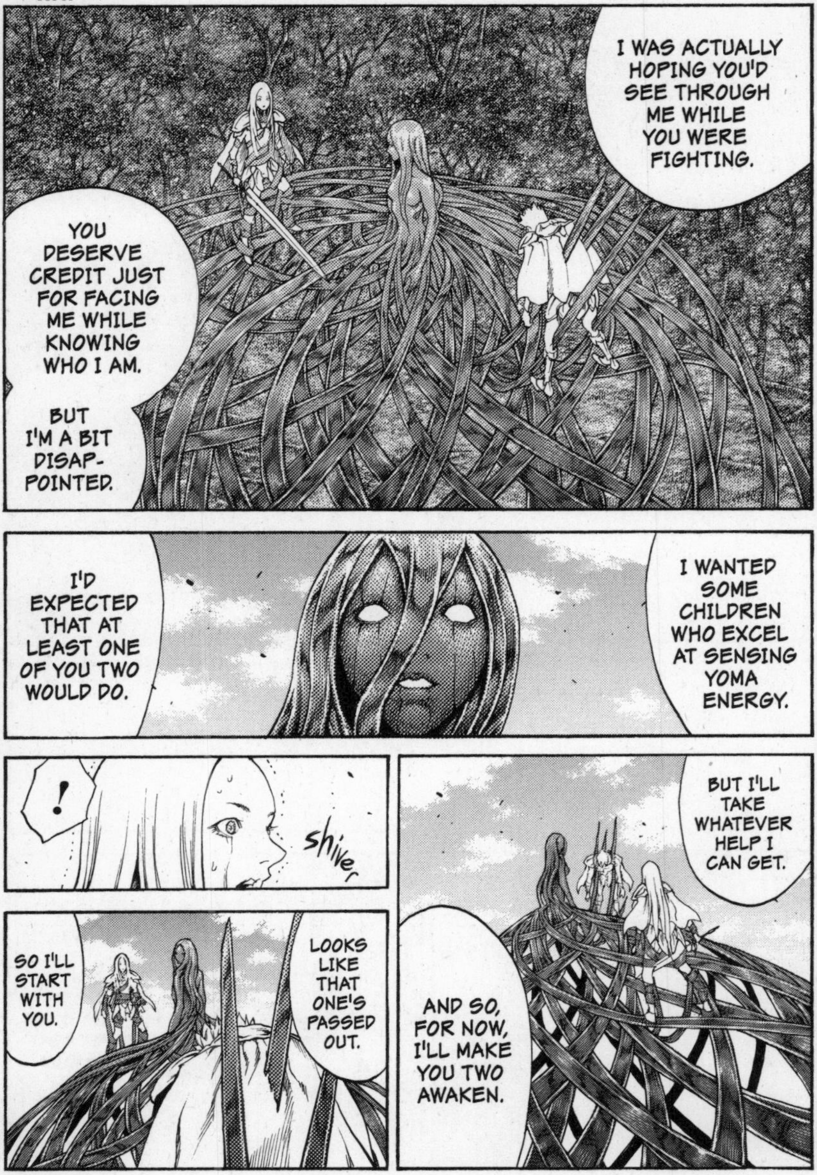
I WAS ACTUALLY HOPING YOU'D SEE THROUGH ME WHILE YOU WERE FIGHTING.
YOU DESERVE CREDIT JUST FOR FACING ME WHILE KNOWING WHO I AM.
BUT I'M A BIT DISAP-POINTED.
I WANTED SOME CHILDREN WHO EXCEL AT SENSING YOMA ENERGY.
I'D EXPECTED THAT AT LEAST ONE OF YOU TWO WOULD DO.
BUT I'LL TAKE WHATEVER HELP I CAN GET.
AND SO, FOR NOW, I'LL MAKE YOU TWO AWAKEN.
!
shiver
LOOKS LIKE THAT ONE'S PASSED OUT.
SO I'LL START WITH YOU.

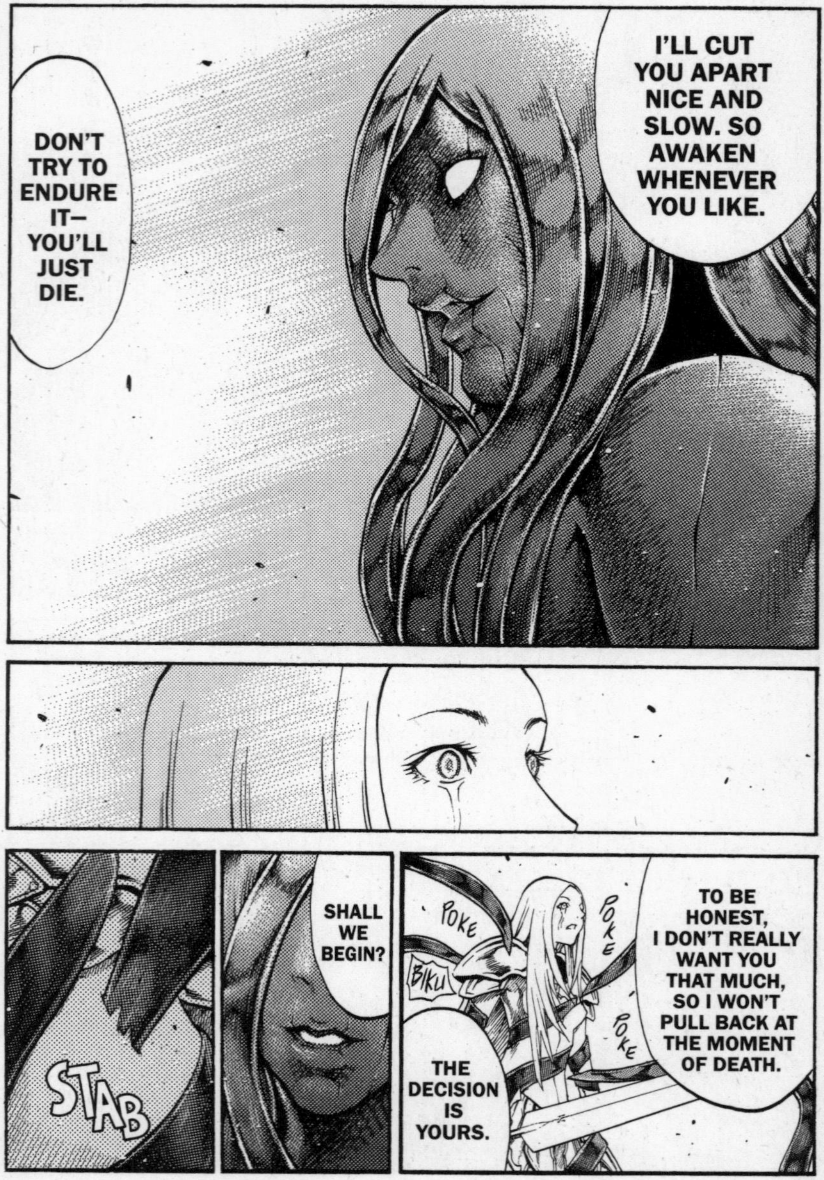
I'LL CUT YOU APART NICE AND SLOW. SO AWAKEN WHENEVER YOU LIKE.
DON'T TRY TO ENDURE IT— YOU'LL JUST DIE.
TO BE HONEST, I DON'T REALLY WANT YOU THAT MUCH, SO I WON'T PULL BACK AT THE MOMENT OF DEATH.
POKE
POKE
POKE
BIKU
THE DECISION IS YOURS.
SHALL WE BEGIN?
STAB

READ THIS WAY

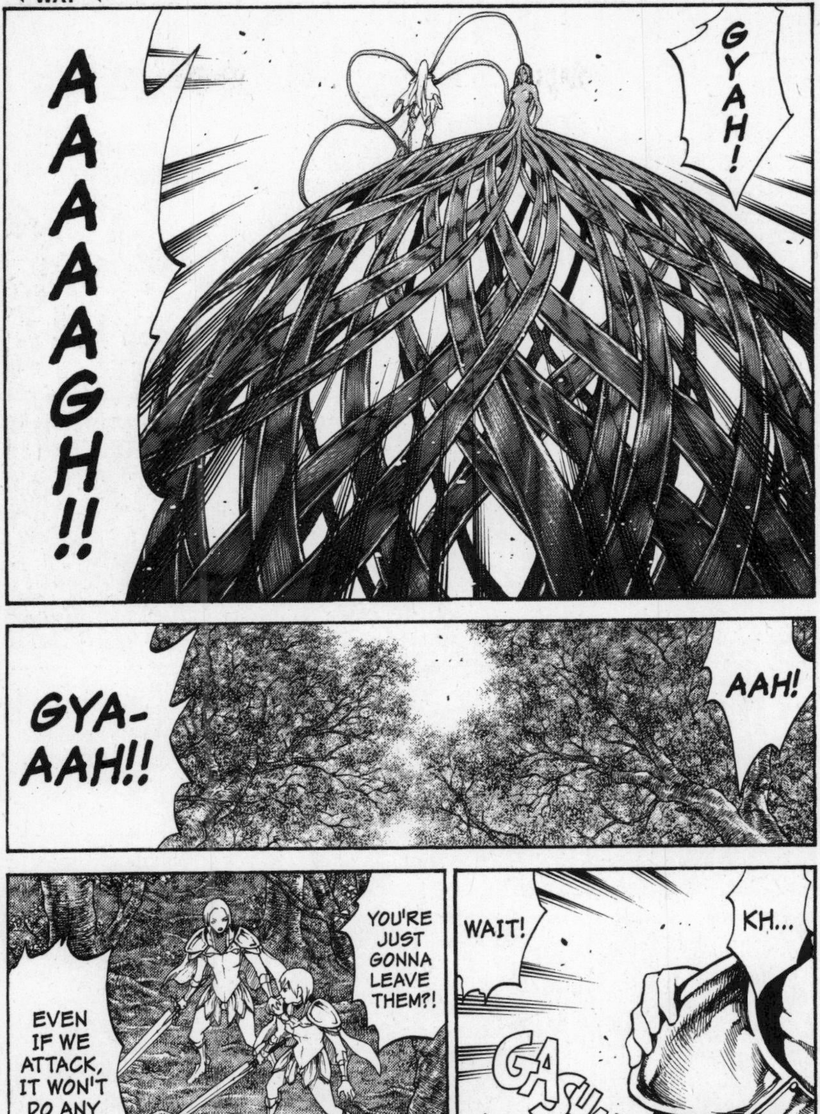
GYAH!
AAAAAGH!!
AAH!
GYA-AAH!!
KH...
WAIT!
GASHAK
YOU'RE JUST GONNA LEAVE THEM?!
EVEN IF WE ATTACK, IT WON'T DO ANY GOOD!

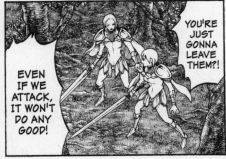

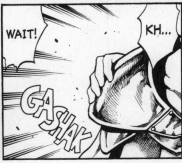

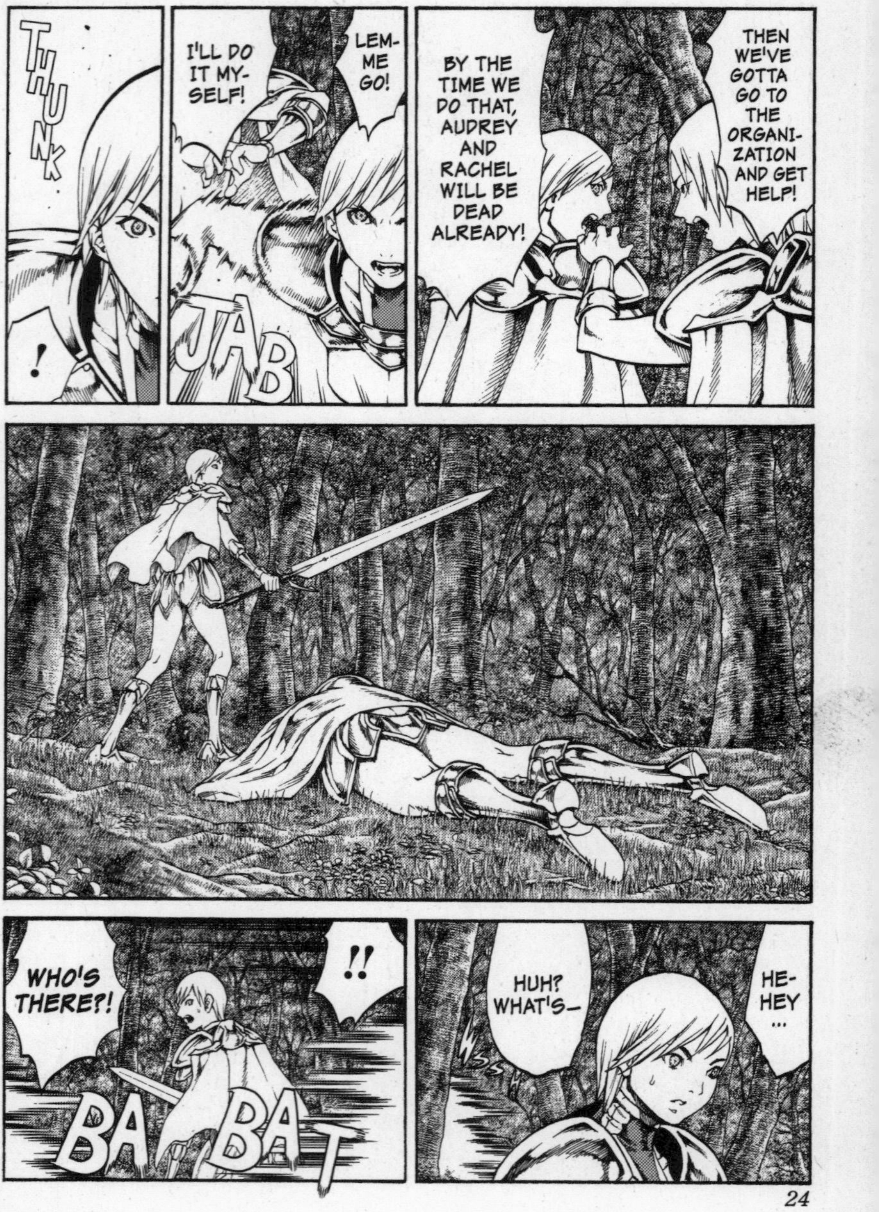
THEN WE'VE GOTTA GO TO THE ORGANIZATION AND GET HELP!
BY THE TIME WE DO THAT, AUDREY AND RACHEL WILL BE DEAD ALREADY!
LEMME GO!
I'LL DO IT MYSELF!
JAB
THUNK
!
HE-HEY ...
HUH? WHAT'S—
!!
WHO'S THERE?!
BA BAT

READ THIS WAY

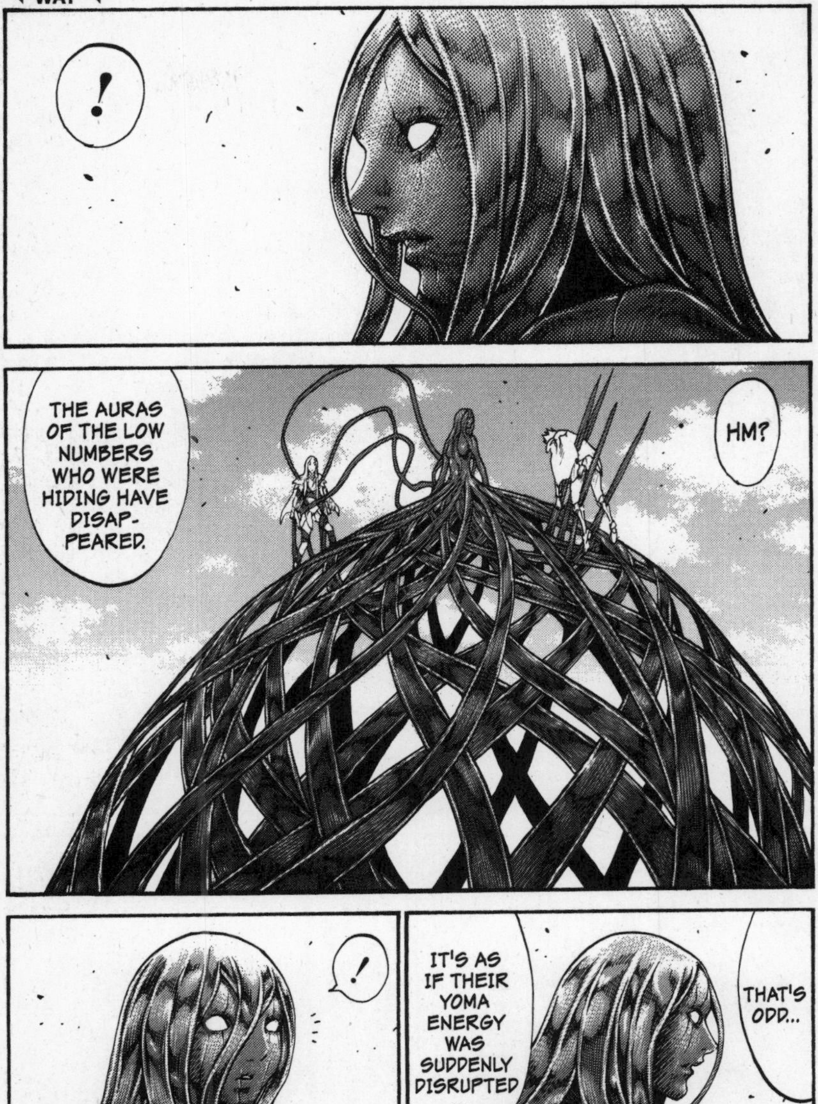
!
HM?
THE AURAS OF THE LOW NUMBERS WHO WERE HIDING HAVE DISAP-PEARED.
THAT'S ODD...
IT'S AS IF THEIR YOMA ENERGY WAS SUDDENLY DISRUPTED ...
!

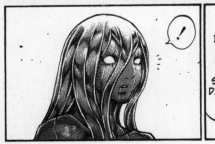

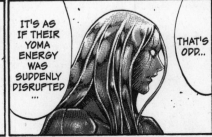

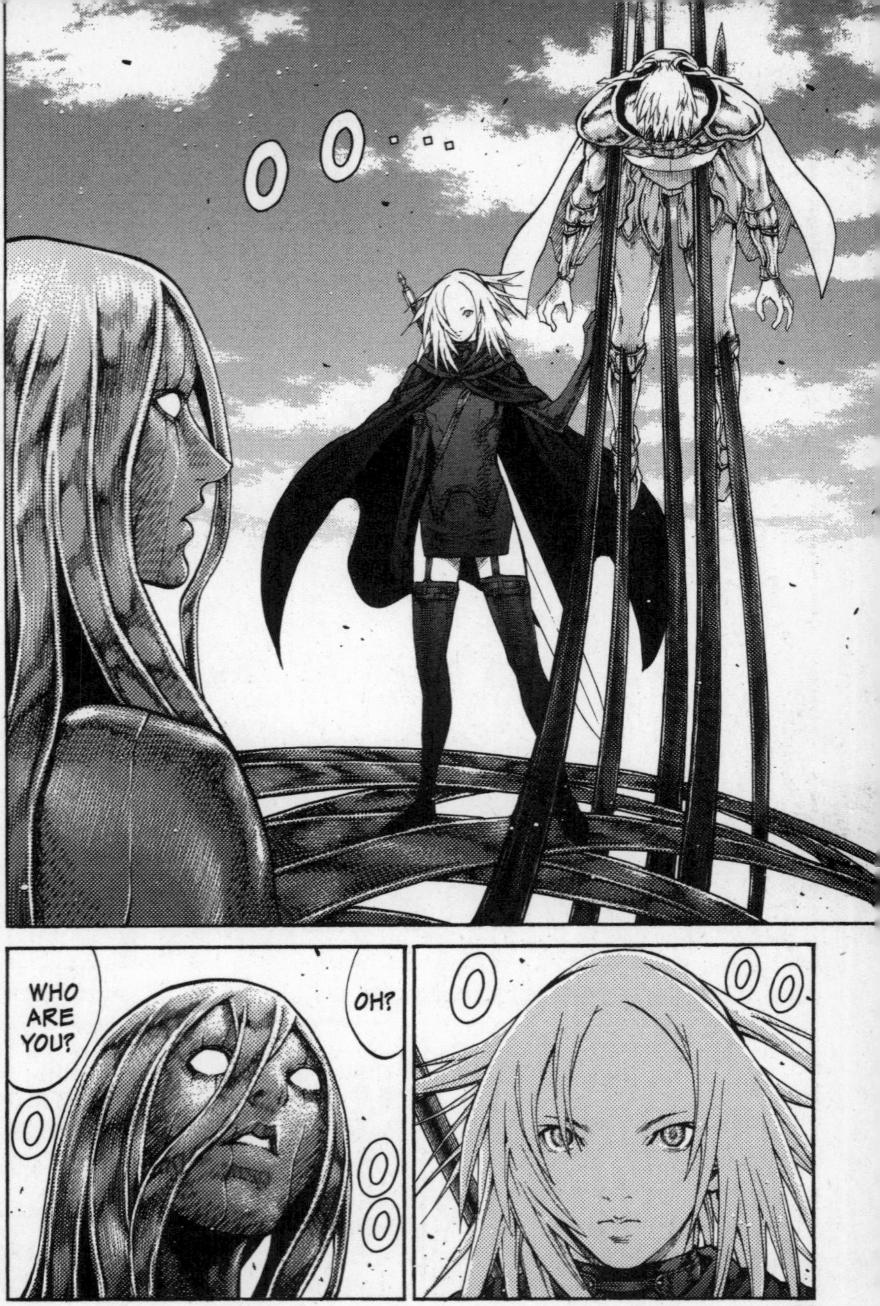
OH?
WHO ARE YOU?

WSSSH

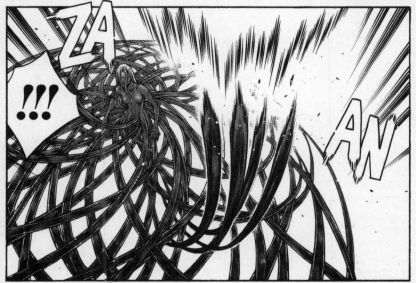

ZA
!!!
AN

WRRR

YOU CAN'T JUST WALTZ OFF WITH MY PREY!

JUST A MINUTE!

27

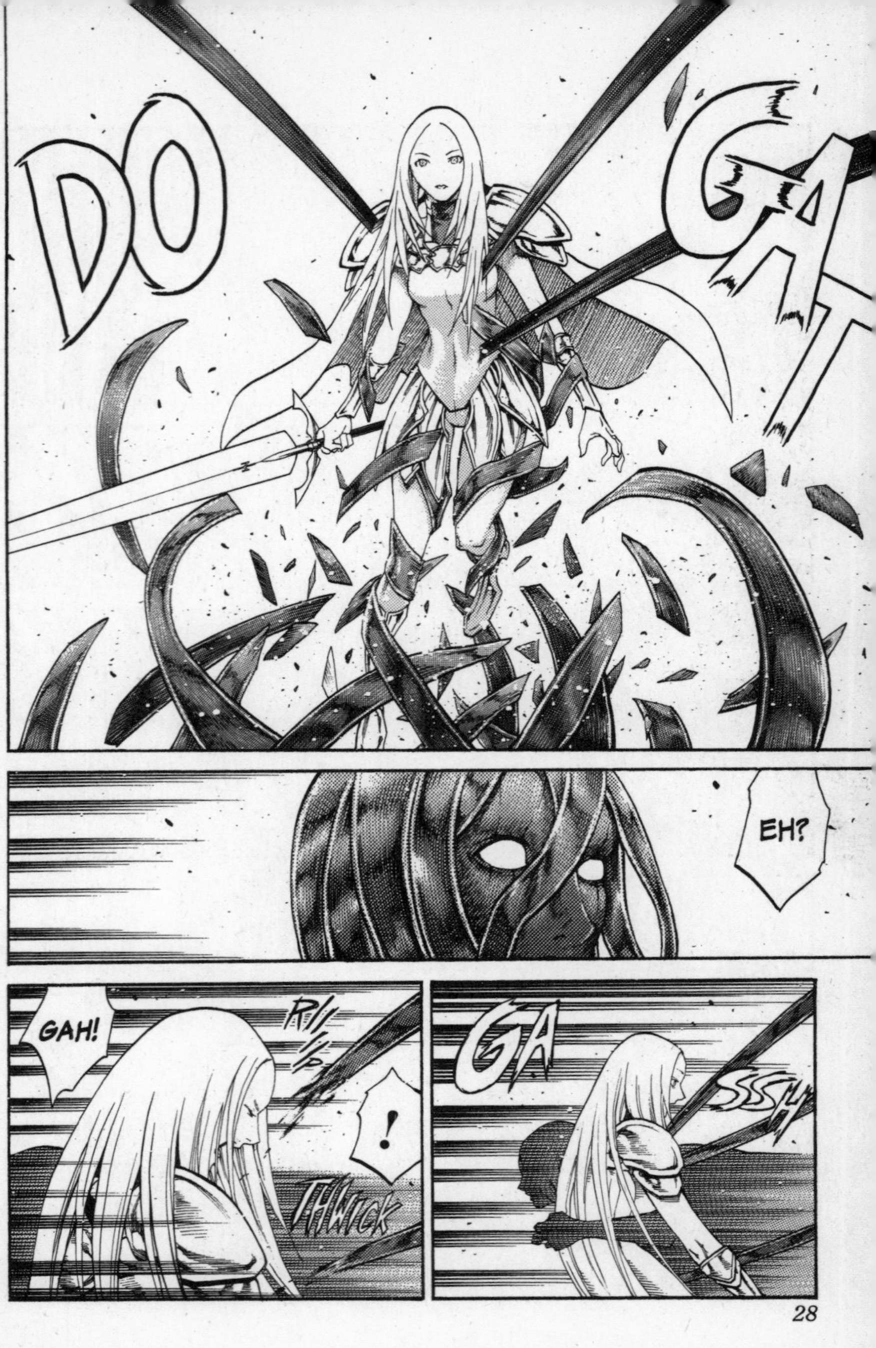
DO
GA
EH?
GA
SSSH
GAH!
RIIP
!
THWICK

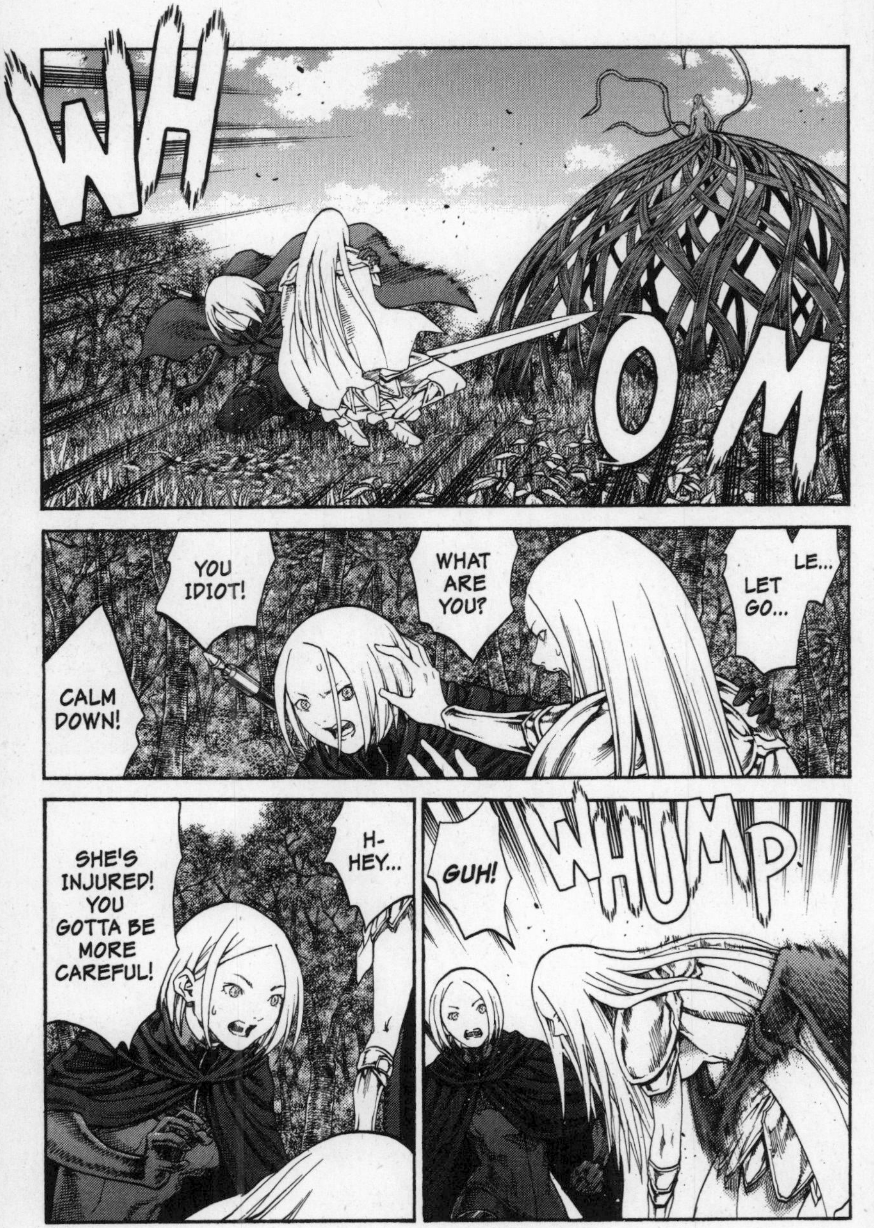
WHOM
LE... LET GO...
WHAT ARE YOU?
YOU IDIOT!
CALM DOWN!
WHUMP
GUH!
H- HEY...
SHE'S INJURED! YOU GOTTA BE MORE CAREFUL!

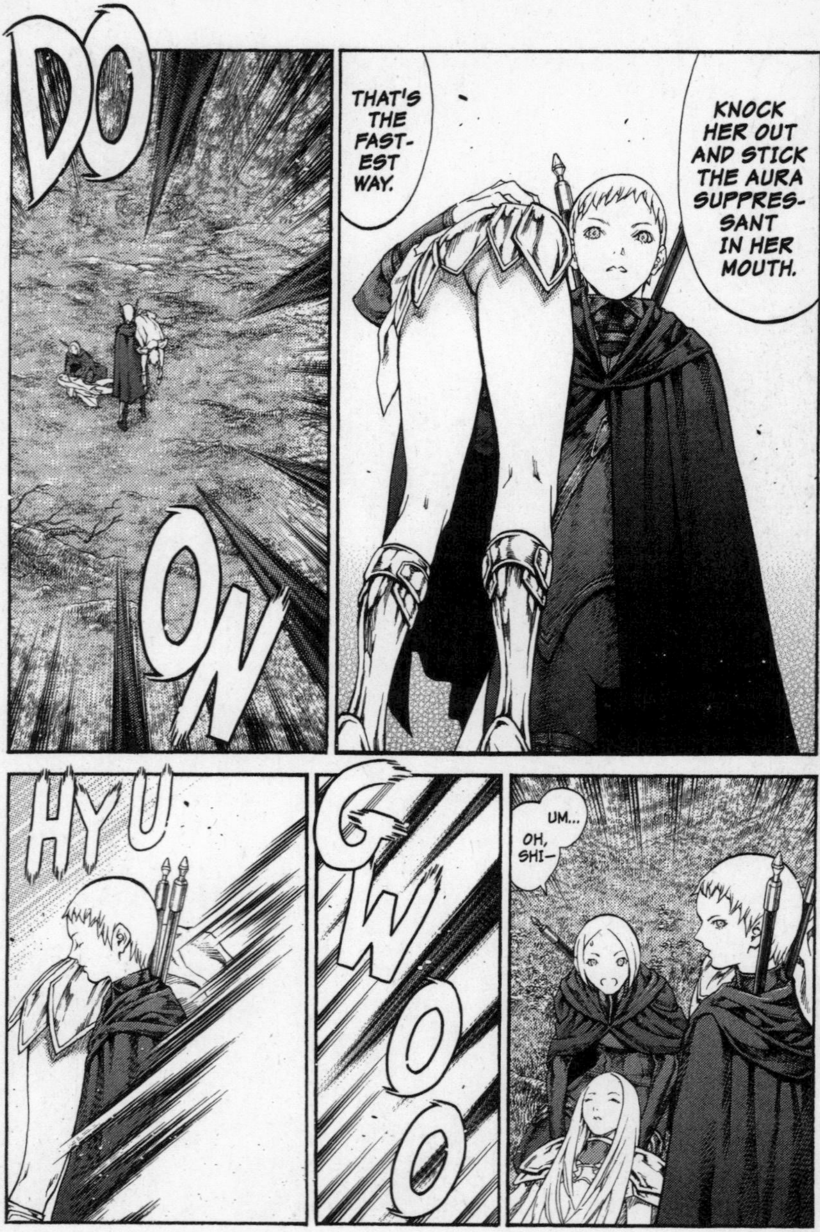
KNOCK HER OUT AND STICK THE AURA SUPPRES-SANT IN HER MOUTH.
THAT'S THE FAST-EST WAY.
DO
ON
UM... OH, SHI-
GWOOO
HYU

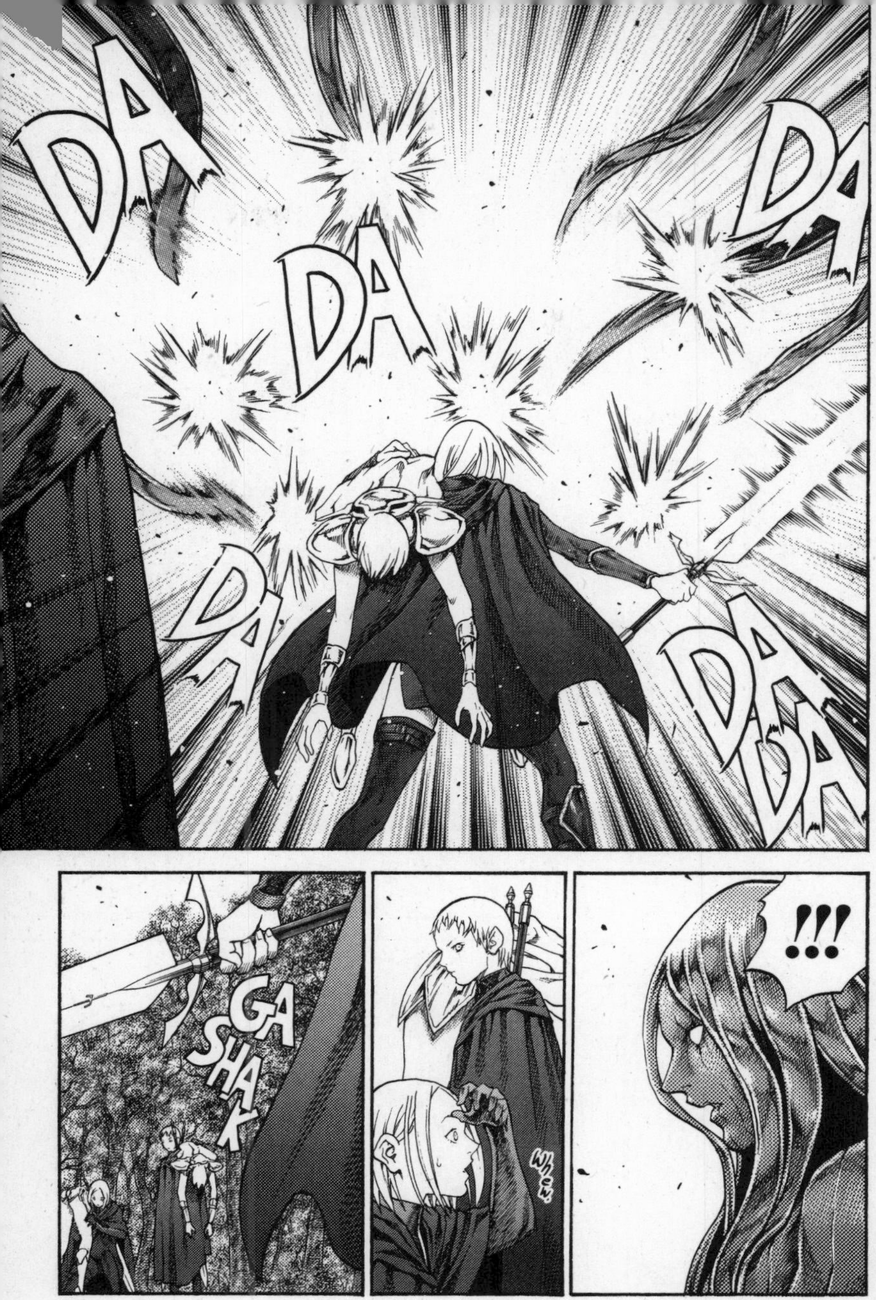
DA
DA
DA
DA
DA
DA DA DA
!!!
Whew.
GA SHAK

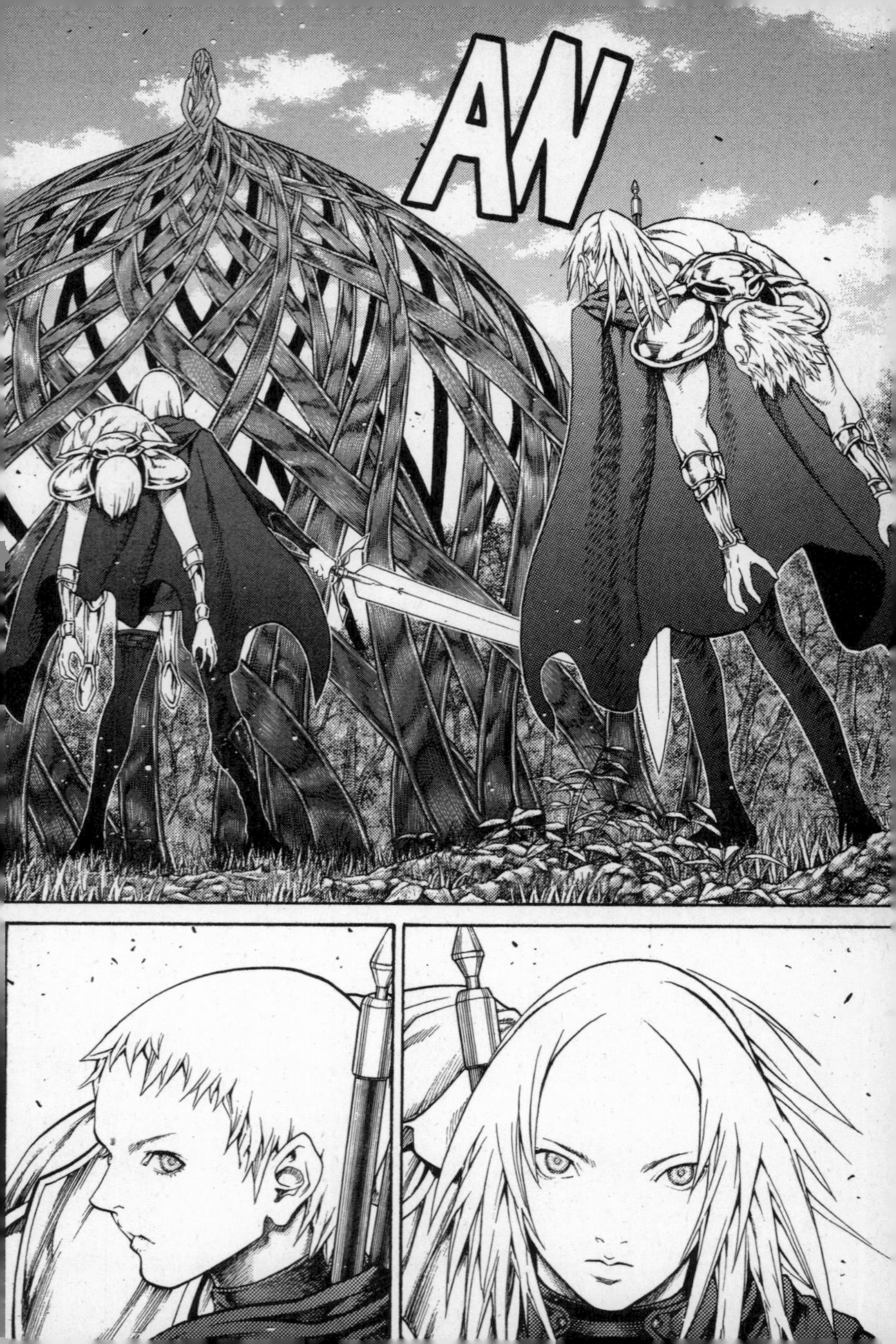
AN

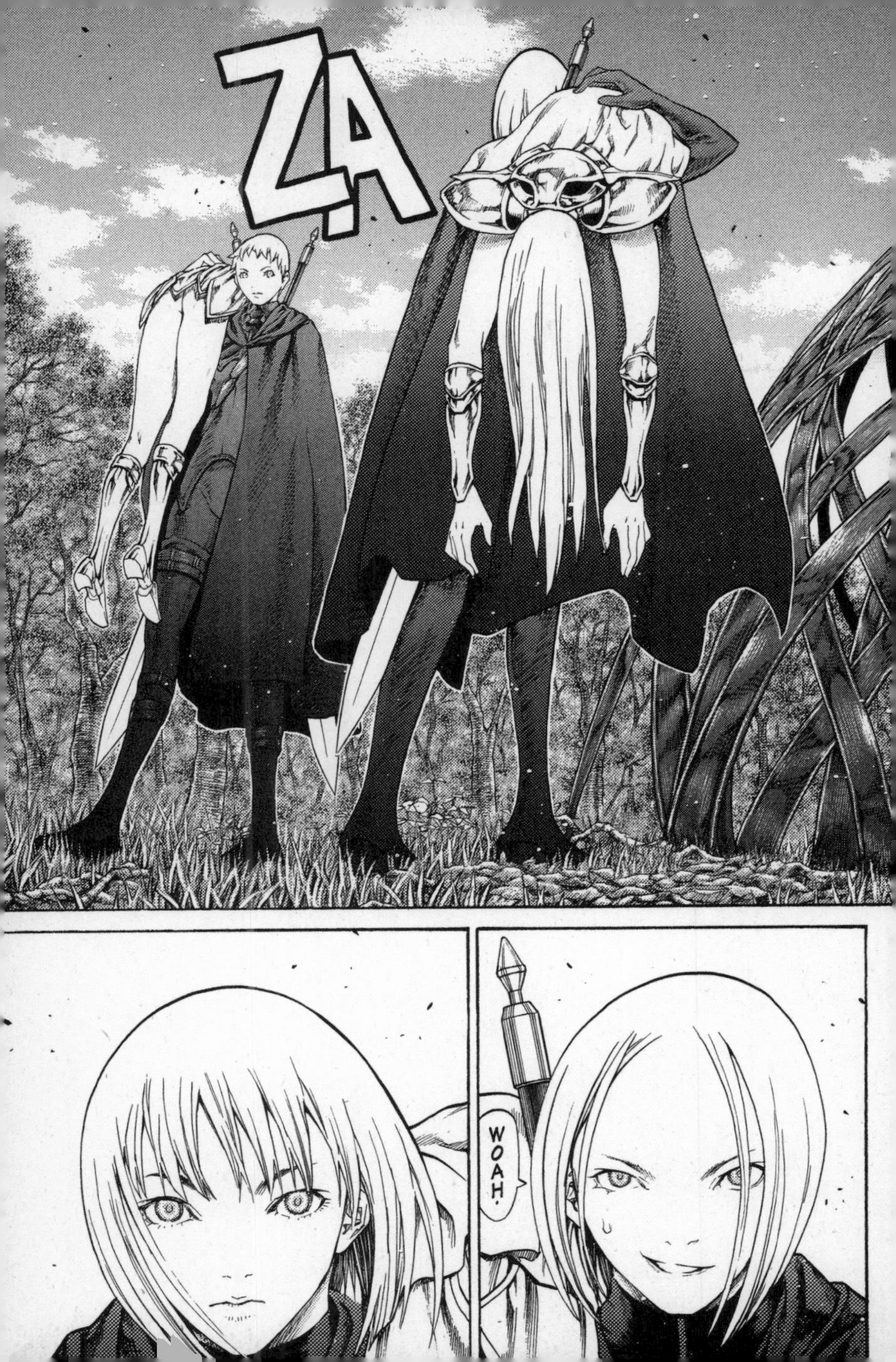
ZA
WOAH!

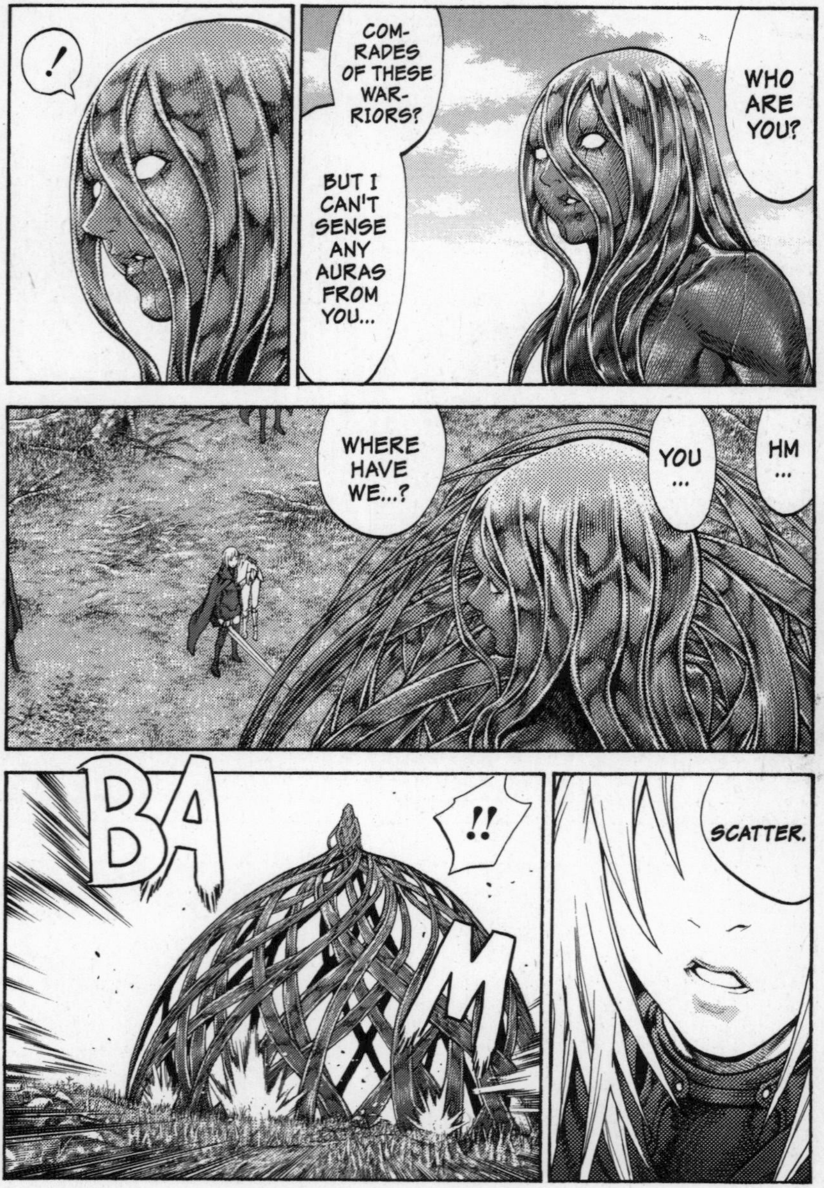
WHO ARE YOU?
COM-RADES OF THESE WAR-RIORS?
BUT I CAN'T SENSE ANY AURAS FROM YOU...
!
HM ...
YOU ...
WHERE HAVE WE...?
SCATTER.
!!
BAM

READ THIS WAY

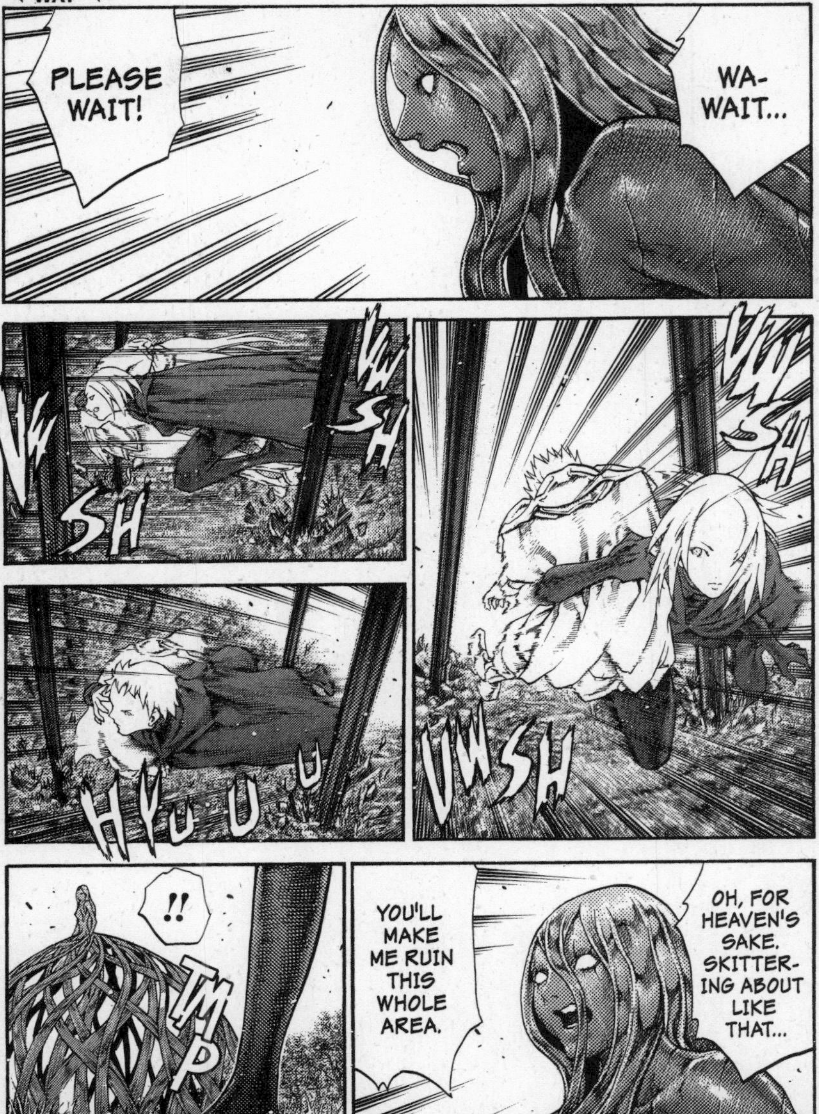
WA-WAIT...
PLEASE WAIT!
VWSH
VWSH
VWSH
VWSH
HYUUU
OH, FOR HEAVEN'S SAKE. SKITTERING ABOUT LIKE THAT...
YOU'LL MAKE ME RUIN THIS WHOLE AREA.
!!
TMP

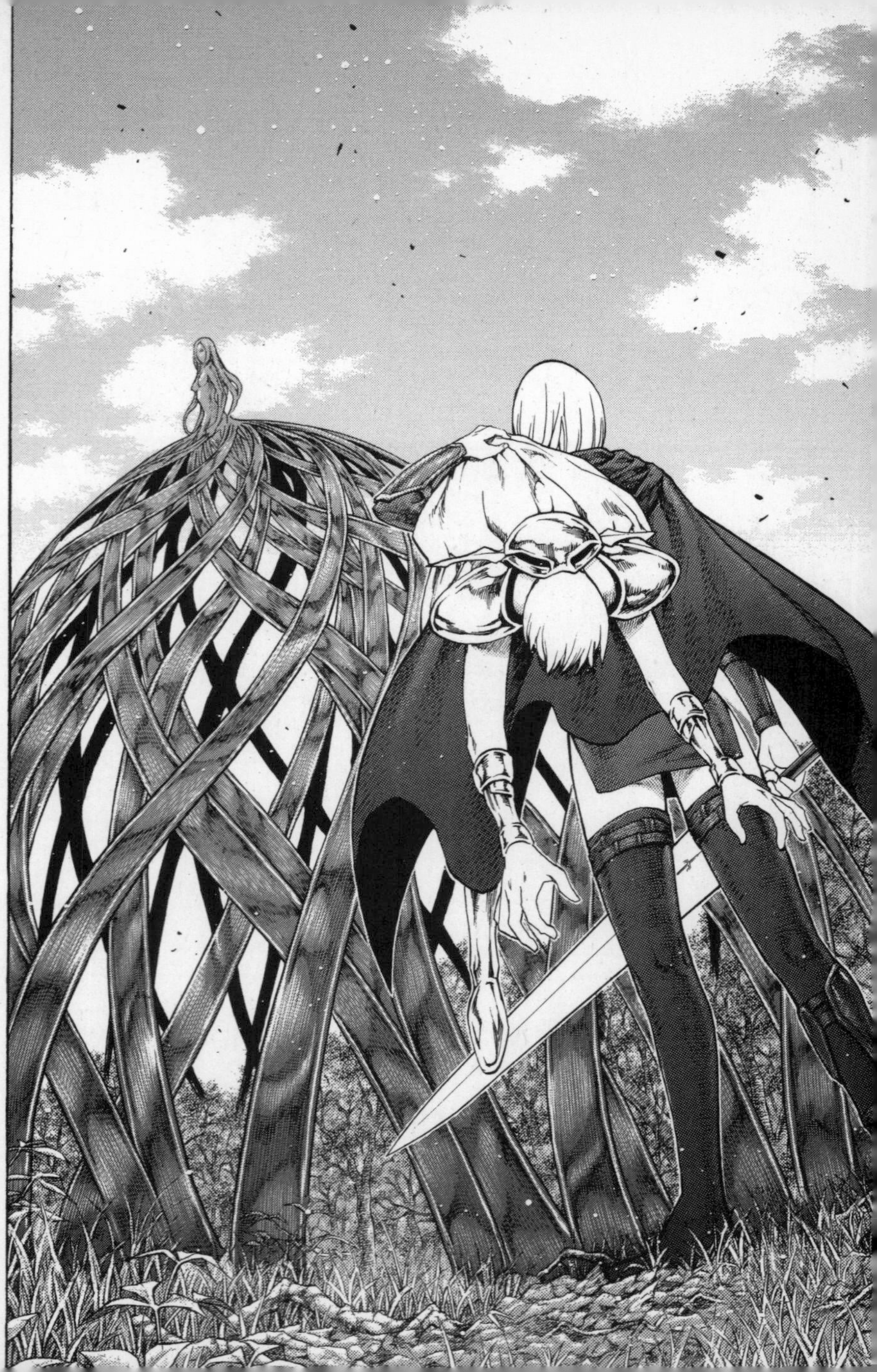

READ THIS WAY

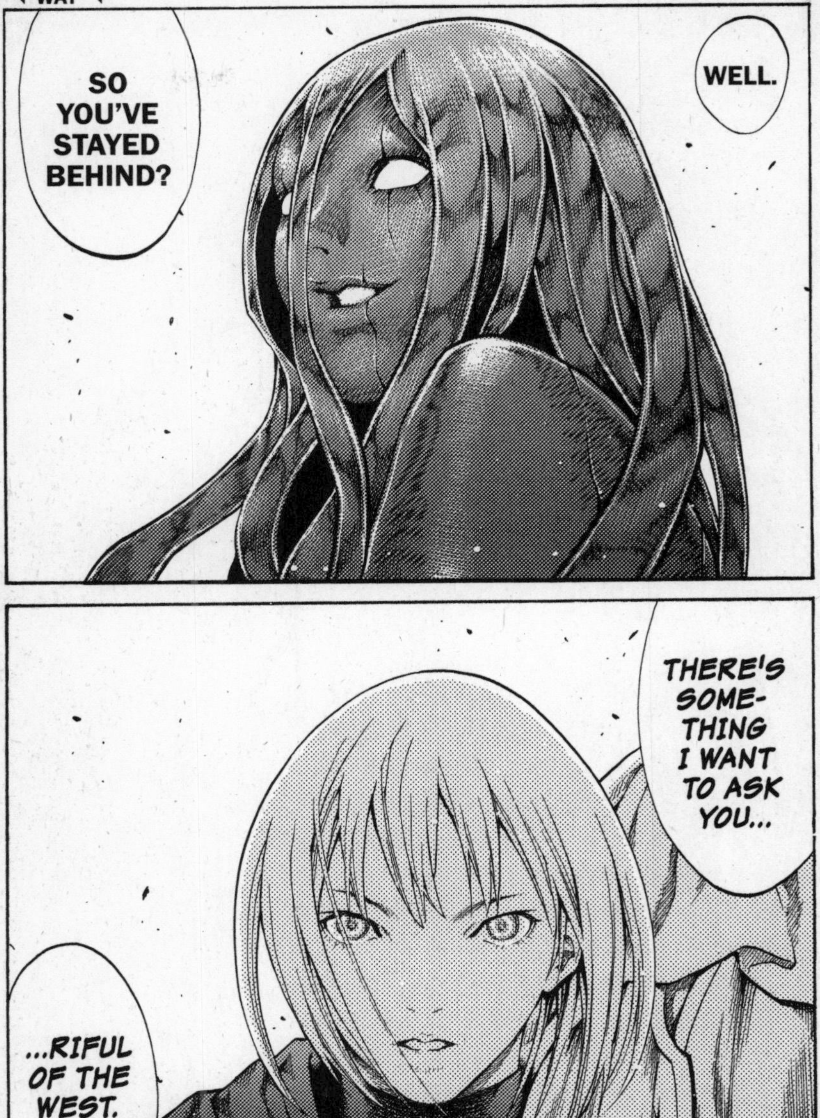
WELL.
SO YOU'VE STAYED BEHIND?
THERE'S SOME-THING I WANT TO ASK YOU...
...RIFUL OF THE WEST.

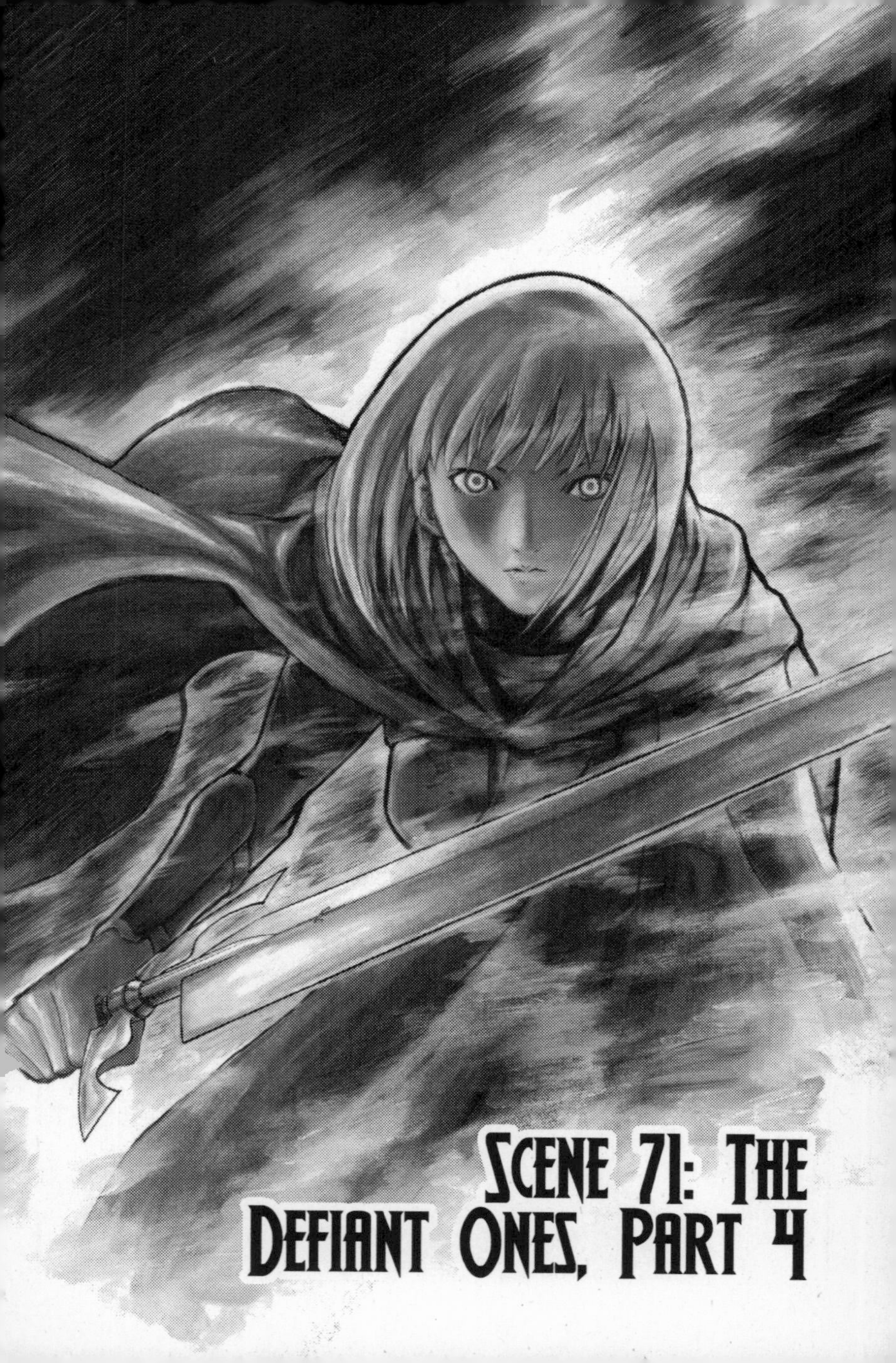
Scene 71: The
Defiant Ones, Part 4

READ THIS WAY

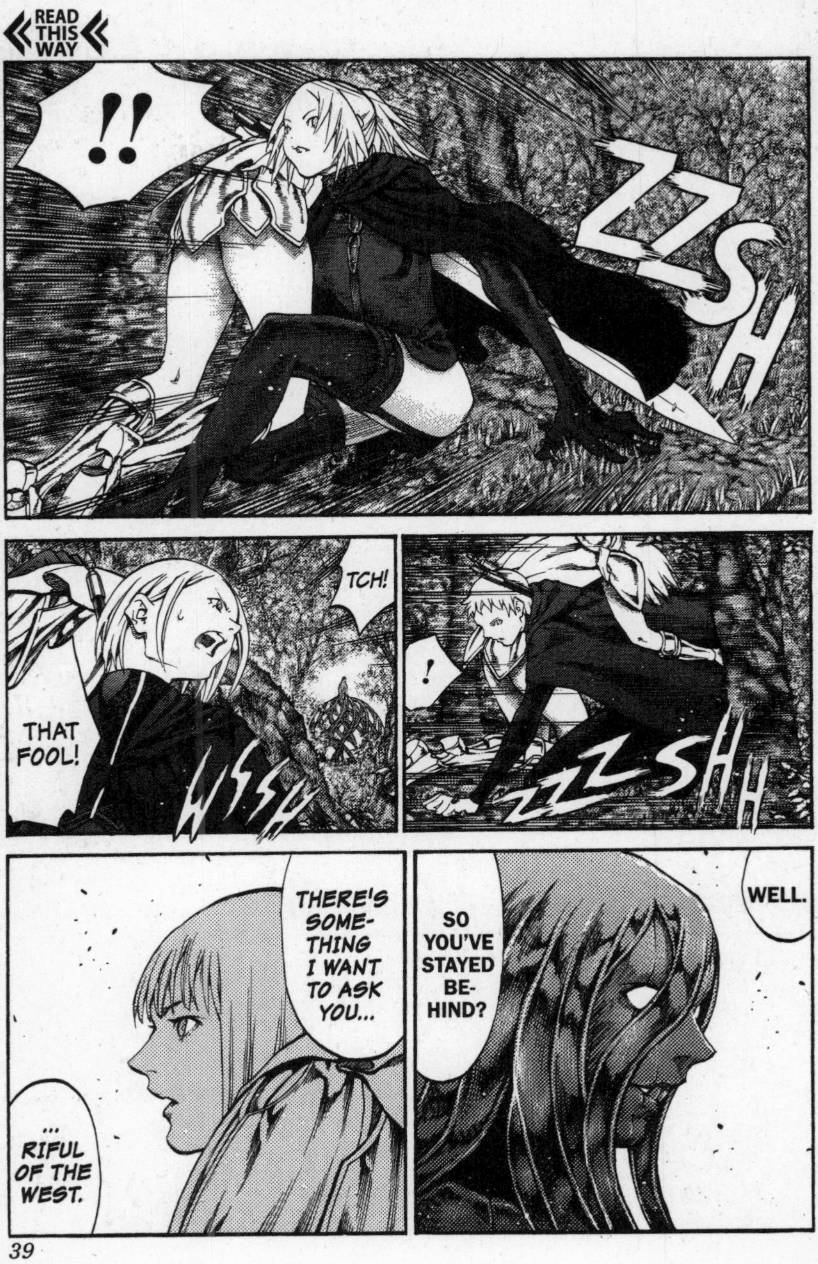

!!
ZZSH
!
ZZZSHH
TCH!
THAT FOOL!
WSSH
WELL.
SO YOU'VE STAYED BE-HIND?
THERE'S SOME-THING I WANT TO ASK YOU...
... RIFUL OF THE WEST.

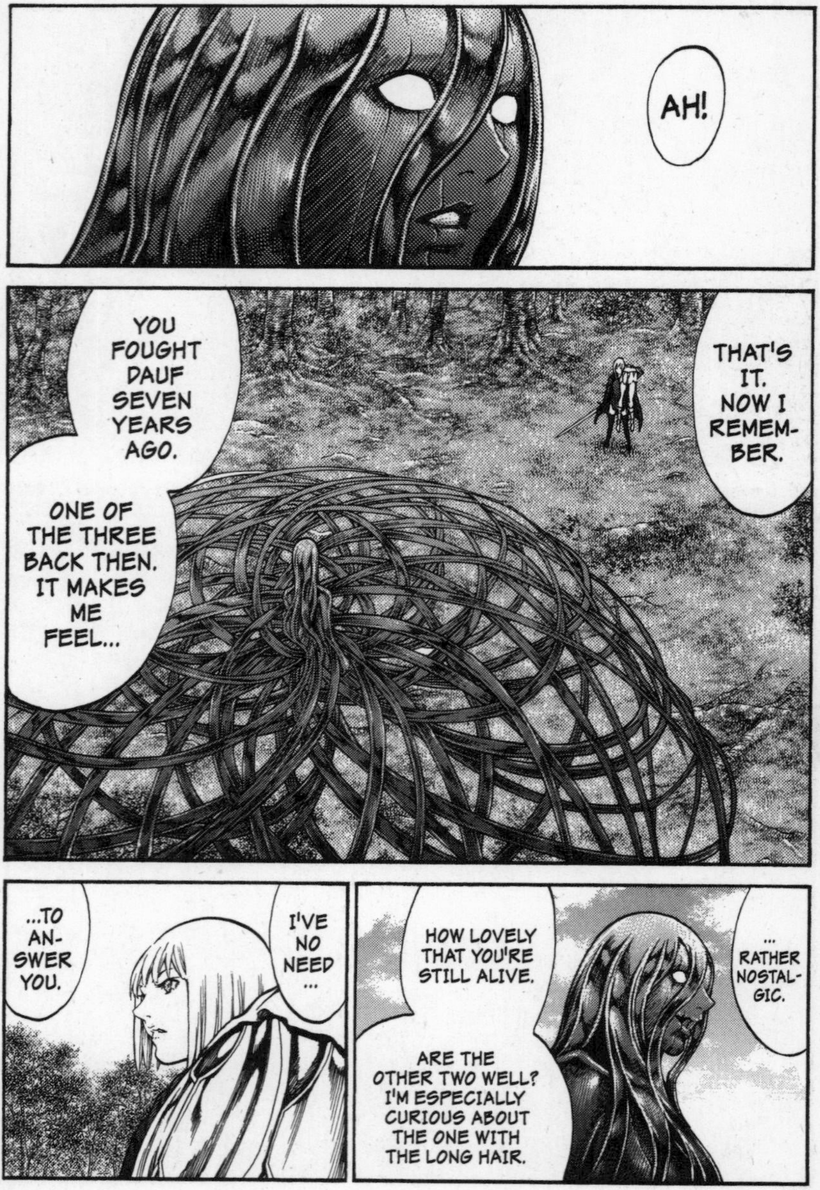
AH!
THAT'S IT. NOW I REMEMBER.
YOU FOUGHT DAUF SEVEN YEARS AGO.
ONE OF THE THREE BACK THEN. IT MAKES ME FEEL...
...RATHER NOSTALGIC.
HOW LOVELY THAT YOU'RE STILL ALIVE.
ARE THE OTHER TWO WELL? I'M ESPECIALLY CURIOUS ABOUT THE ONE WITH THE LONG HAIR.
I'VE NO NEED...
...TO ANSWER YOU.

READ THIS WAY

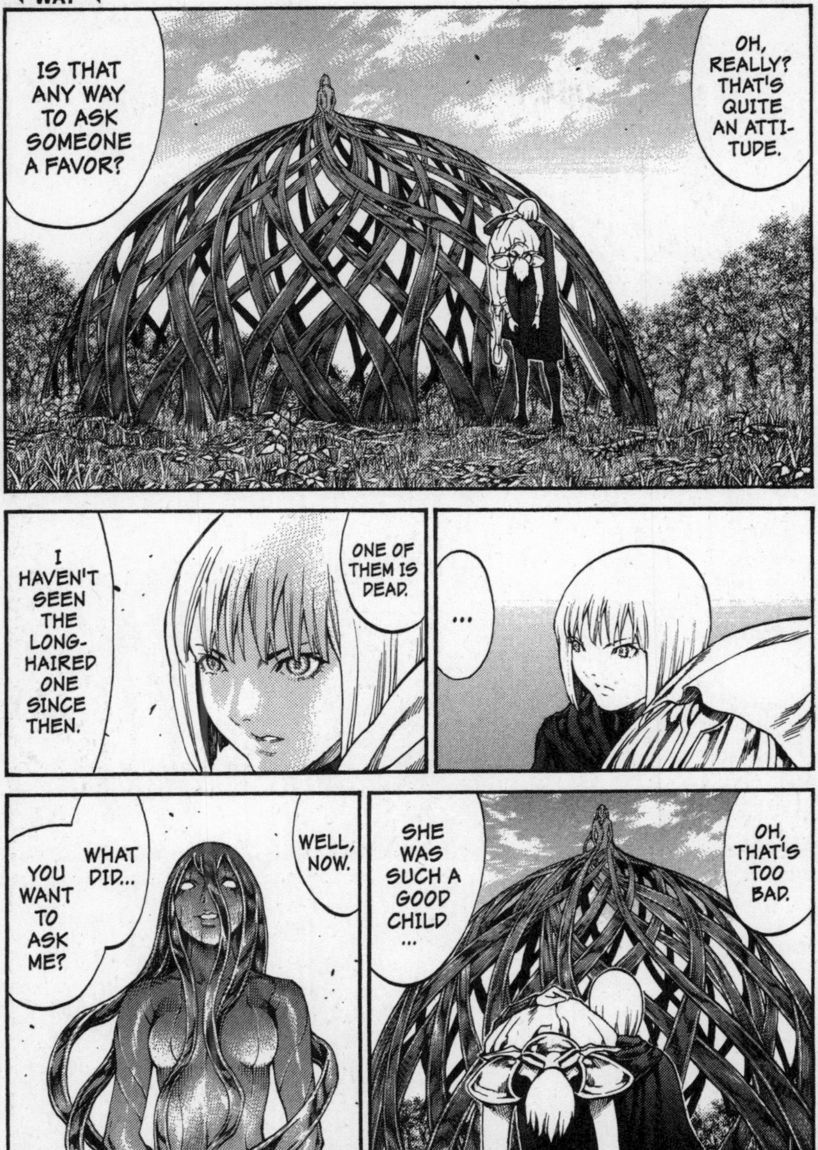
OH, REALLY? THAT'S QUITE AN ATTITUDE.
IS THAT ANY WAY TO ASK SOMEONE A FAVOR?
...
ONE OF THEM IS DEAD.
I HAVEN'T SEEN THE LONG-HAIRED ONE SINCE THEN.
OH, THAT'S TOO BAD.
SHE WAS SUCH A GOOD CHILD ...
WELL, NOW.
WHAT DID...
YOU WANT TO ASK ME?

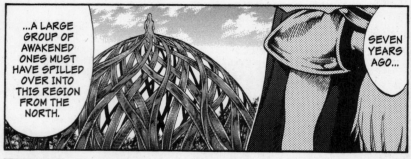

SEVEN YEARS AGO...
...A LARGE GROUP OF AWAKENED ONES MUST HAVE SPILLED OVER INTO THIS REGION FROM THE NORTH.
I WANT TO KNOW WHAT HAP-PENED.
YOU CREATURES OF THE ABYSS MUST HAVE FACED THEM. HOW DID IT END?
AND WHAT IS THE PRESENT CONDI-TION OF THE ORGANI-ZATION?
!
A HA HA! I SEE!
SO THAT'S IT...

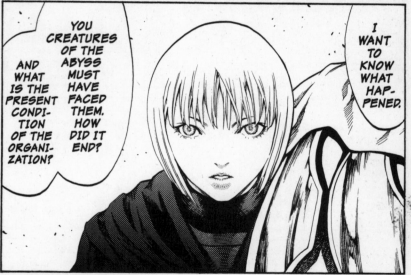

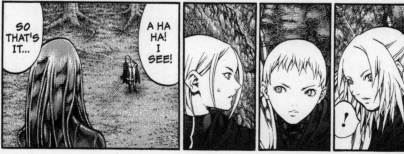

READ THIS WAY

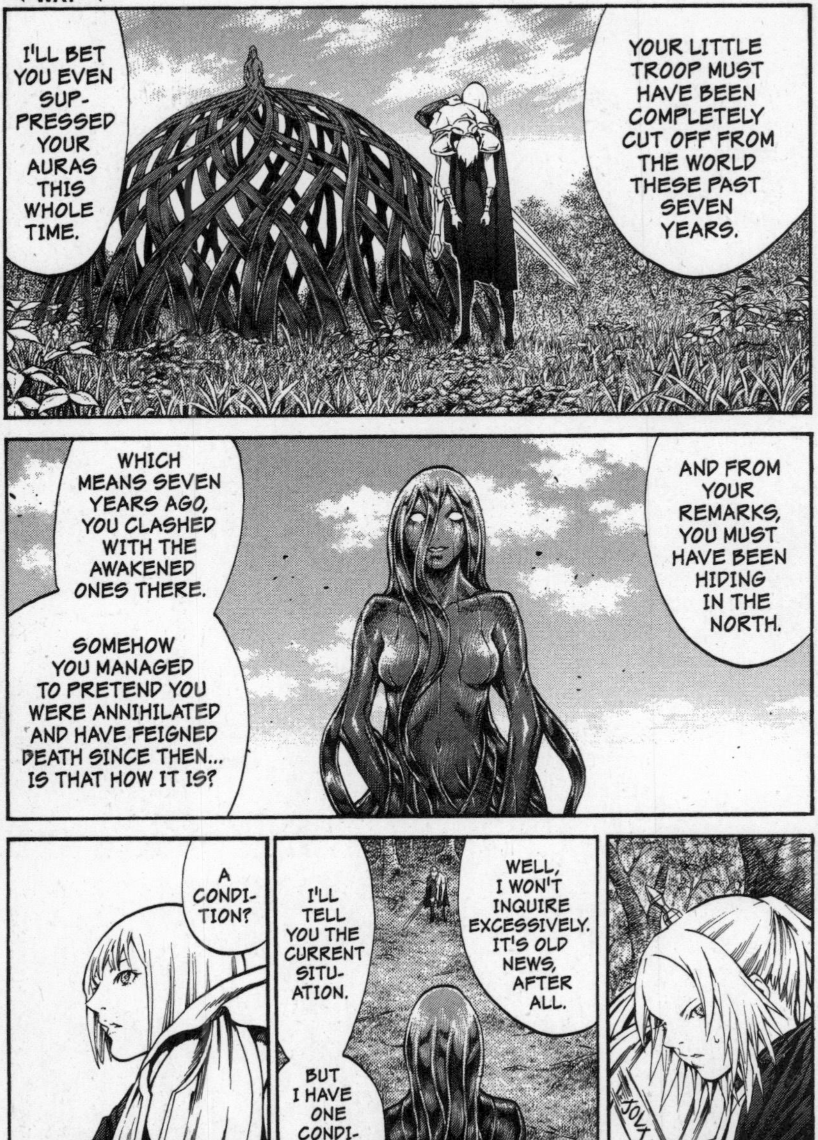

YOUR LITTLE TROOP MUST HAVE BEEN COMPLETELY CUT OFF FROM THE WORLD THESE PAST SEVEN YEARS.
I'LL BET YOU EVEN SUP-PRESSED YOUR AURAS THIS WHOLE TIME.
AND FROM YOUR REMARKS, YOU MUST HAVE BEEN HIDING IN THE NORTH.
WHICH MEANS SEVEN YEARS AGO, YOU CLASHED WITH THE AWAKENED ONES THERE.
SOMEHOW YOU MANAGED TO PRETEND YOU WERE ANNIHILATED AND HAVE FEIGNED DEATH SINCE THEN... IS THAT HOW IT IS?
JOLT
WELL, I WON'T INQUIRE EXCESSIVELY. IT'S OLD NEWS, AFTER ALL.
I'LL TELL YOU THE CURRENT SITU-ATION.
BUT I HAVE ONE CONDI-TION.
A CONDI-TION?

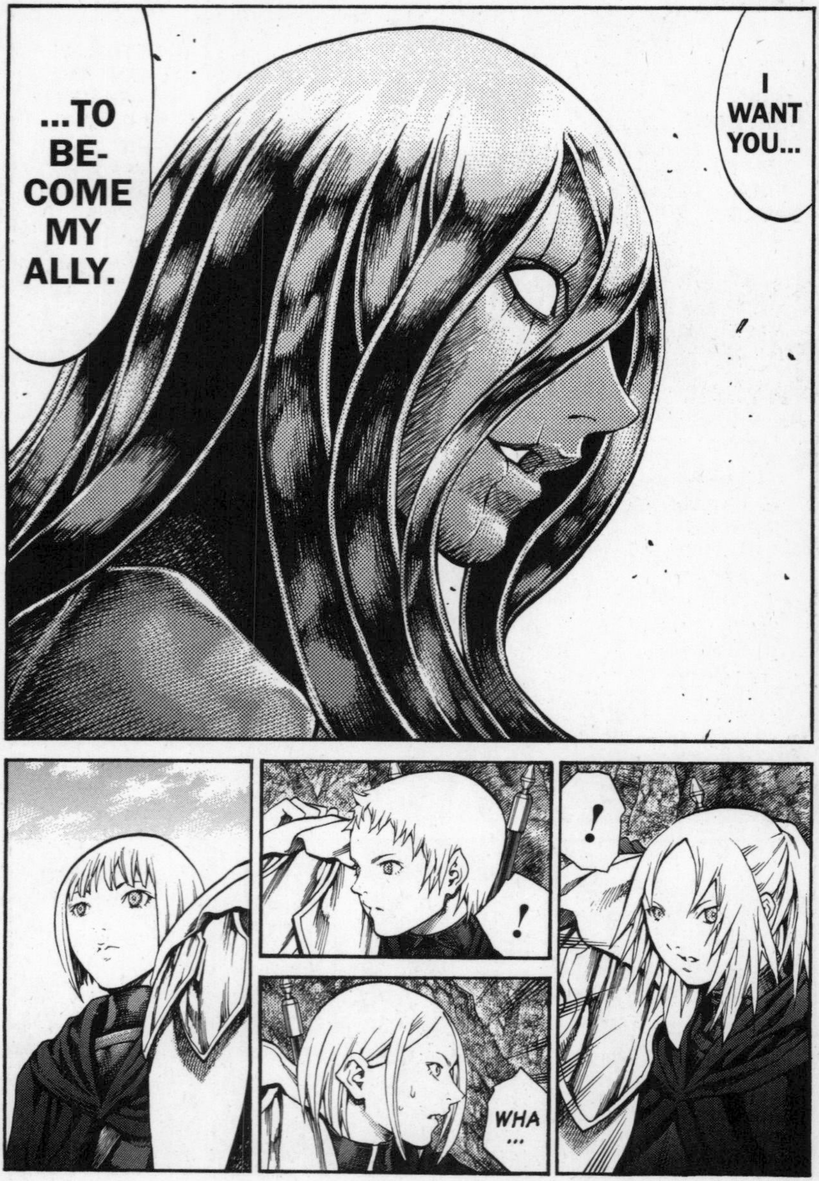
I WANT YOU...
...TO BE-COME MY ALLY.
!
!
WHA ...

READ THIS WAY

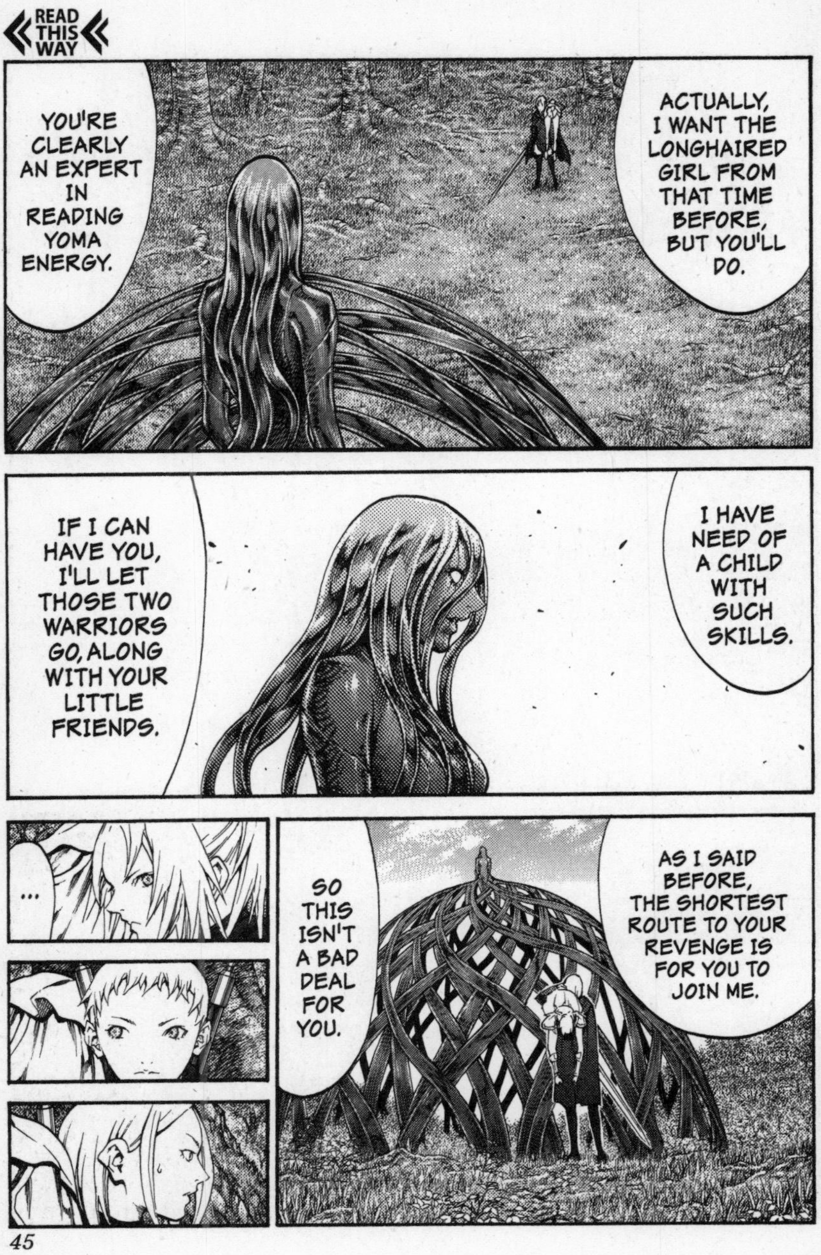
ACTUALLY, I WANT THE LONGHAIRED GIRL FROM THAT TIME BEFORE, BUT YOU'LL DO.
YOU'RE CLEARLY AN EXPERT IN READING YOMA ENERGY.
I HAVE NEED OF A CHILD WITH SUCH SKILLS.
IF I CAN HAVE YOU, I'LL LET THOSE TWO WARRIORS GO, ALONG WITH YOUR LITTLE FRIENDS.
AS I SAID BEFORE, THE SHORTEST ROUTE TO YOUR REVENGE IS FOR YOU TO JOIN ME.
SO THIS ISN'T A BAD DEAL FOR YOU.
...

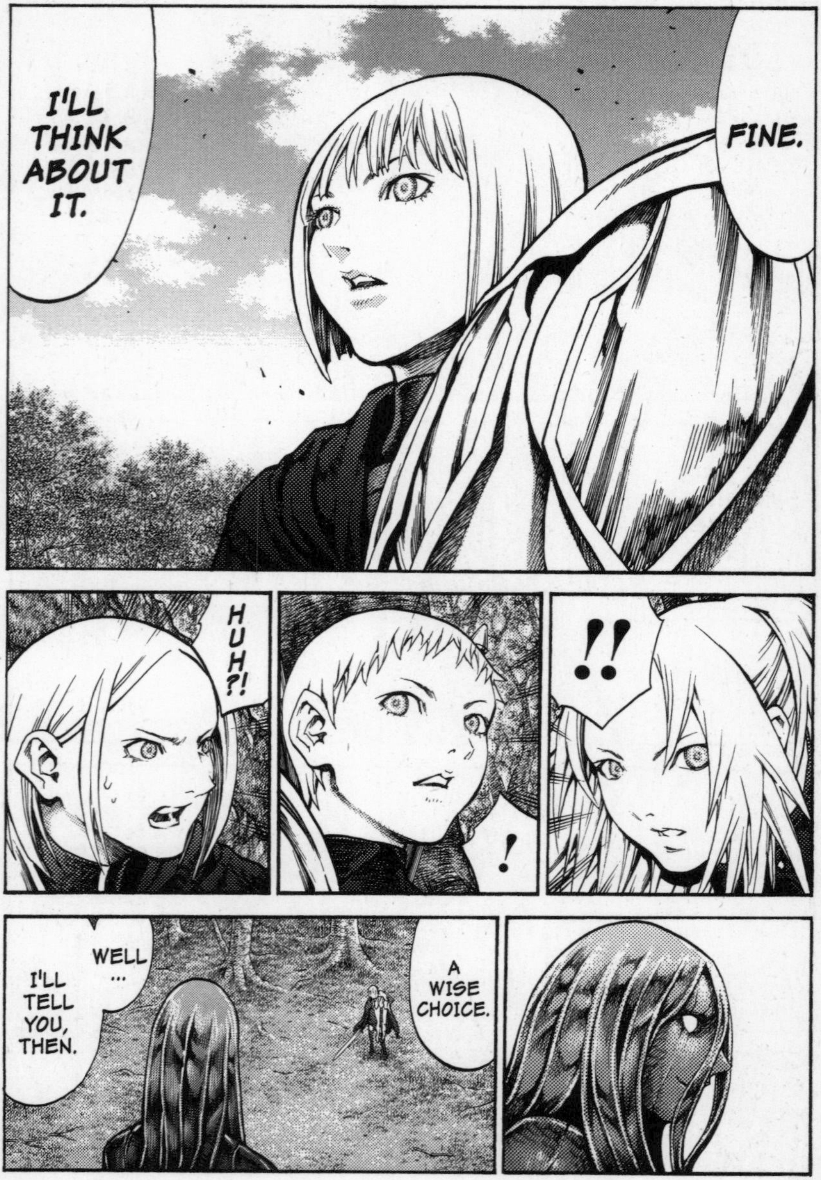

FINE.
I'LL THINK ABOUT IT.
!!
!
HUH?!
A WISE CHOICE.
WELL ...
I'LL TELL YOU, THEN.

READ THIS WAY

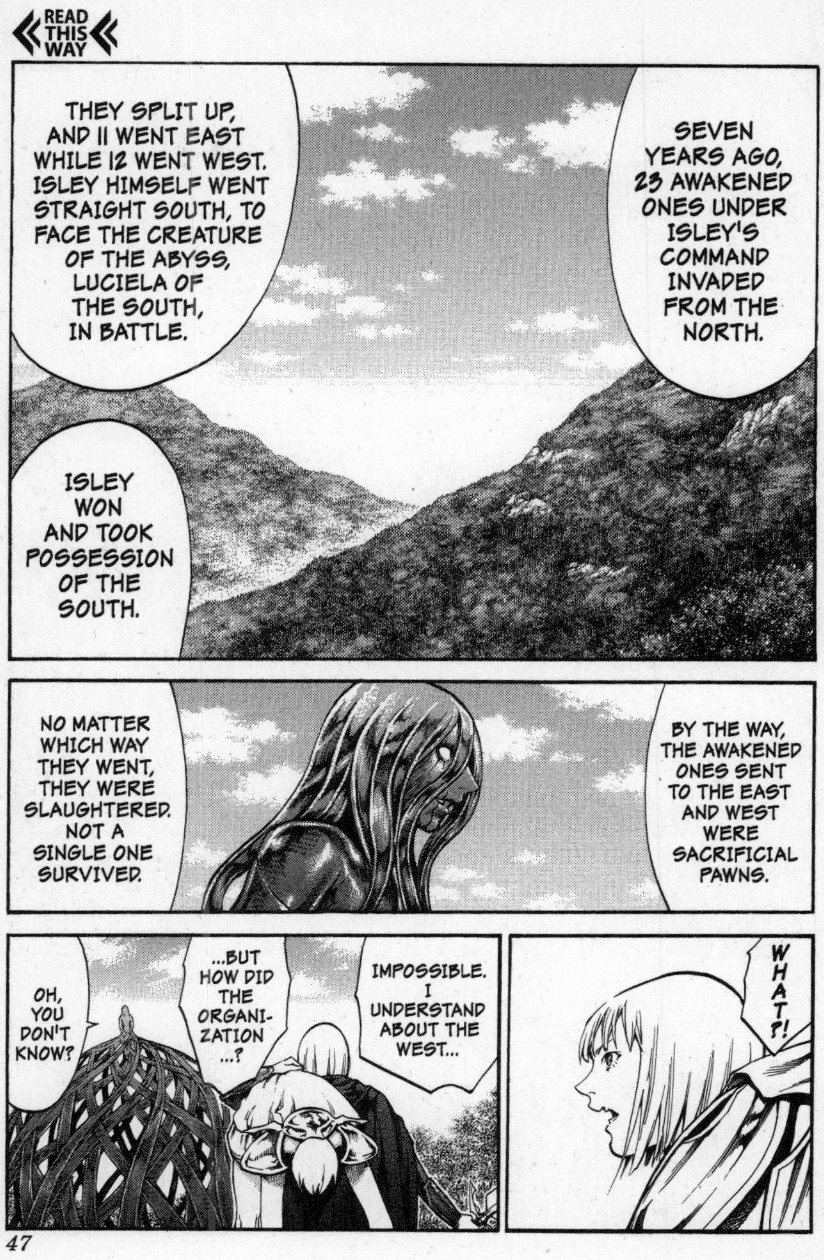
SEVEN YEARS AGO, 23 AWAKENED ONES UNDER ISLEY'S COMMAND INVADED FROM THE NORTH.
THEY SPLIT UP, AND 11 WENT EAST WHILE 12 WENT WEST. ISLEY HIMSELF WENT STRAIGHT SOUTH, TO FACE THE CREATURE OF THE ABYSS, LUCIELA OF THE SOUTH, IN BATTLE.
ISLEY WON AND TOOK POSSESSION OF THE SOUTH.
BY THE WAY, THE AWAKENED ONES SENT TO THE EAST AND WEST WERE SACRIFICIAL PAWNS.
NO MATTER WHICH WAY THEY WENT, THEY WERE SLAUGHTERED. NOT A SINGLE ONE SURVIVED.
WHAT?!
IMPOSSIBLE. I UNDERSTAND ABOUT THE WEST...
...BUT HOW DID THE ORGANIZATION ...?
OH, YOU DON'T KNOW?

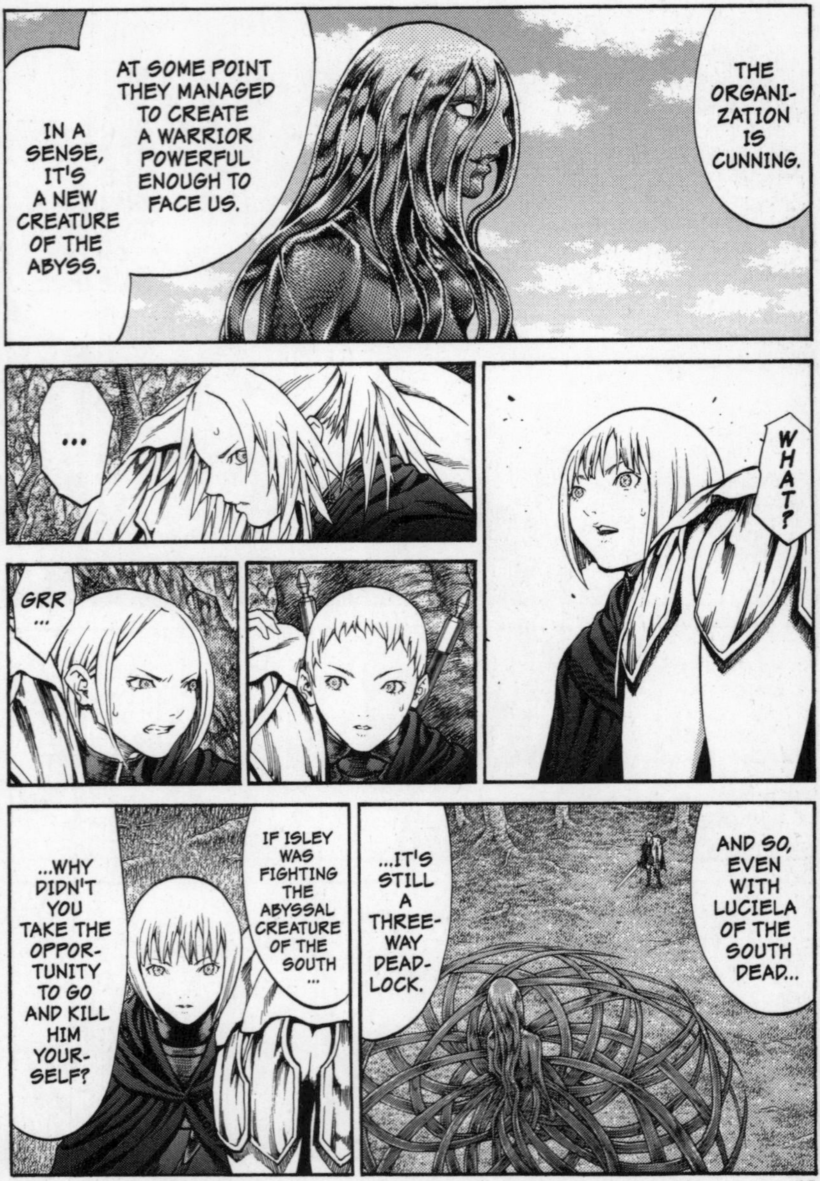
THE ORGANIZATION IS CUNNING.
AT SOME POINT THEY MANAGED TO CREATE A WARRIOR POWERFUL ENOUGH TO FACE US.
IN A SENSE, IT'S A NEW CREATURE OF THE ABYSS.
WHAT?
...
GRR ...
AND SO, EVEN WITH LUCIELA OF THE SOUTH DEAD...
...IT'S STILL A THREE-WAY DEADLOCK.
IF ISLEY WAS FIGHTING THE ABYSSAL CREATURE OF THE SOUTH ...
...WHY DIDN'T YOU TAKE THE OPPORTUNITY TO GO AND KILL HIM YOURSELF?

READ THIS WAY

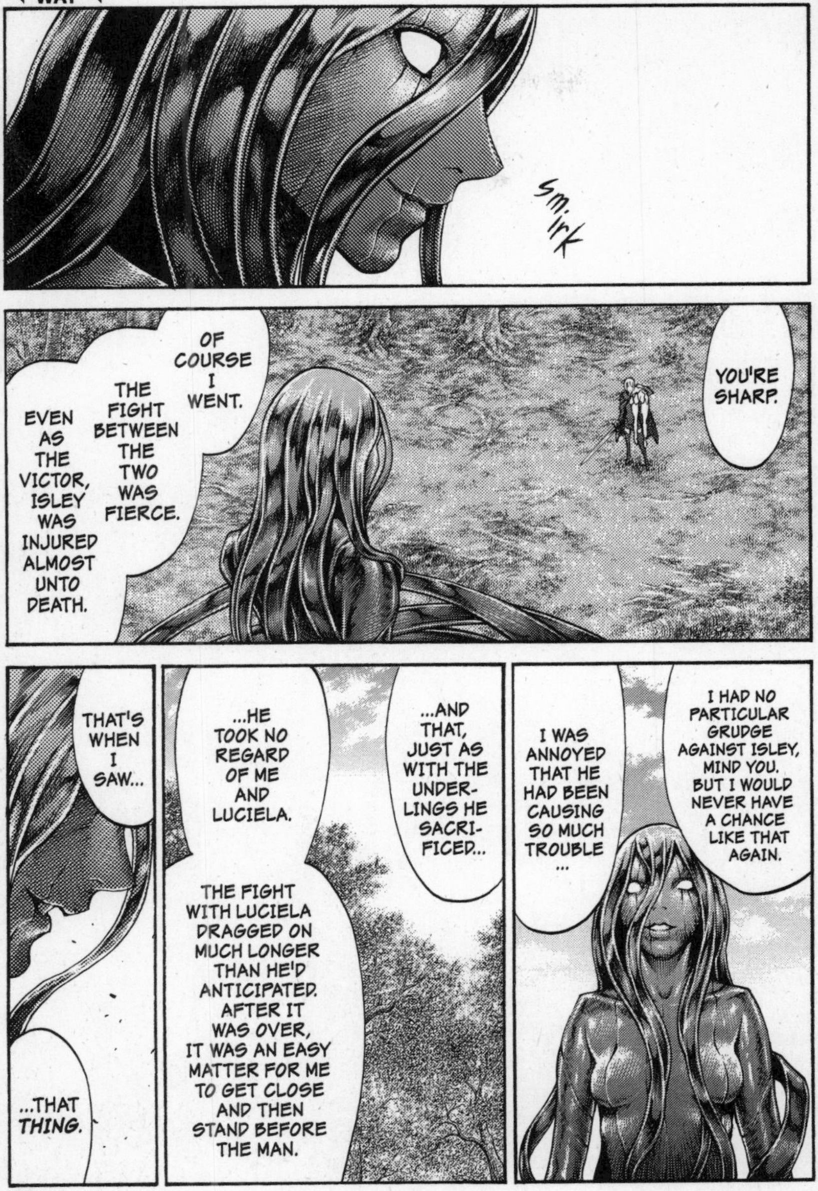
smirk
YOU'RE SHARP.
OF COURSE I WENT.
THE FIGHT BETWEEN THE TWO WAS FIERCE.
EVEN AS THE VICTOR, ISLEY WAS INJURED ALMOST UNTO DEATH.
I HAD NO PARTICULAR GRUDGE AGAINST ISLEY, MIND YOU. BUT I WOULD NEVER HAVE A CHANCE LIKE THAT AGAIN.
I WAS ANNOYED THAT HE HAD BEEN CAUSING SO MUCH TROUBLE ...
...AND THAT, JUST AS WITH THE UNDER-LINGS HE SACRI-FICED...
...HE TOOK NO REGARD OF ME AND LUCIELA.
THE FIGHT WITH LUCIELA DRAGGED ON MUCH LONGER THAN HE'D ANTICIPATED. AFTER IT WAS OVER, IT WAS AN EASY MATTER FOR ME TO GET CLOSE AND THEN STAND BEFORE THE MAN.
THAT'S WHEN I SAW...
...THAT THING.

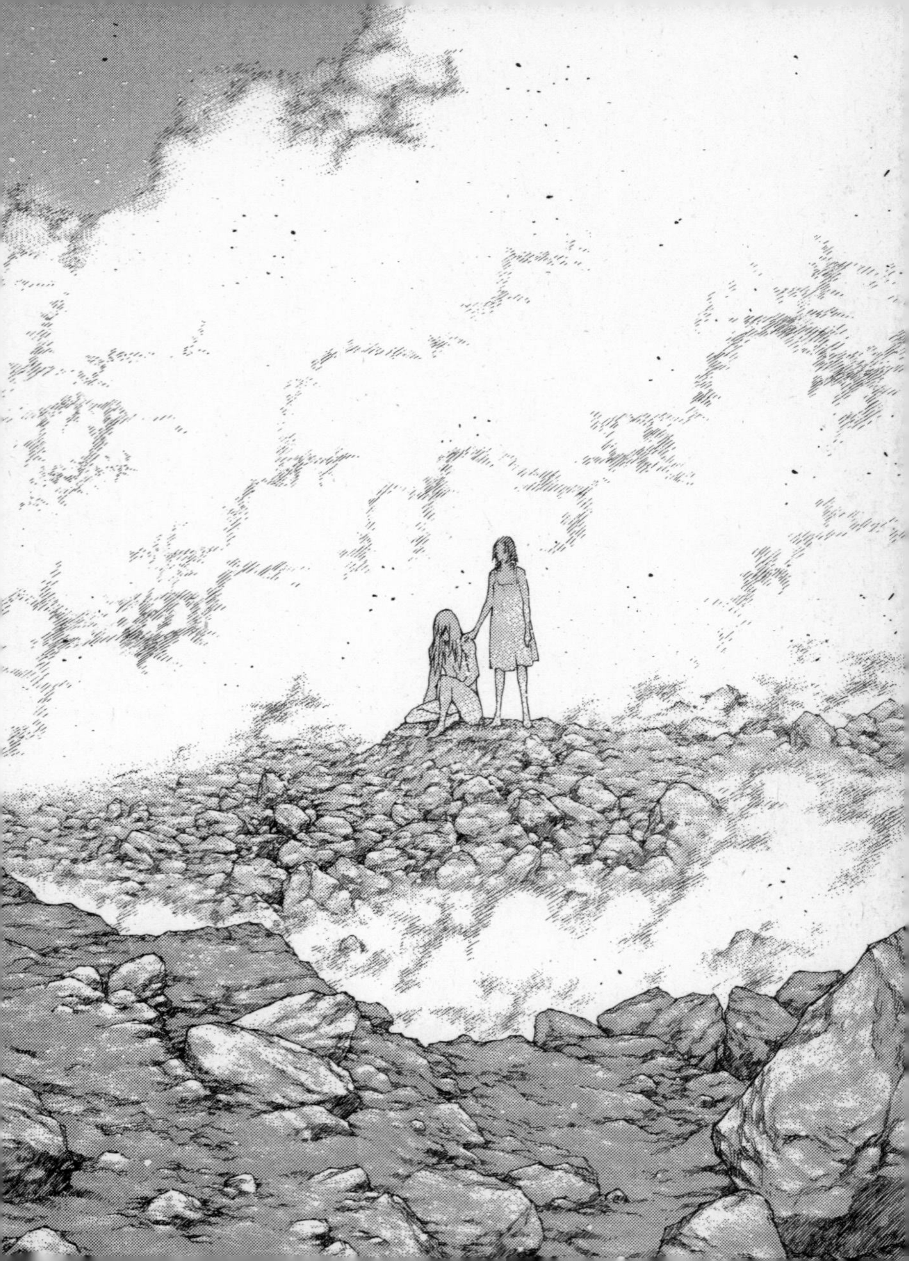

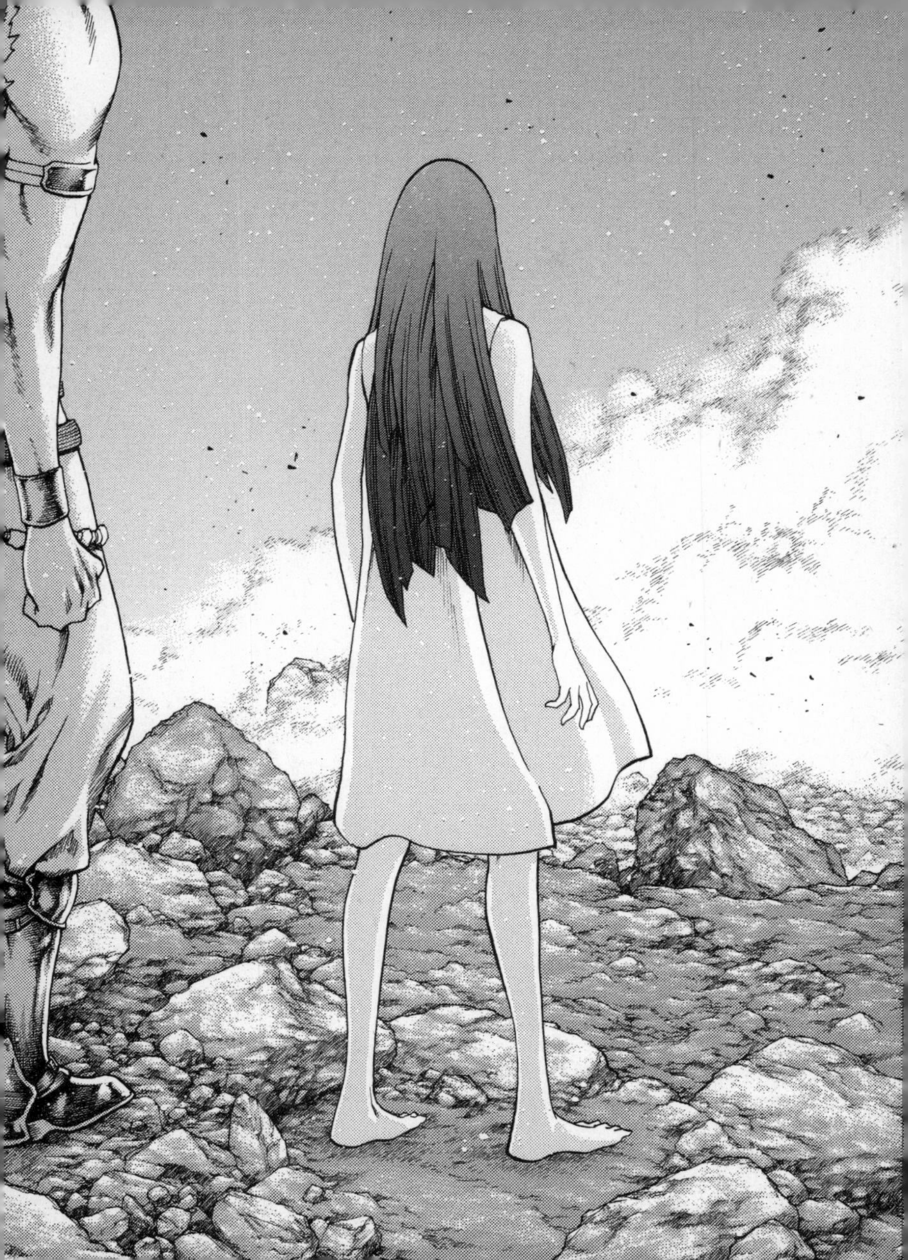

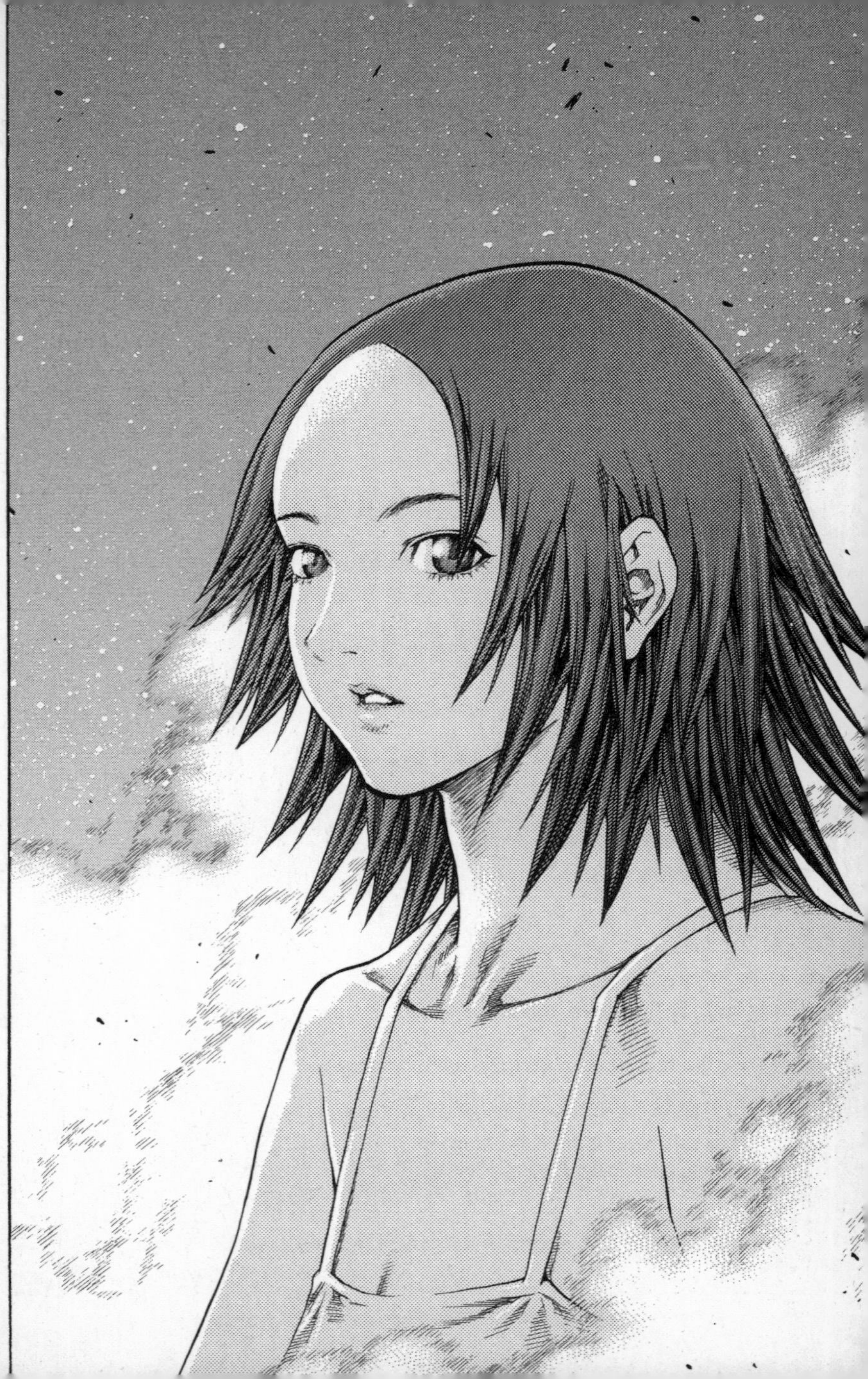

READ THIS WAY

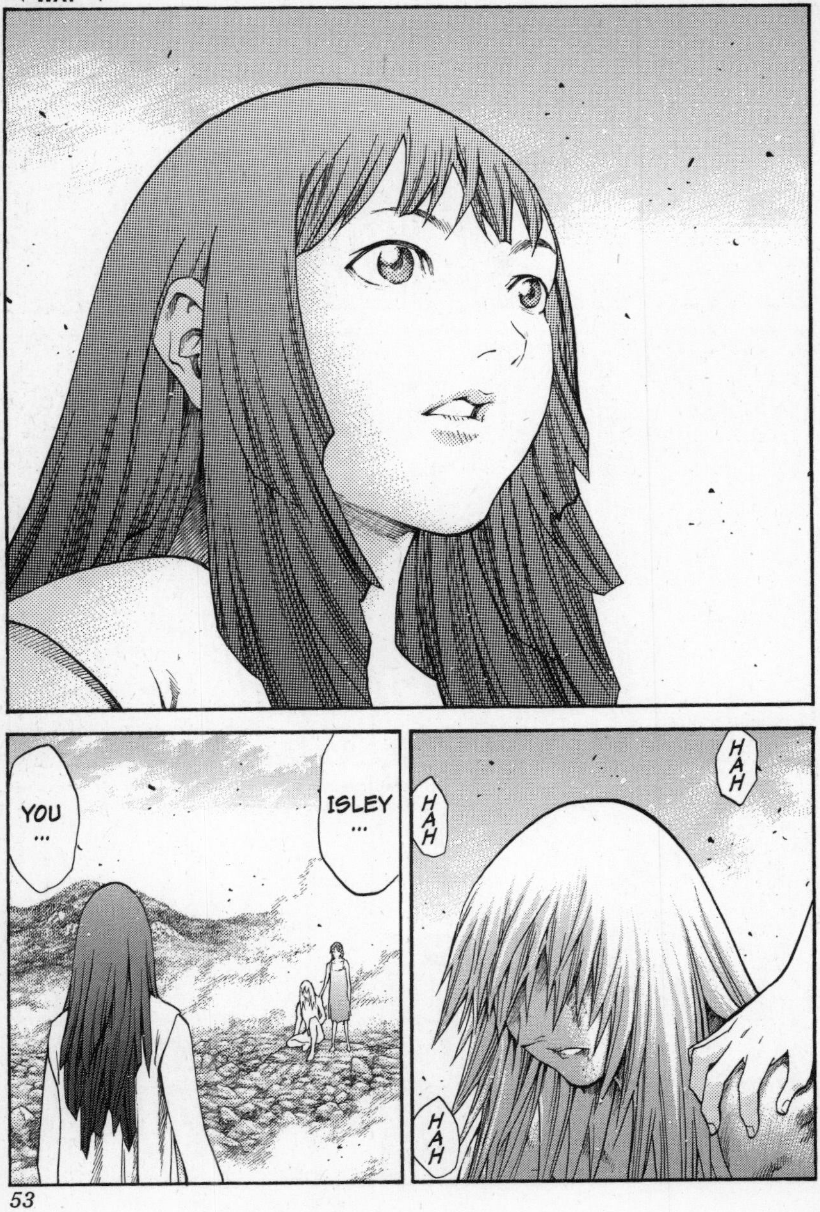

HAH
HAH
HAH
ISLEY ...
YOU ...

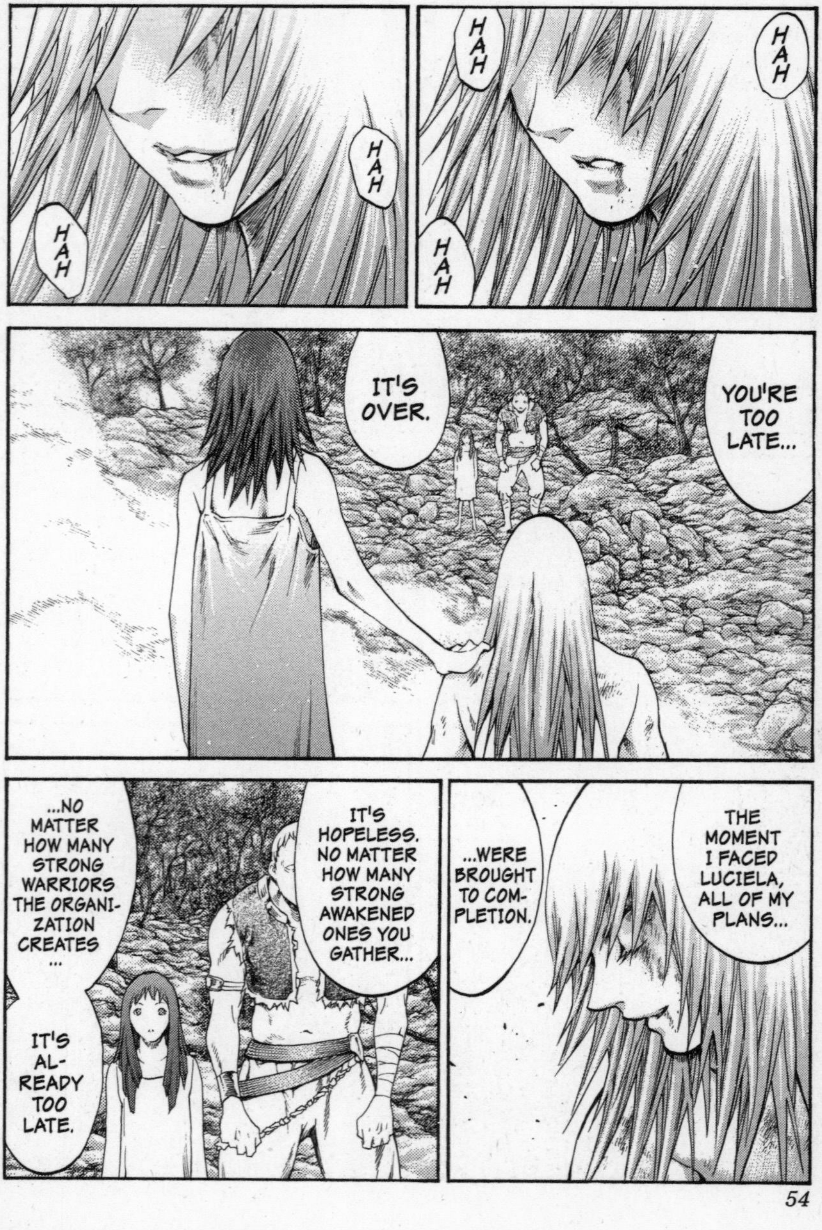
HAH HAH
HAH HAH
HAH HAH
HAH HAH
HAH HAH
YOU'RE TOO LATE...
IT'S OVER.
THE MOMENT I FACED LUCIELA, ALL OF MY PLANS...
...WERE BROUGHT TO COMPLETION.
IT'S HOPELESS. NO MATTER HOW MANY STRONG AWAKENED ONES YOU GATHER...
...NO MATTER HOW MANY STRONG WARRIORS THE ORGANIZATION CREATES...
IT'S ALREADY TOO LATE.

READ THIS WAY

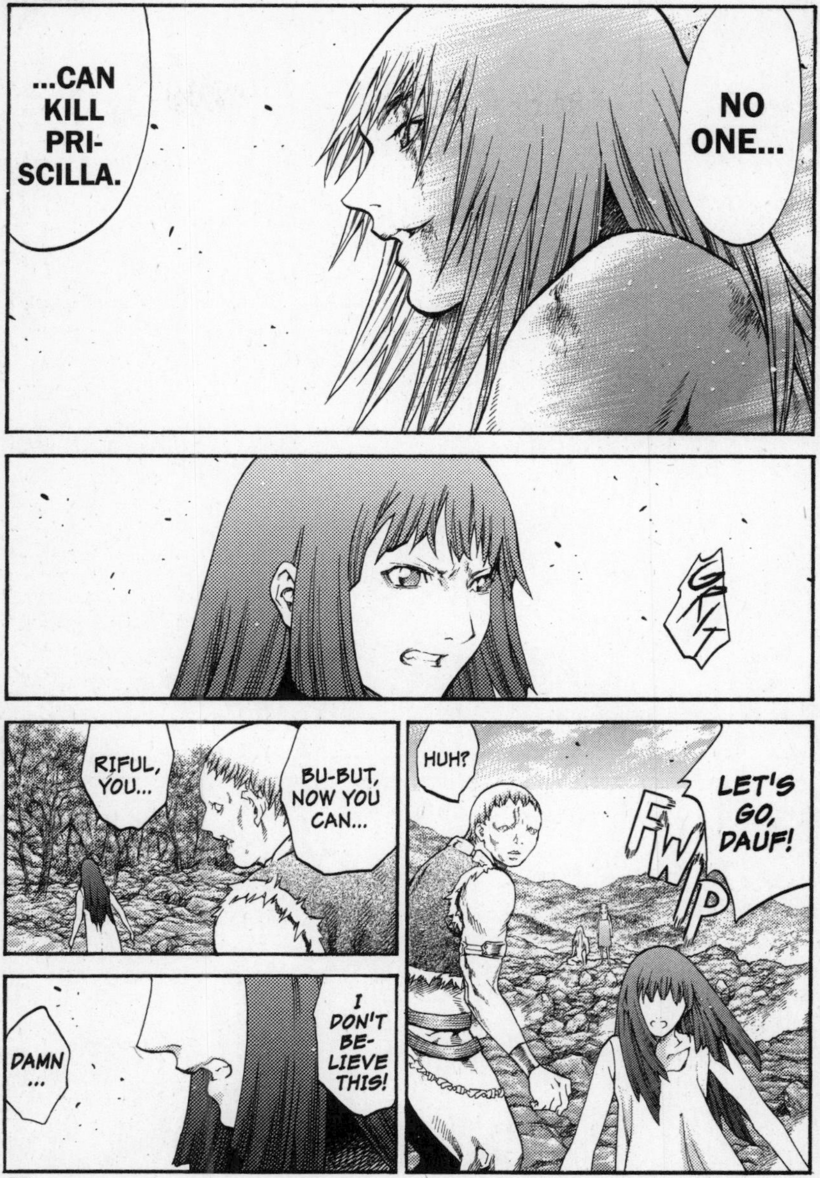
NO ONE...
...CAN KILL PRI-SCILLA.
GRIT
LET'S GO, DAUF!
FWIP
HUH?
BU-BUT, NOW YOU CAN...
RIFUL, YOU...
I DON'T BE-LIEVE THIS!
DAMN...

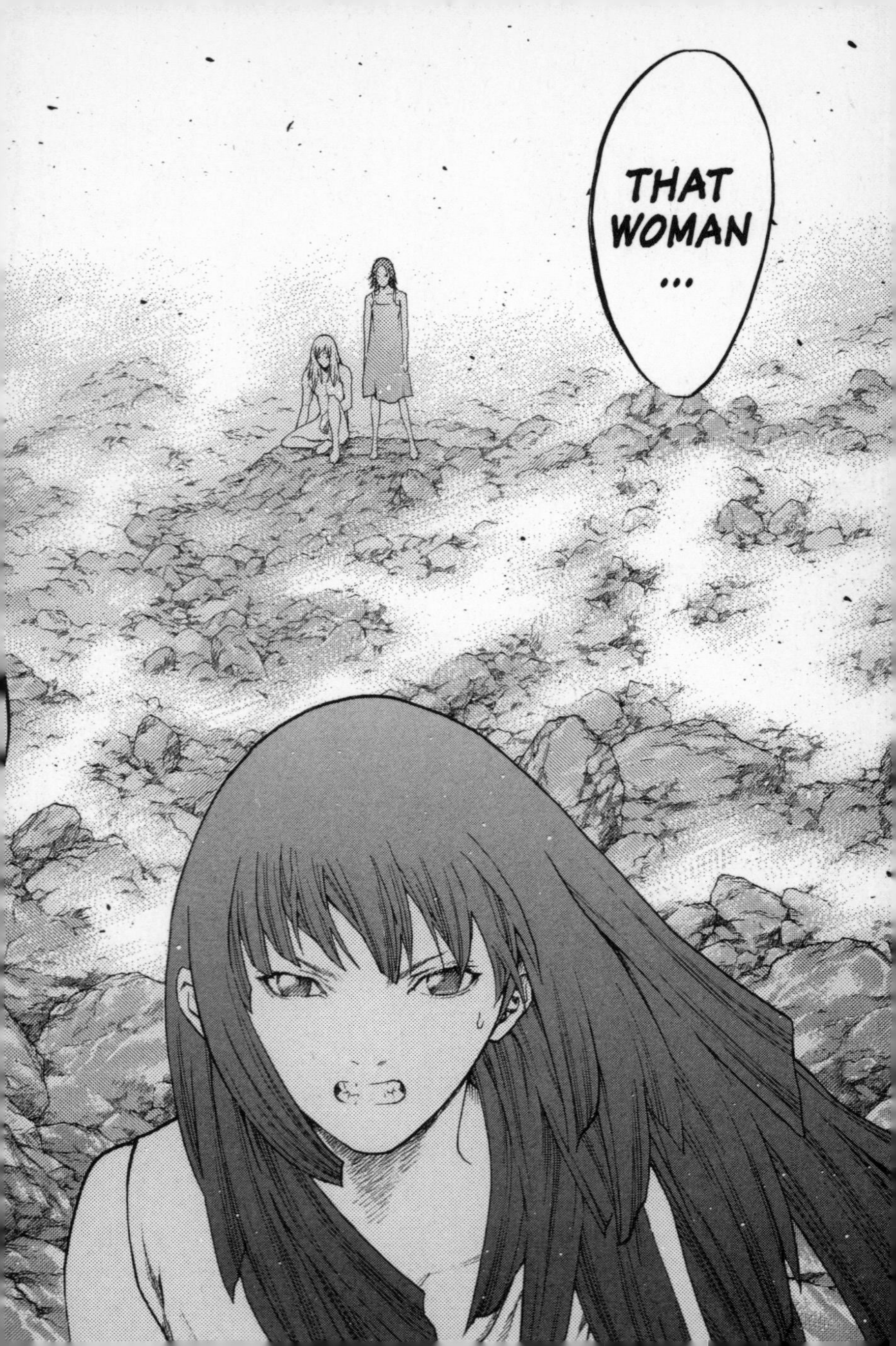
THAT WOMAN ...

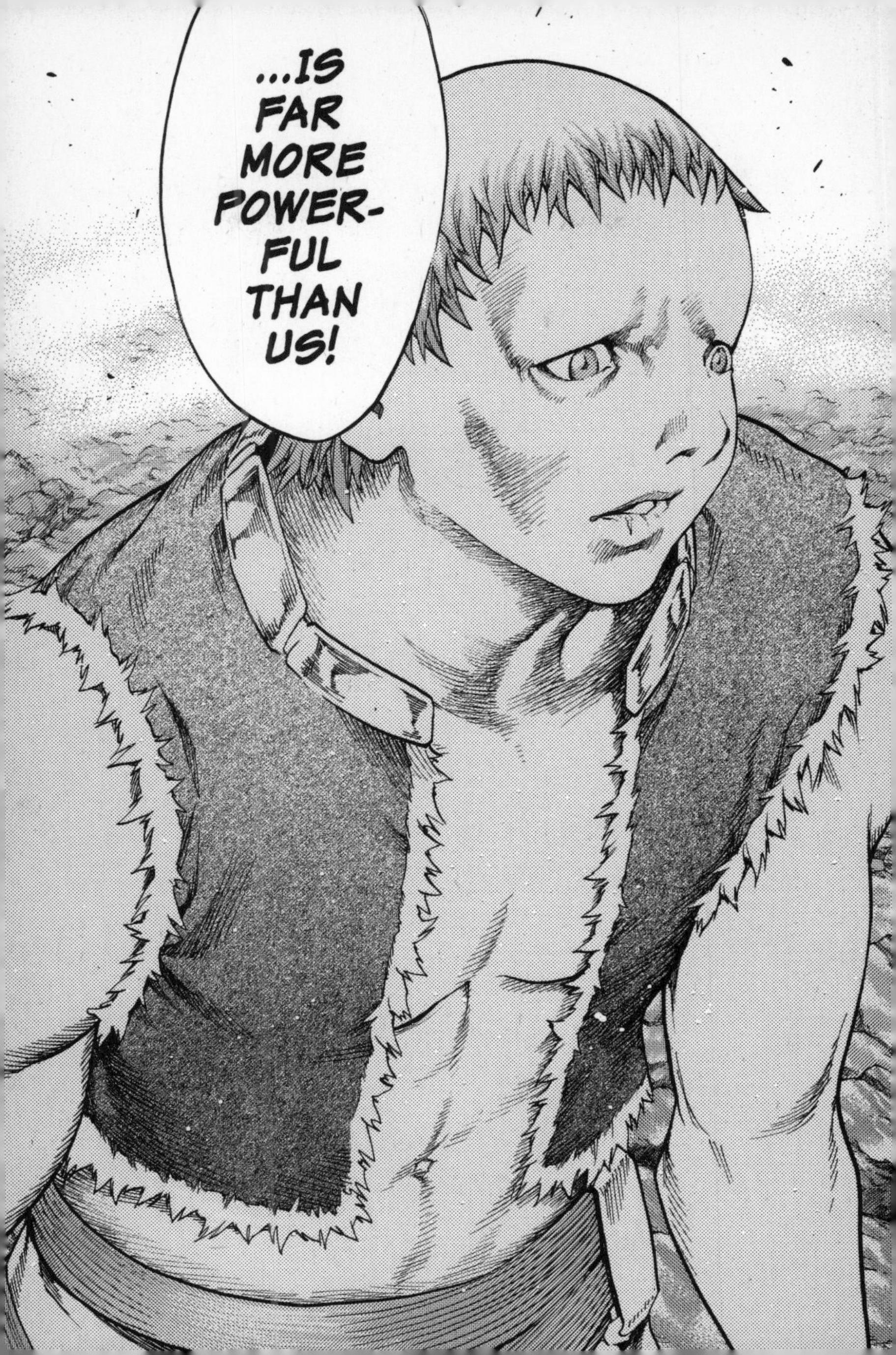
...IS FAR MORE POWER-FUL THAN US!

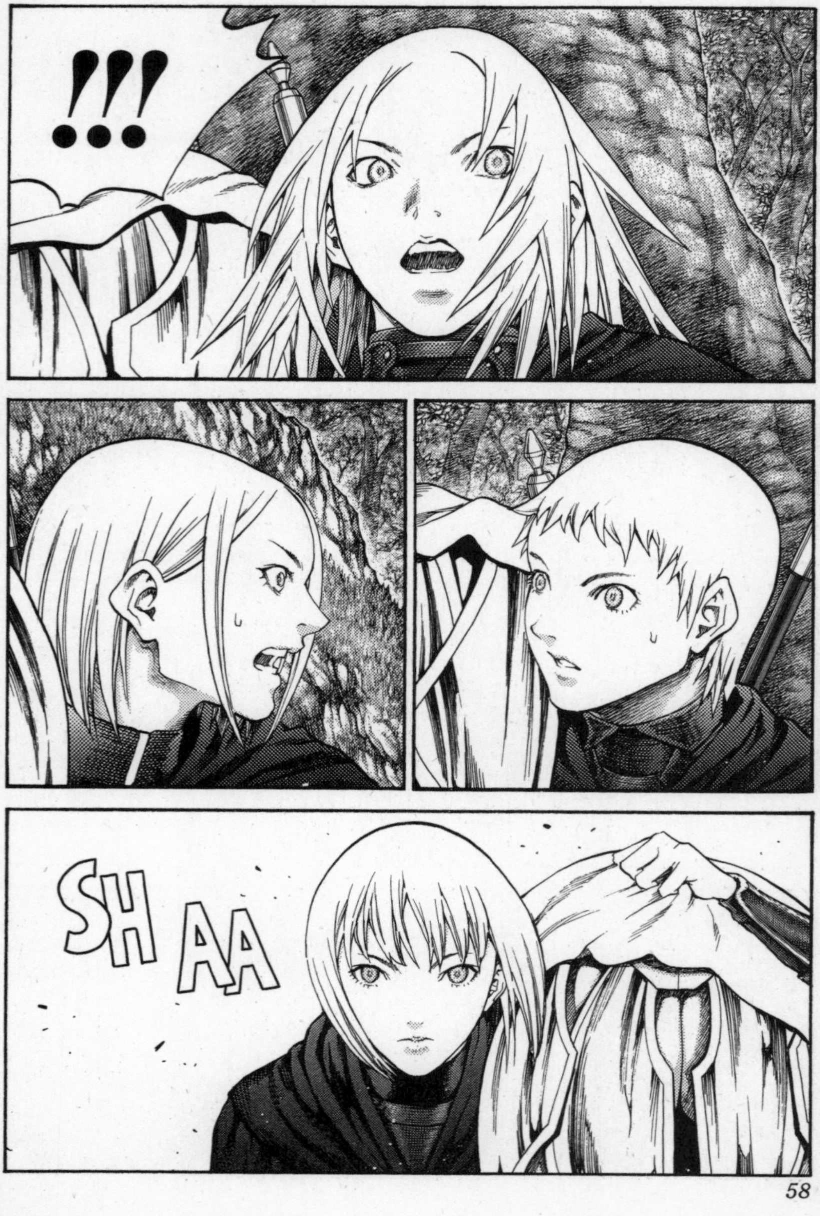
!!!
SHAA

READ THIS WAY

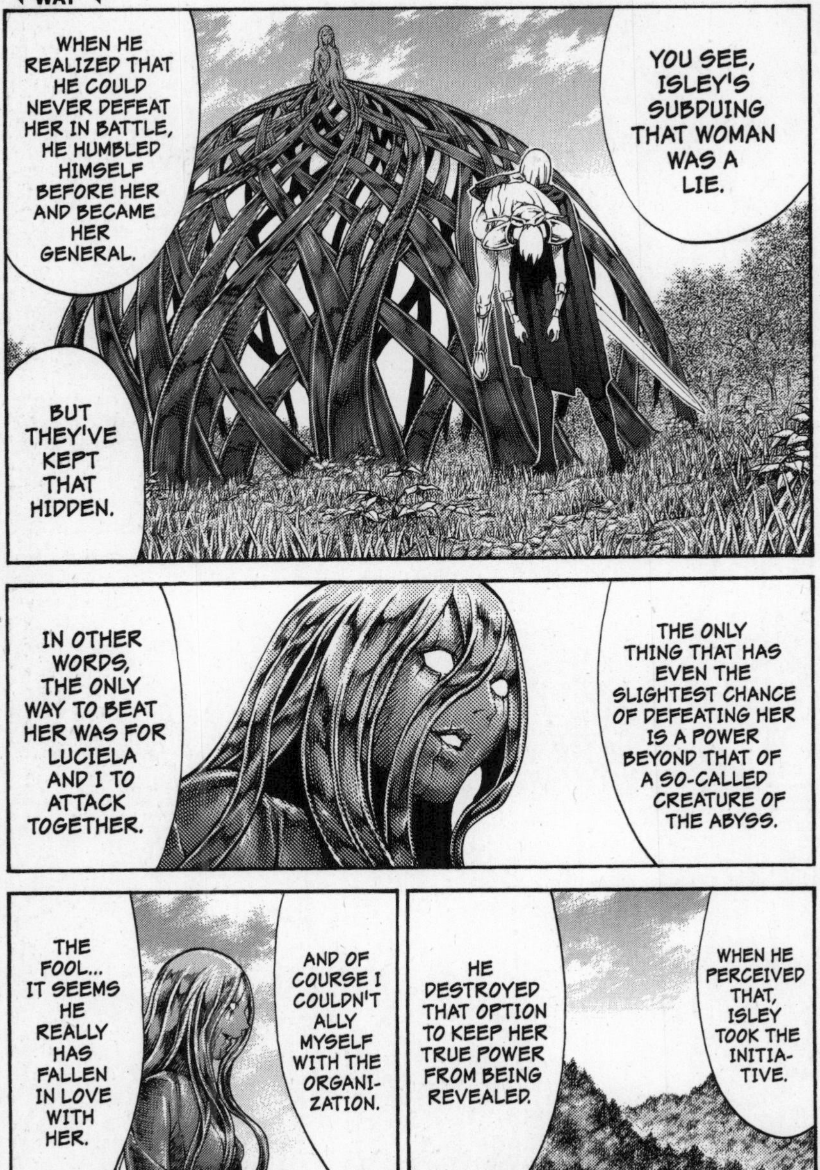
YOU SEE, ISLEY'S SUBDUING THAT WOMAN WAS A LIE.
WHEN HE REALIZED THAT HE COULD NEVER DEFEAT HER IN BATTLE, HE HUMBLED HIMSELF BEFORE HER AND BECAME HER GENERAL.
BUT THEY'VE KEPT THAT HIDDEN.
THE ONLY THING THAT HAS EVEN THE SLIGHTEST CHANCE OF DEFEATING HER IS A POWER BEYOND THAT OF A SO-CALLED CREATURE OF THE ABYSS.
IN OTHER WORDS, THE ONLY WAY TO BEAT HER WAS FOR LUCIELA AND I TO ATTACK TOGETHER.
WHEN HE PERCEIVED THAT, ISLEY TOOK THE INITIA-TIVE.
HE DESTROYED THAT OPTION TO KEEP HER TRUE POWER FROM BEING REVEALED.
AND OF COURSE I COULDN'T ALLY MYSELF WITH THE ORGANI-ZATION.
THE FOOL... IT SEEMS HE REALLY HAS FALLEN IN LOVE WITH HER.

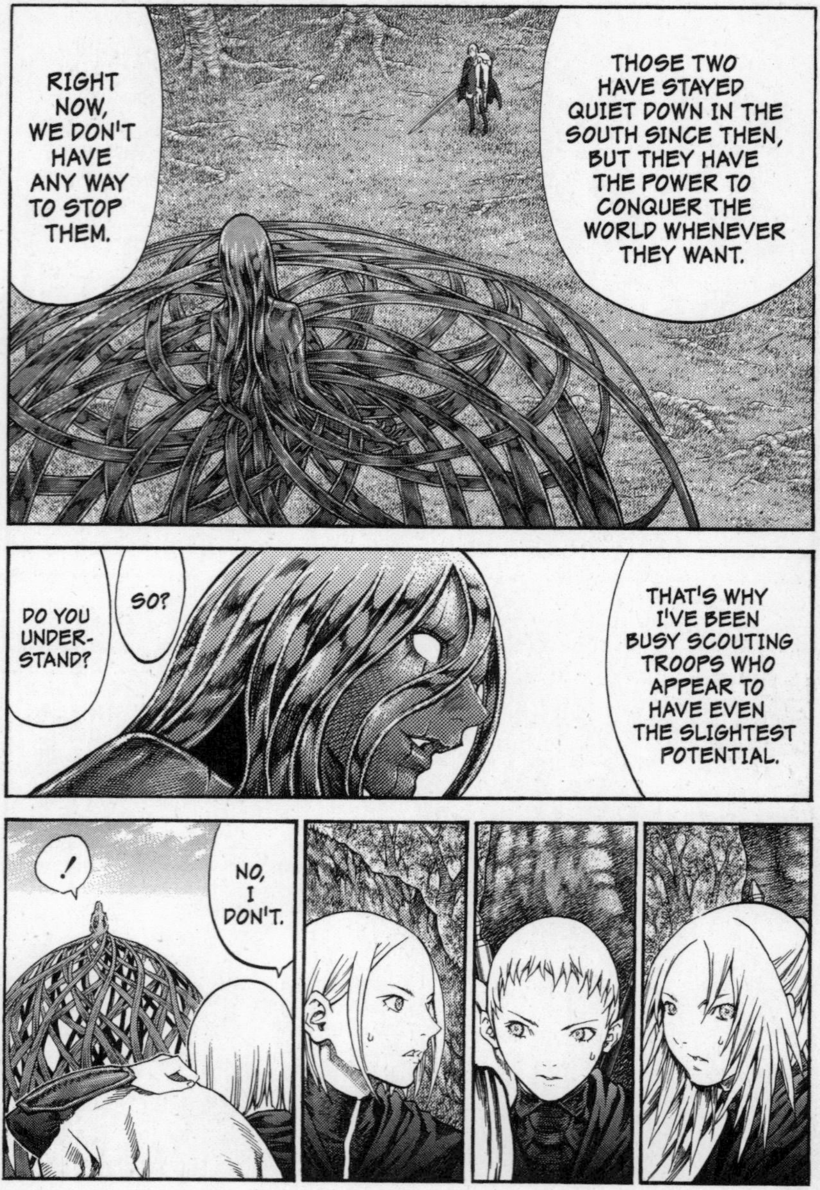
THOSE TWO HAVE STAYED QUIET DOWN IN THE SOUTH SINCE THEN, BUT THEY HAVE THE POWER TO CONQUER THE WORLD WHENEVER THEY WANT.
RIGHT NOW, WE DON'T HAVE ANY WAY TO STOP THEM.
THAT'S WHY I'VE BEEN BUSY SCOUTING TROOPS WHO APPEAR TO HAVE EVEN THE SLIGHTEST POTENTIAL.
SO?
DO YOU UNDER-STAND?
NO, I DON'T.
!

READ THIS WAY

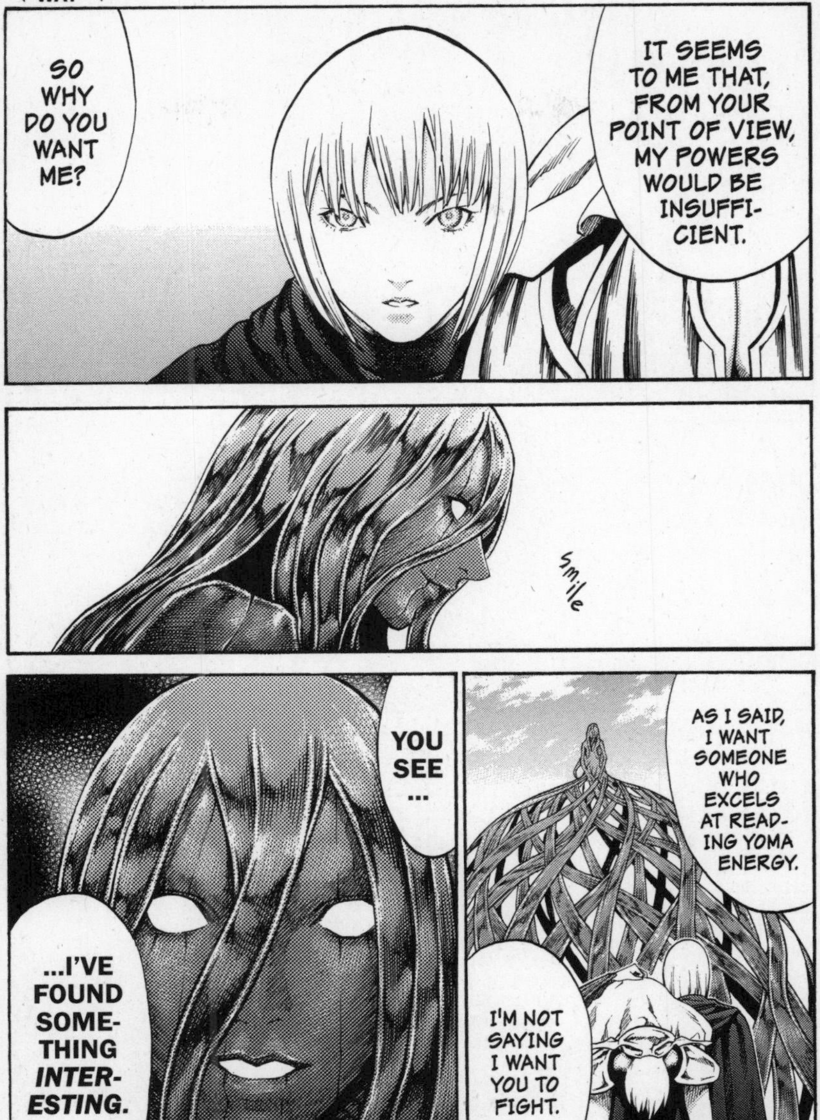

IT SEEMS TO ME THAT, FROM YOUR POINT OF VIEW, MY POWERS WOULD BE INSUFFICIENT.
SO WHY DO YOU WANT ME?
Smile
AS I SAID, I WANT SOMEONE WHO EXCELS AT READING YOMA ENERGY.
I'M NOT SAYING I WANT YOU TO FIGHT.
YOU SEE...
...I'VE FOUND SOMETHING *INTERESTING.*

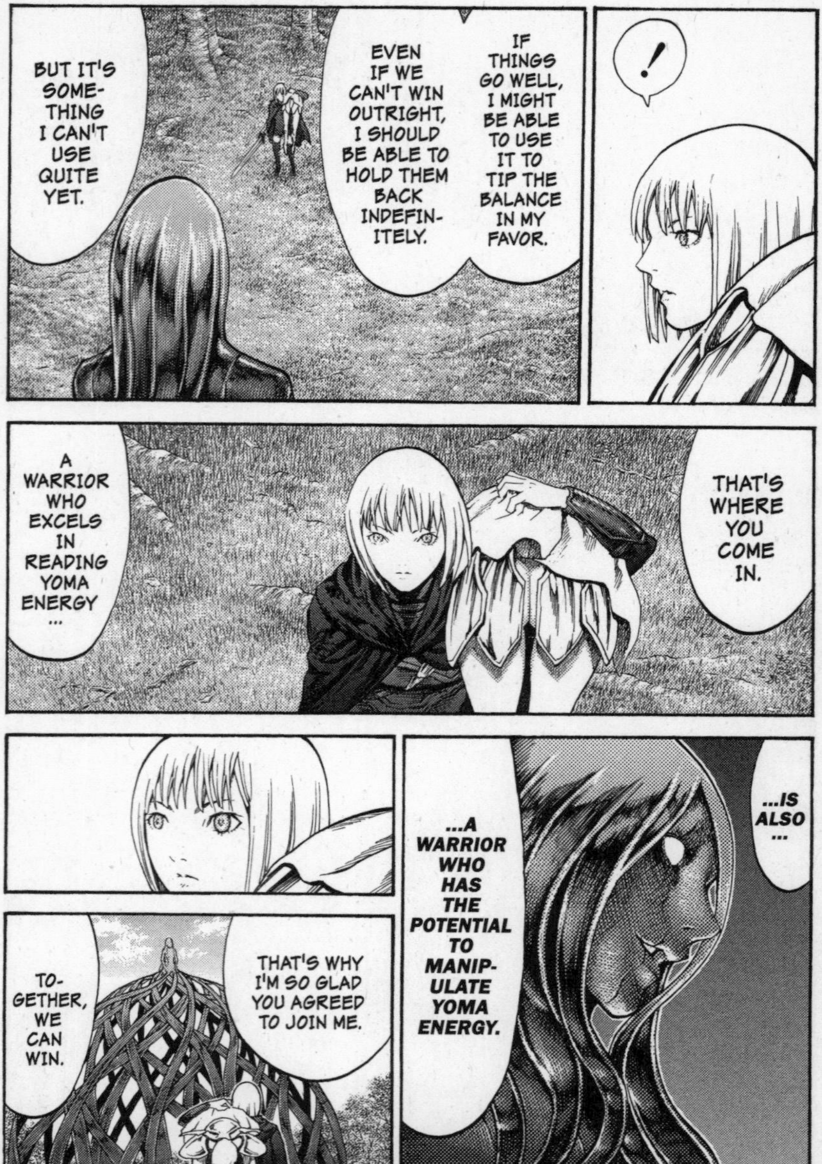
!
IF THINGS GO WELL, I MIGHT BE ABLE TO USE IT TO TIP THE BALANCE IN MY FAVOR.
EVEN IF WE CAN'T WIN OUTRIGHT, I SHOULD BE ABLE TO HOLD THEM BACK INDEFIN-ITELY.
BUT IT'S SOME-THING I CAN'T USE QUITE YET.
THAT'S WHERE YOU COME IN.
A WARRIOR WHO EXCELS IN READING YOMA ENERGY ...
...IS ALSO ...
...A WARRIOR WHO HAS THE POTENTIAL TO MANIP-ULATE YOMA ENERGY.
THAT'S WHY I'M SO GLAD YOU AGREED TO JOIN ME.
TO-GETHER, WE CAN WIN.

READ THIS WAY

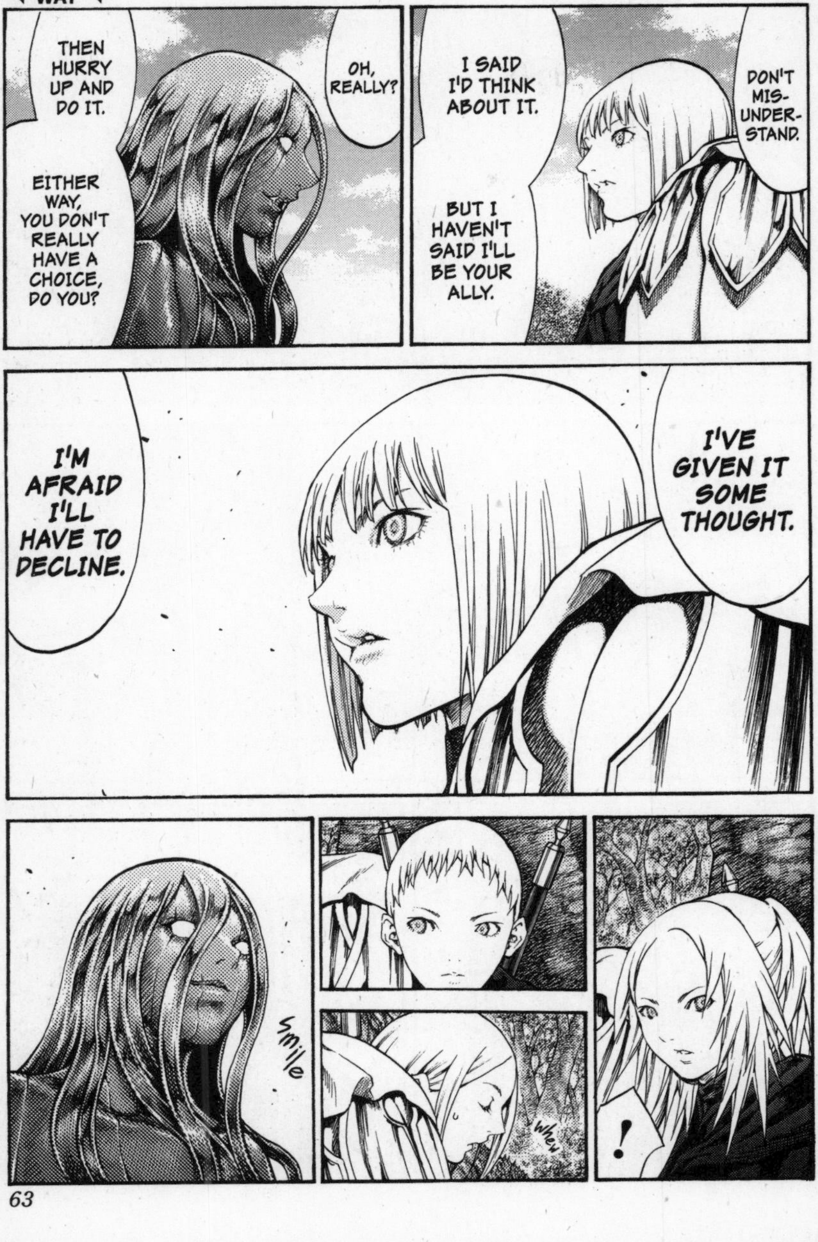

DON'T MIS-UNDERSTAND.
I SAID I'D THINK ABOUT IT.
BUT I HAVEN'T SAID I'LL BE YOUR ALLY.
OH, REALLY?
THEN HURRY UP AND DO IT.
EITHER WAY, YOU DON'T REALLY HAVE A CHOICE, DO YOU?
I'VE GIVEN IT SOME THOUGHT.
I'M AFRAID I'LL HAVE TO DECLINE.
!
whew
Smile

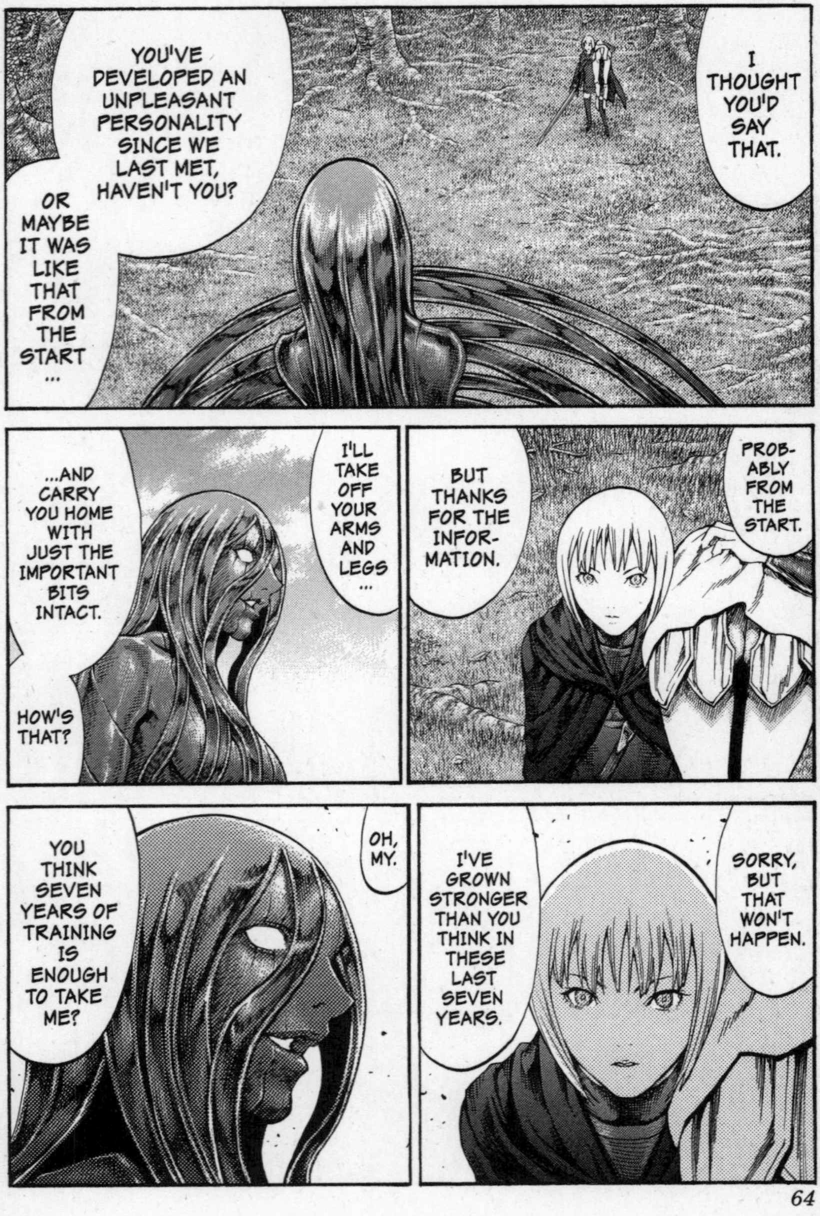
I THOUGHT YOU'D SAY THAT.
YOU'VE DEVELOPED AN UNPLEASANT PERSONALITY SINCE WE LAST MET, HAVEN'T YOU?
OR MAYBE IT WAS LIKE THAT FROM THE START ...
PROB-ABLY FROM THE START.
BUT THANKS FOR THE INFOR-MATION.
I'LL TAKE OFF YOUR ARMS AND LEGS ...
...AND CARRY YOU HOME WITH JUST THE IMPORTANT BITS INTACT.
HOW'S THAT?
SORRY, BUT THAT WON'T HAPPEN.
I'VE GROWN STRONGER THAN YOU THINK IN THESE LAST SEVEN YEARS.
OH, MY.
YOU THINK SEVEN YEARS OF TRAINING IS ENOUGH TO TAKE ME?

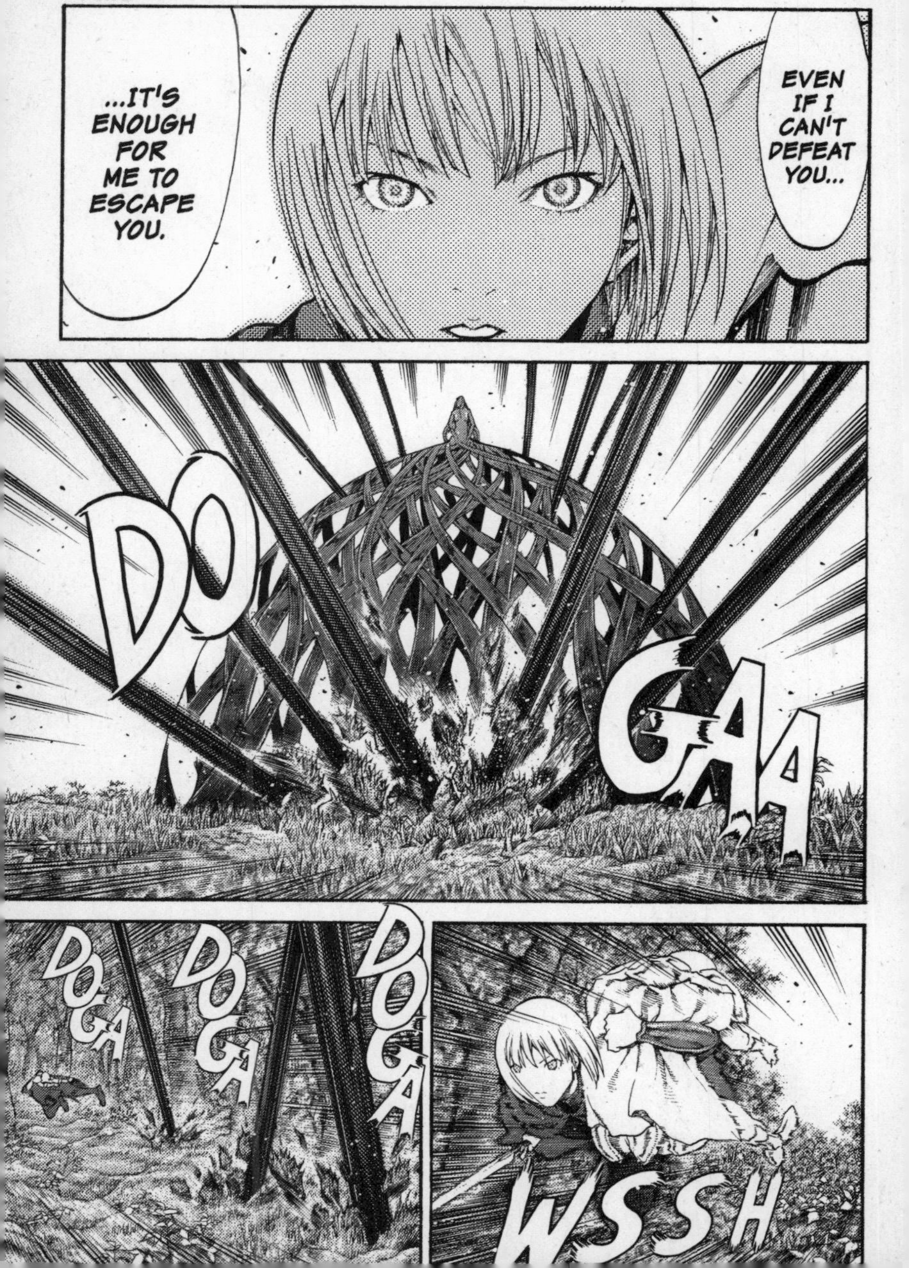
READ THIS WAY
EVEN IF I CAN'T DEFEAT YOU...
...IT'S ENOUGH FOR ME TO ESCAPE YOU.
DO
GAA
WSSH
DOGA
DOGA
DOGA

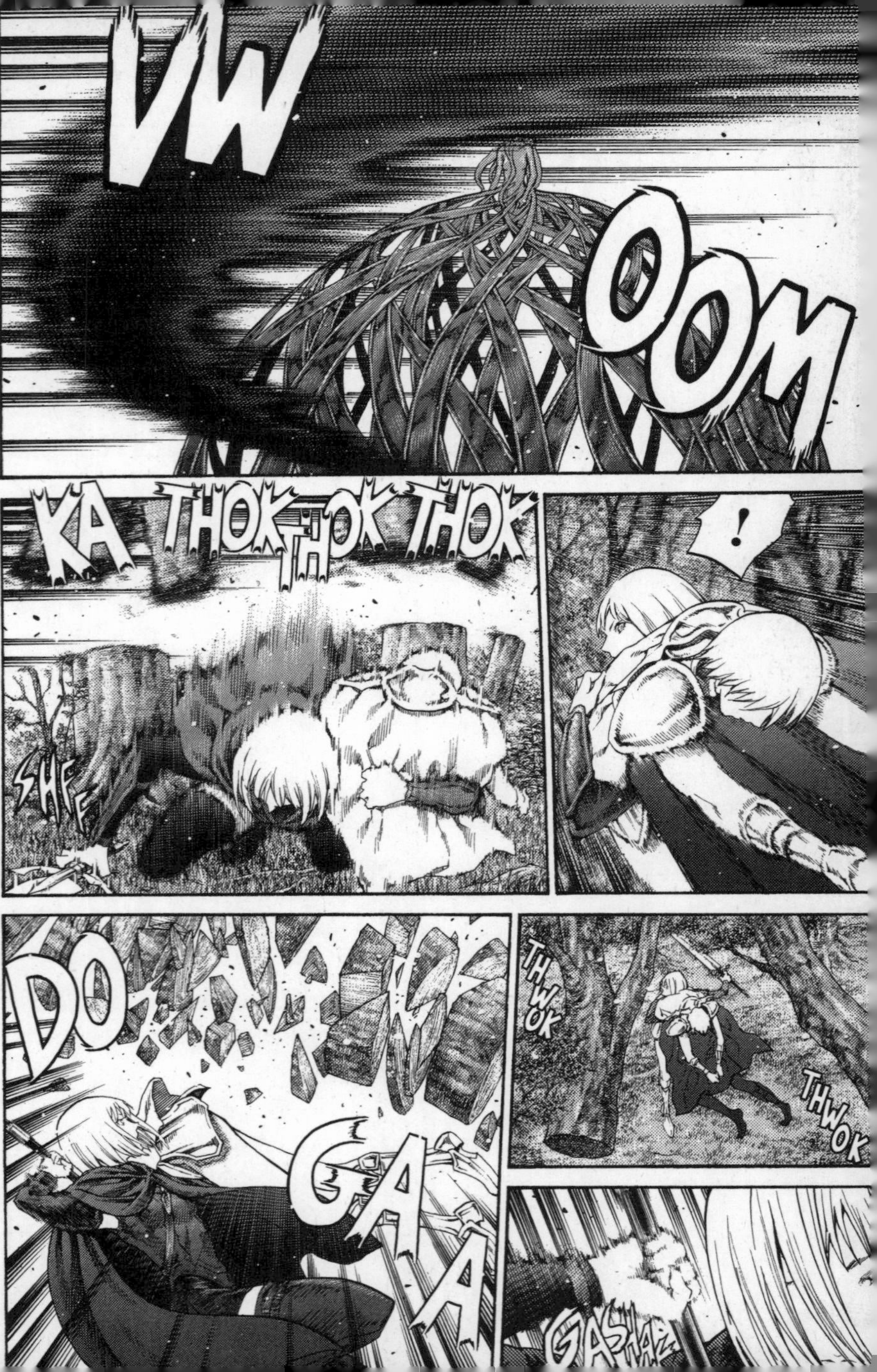
VWOOM
!
KA THOK THOK THOK
SHFF
THWOK
THWOK
GASHAZ
DO
GAA

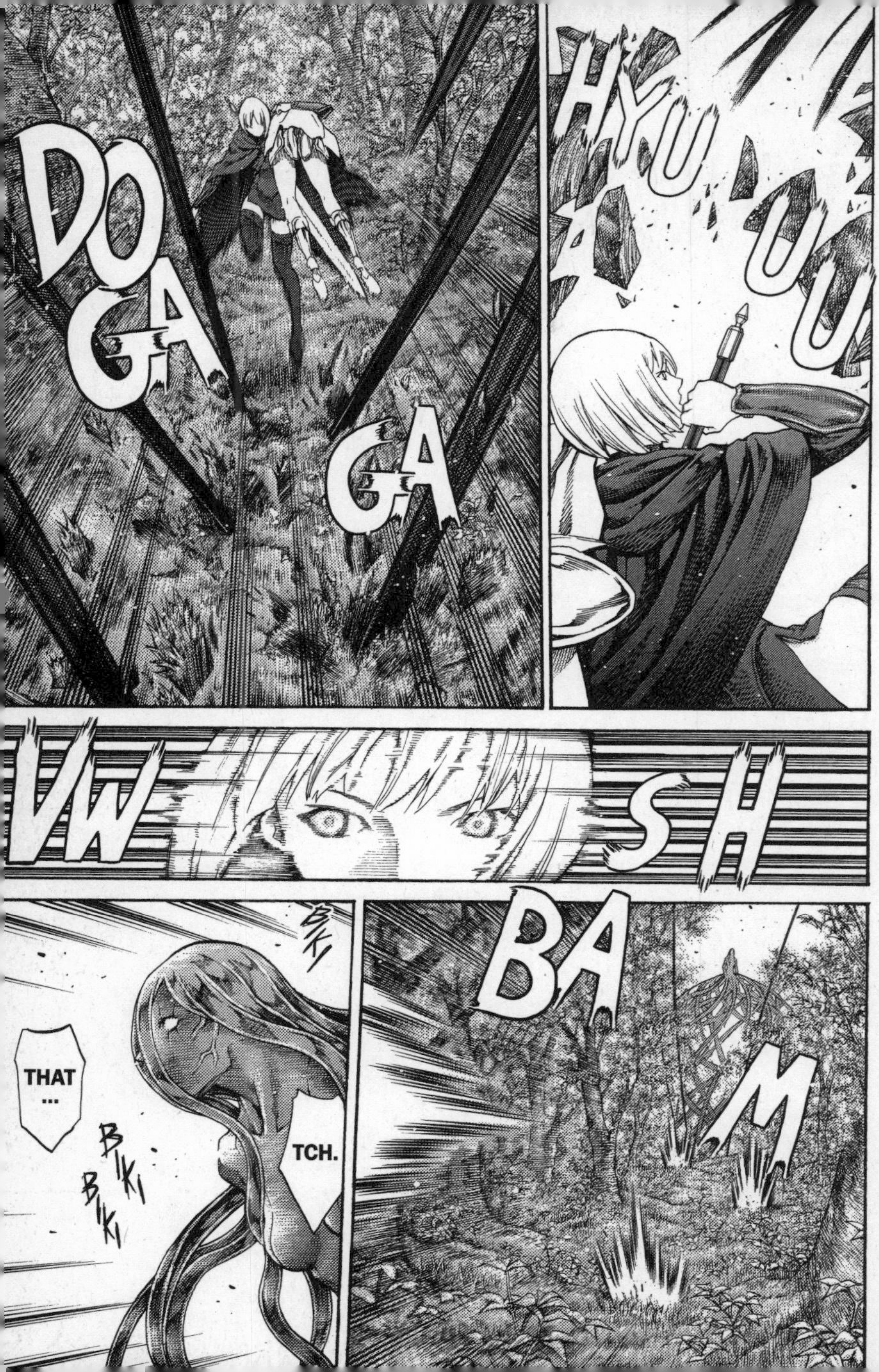
HYUUUU
DOGA
GA
VWSH
BAM
BIKI
TCH.
THAT ...
BIKI
BIKI

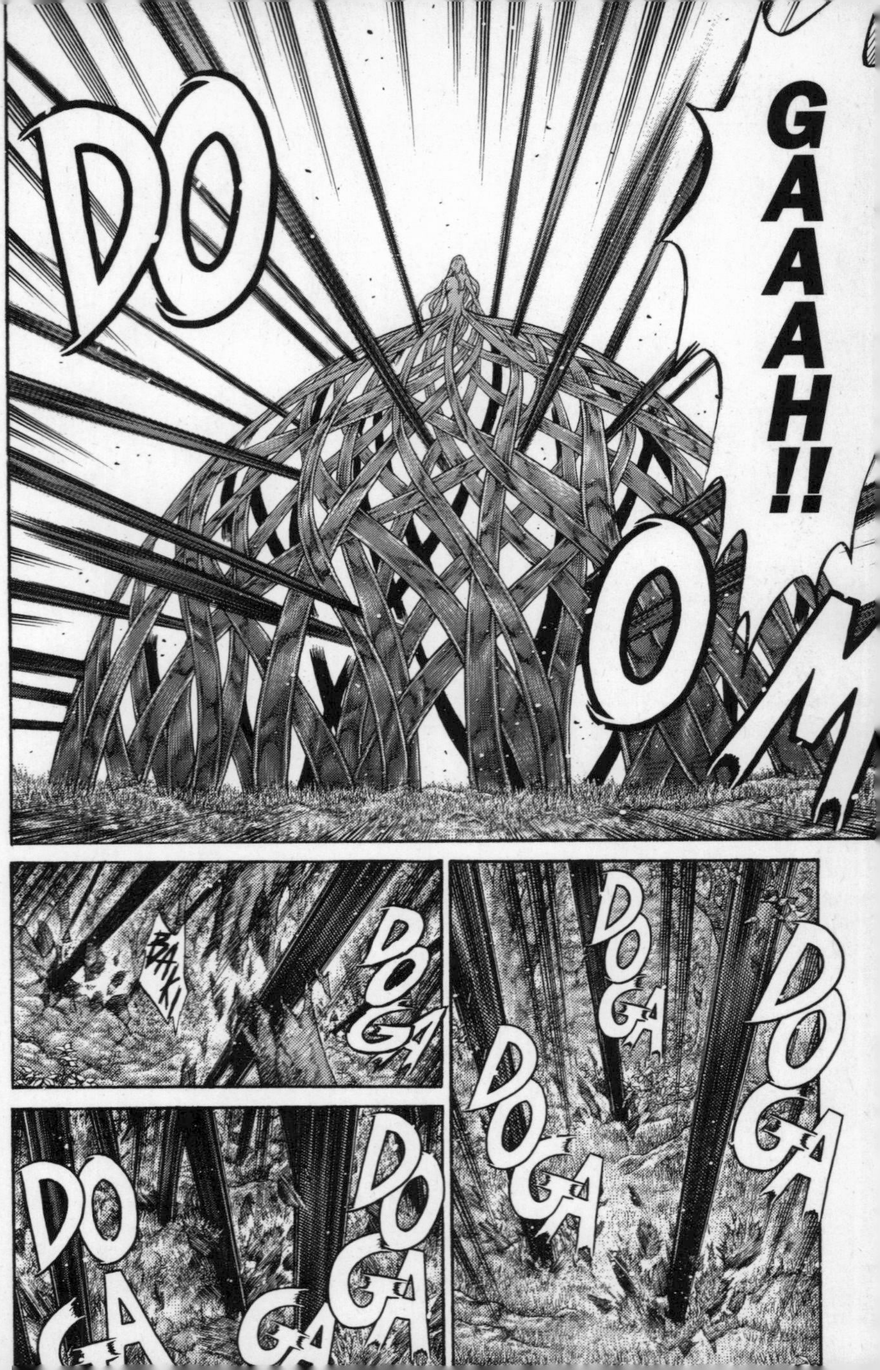
GAAAH!!
DOOM
DOGA
DOGA
DOGA
DOGA
BAKI
DOGA
DO
GA

READ THIS WAY

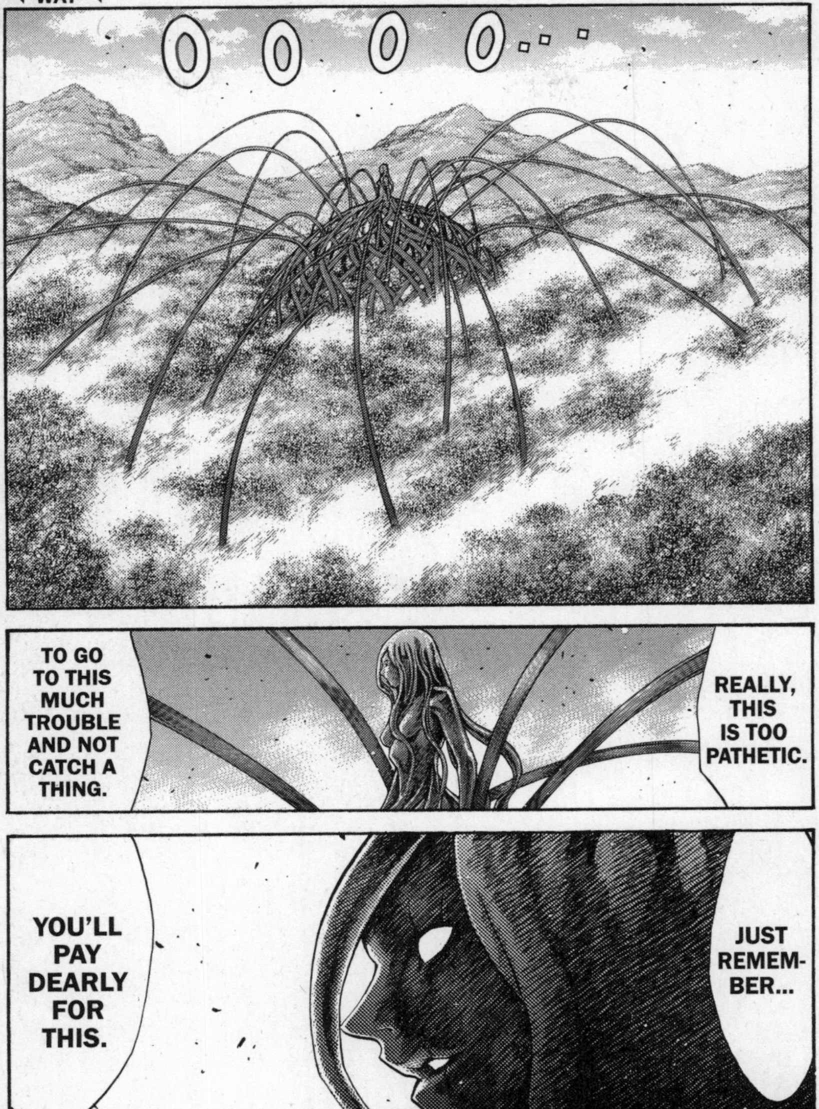
OOOO...
REALLY, THIS IS TOO PATHETIC.
TO GO TO THIS MUCH TROUBLE AND NOT CATCH A THING.
JUST REMEMBER...
YOU'LL PAY DEARLY FOR THIS.

クレイモア
Claymore

Scene 72: The Defiant Ones, Part 5

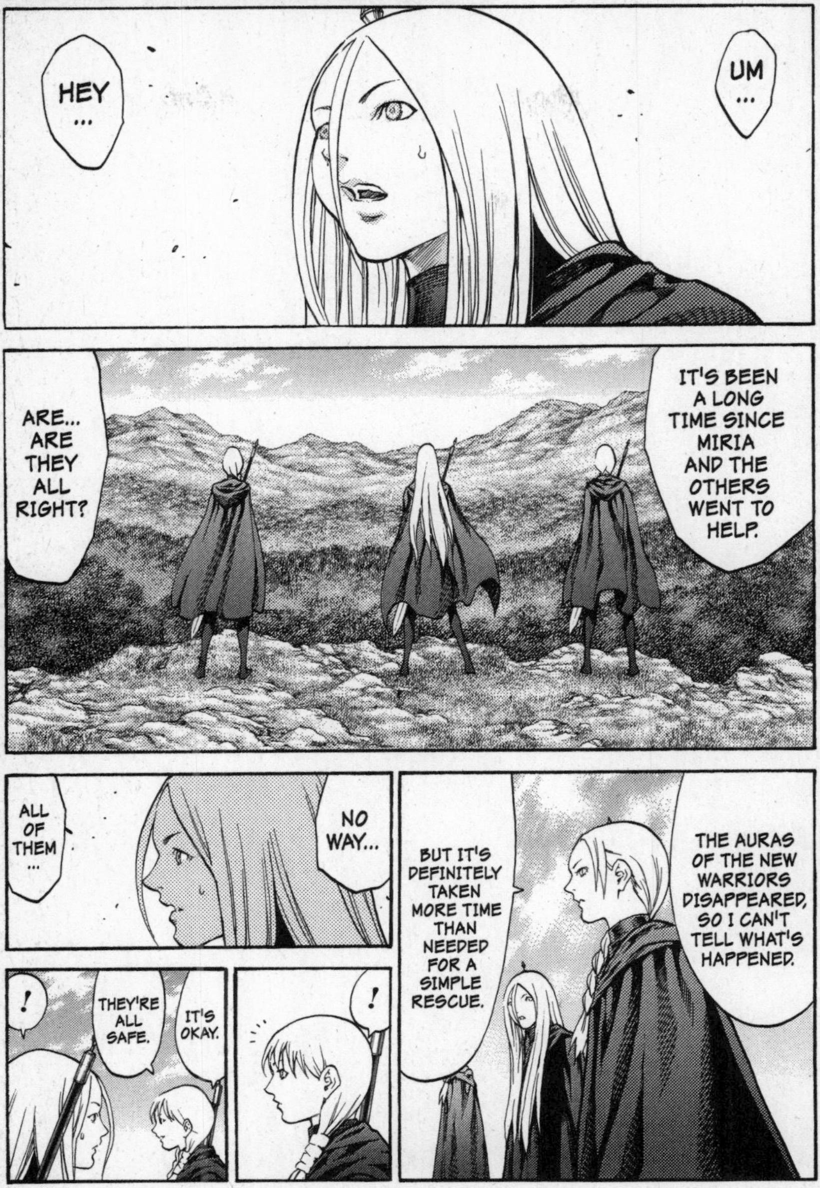

UM ...
HEY ...
IT'S BEEN A LONG TIME SINCE MIRIA AND THE OTHERS WENT TO HELP.
ARE... ARE THEY ALL RIGHT?
THE AURAS OF THE NEW WARRIORS DISAPPEARED, SO I CAN'T TELL WHAT'S HAPPENED.
BUT IT'S DEFINITELY TAKEN MORE TIME THAN NEEDED FOR A SIMPLE RESCUE.
NO WAY...
ALL OF THEM ...
!
IT'S OKAY.
THEY'RE ALL SAFE.
!

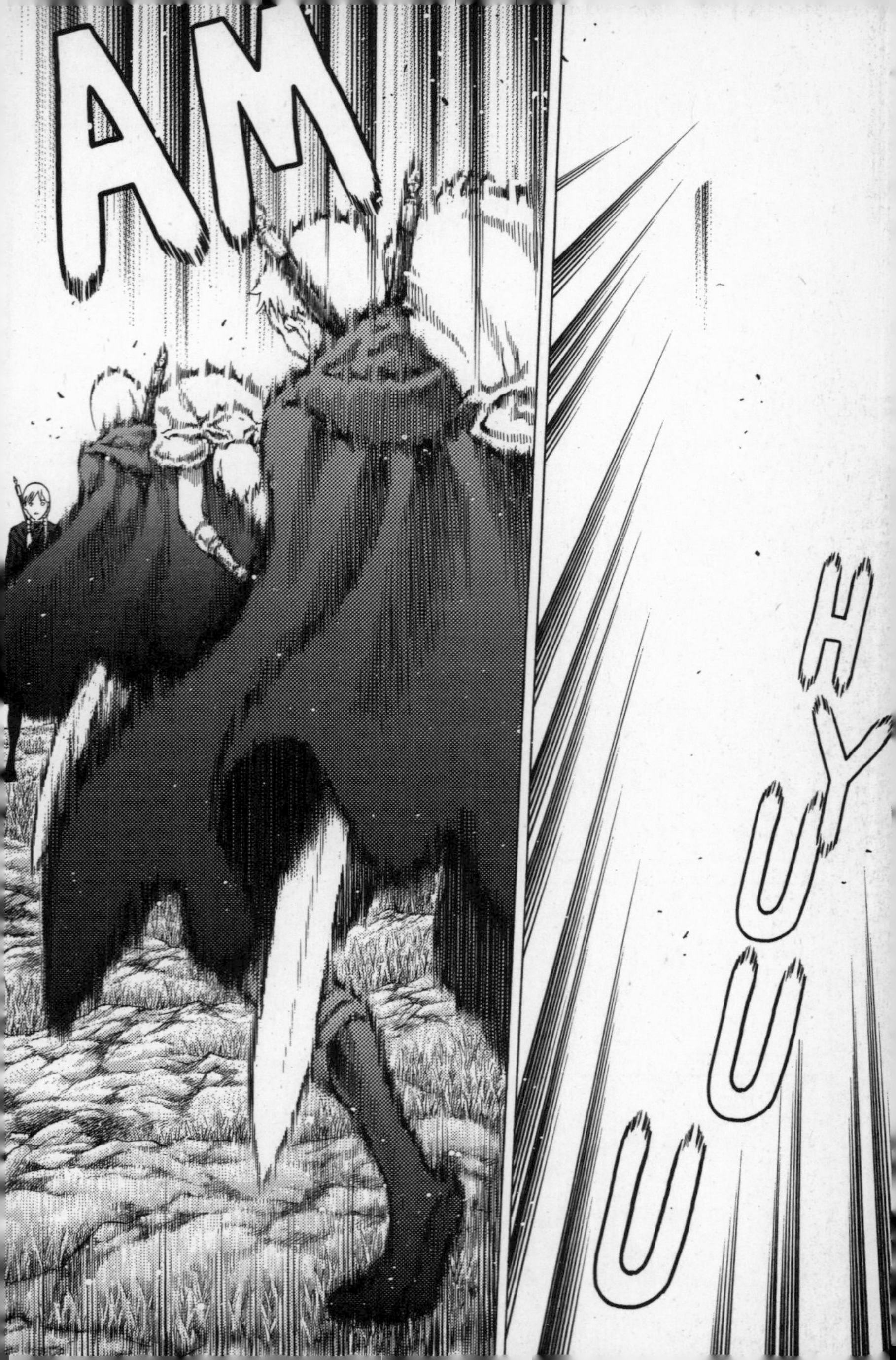
HYUUUU
AM

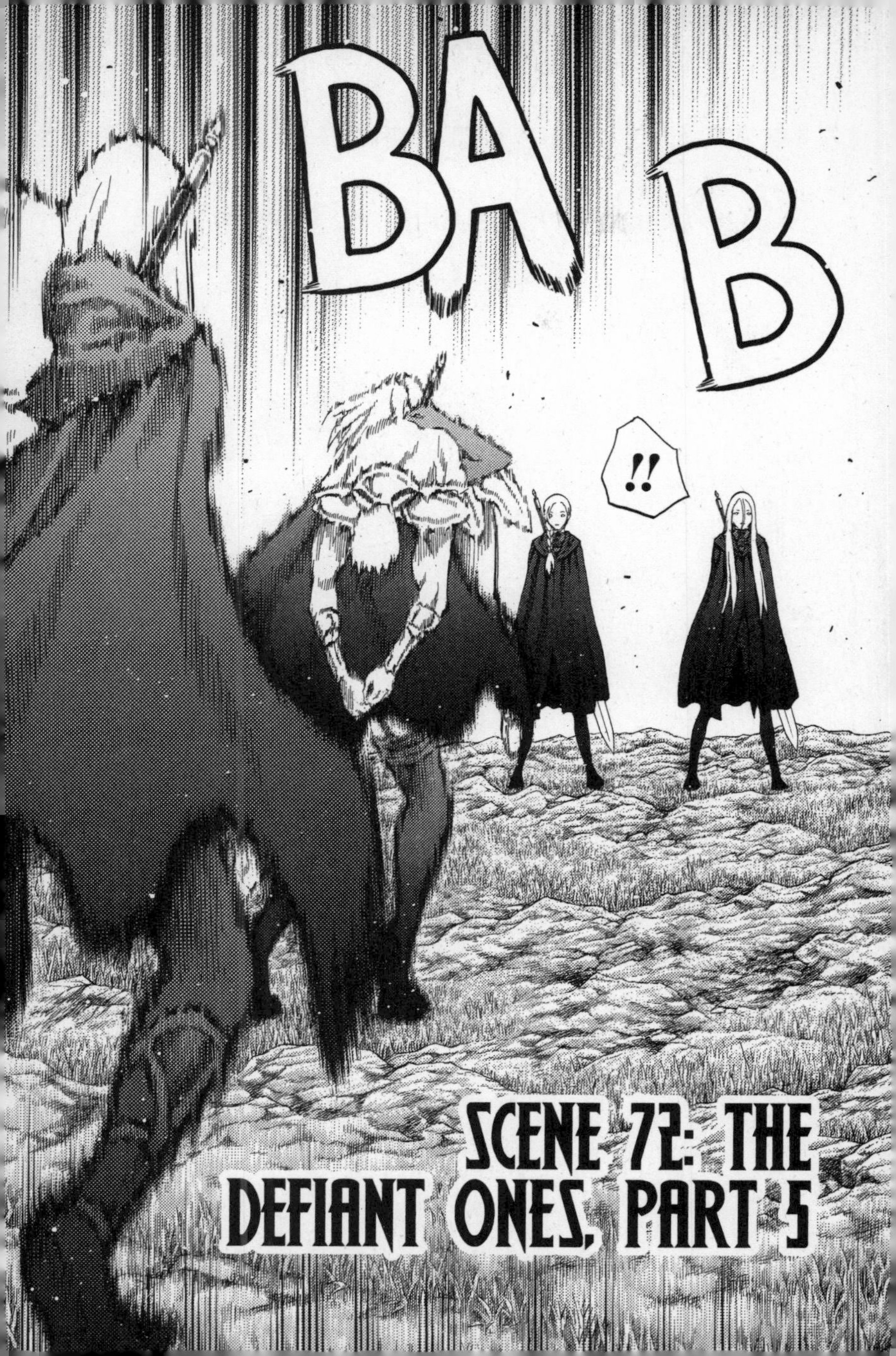
BA
B
!!
SCENE 72: THE DEFIANT ONES, PART 5

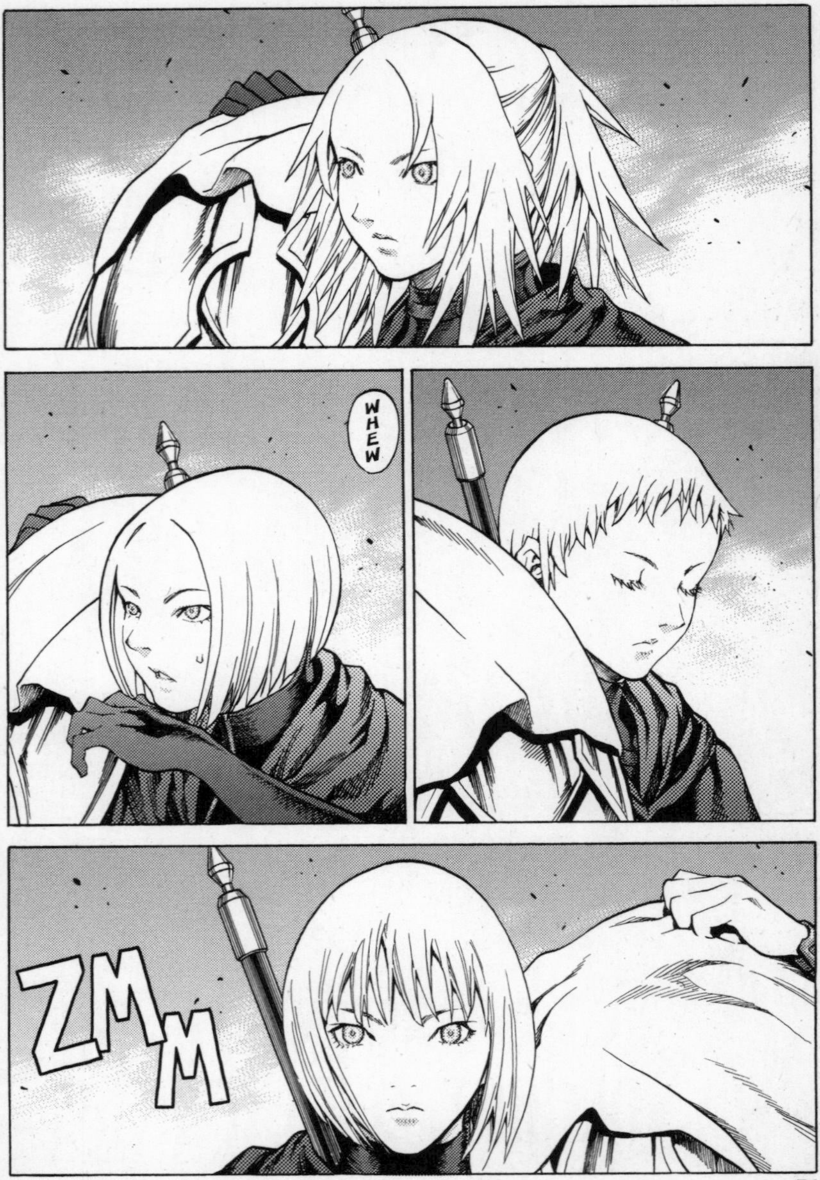
WHEW
ZMM

READ THIS WAY

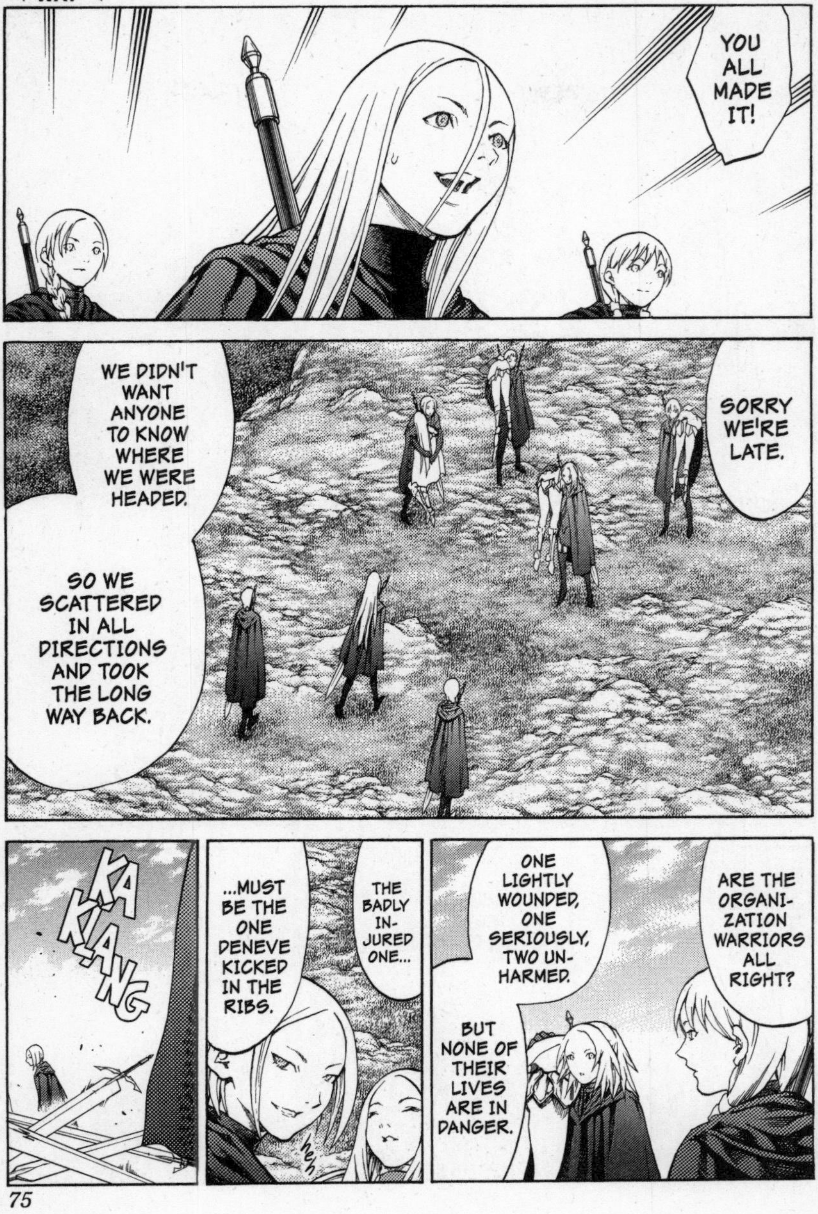
YOU ALL MADE IT!
SORRY WE'RE LATE.
WE DIDN'T WANT ANYONE TO KNOW WHERE WE WERE HEADED.
SO WE SCATTERED IN ALL DIRECTIONS AND TOOK THE LONG WAY BACK.
ARE THE ORGANIZATION WARRIORS ALL RIGHT?
ONE LIGHTLY WOUNDED, ONE SERIOUSLY, TWO UNHARMED.
BUT NONE OF THEIR LIVES ARE IN DANGER.
THE BADLY INJURED ONE...
...MUST BE THE ONE DENEVE KICKED IN THE RIBS.
heh
KA KLANG

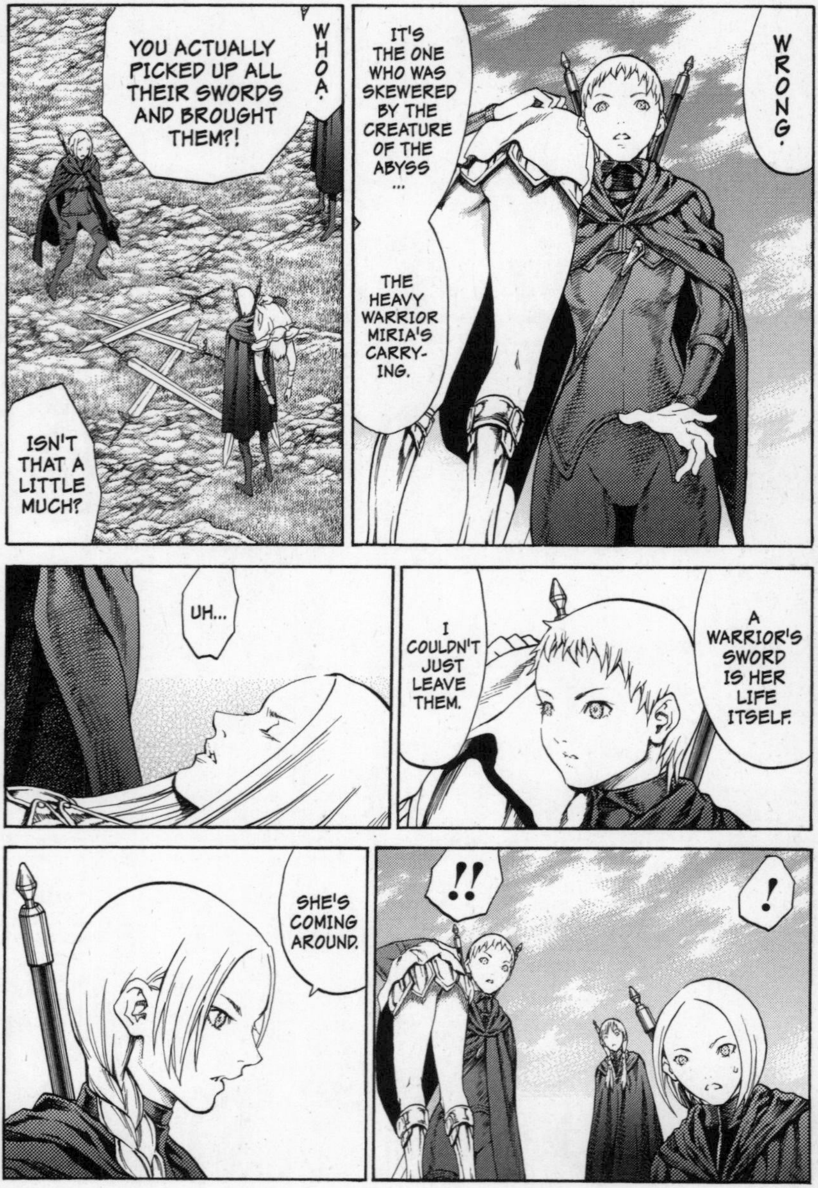
WRONG.
IT'S THE ONE WHO WAS SKEWERED BY THE CREATURE OF THE ABYSS ...
THE HEAVY WARRIOR MIRIA'S CARRYING.
WHOA.
YOU ACTUALLY PICKED UP ALL THEIR SWORDS AND BROUGHT THEM?!
ISN'T THAT A LITTLE MUCH?
A WARRIOR'S SWORD IS HER LIFE ITSELF.
I COULDN'T JUST LEAVE THEM.
UH...
!
!!
SHE'S COMING AROUND.

READ THIS WAY

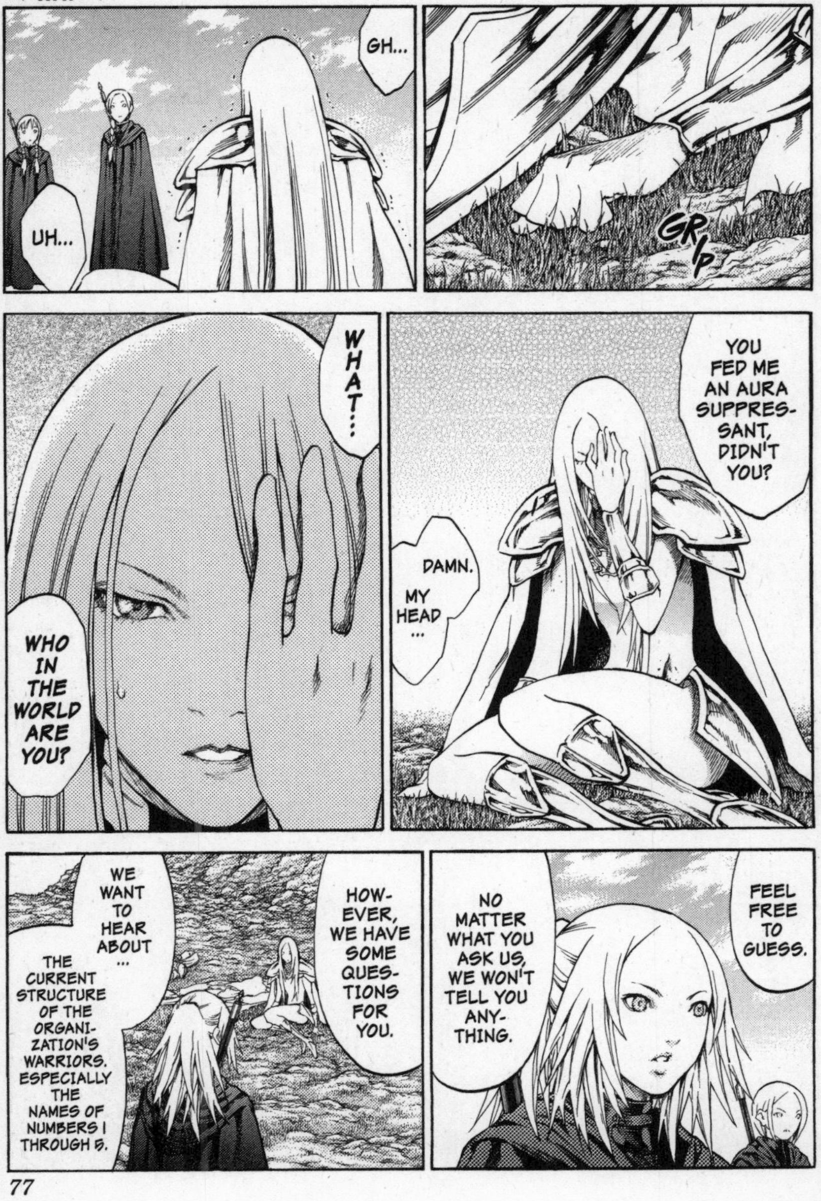

GRIP
GH...
UH...
YOU FED ME AN AURA SUPPRESSANT, DIDN'T YOU?
DAMN.
MY HEAD...
WHAT...
WHO IN THE WORLD ARE YOU?
FEEL FREE TO GUESS.
NO MATTER WHAT YOU ASK US, WE WON'T TELL YOU ANYTHING.
HOWEVER, WE HAVE SOME QUESTIONS FOR YOU.
WE WANT TO HEAR ABOUT...
THE CURRENT STRUCTURE OF THE ORGANIZATION'S WARRIORS. ESPECIALLY THE NAMES OF NUMBERS 1 THROUGH 5.

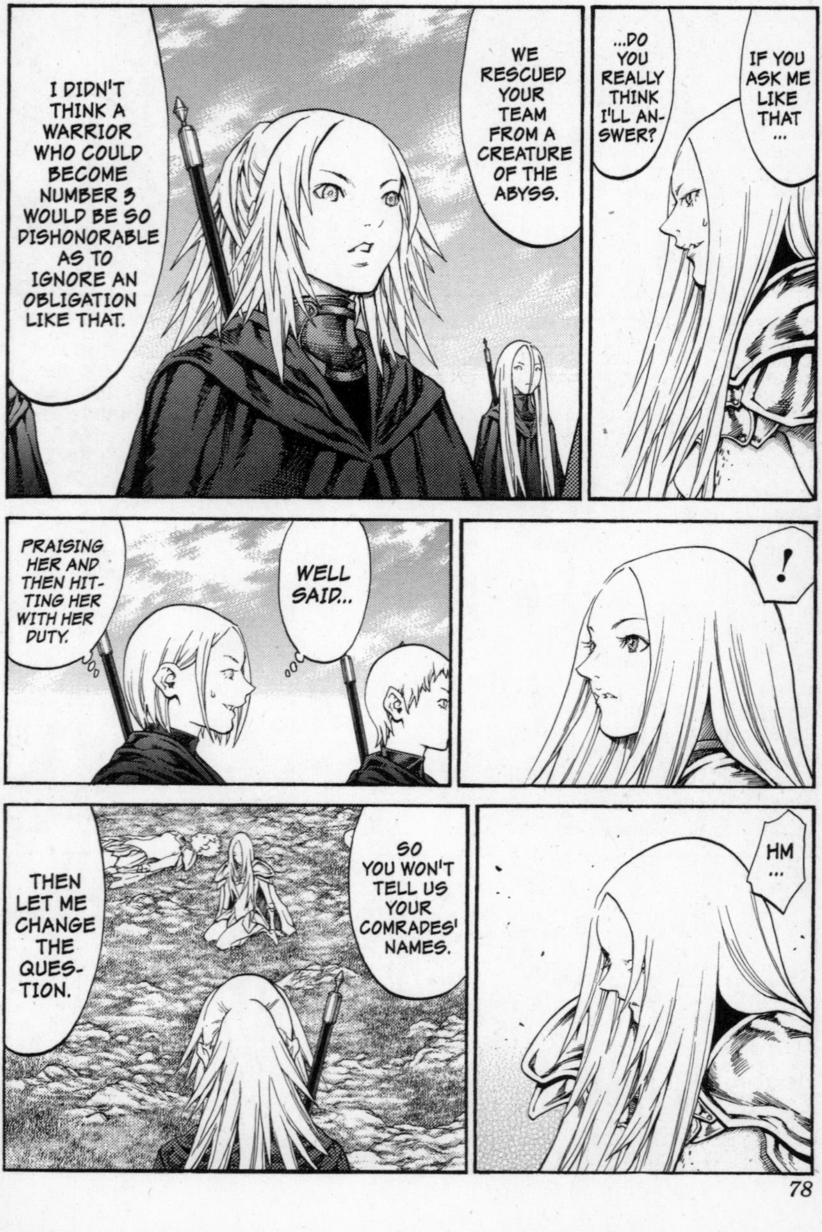
IF YOU ASK ME LIKE THAT ...
...DO YOU REALLY THINK I'LL AN-SWER?
WE RESCUED YOUR TEAM FROM A CREATURE OF THE ABYSS.
I DIDN'T THINK A WARRIOR WHO COULD BECOME NUMBER 3 WOULD BE SO DISHONORABLE AS TO IGNORE AN OBLIGATION LIKE THAT.
!
WELL SAID...
PRAISING HER AND THEN HIT-TING HER WITH HER DUTY.
HM ...
SO YOU WON'T TELL US YOUR COMRADES' NAMES.
THEN LET ME CHANGE THE QUES-TION.

READ THIS WAY

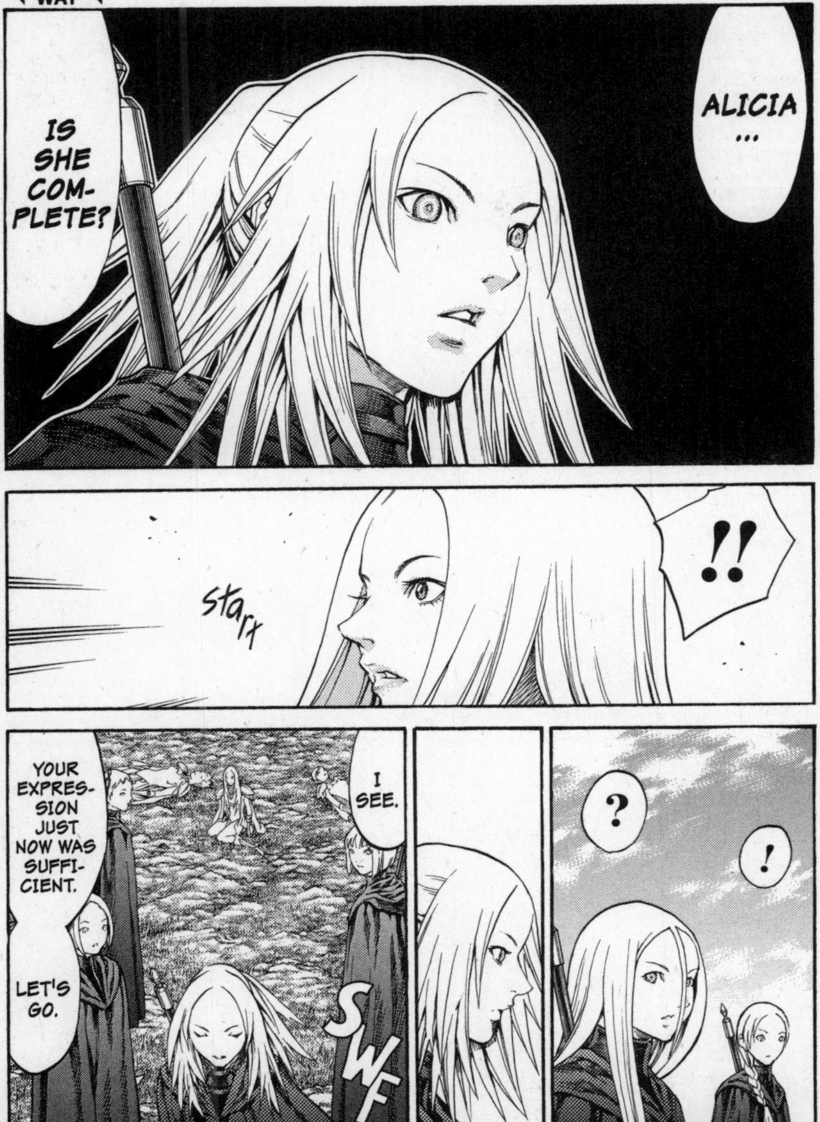

ALICIA ...
IS SHE COMPLETE?
!!
starx
?
!
I SEE.
YOUR EXPRESSION JUST NOW WAS SUFFICIENT.
LET'S GO.
SWF

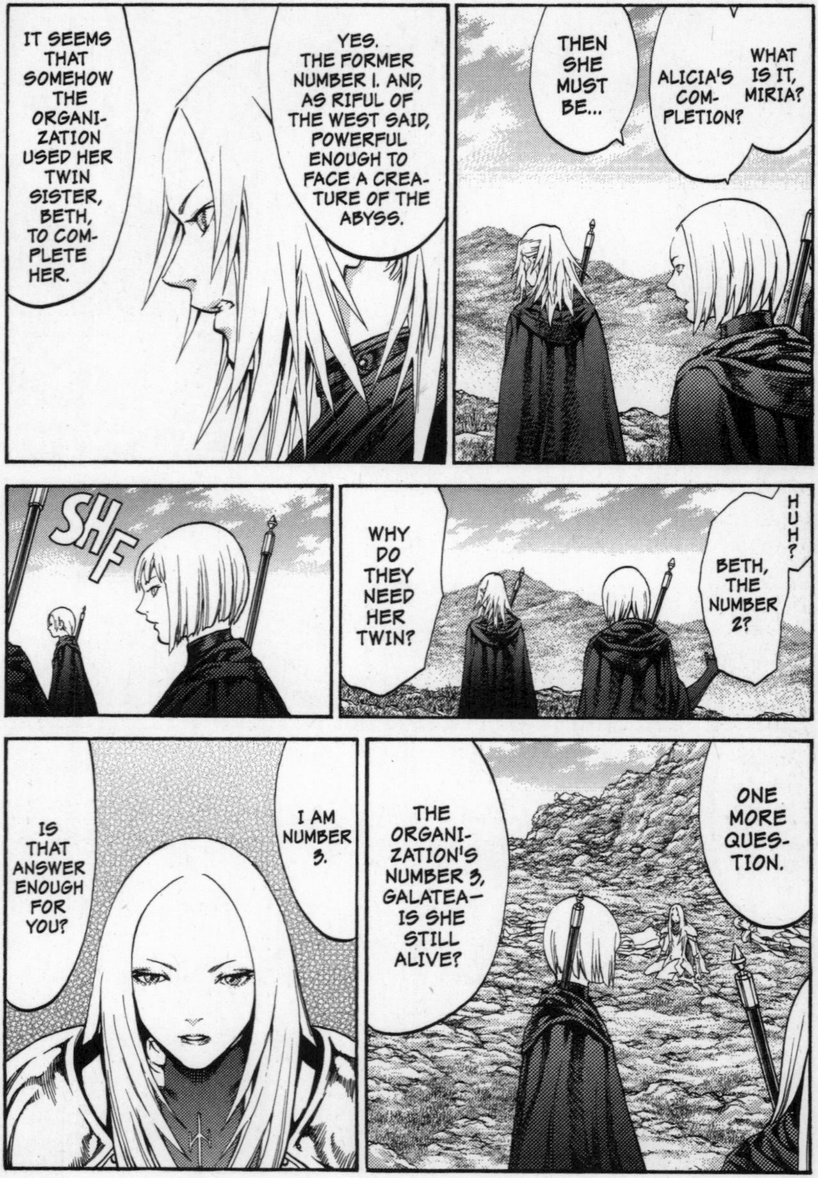
WHAT IS IT, MIRIA?
ALICIA'S COMPLETION?
THEN SHE MUST BE...
YES. THE FORMER NUMBER 1. AND, AS RIFUL OF THE WEST SAID, POWERFUL ENOUGH TO FACE A CREATURE OF THE ABYSS.
IT SEEMS THAT SOMEHOW THE ORGANIZATION USED HER TWIN SISTER, BETH, TO COMPLETE HER.
HUH?
BETH, THE NUMBER 2?
WHY DO THEY NEED HER TWIN?
SHF
ONE MORE QUESTION.
THE ORGANIZATION'S NUMBER 3, GALATEA— IS SHE STILL ALIVE?
I AM NUMBER 3.
IS THAT ANSWER ENOUGH FOR YOU?

READ THIS WAY

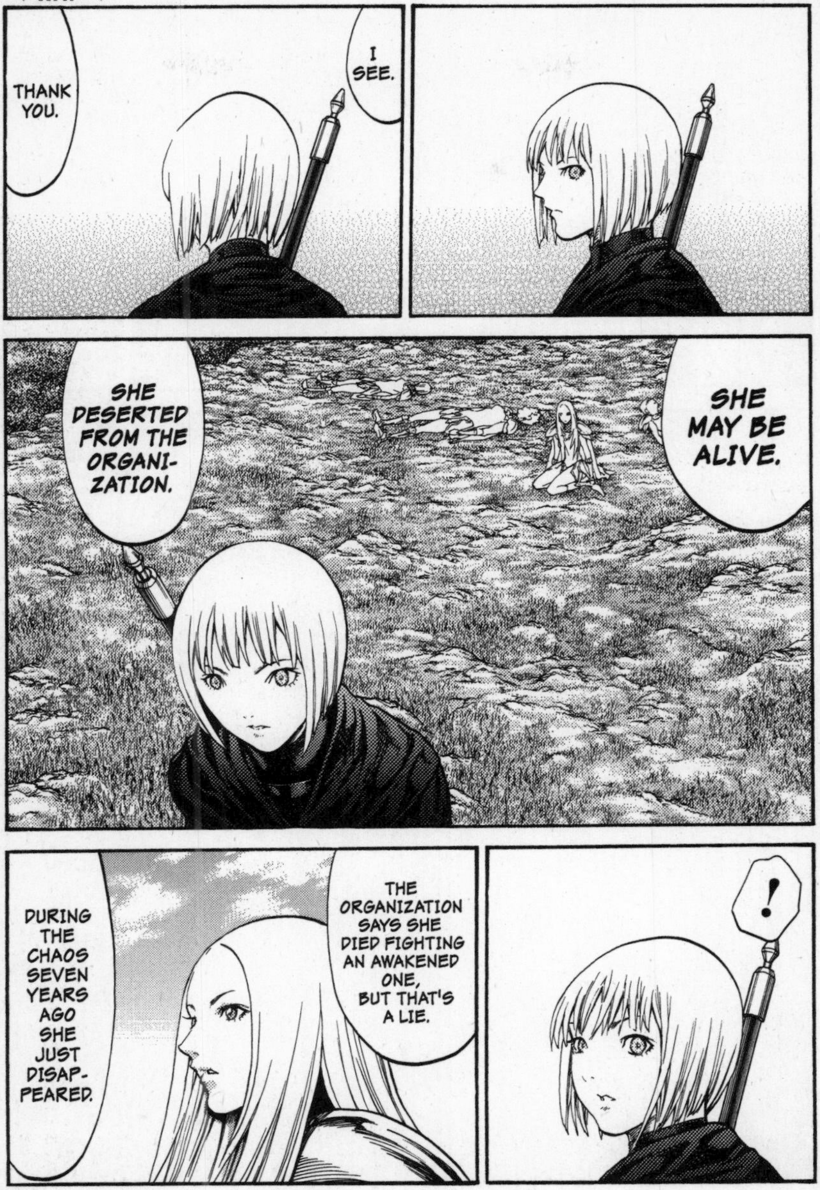

I SEE.
THANK YOU.
SHE MAY BE ALIVE.
SHE DESERTED FROM THE ORGANIZATION.
!
THE ORGANIZATION SAYS SHE DIED FIGHTING AN AWAKENED ONE, BUT THAT'S A LIE.
DURING THE CHAOS SEVEN YEARS AGO SHE JUST DISAPPEARED.

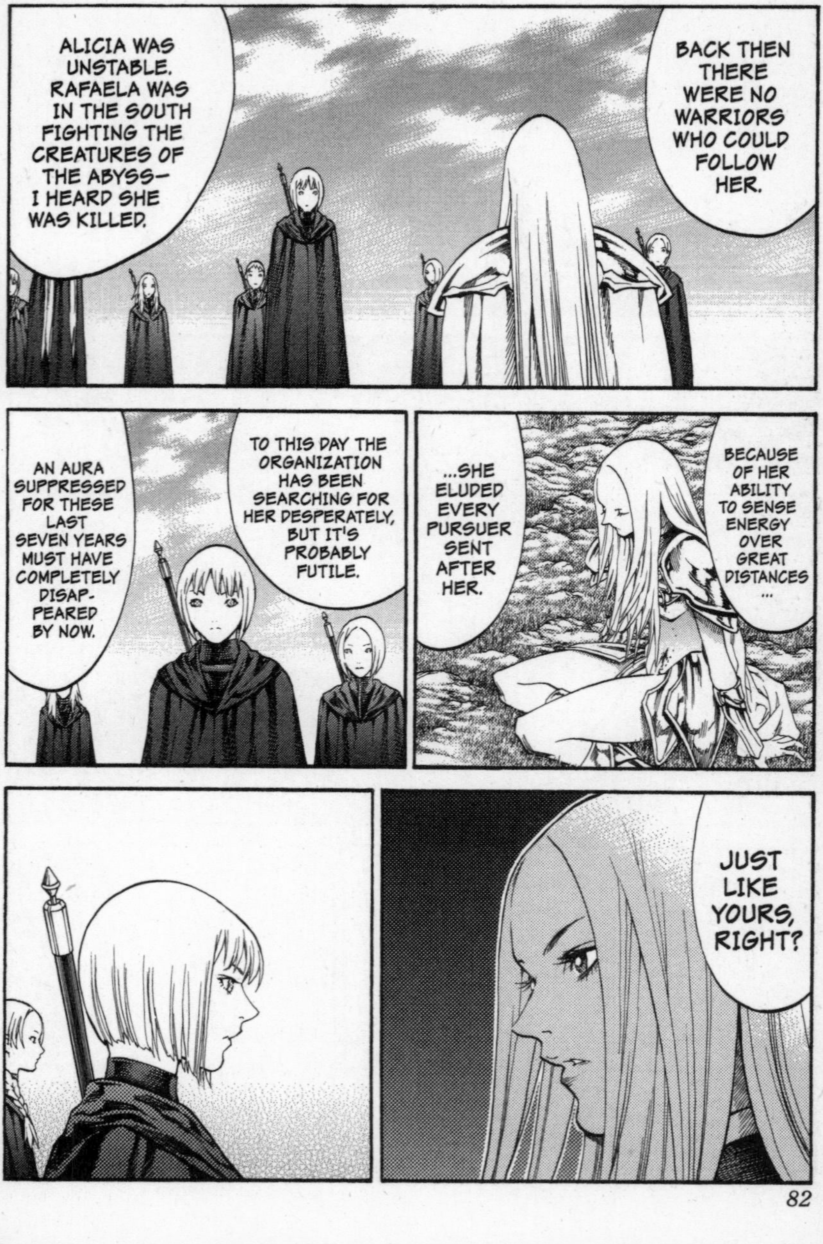
BACK THEN THERE WERE NO WARRIORS WHO COULD FOLLOW HER.
ALICIA WAS UNSTABLE. RAFAELA WAS IN THE SOUTH FIGHTING THE CREATURES OF THE ABYSS— I HEARD SHE WAS KILLED.
BECAUSE OF HER ABILITY TO SENSE ENERGY OVER GREAT DISTANCES ...
...SHE ELUDED EVERY PURSUER SENT AFTER HER.
TO THIS DAY THE ORGANIZATION HAS BEEN SEARCHING FOR HER DESPERATELY, BUT IT'S PROBABLY FUTILE.
AN AURA SUPPRESSED FOR THESE LAST SEVEN YEARS MUST HAVE COMPLETELY DISAP-PEARED BY NOW.
JUST LIKE YOURS, RIGHT?

READ THIS WAY

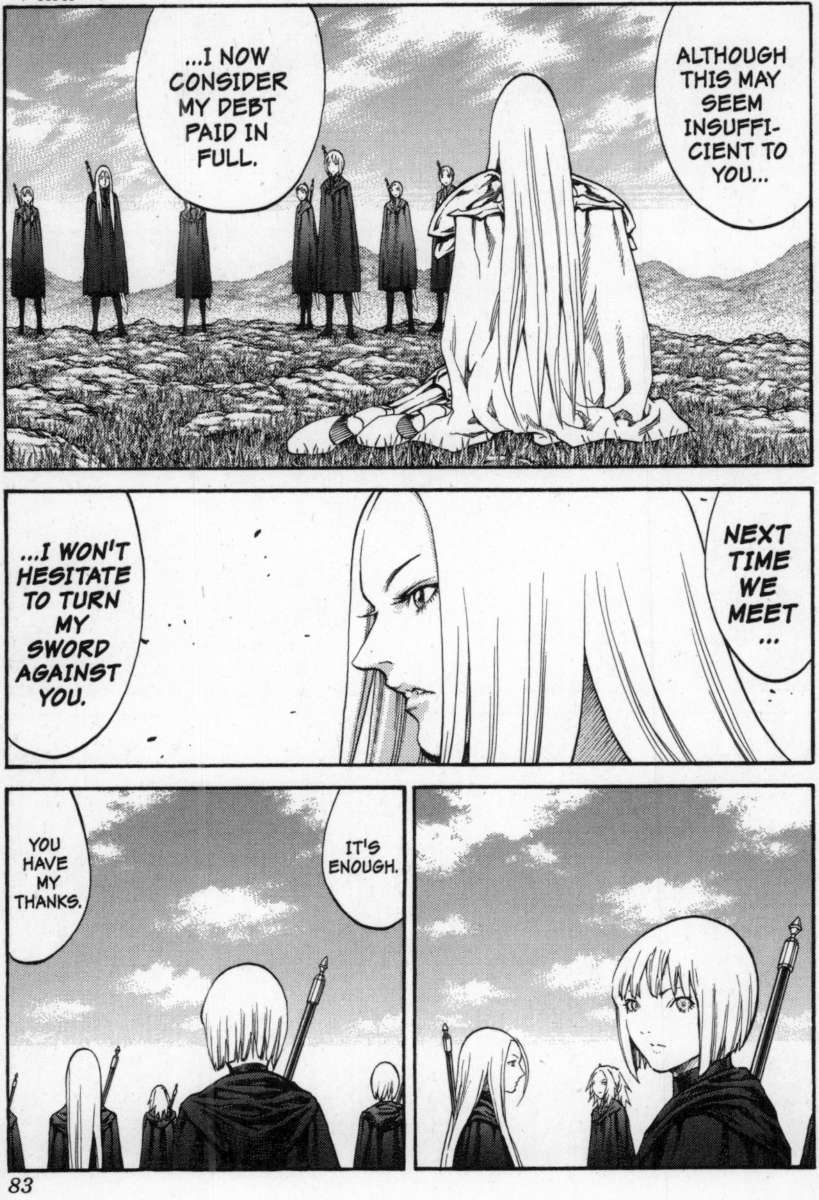
ALTHOUGH THIS MAY SEEM INSUFFI-CIENT TO YOU...
...I NOW CONSIDER MY DEBT PAID IN FULL.
NEXT TIME WE MEET ...
...I WON'T HESITATE TO TURN MY SWORD AGAINST YOU.
IT'S ENOUGH.
YOU HAVE MY THANKS.

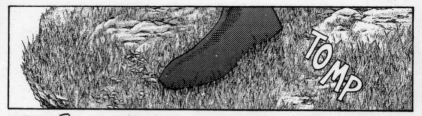

TOMP

BA

M

! UH UGH ...

GH ...

KH ...

TCH.

READ THIS WAY

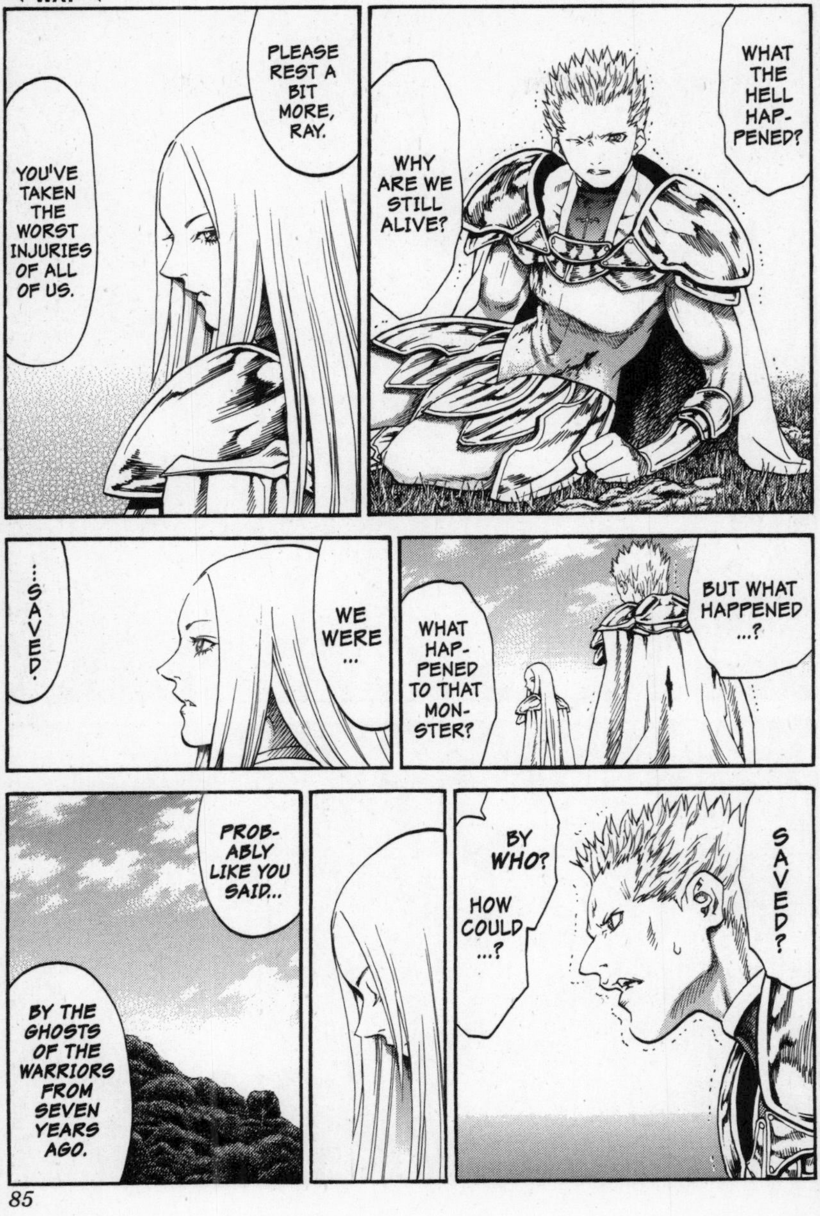
WHAT THE HELL HAP-PENED?
WHY ARE WE STILL ALIVE?
PLEASE REST A BIT MORE, RAY.
YOU'VE TAKEN THE WORST INJURIES OF ALL OF US.
BUT WHAT HAPPENED ...?
WHAT HAP-PENED TO THAT MON-STER?
WE WERE ...
...SAVED.
SAVED?
BY WHO?
HOW COULD ...?
PROB-ABLY LIKE YOU SAID...
BY THE GHOSTS OF THE WARRIORS FROM SEVEN YEARS AGO.

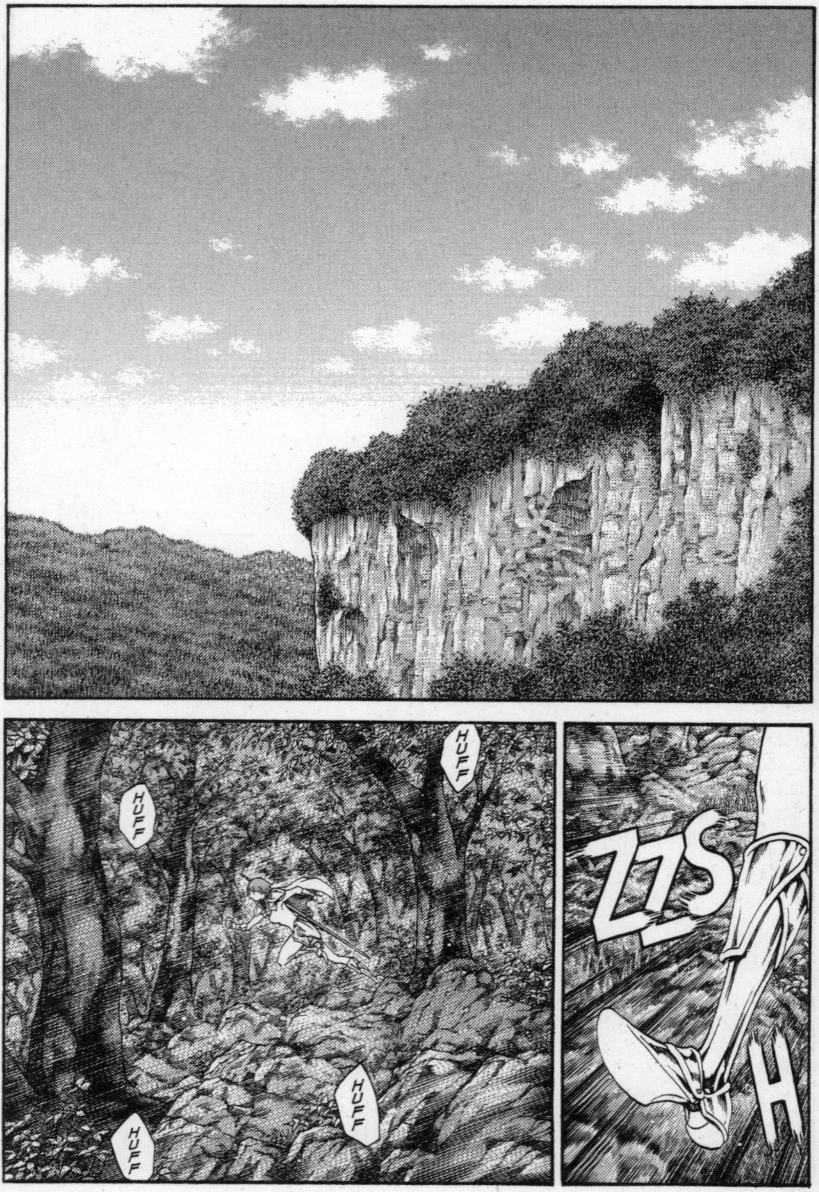
ZZSH
HUFF
HUFF
HUFF
HUFF

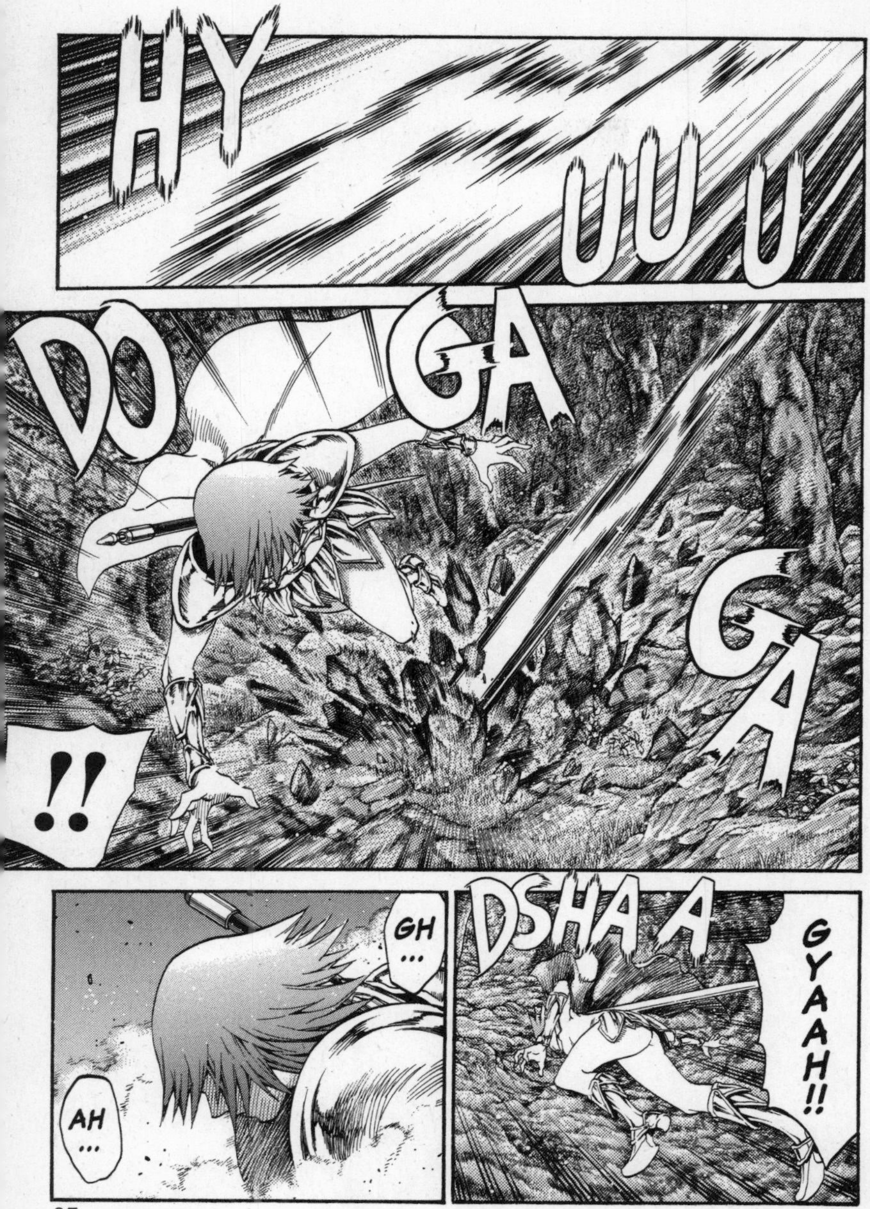
HYUUUU
DOGAGA
!!
DSHAAA
GYAAH!!
GH...
AH...

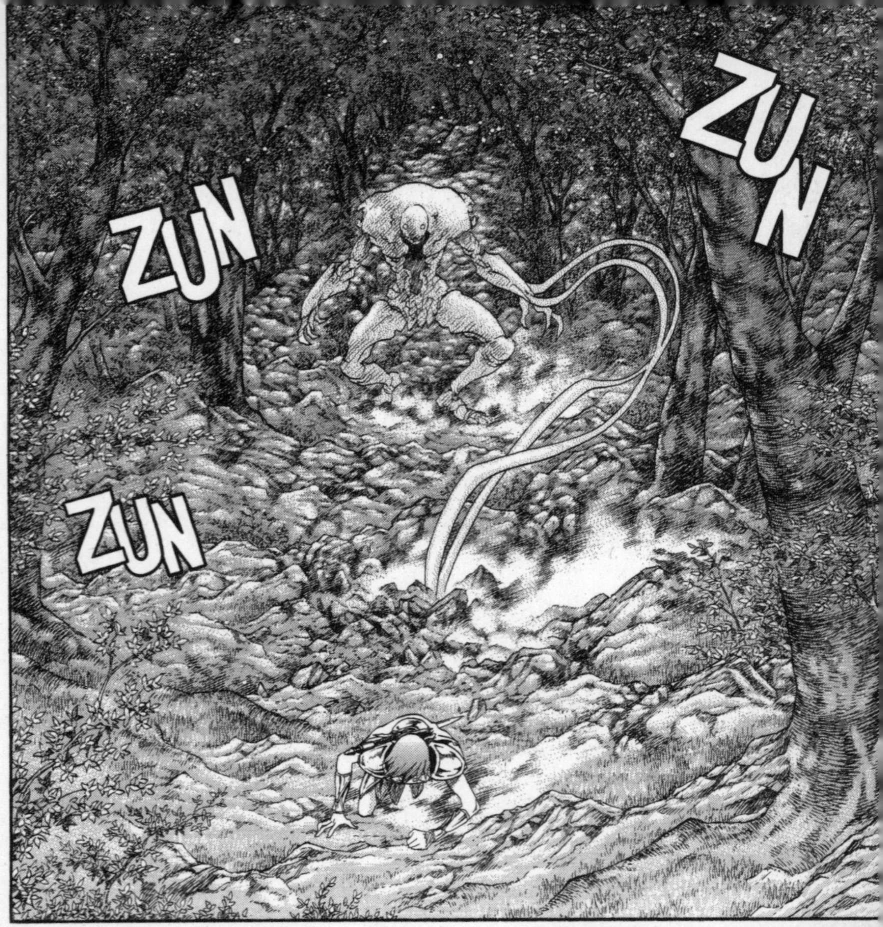
ZUN
ZUN
ZUN
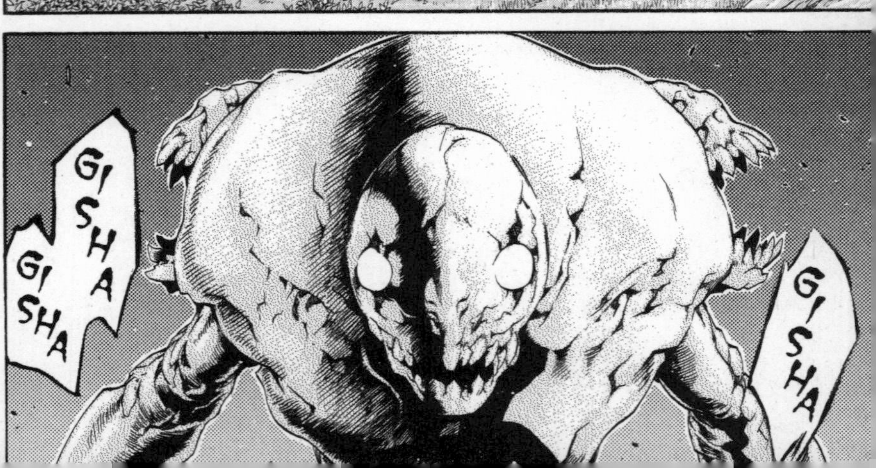
GISHA
GISHA GISHA

READ THIS WAY

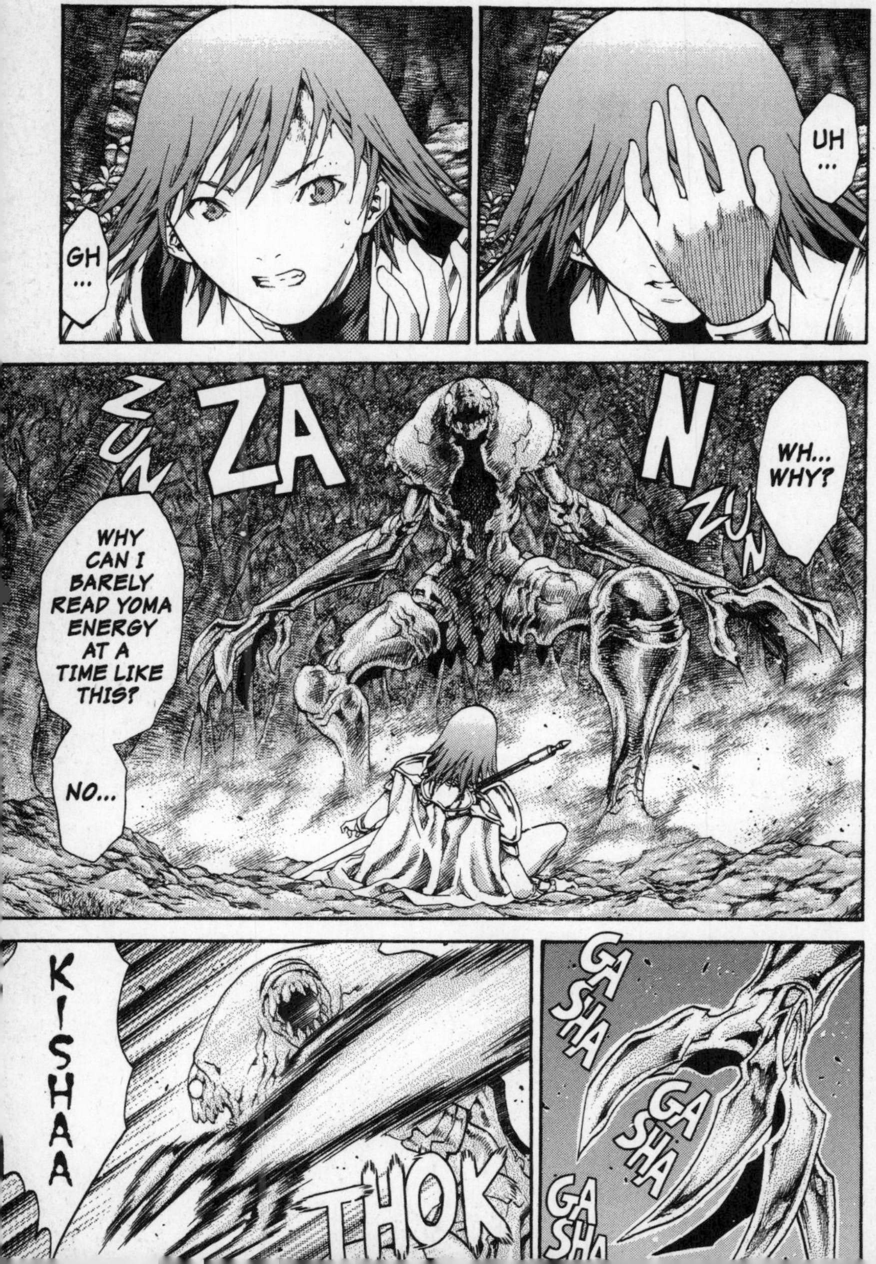
UH...
GH...
WH... WHY?
ZUN ZA N ZUN
WHY CAN I BARELY READ YOMA ENERGY AT A TIME LIKE THIS?
NO...
GASHA GASHA GASHA
KISHAA
THOK

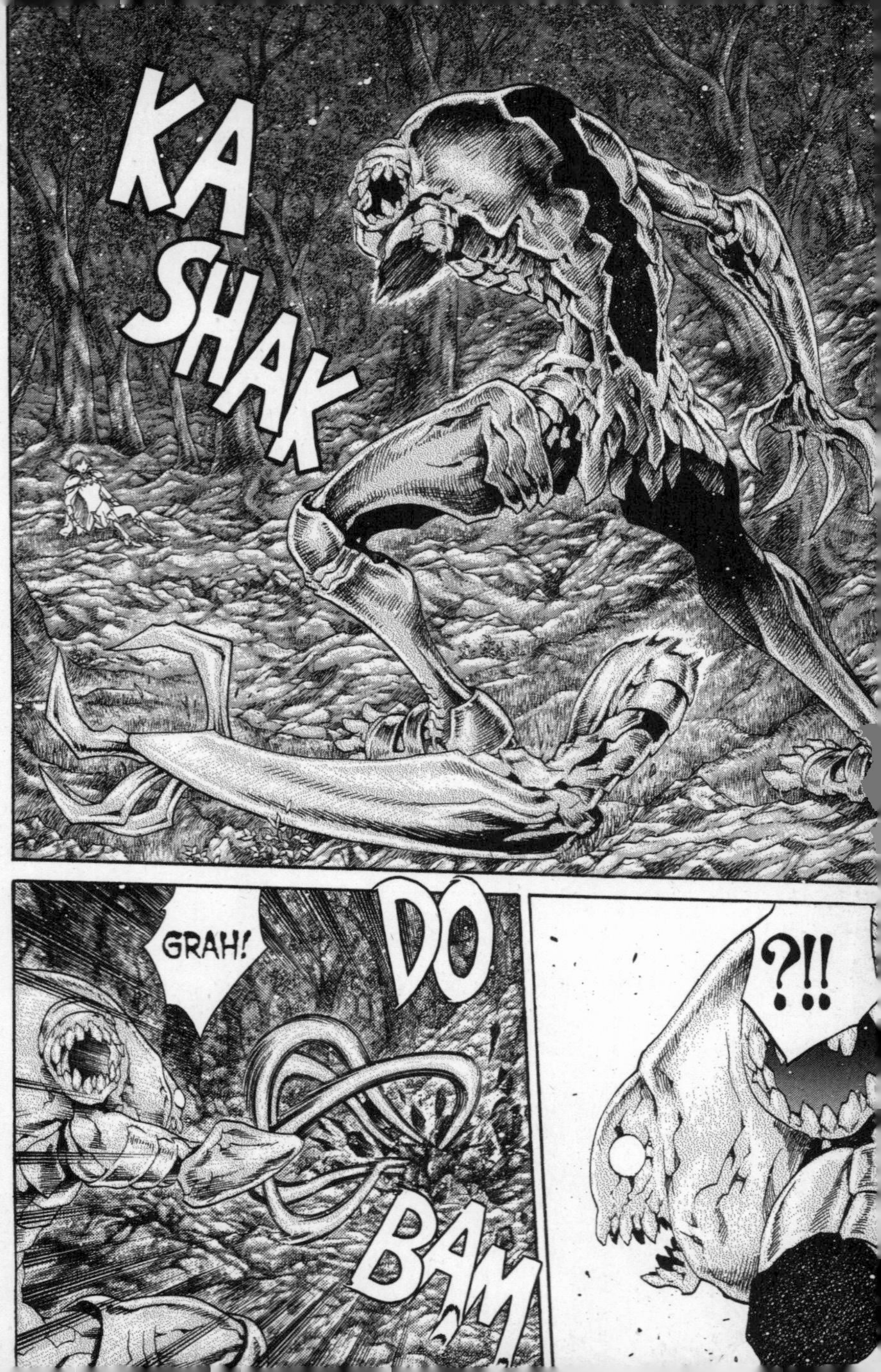
KA
SHAK
?!!
DO
GRAH!
BAM

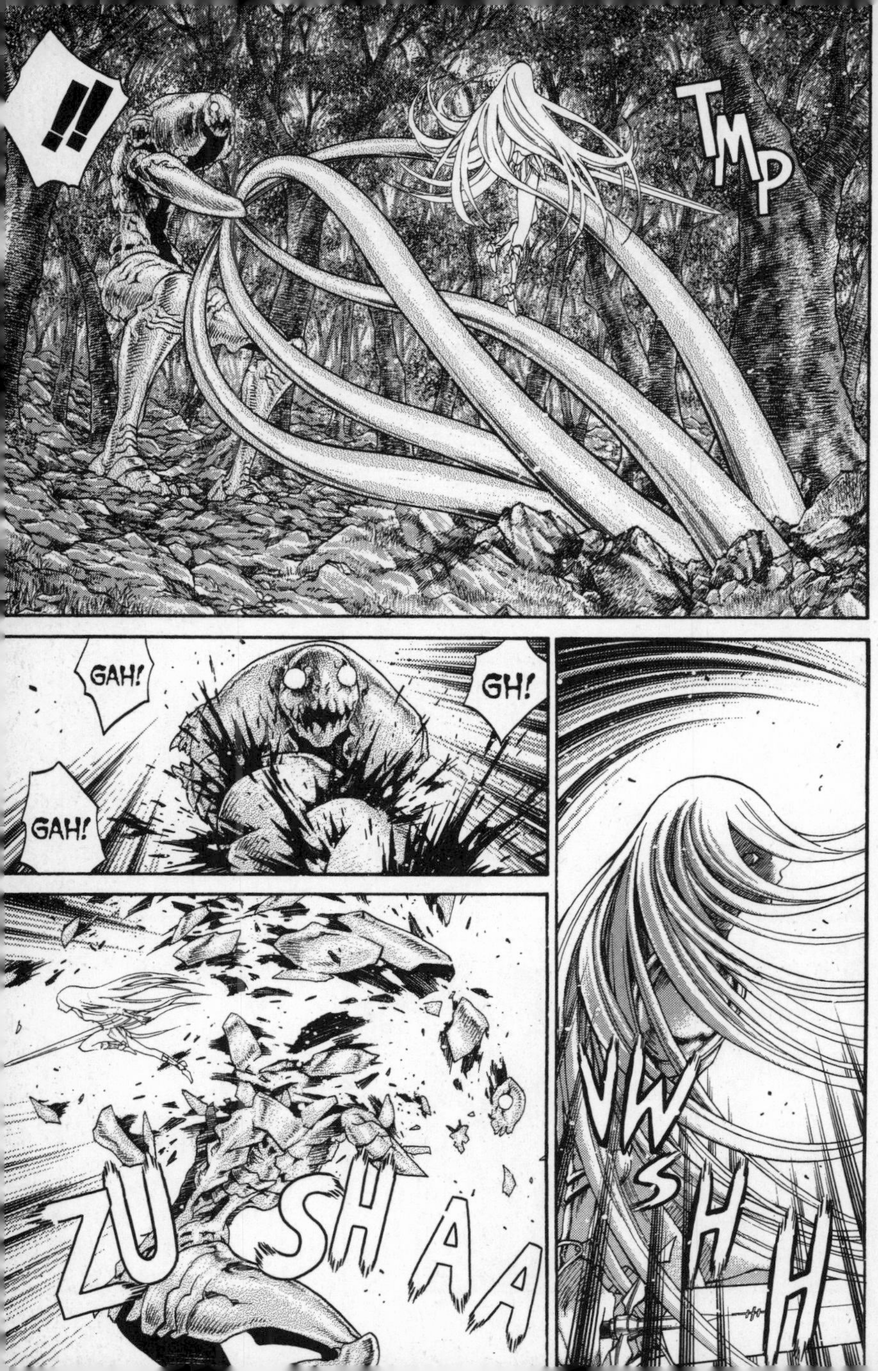
TMP
!!
VWSHH
GH!
GAH!
GAH!
ZUSHAA

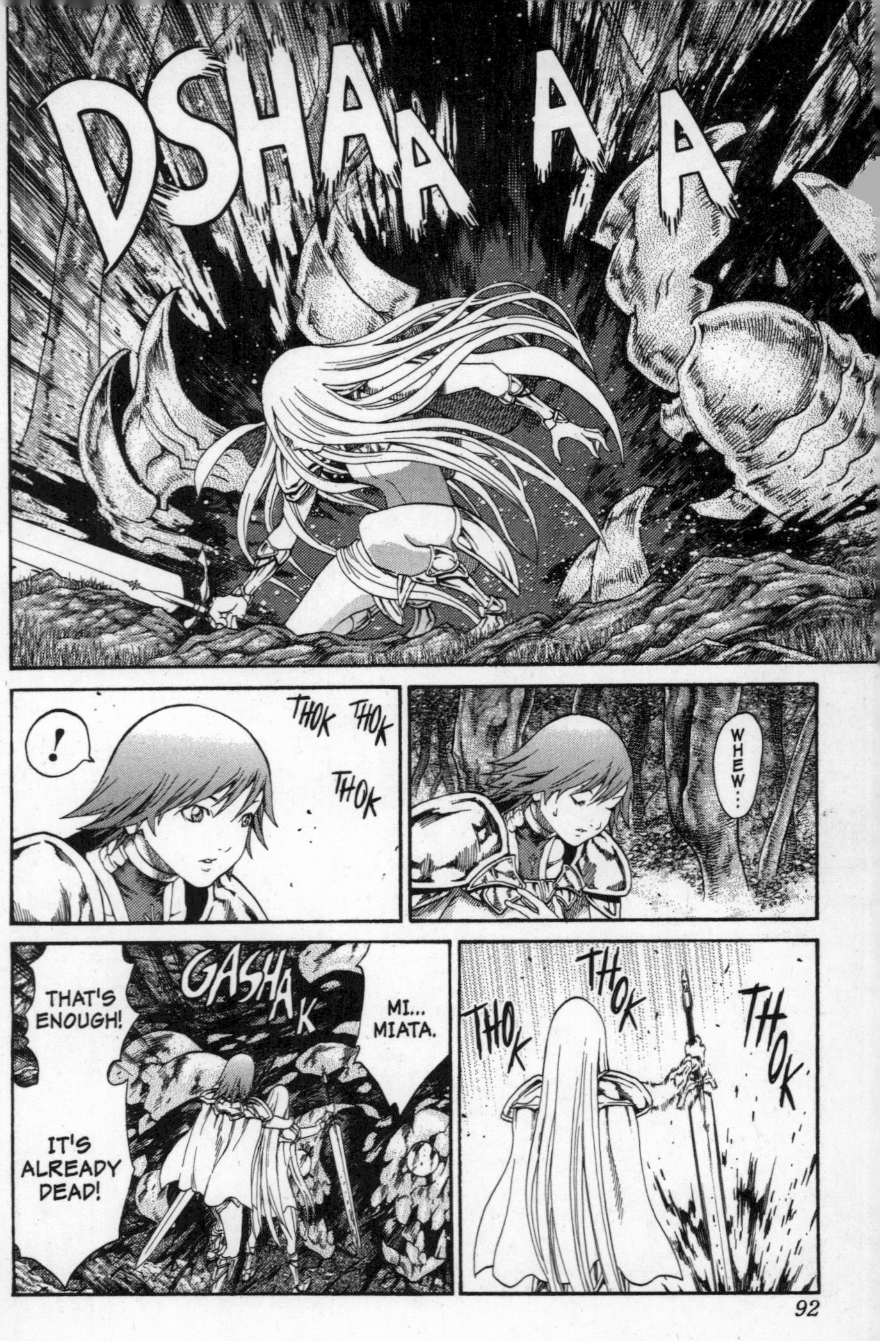
DSHAAAA
WHEW...
THOK THOK
THOK
!
THOK
THOK
THOK
MI... MIATA.
GASHAK
THAT'S ENOUGH!
IT'S ALREADY DEAD!

READ THIS WAY

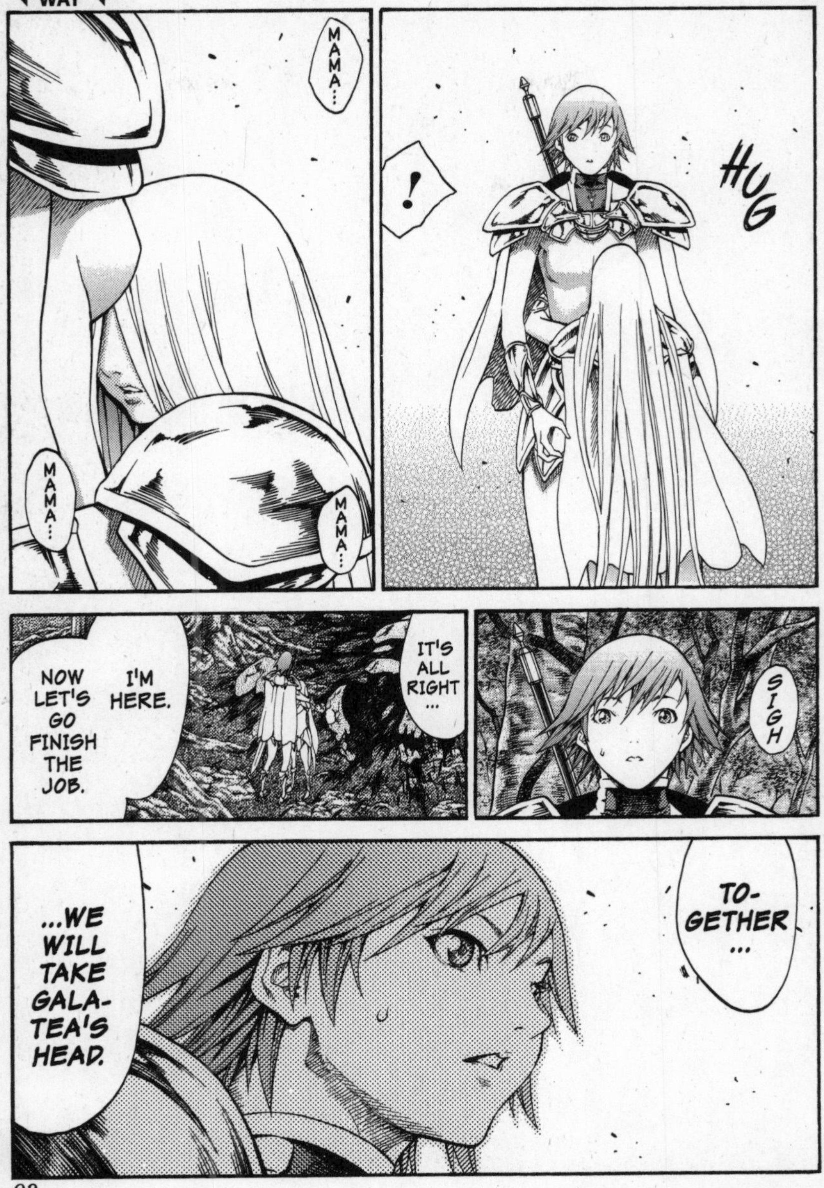
!
HUG
MAMA...
MAMA...
MAMA...
SIGH
IT'S ALL RIGHT...
I'M HERE.
NOW LET'S GO FINISH THE JOB.
TO-GETHER...
...WE WILL TAKE GALA-TEA'S HEAD.

Claymore
クレイモア

Scene 73: A Child Weapon, Part 1

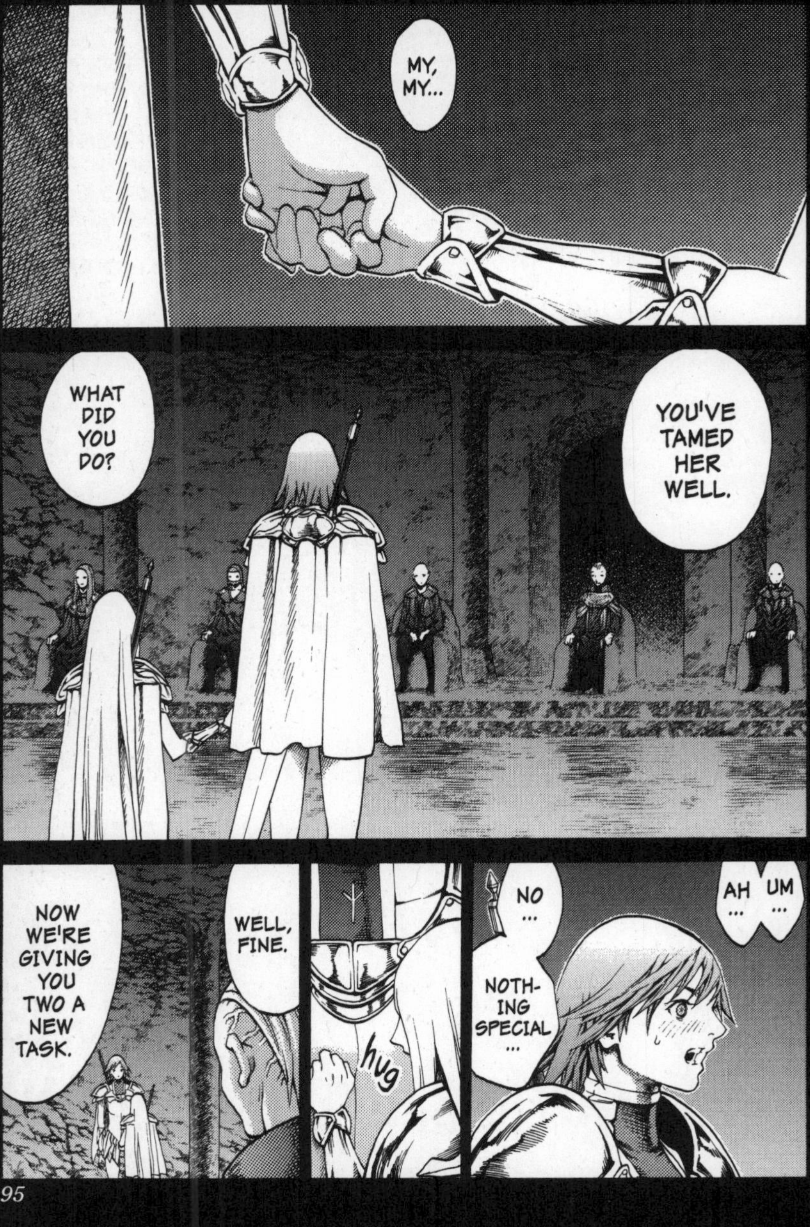
MY, MY...
YOU'VE TAMED HER WELL.
WHAT DID YOU DO?
UM ...
AH ...
NO ...
NOTH-ING SPECIAL ...
WELL, FINE.
hug
NOW WE'RE GIVING YOU TWO A NEW TASK.

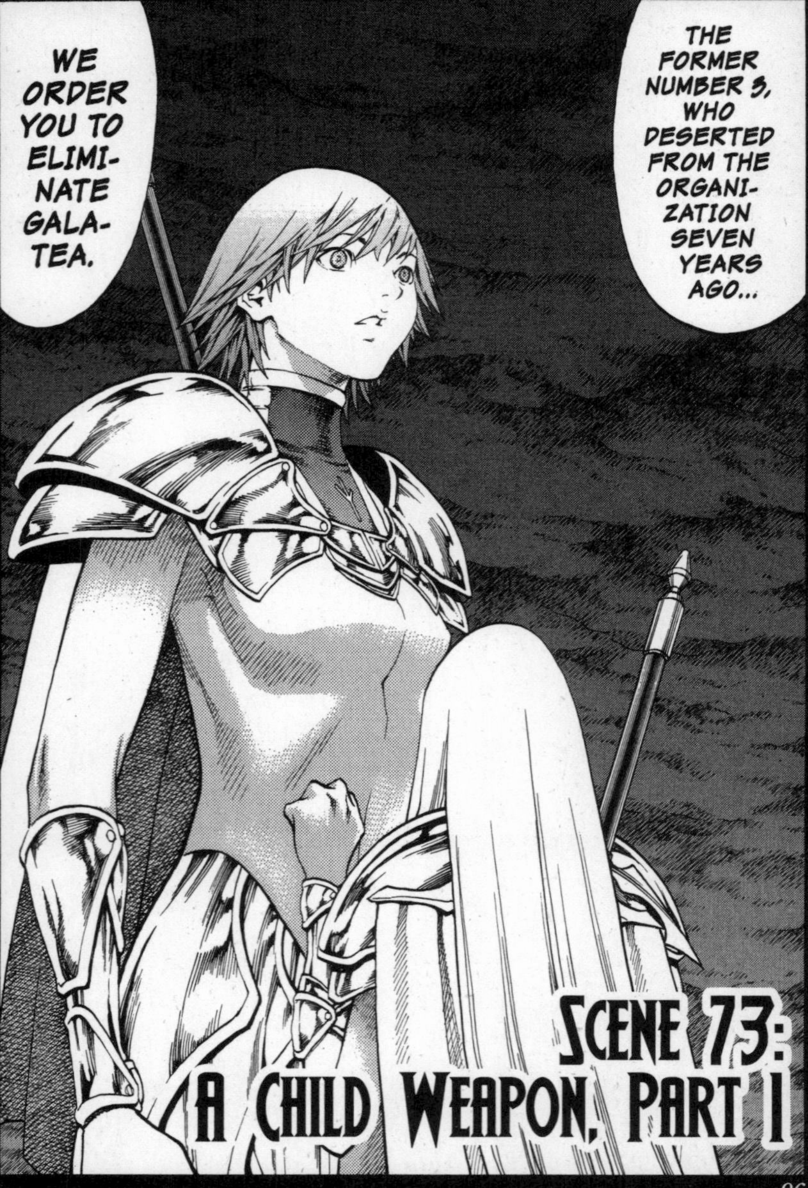
THE FORMER NUMBER 3, WHO DESERTED FROM THE ORGANIZATION SEVEN YEARS AGO...
WE ORDER YOU TO ELIMINATE GALATEA.
SCENE 73: A CHILD WEAPON, PART 1

READ THIS WAY

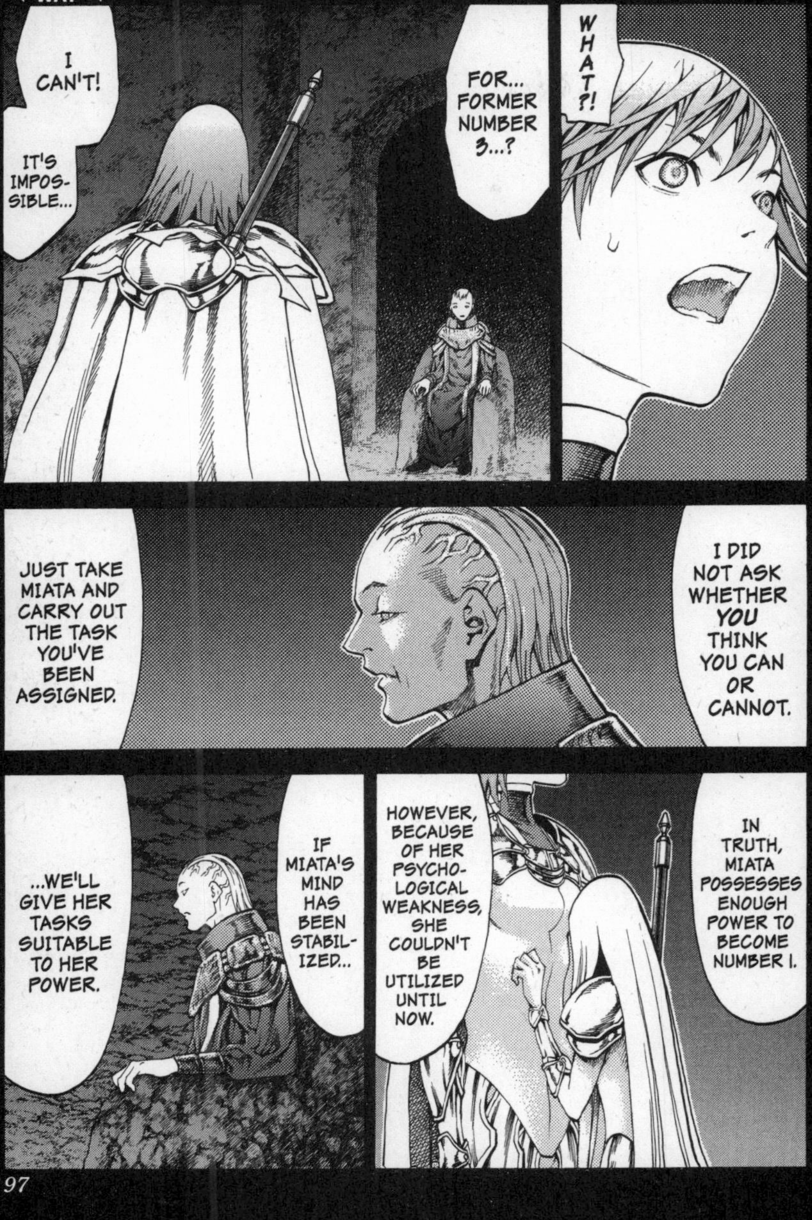
WHAT?!
FOR... FORMER NUMBER 3...?
I CAN'T!
IT'S IMPOSSIBLE...
I DID NOT ASK WHETHER YOU THINK YOU CAN OR CANNOT.
JUST TAKE MIATA AND CARRY OUT THE TASK YOU'VE BEEN ASSIGNED.
IN TRUTH, MIATA POSSESSES ENOUGH POWER TO BECOME NUMBER 1.
HOWEVER, BECAUSE OF HER PSYCHOLOGICAL WEAKNESS, SHE COULDN'T BE UTILIZED UNTIL NOW.
IF MIATA'S MIND HAS BEEN STABILIZED...
...WE'LL GIVE HER TASKS SUITABLE TO HER POWER.

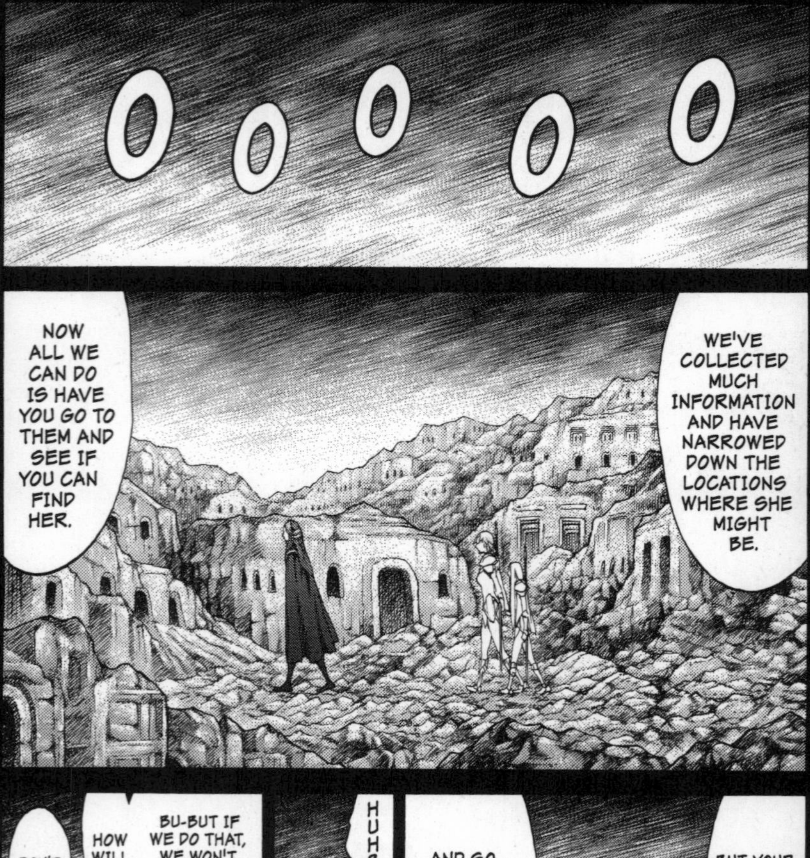
OOOOO
WE'VE COLLECTED MUCH INFORMATION AND HAVE NARROWED DOWN THE LOCATIONS WHERE SHE MIGHT BE.
NOW ALL WE CAN DO IS HAVE YOU GO TO THEM AND SEE IF YOU CAN FIND HER.
BUT YOUR OPPONENT EXCELS AT SENSING AURAS OVER A LONG RANGE.
AND SO, YOU WILL CONTINUALLY TAKE AURA SUPPRES-SANTS WHILE ON THE JOB.
HUH?
BU-BUT IF WE DO THAT, WE WON'T BE ABLE TO SENSE AURAS EITHER.
HOW WILL WE–
DON'T WORRY.

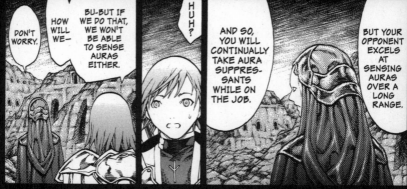

READ THIS WAY

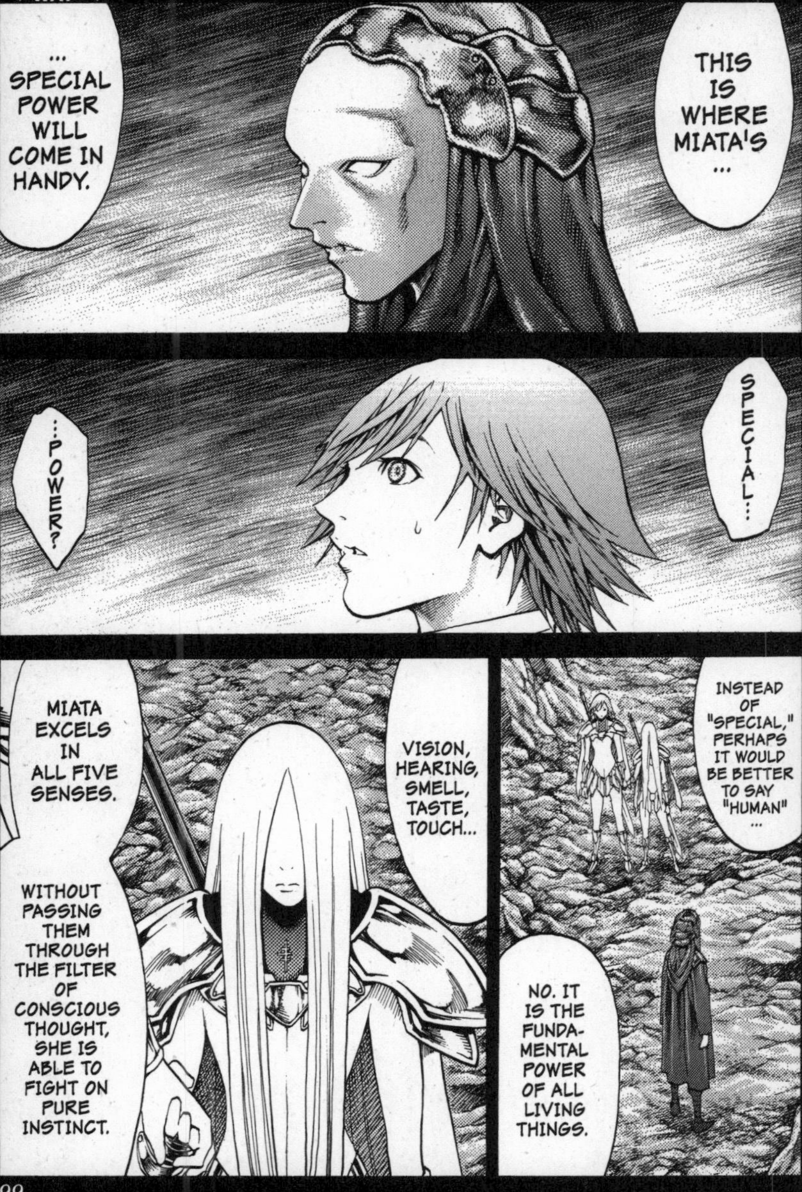

THIS IS WHERE MIATA'S ...
... SPECIAL POWER WILL COME IN HANDY.
SPECIAL...
...POWER?
INSTEAD OF "SPECIAL," PERHAPS IT WOULD BE BETTER TO SAY "HUMAN" ...
NO. IT IS THE FUNDAMENTAL POWER OF ALL LIVING THINGS.
VISION, HEARING, SMELL, TASTE, TOUCH...
MIATA EXCELS IN ALL FIVE SENSES.
WITHOUT PASSING THEM THROUGH THE FILTER OF CONSCIOUS THOUGHT, SHE IS ABLE TO FIGHT ON PURE INSTINCT.

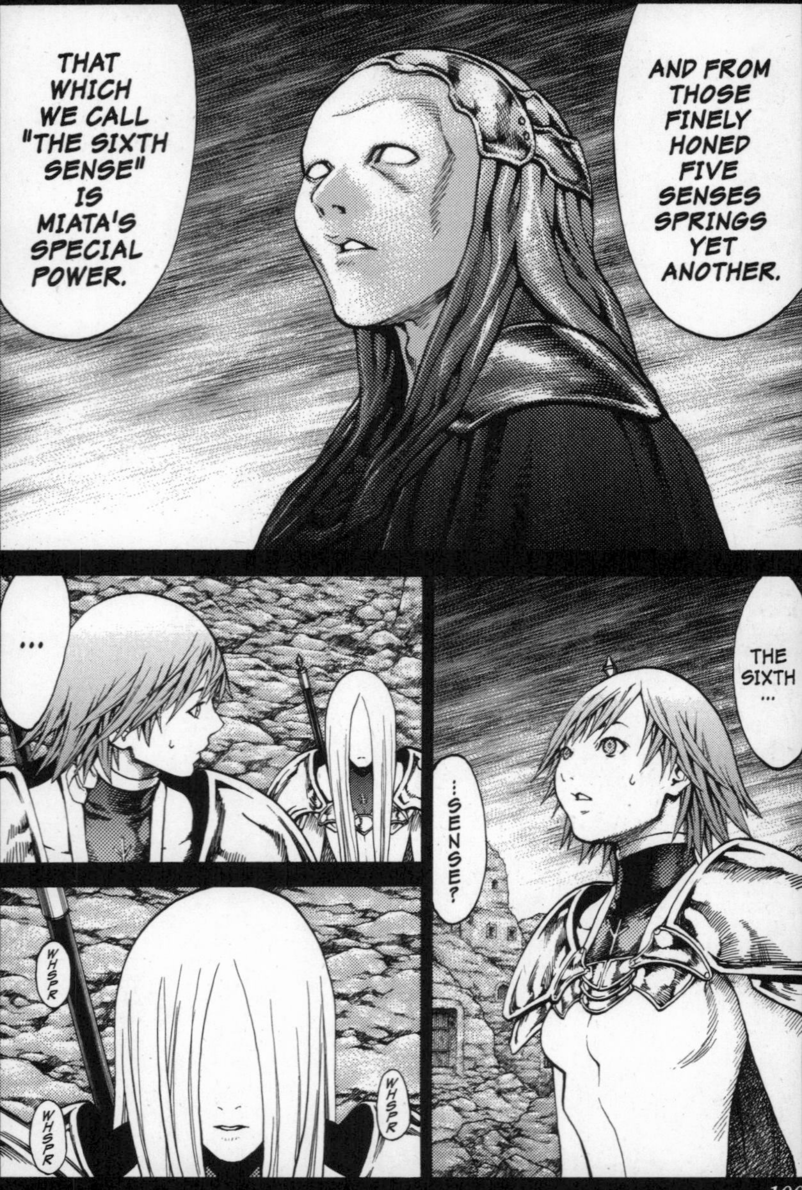
AND FROM THOSE FINELY HONED FIVE SENSES SPRINGS YET ANOTHER.
THAT WHICH WE CALL "THE SIXTH SENSE" IS MIATA'S SPECIAL POWER.
THE SIXTH ...
...SENSE?
...
WHSPR
WHSPR
WHSPR

READ THIS WAY

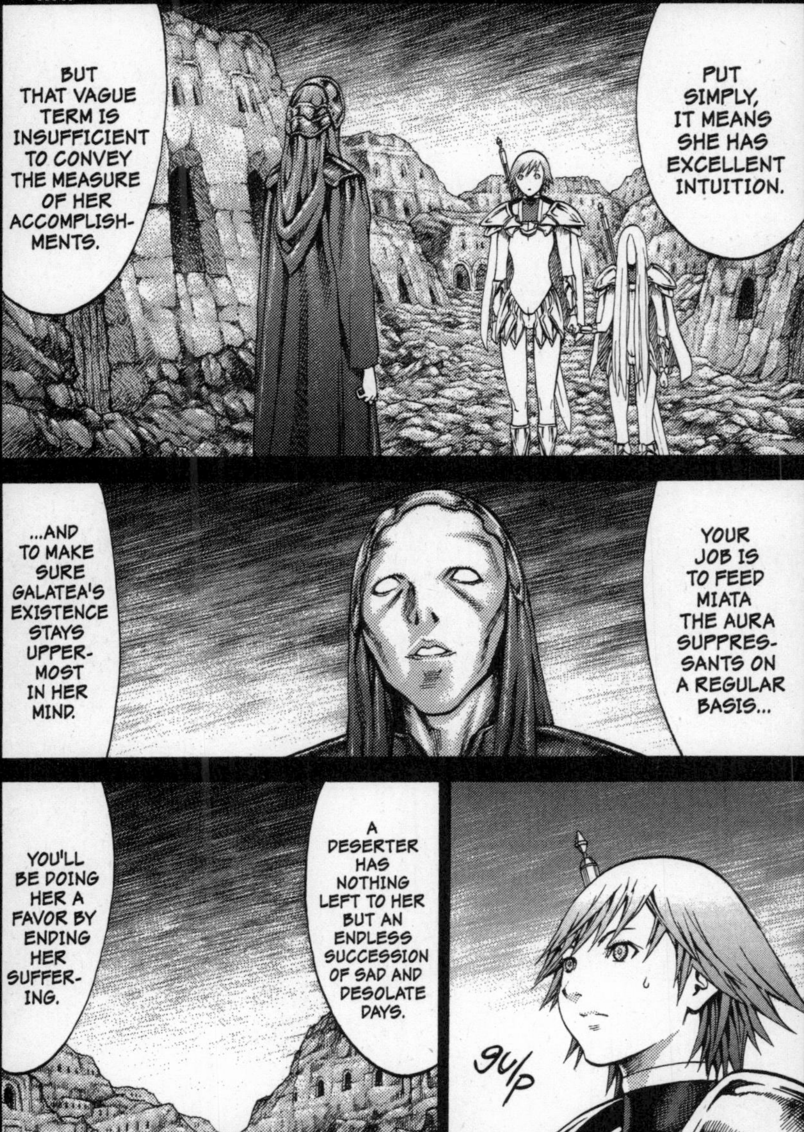
PUT SIMPLY, IT MEANS SHE HAS EXCELLENT INTUITION.
BUT THAT VAGUE TERM IS INSUFFICIENT TO CONVEY THE MEASURE OF HER ACCOMPLISHMENTS.
YOUR JOB IS TO FEED MIATA THE AURA SUPPRESSANTS ON A REGULAR BASIS...
...AND TO MAKE SURE GALATEA'S EXISTENCE STAYS UPPERMOST IN HER MIND.
gulp
A DESERTER HAS NOTHING LEFT TO HER BUT AN ENDLESS SUCCESSION OF SAD AND DESOLATE DAYS.
YOU'LL BE DOING HER A FAVOR BY ENDING HER SUFFERING.

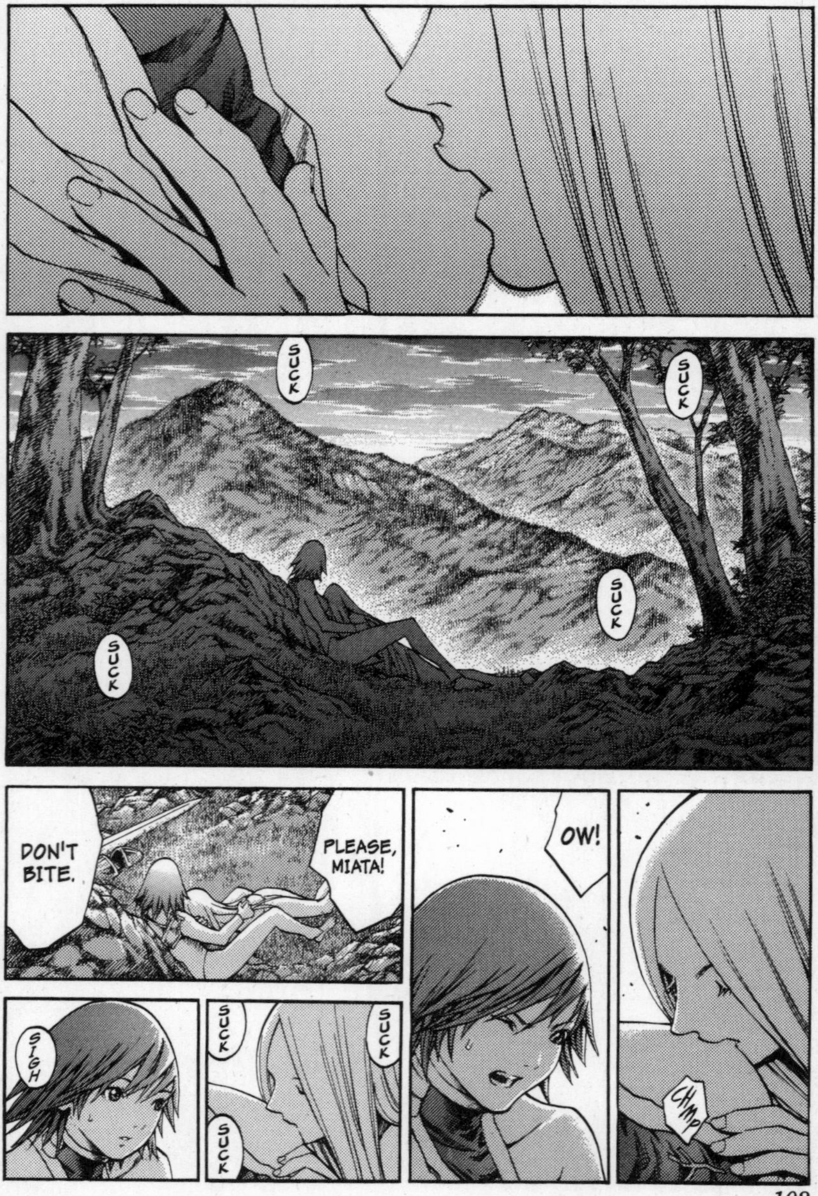
SUCK
SUCK
SUCK
SUCK
CHMP
OW!
PLEASE, MIATA!
DON'T BITE.
SUCK
SUCK
SUCK
SIGH

READ THIS WAY

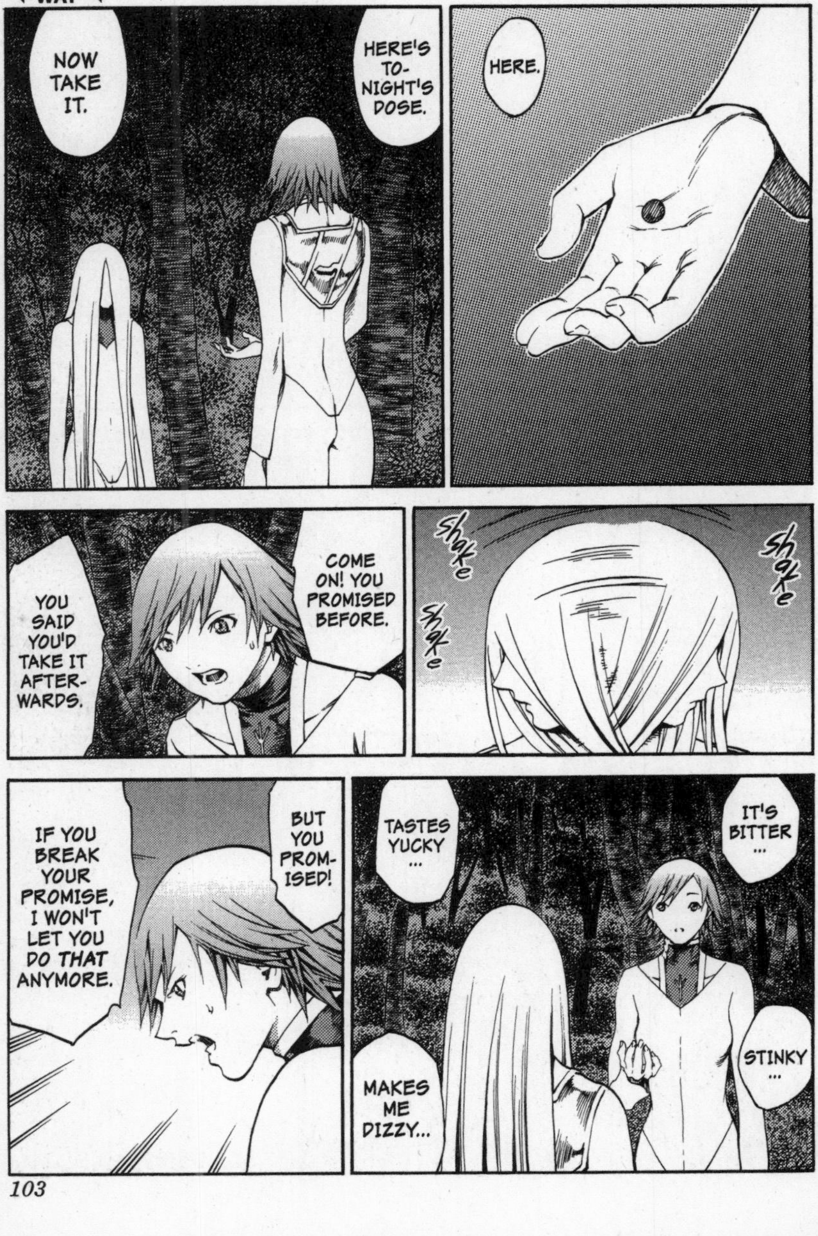

HERE.
HERE'S TO-NIGHT'S DOSE.
NOW TAKE IT.
shake
shake
shake
COME ON! YOU PROMISED BEFORE.
YOU SAID YOU'D TAKE IT AFTER-WARDS.
IT'S BITTER...
TASTES YUCKY...
STINKY...
MAKES ME DIZZY...
BUT YOU PROM-ISED!
IF YOU BREAK YOUR PROMISE, I WON'T LET YOU DO THAT ANYMORE.

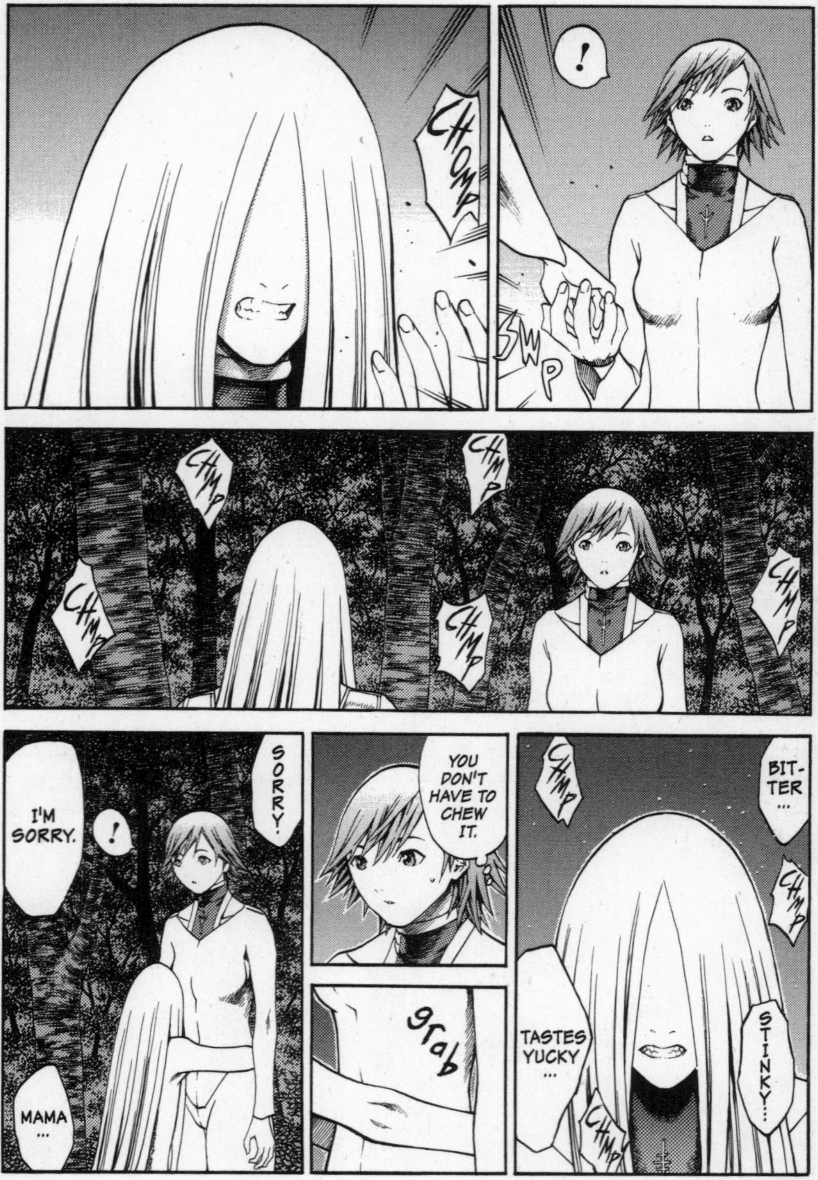
!
SWP
CHOMP
CHMP
CHMP
CHMP
CHMP
BIT-TER...
CHMP
STINKY...
TASTES YUCKY...
CHMP
YOU DON'T HAVE TO CHEW IT.
grab
SORRY.
I'M SORRY.
!
MAMA...

READ THIS WAY

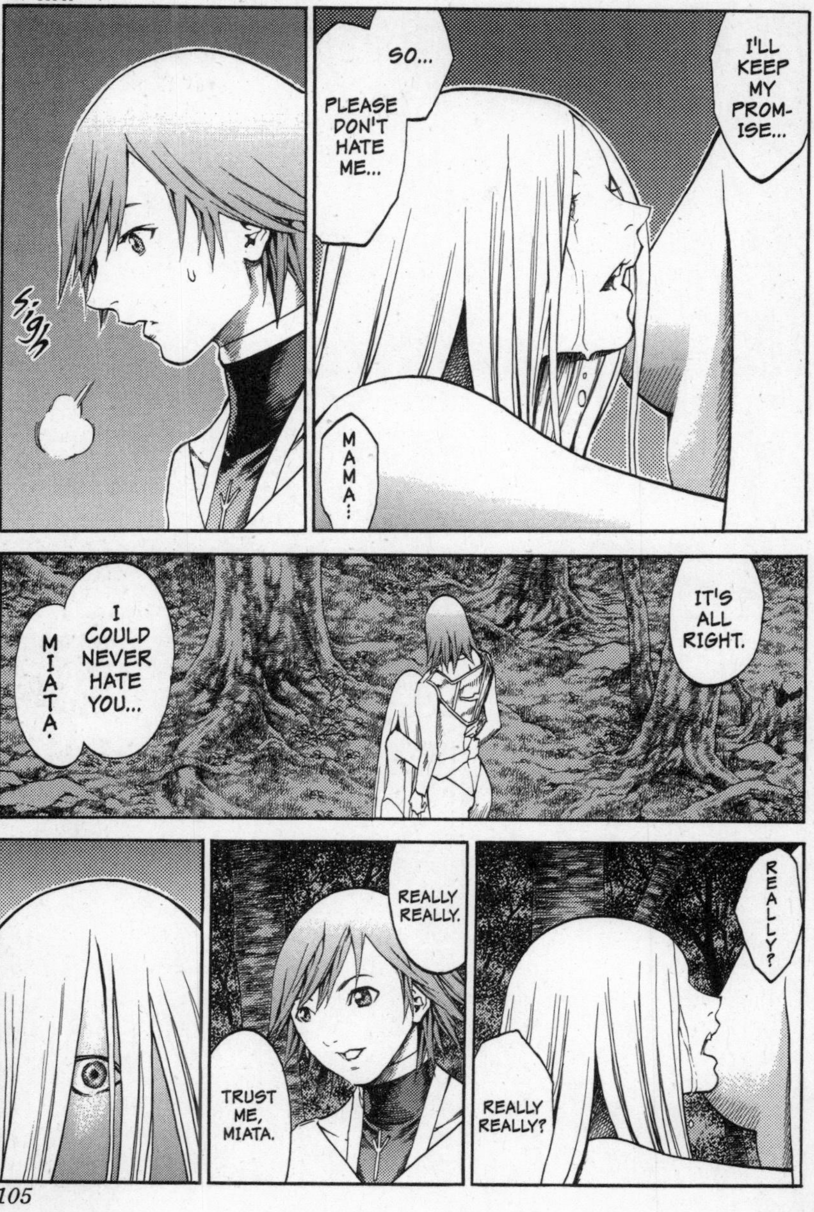

I'LL KEEP MY PROMISE...
SO...
PLEASE DON'T HATE ME...
MAMA...
sigh
IT'S ALL RIGHT.
I COULD NEVER HATE YOU...
MIATA.
REALLY?
REALLY REALLY?
REALLY REALLY.
TRUST ME, MIATA.

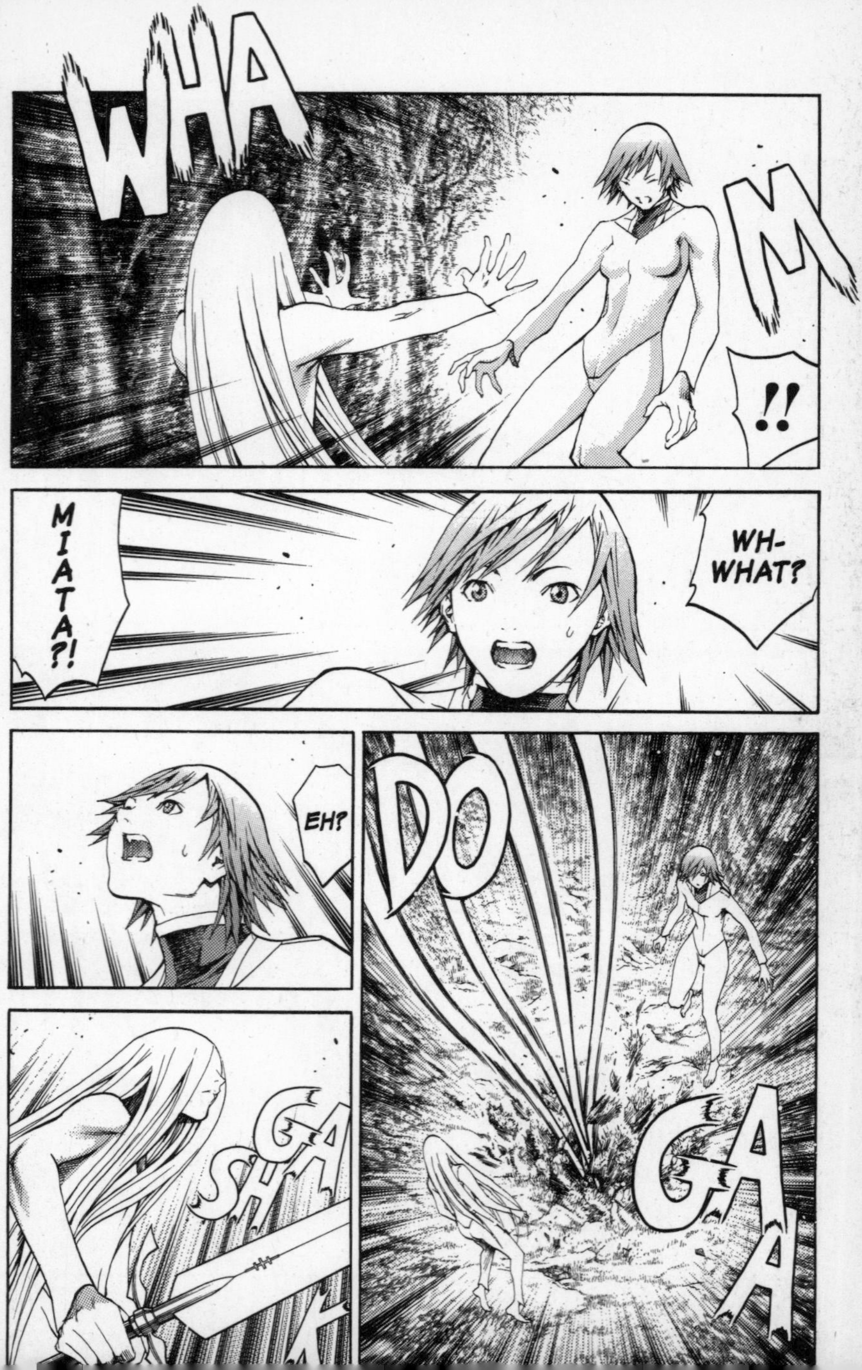
WHAM
!!
WH-
WHAT?
MIATA?!
DO
GAGA
EH?
GASHA

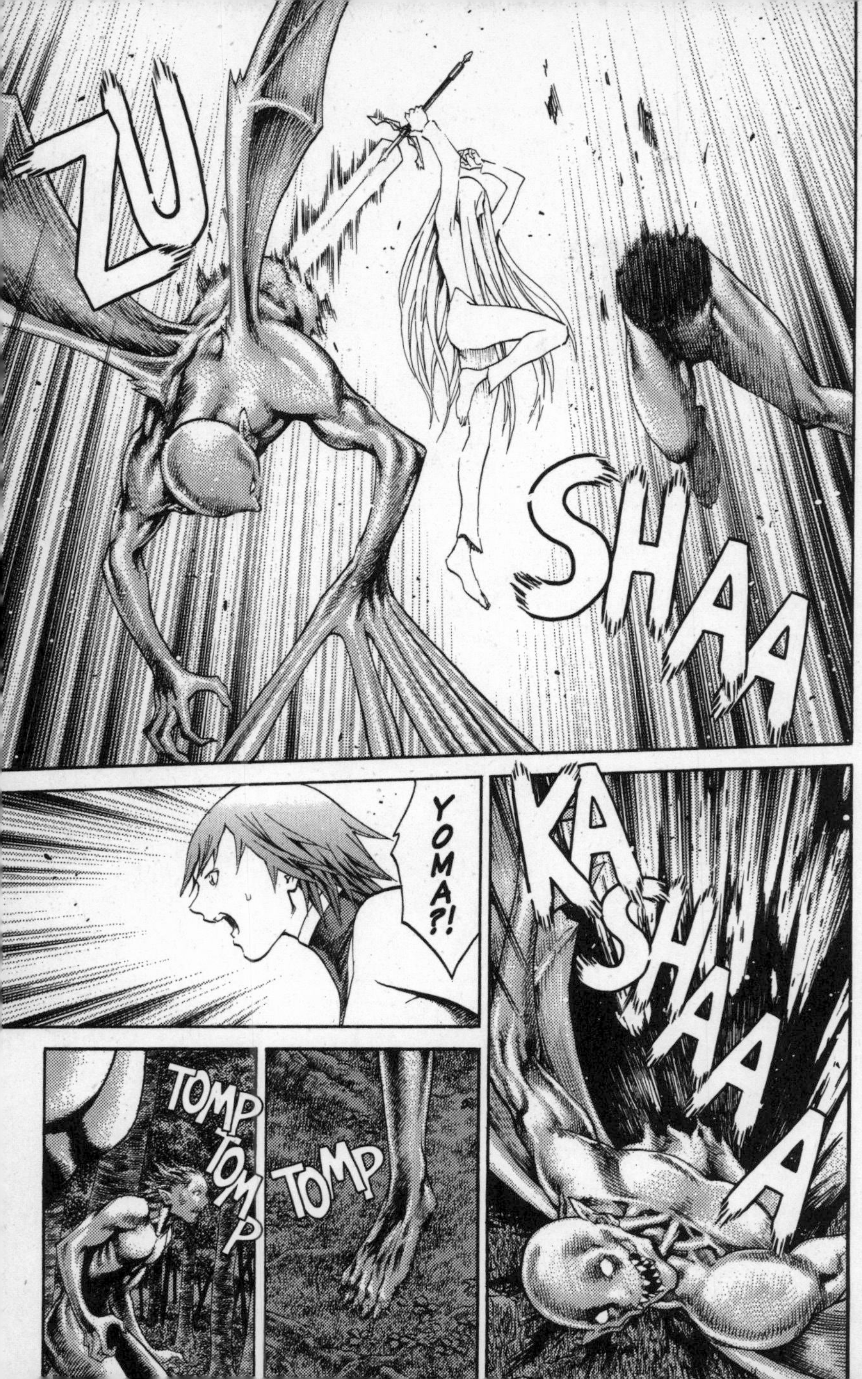
ZU
SHAA
KASHAAAA
YOMA?!
TOMP
TOMP TOMP TOMP

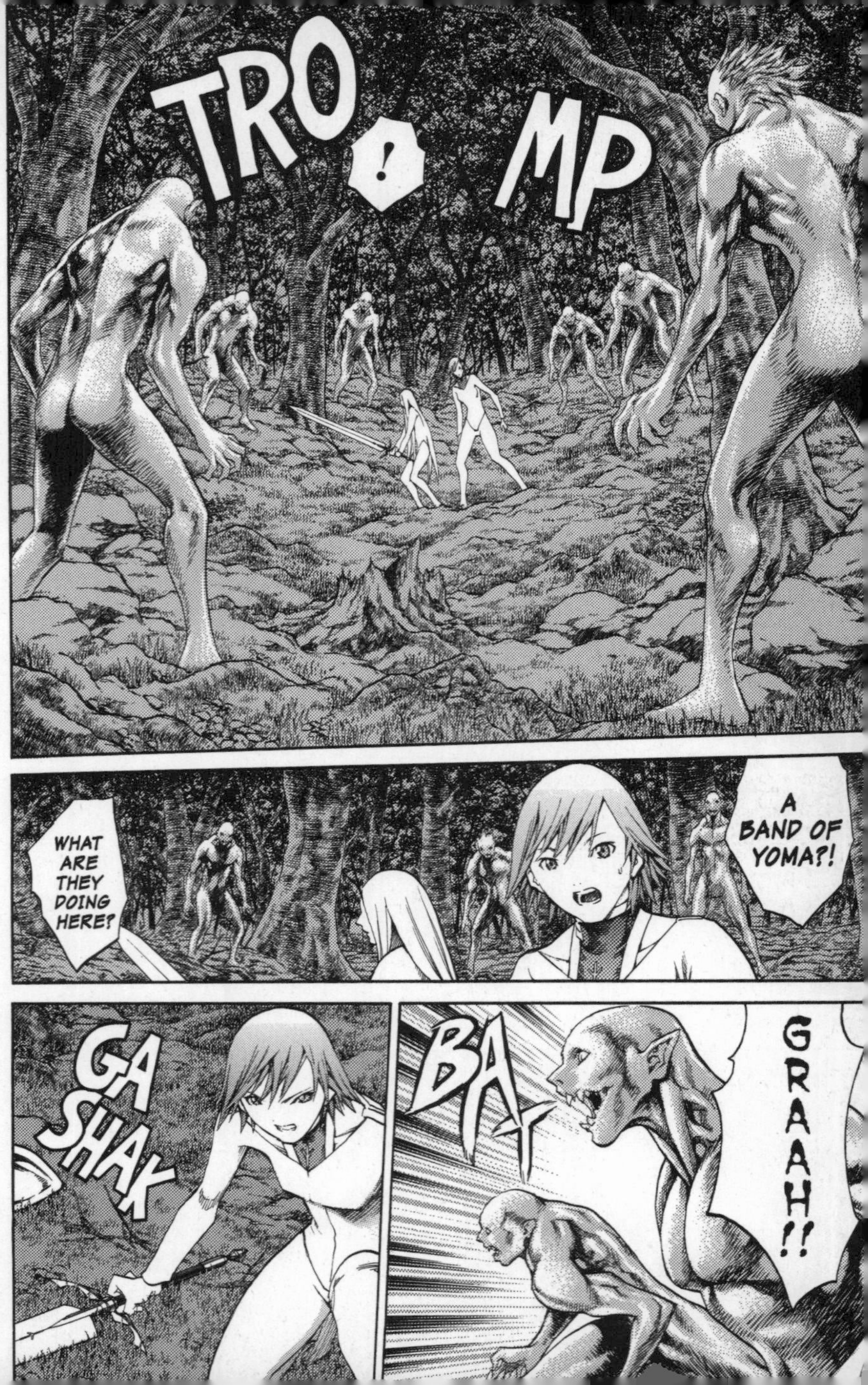
TRO
!
MP
A BAND OF YOMA?!
WHAT ARE THEY DOING HERE?
GRAAH!!
BA
GA SHAK

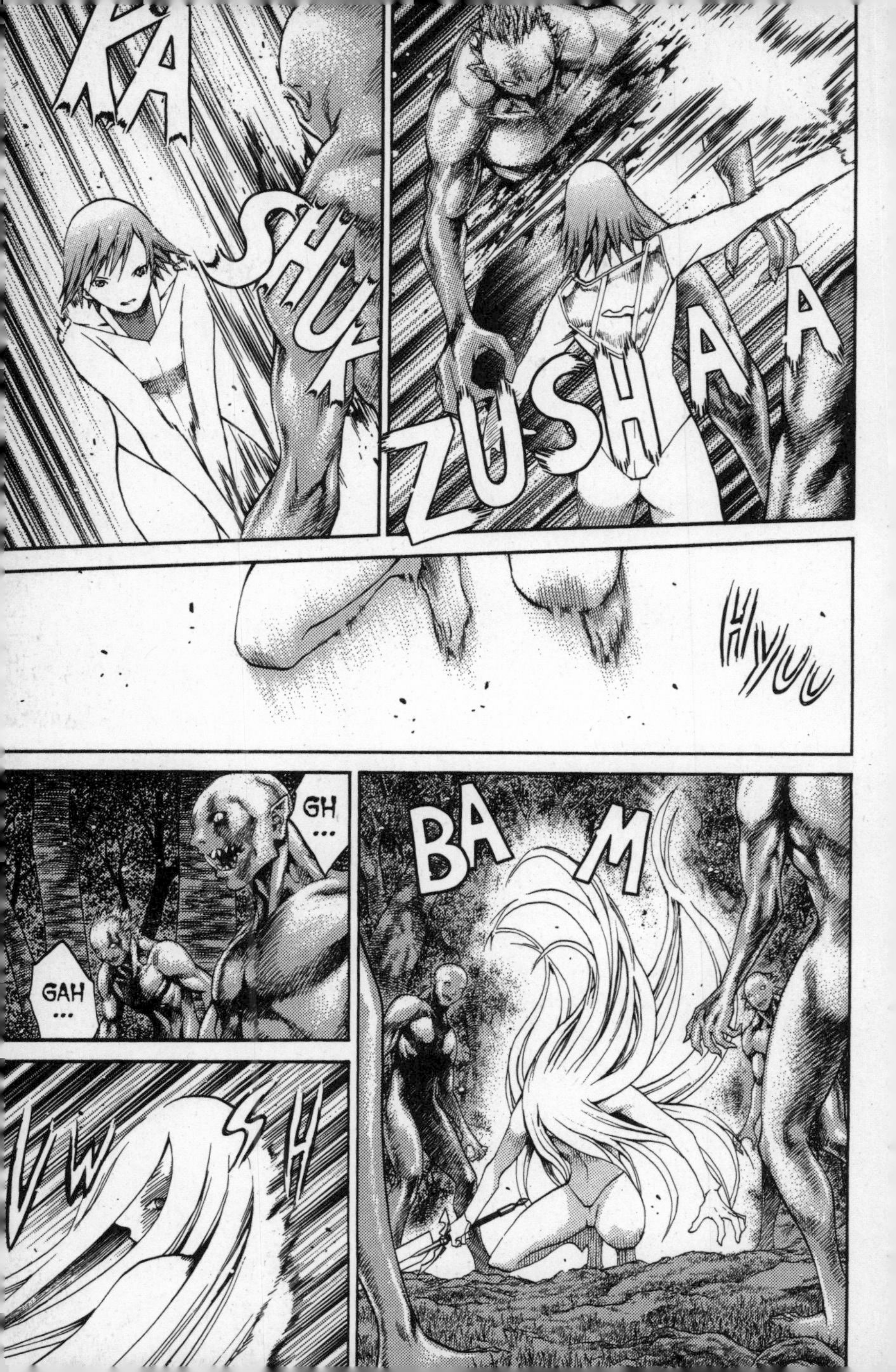
ZUSHAAA
KA
SHUK
HYUU
BAM
GH...
GAH...
VWSH

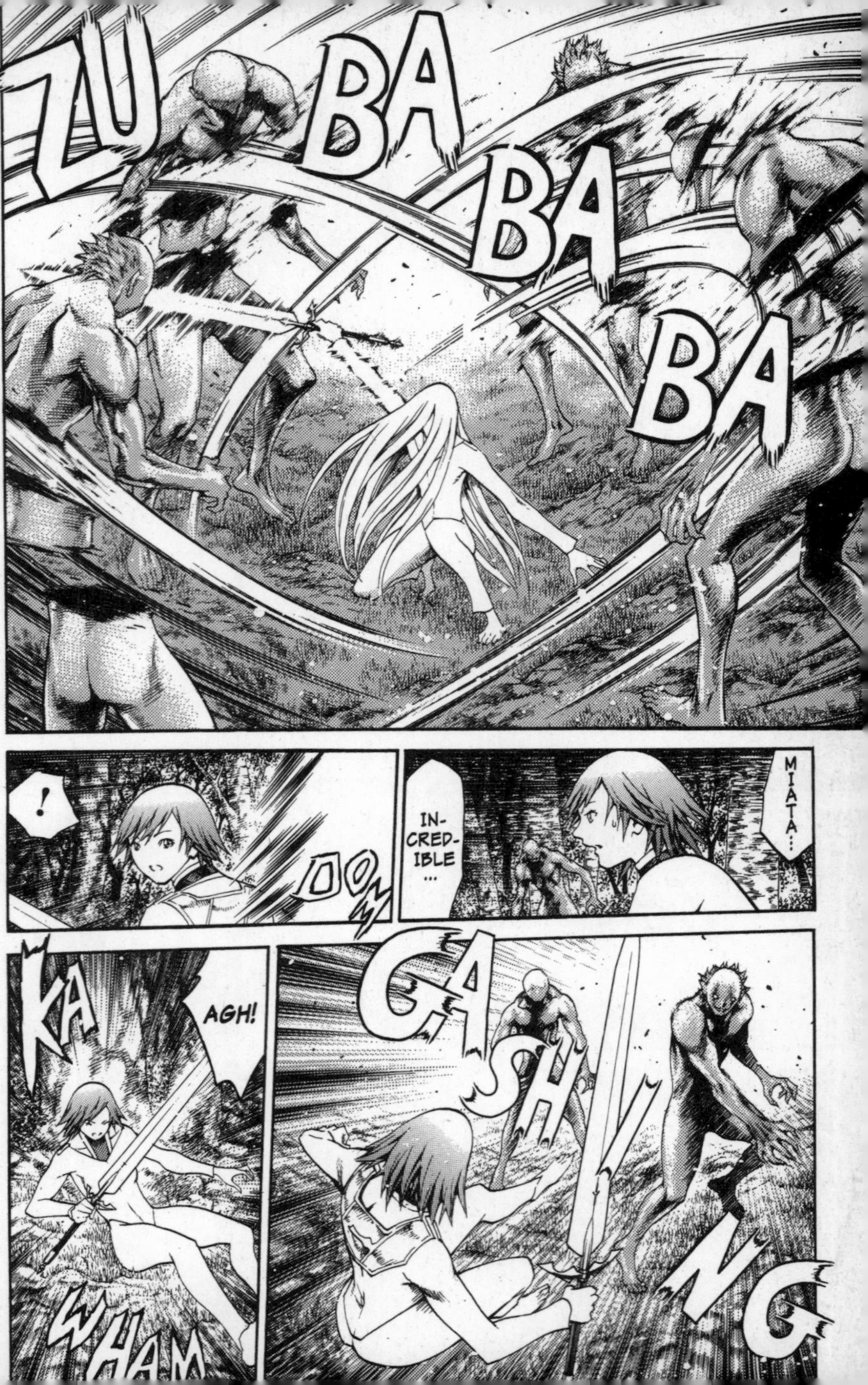
ZUBABABABA
MIATA...
IN-CRED-IBLE...
!
DOM
GASHING
KA
AGH!
WHAM

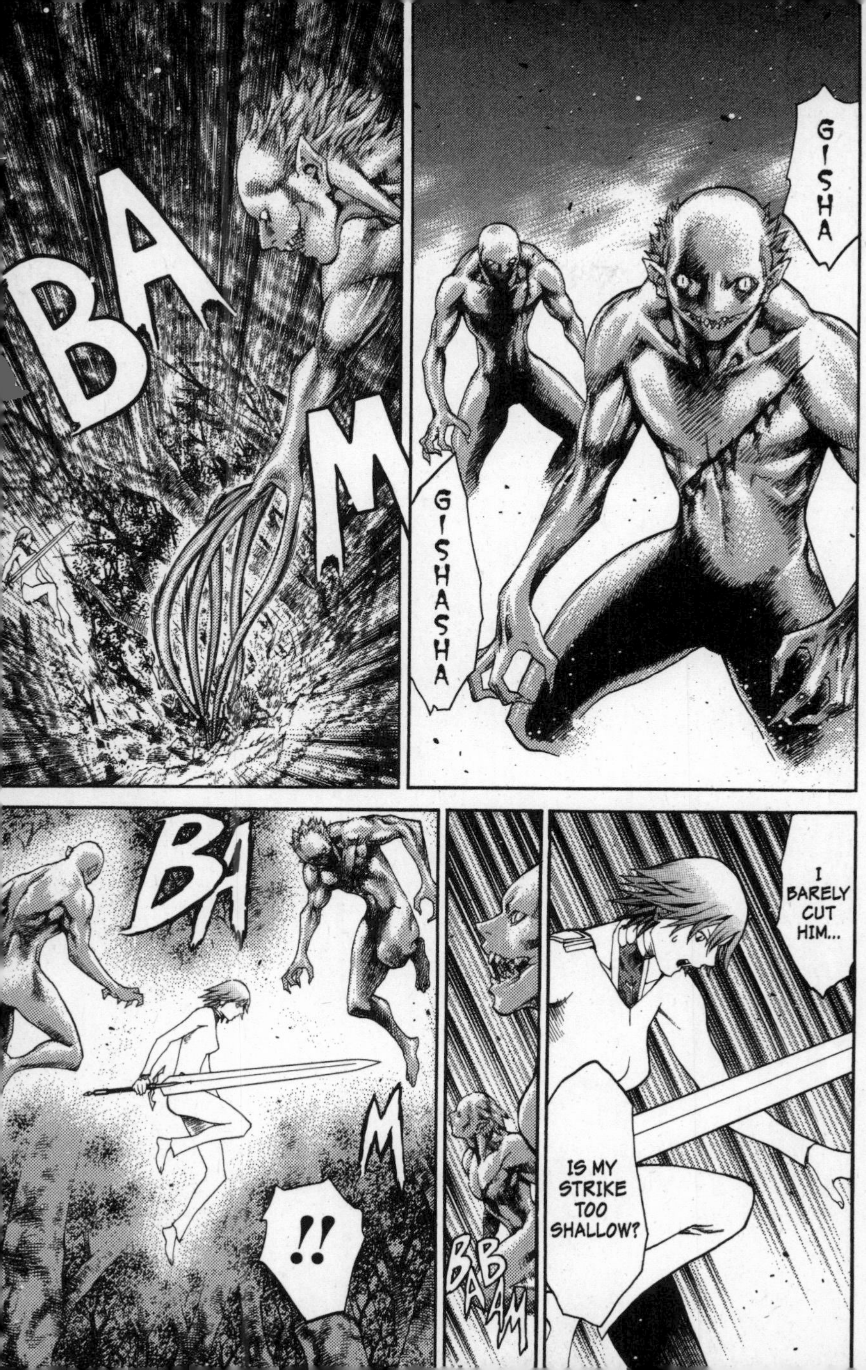
GISHA
GISHASHA
BAM
I BARELY CUT HIM...
IS MY STRIKE TOO SHALLOW?
BABAM
BAM
!!

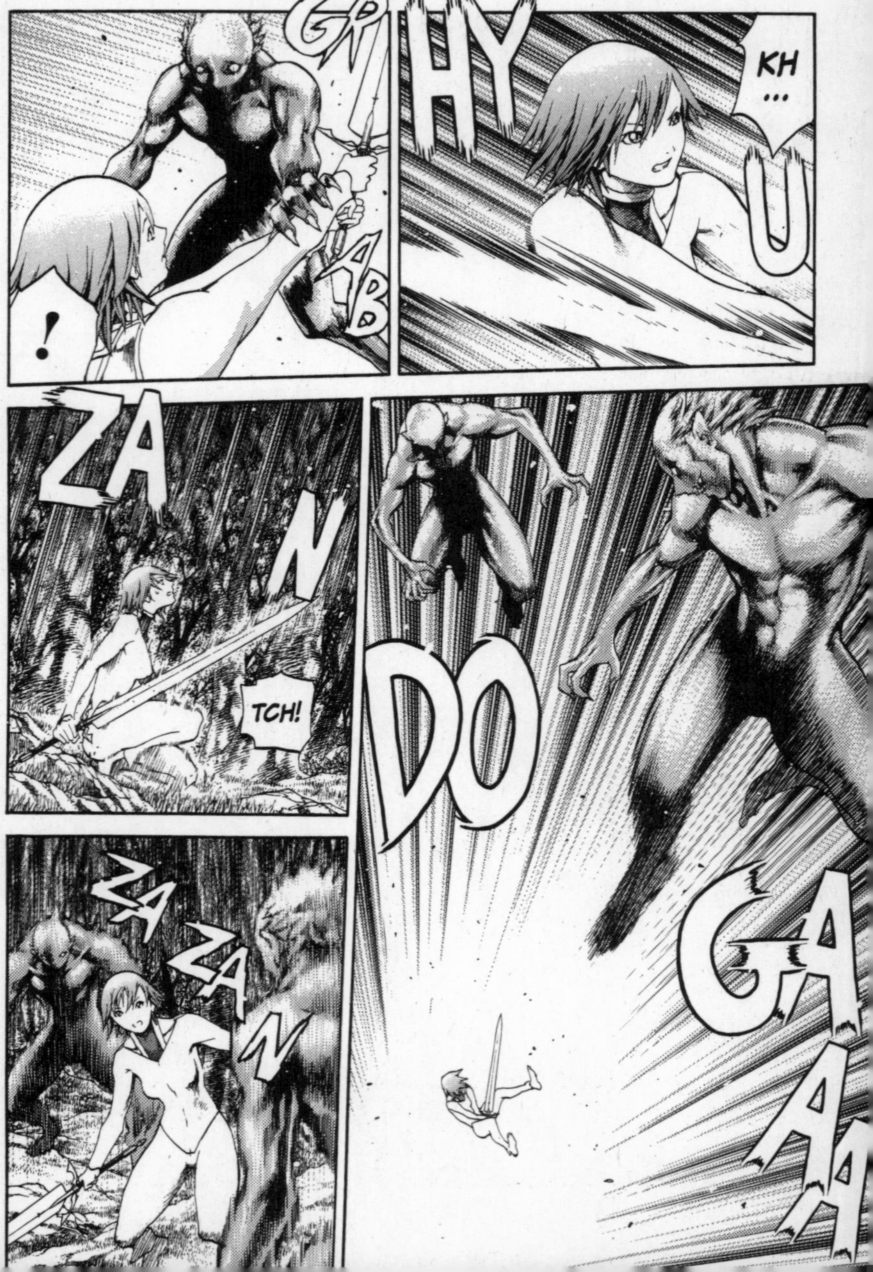
HYU
KH ...
GRAB
!
DO
GAAA
ZAN
TCH!
ZAZAN

READ THIS WAY

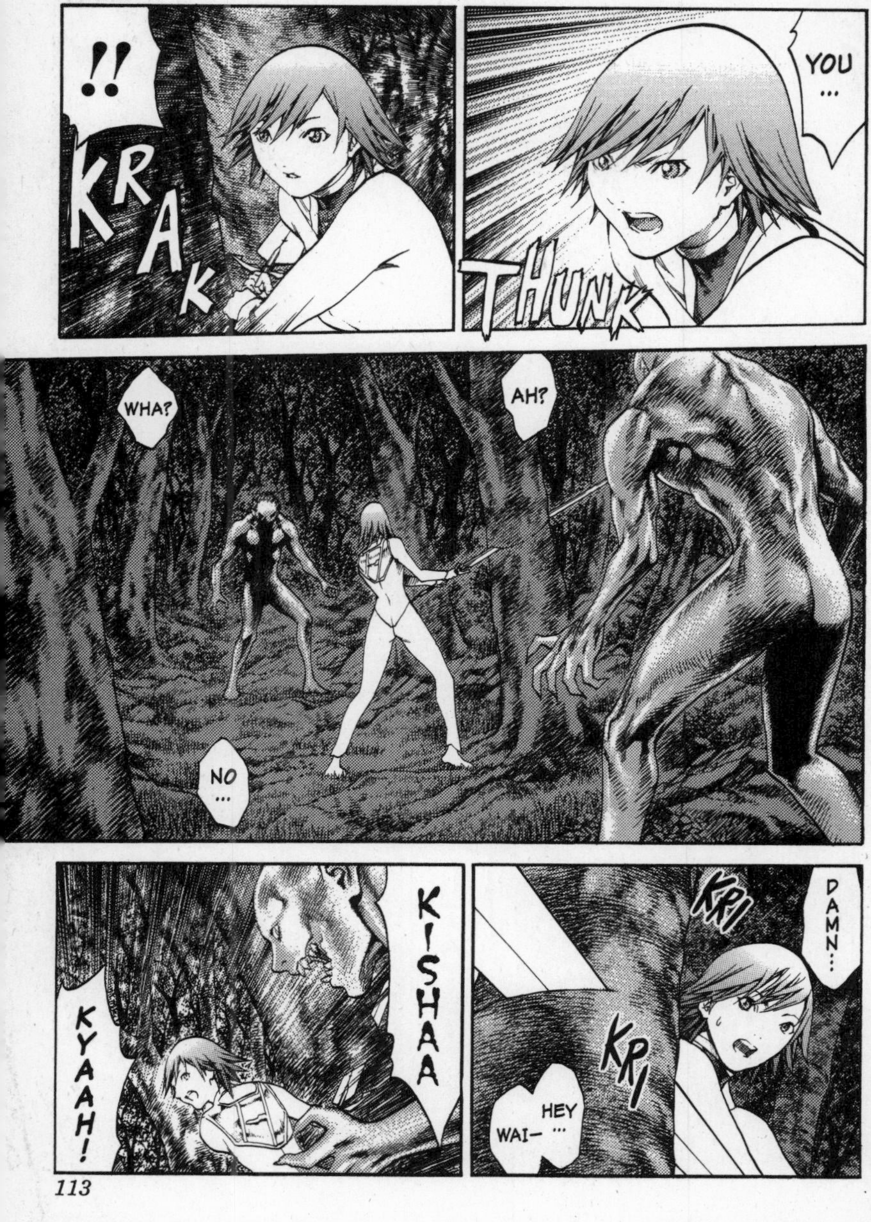

YOU ...
THUNK
!!
KRAK
AH?
WHA?
NO ...
DAMN...
KRI
KRI
HEY ...
WAI—
KISHAA
KYAAH!

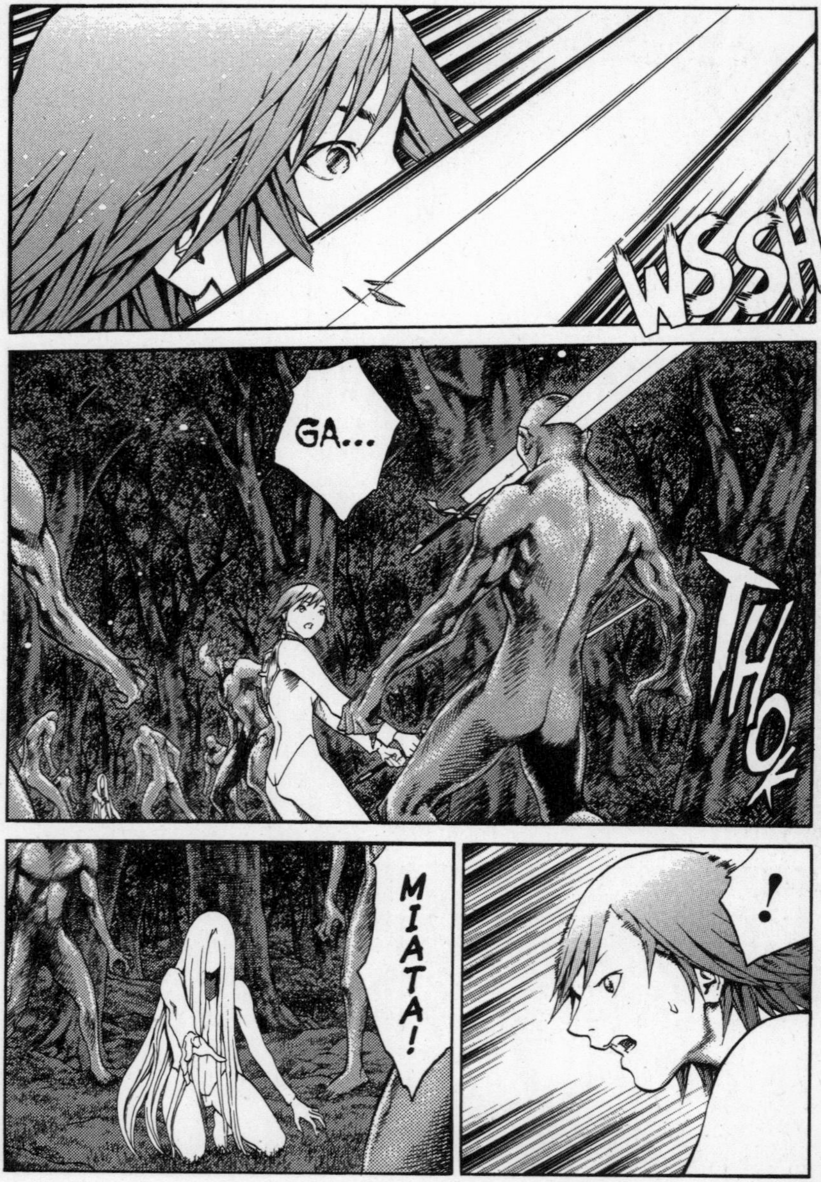
WSSH
GA...
THOK
!
MIATA!

READ THIS WAY

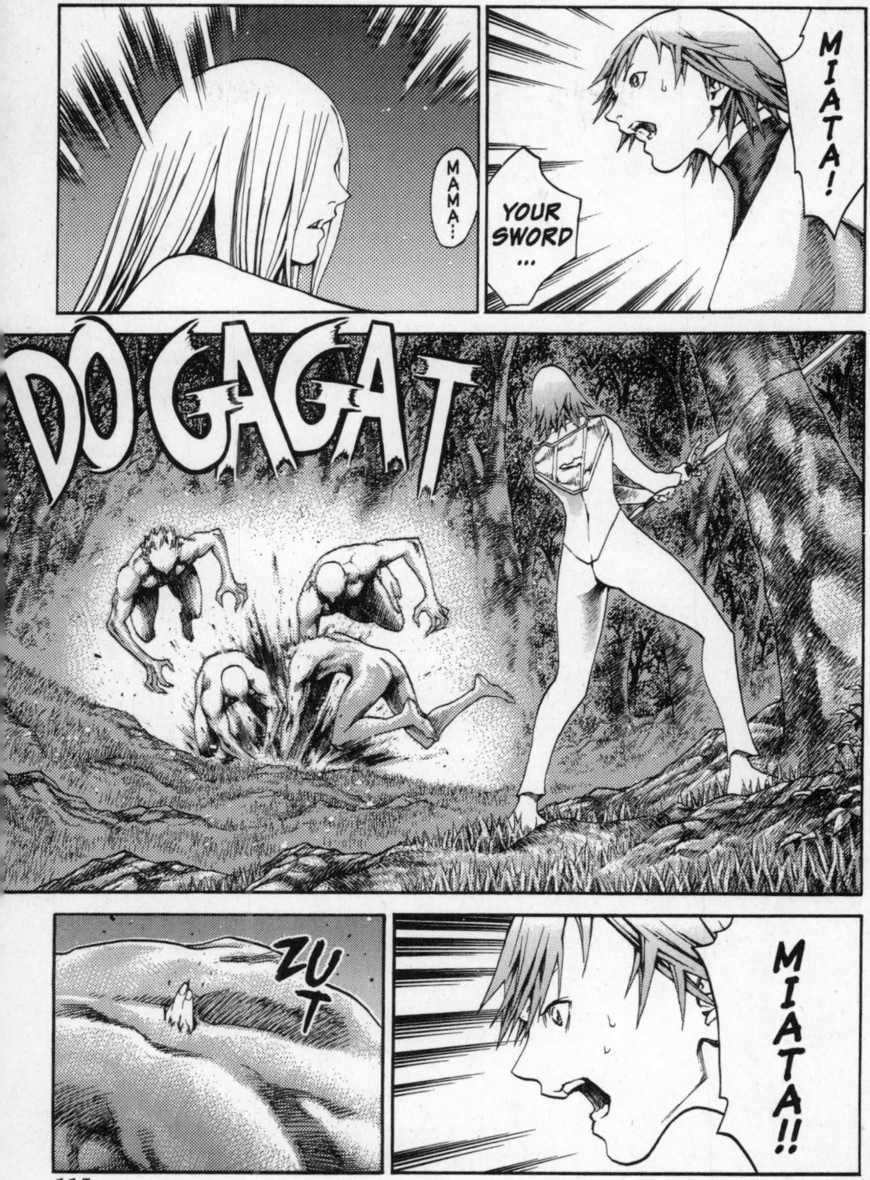

MIATA!
YOUR SWORD ...
MAMA...
DOGAGAT
MIATA!!
ZUT

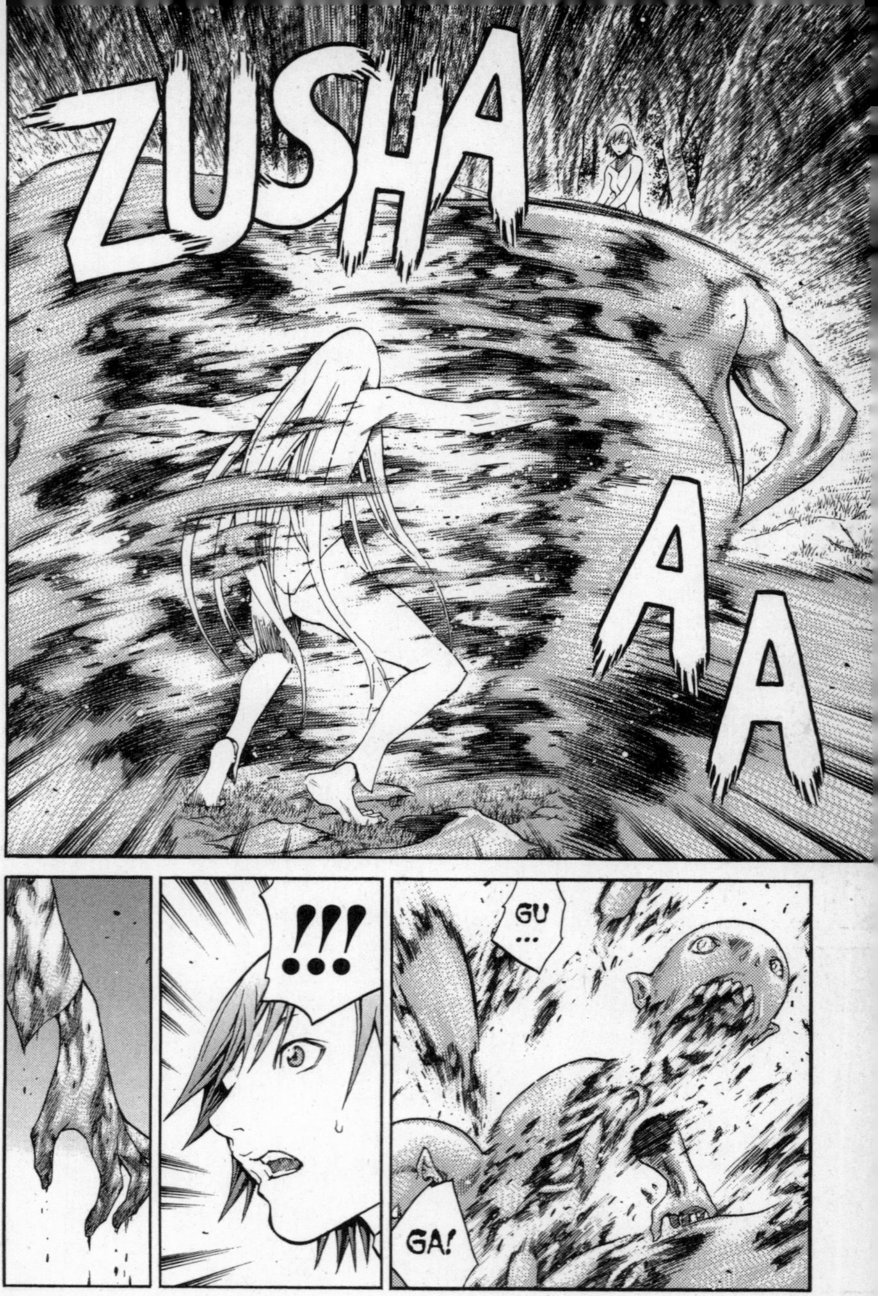
ZUSHA
AAA
GU...
GA!
!!!

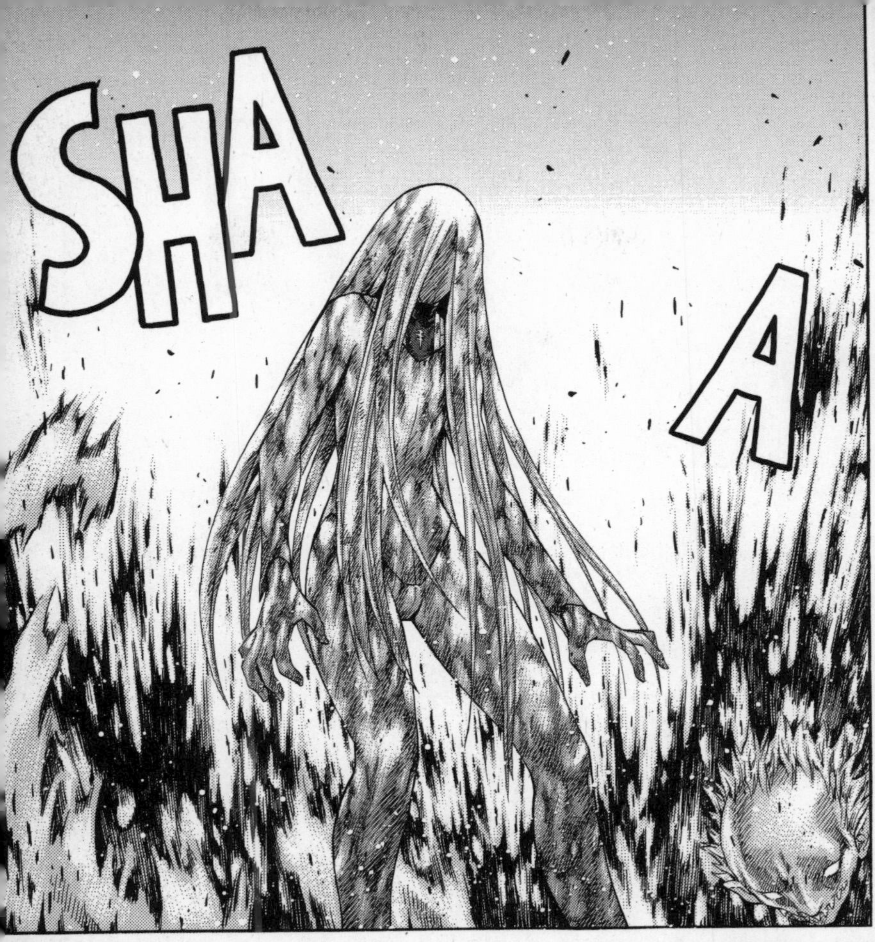
SHAA
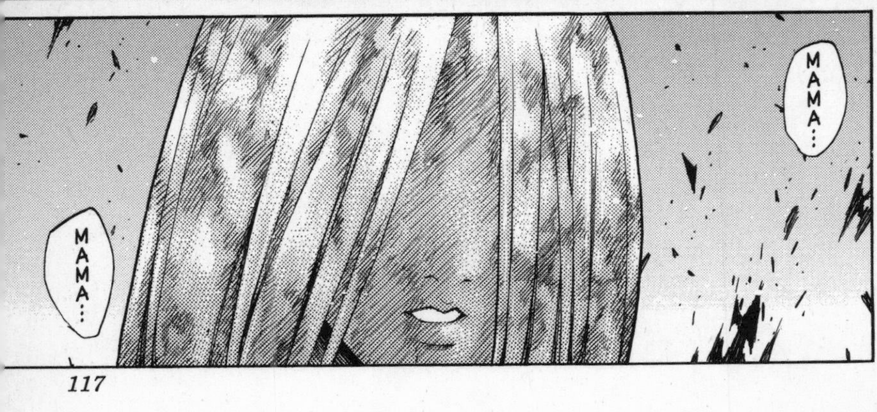
MAMA...
MAMA...

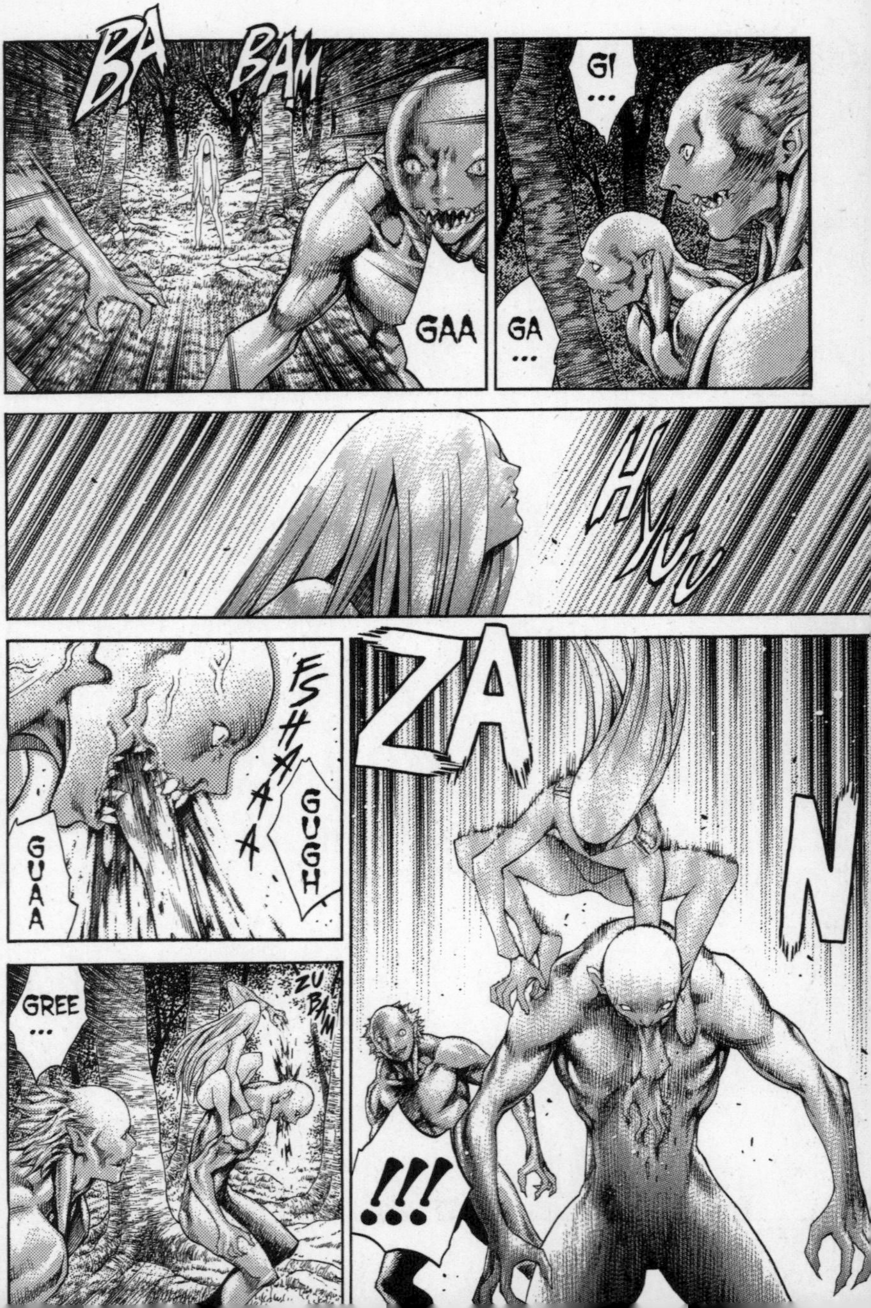
GI ...
GA ...
BA BAM
GAA
HYUU
ZAN
!!!
FSHAAAA
GUGH
GUAA
ZUBAM
GREE ...

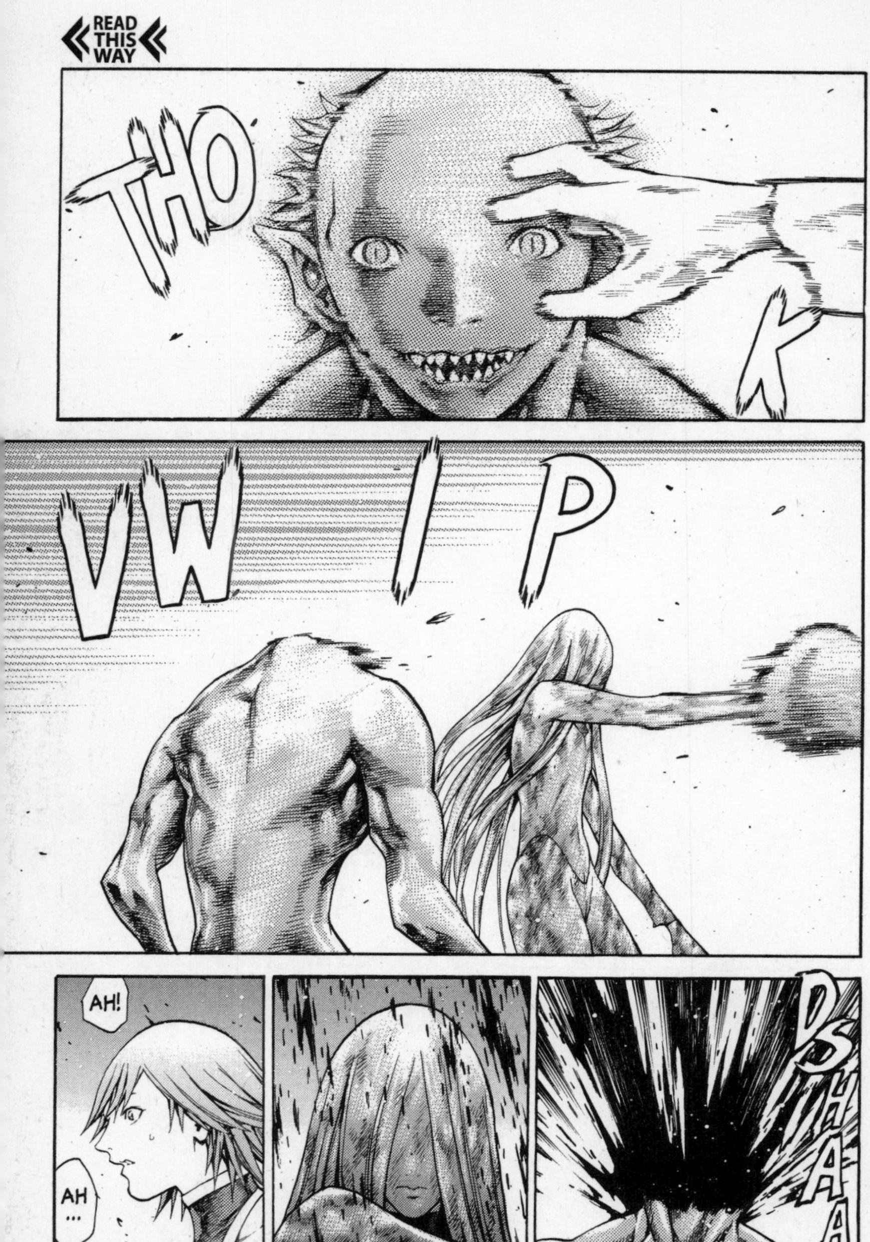
READ THIS WAY
THOK
VWIP
DSHAAA
AH!
AH ...

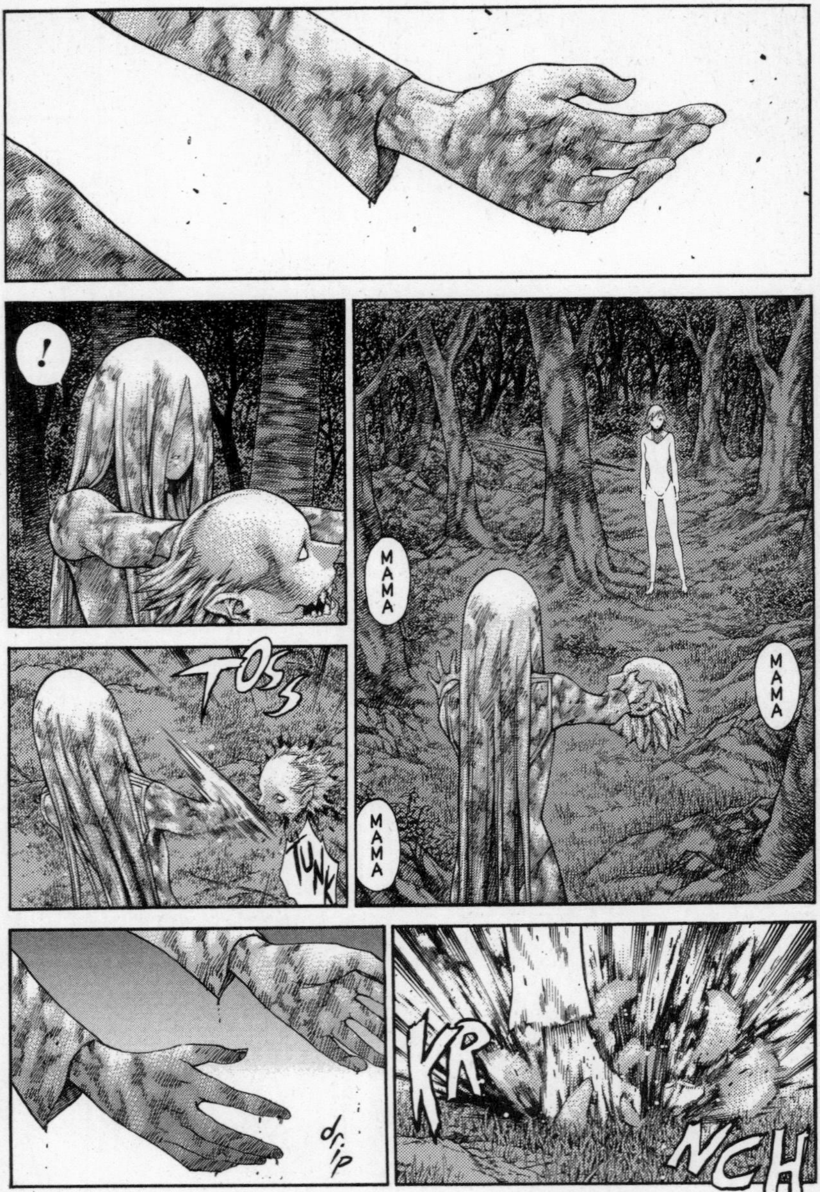
MAMA
MAMA
MAMA
!
TOSS
TUNK
KRNCH
drip

READ THIS WAY

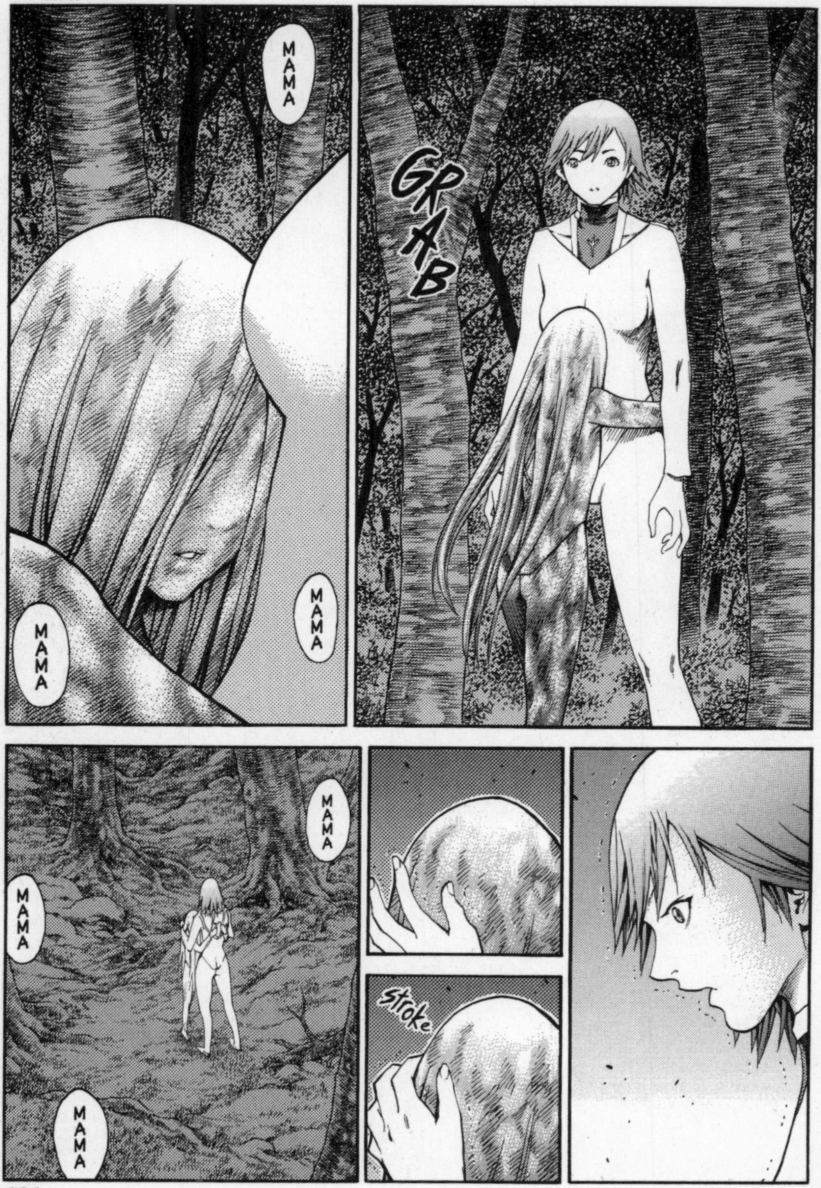

GRAB
MAMA
MAMA
MAMA
stroke
MAMA
MAMA
MAMA

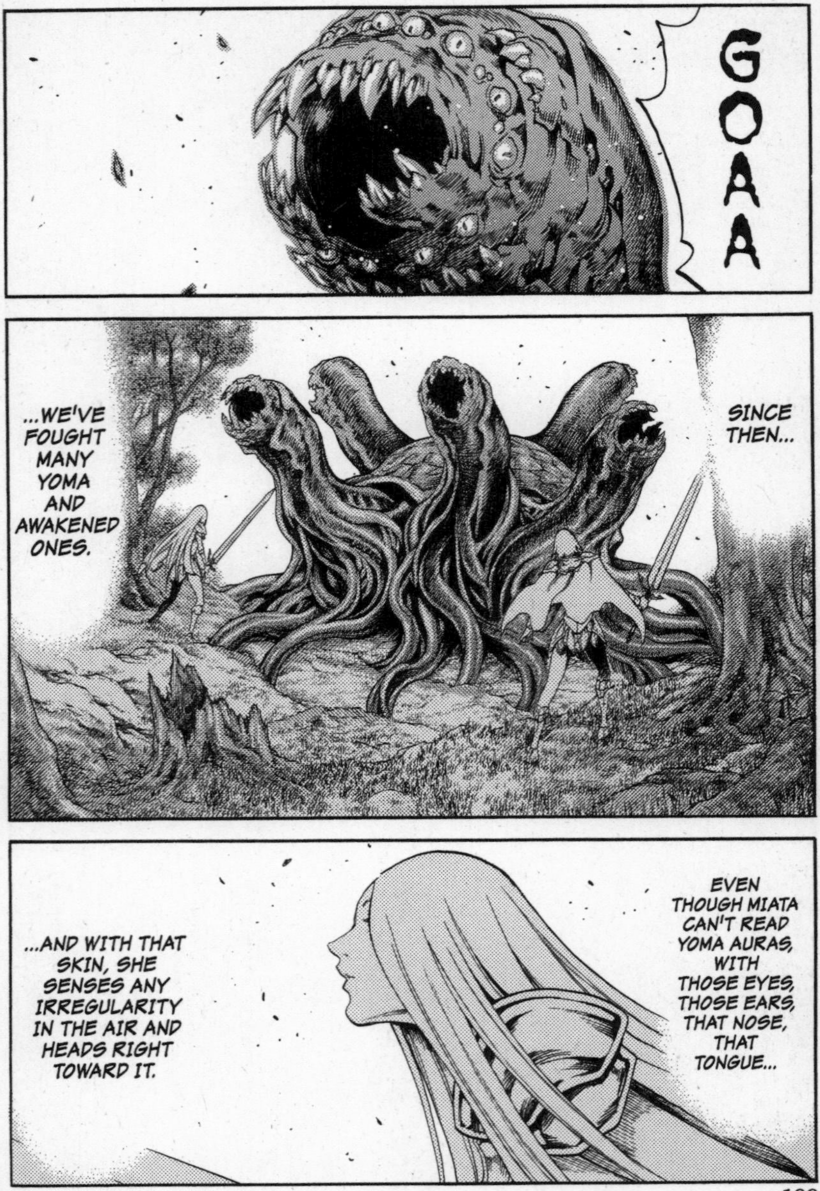
GOAA
SINCE THEN...
...WE'VE FOUGHT MANY YOMA AND AWAKENED ONES.
EVEN THOUGH MIATA CAN'T READ YOMA AURAS, WITH THOSE EYES, THOSE EARS, THAT NOSE, THAT TONGUE...
...AND WITH THAT SKIN, SHE SENSES ANY IRREGULARITY IN THE AIR AND HEADS RIGHT TOWARD IT.

READ THIS WAY

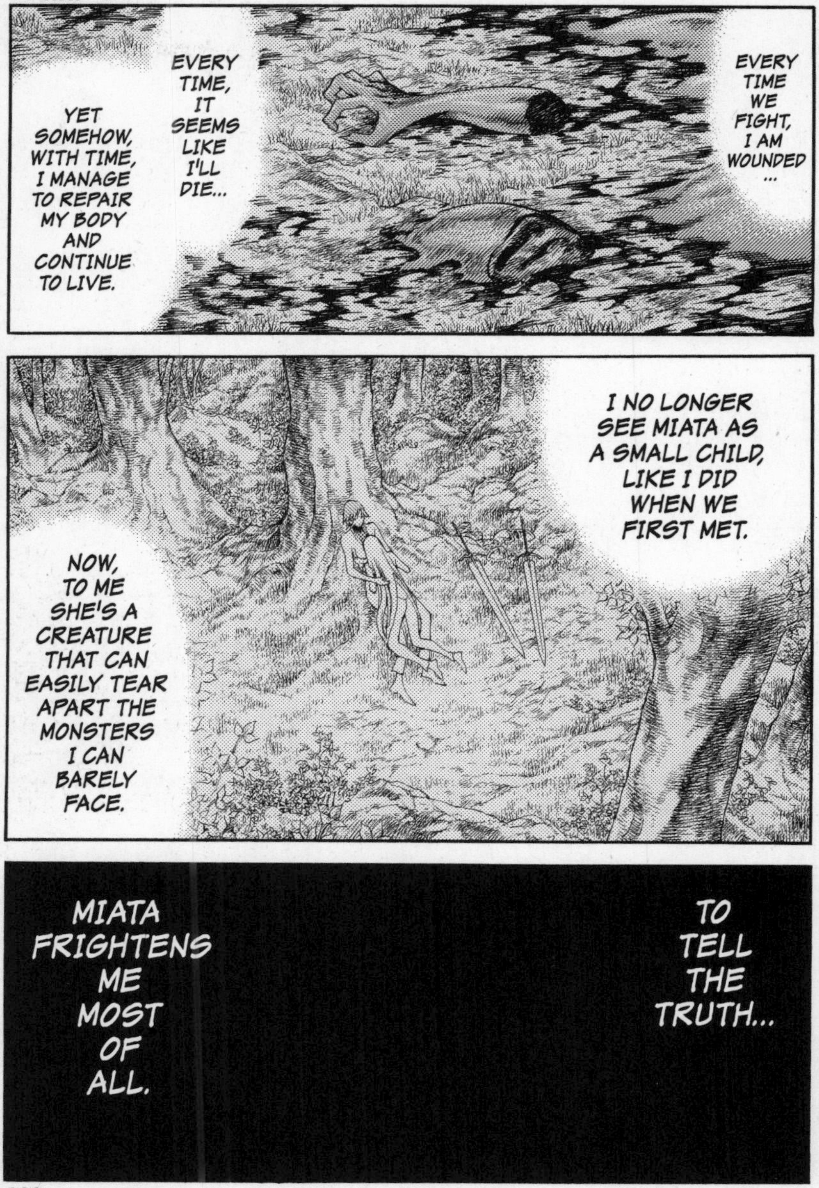
EVERY TIME WE FIGHT, I AM WOUNDED...
EVERY TIME, IT SEEMS LIKE I'LL DIE...
YET SOMEHOW, WITH TIME, I MANAGE TO REPAIR MY BODY AND CONTINUE TO LIVE.
I NO LONGER SEE MIATA AS A SMALL CHILD, LIKE I DID WHEN WE FIRST MET.
NOW, TO ME SHE'S A CREATURE THAT CAN EASILY TEAR APART THE MONSTERS I CAN BARELY FACE.
TO TELL THE TRUTH...
MIATA FRIGHTENS ME MOST OF ALL.

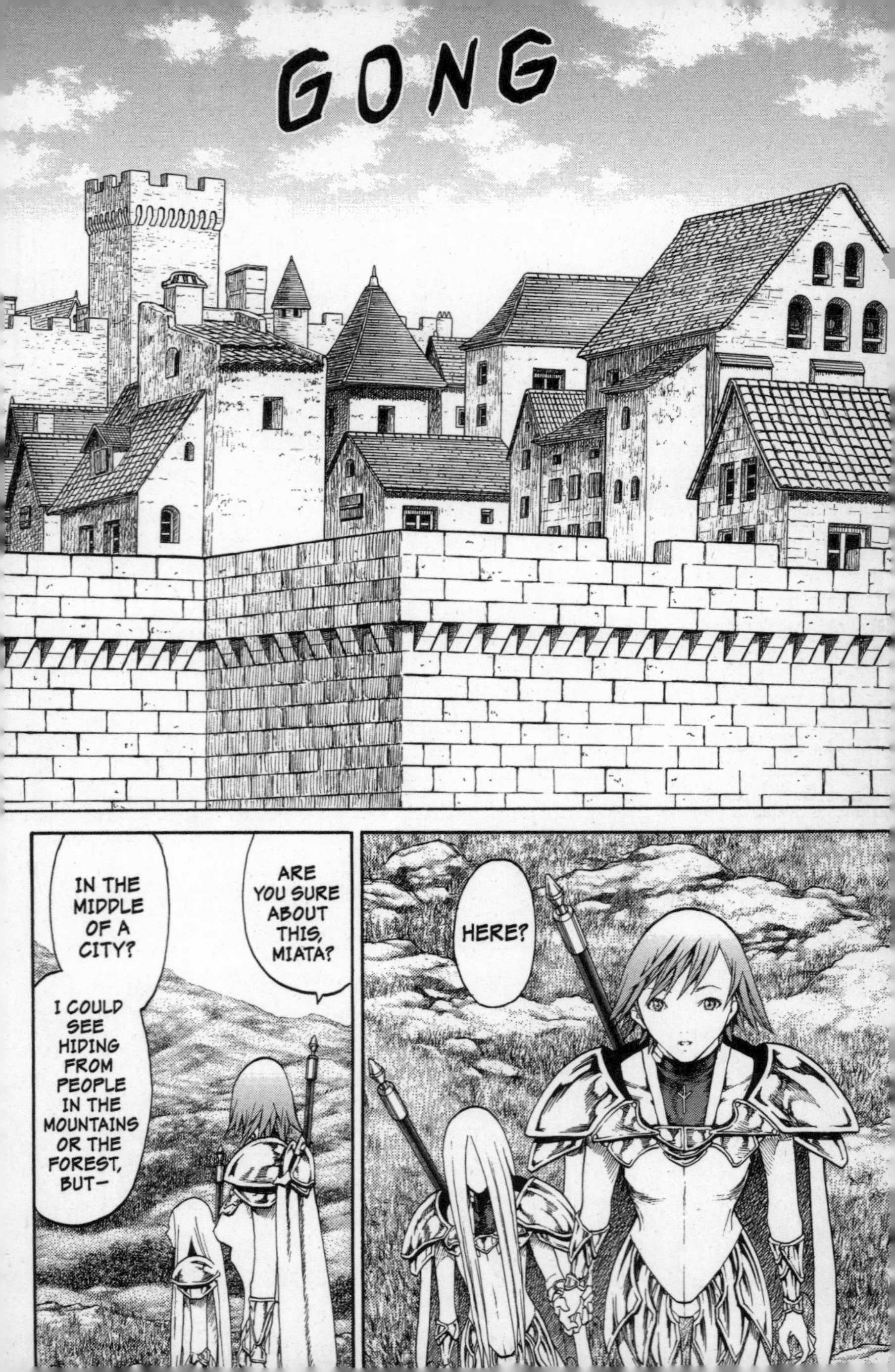
GONG
HERE?
ARE YOU SURE ABOUT THIS, MIATA?
IN THE MIDDLE OF A CITY?
I COULD SEE HIDING FROM PEOPLE IN THE MOUNTAINS OR THE FOREST, BUT—

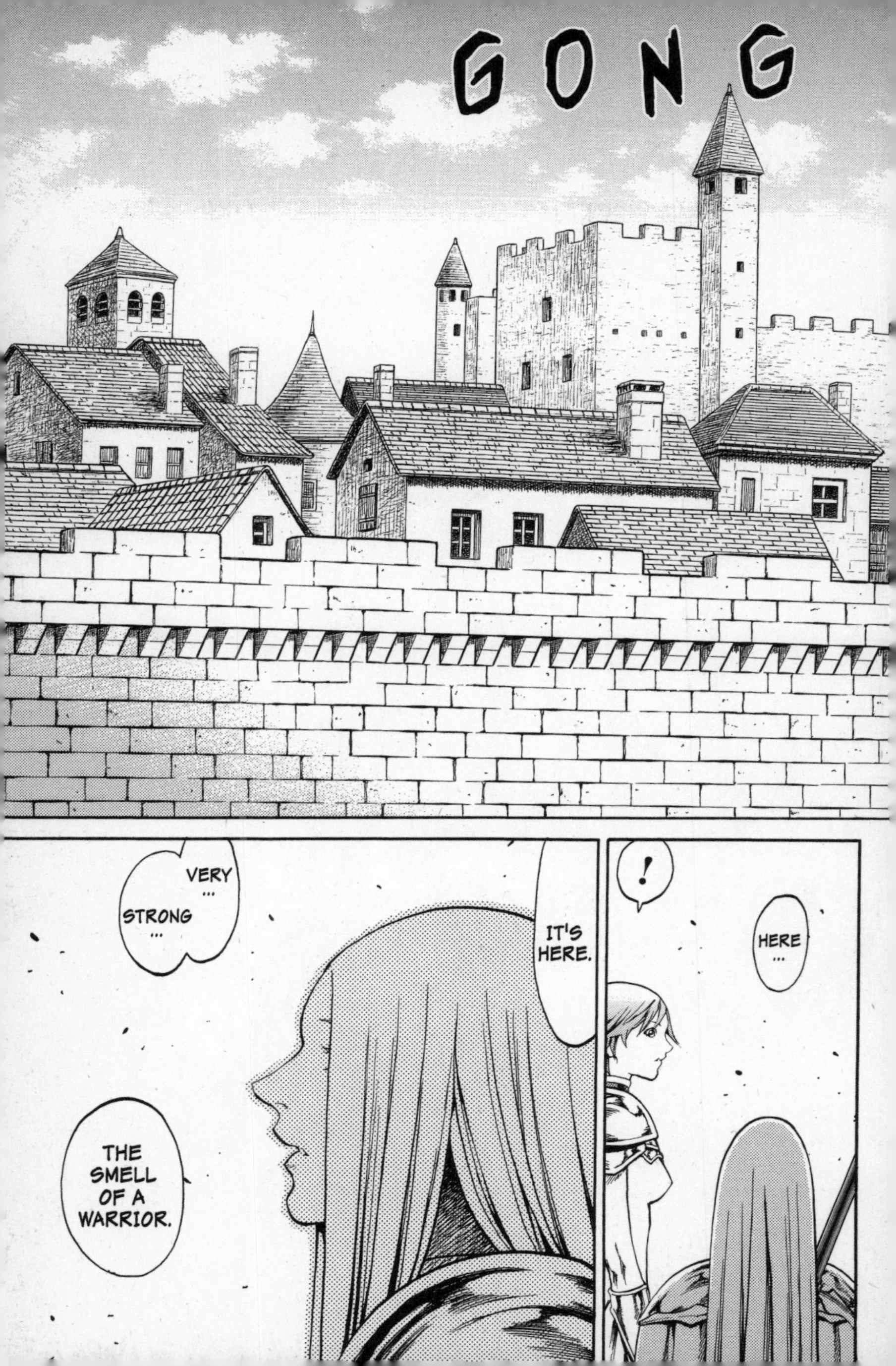
GONG
!
HERE ...
IT'S HERE.
VERY ... STRONG ...
THE SMELL OF A WARRIOR.

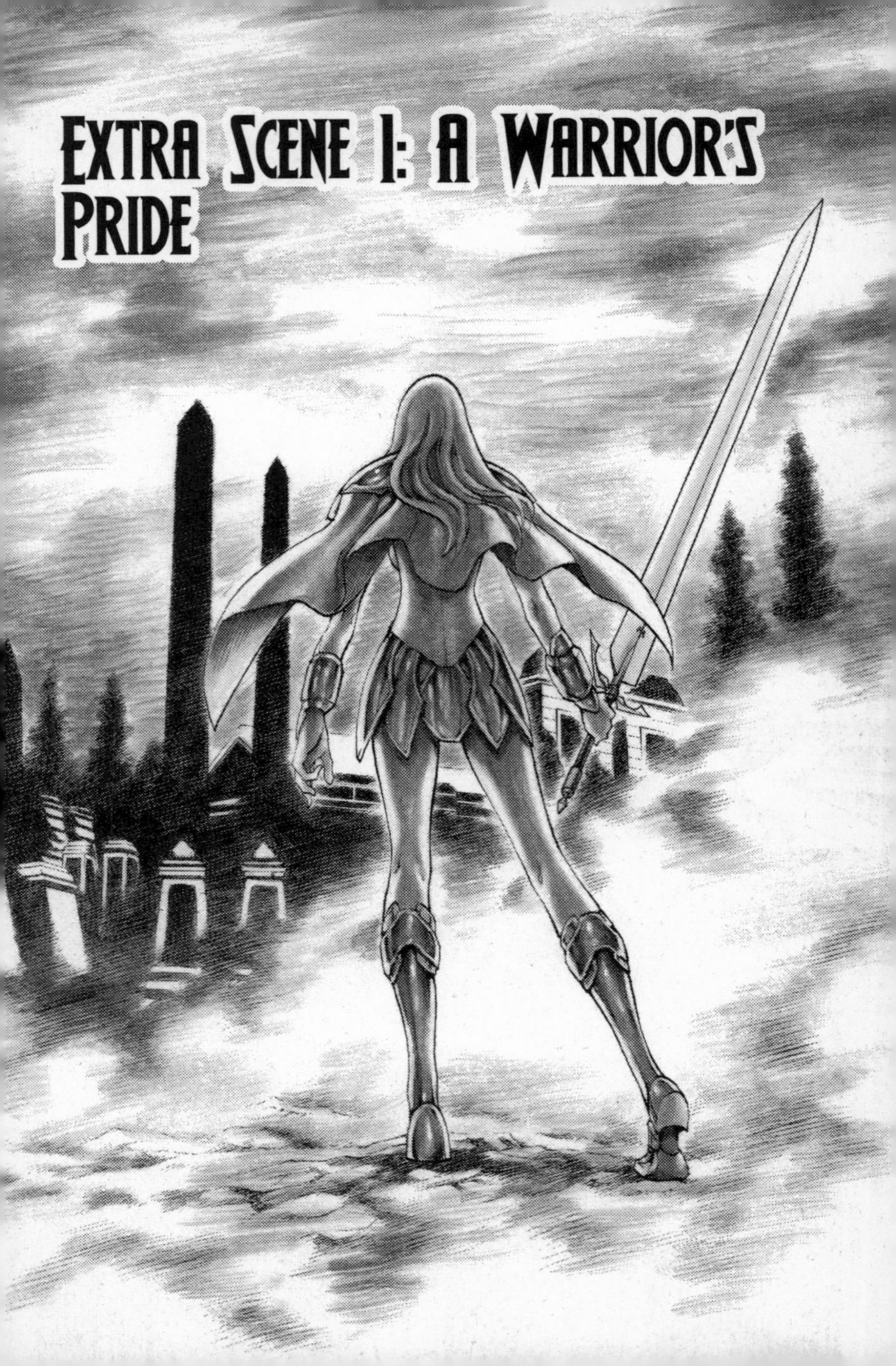
Extra Scene 1: A Warrior's Pride

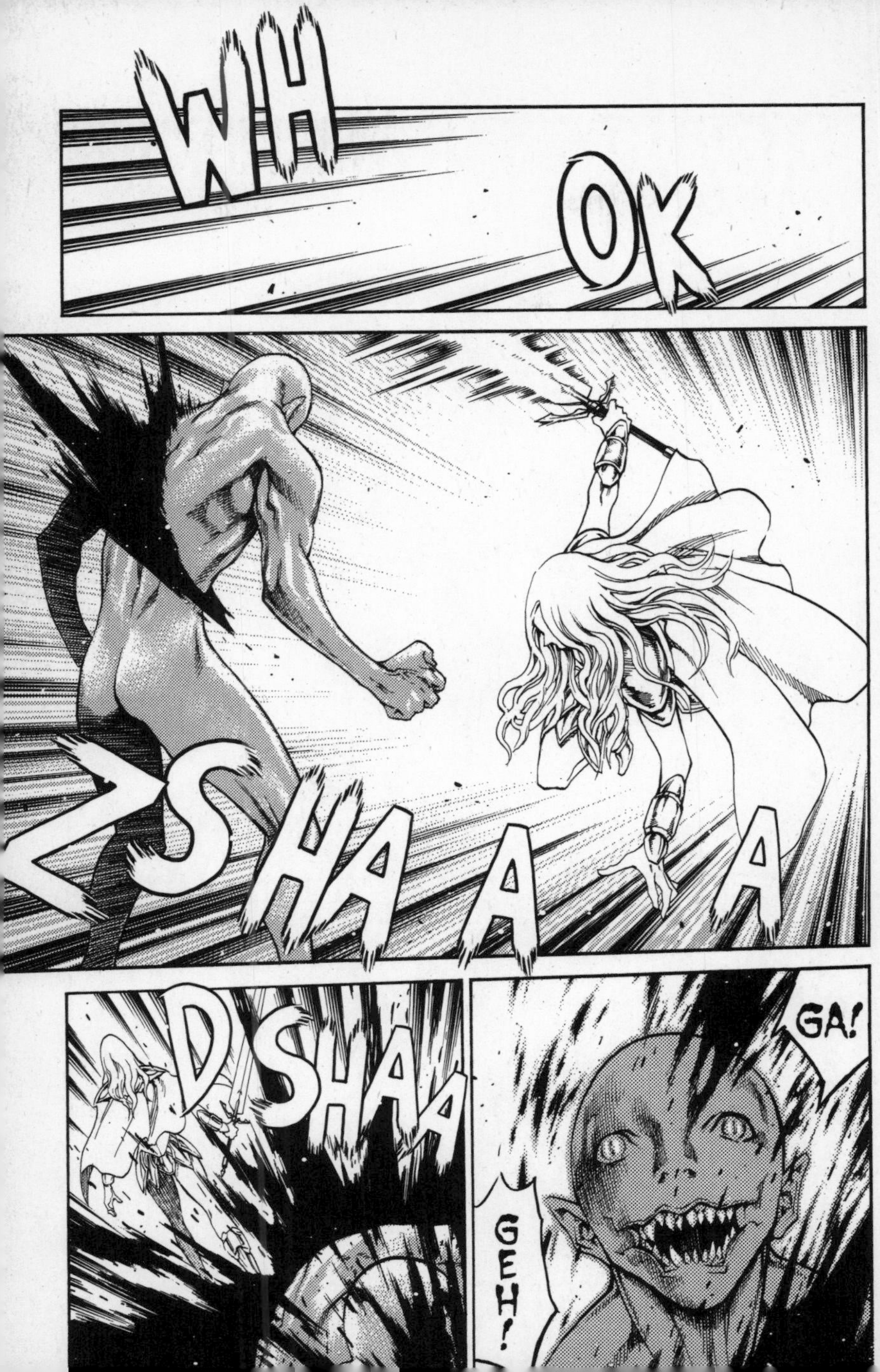
WH OK
ZSHA A A
GA!
GEH!
DSHAA

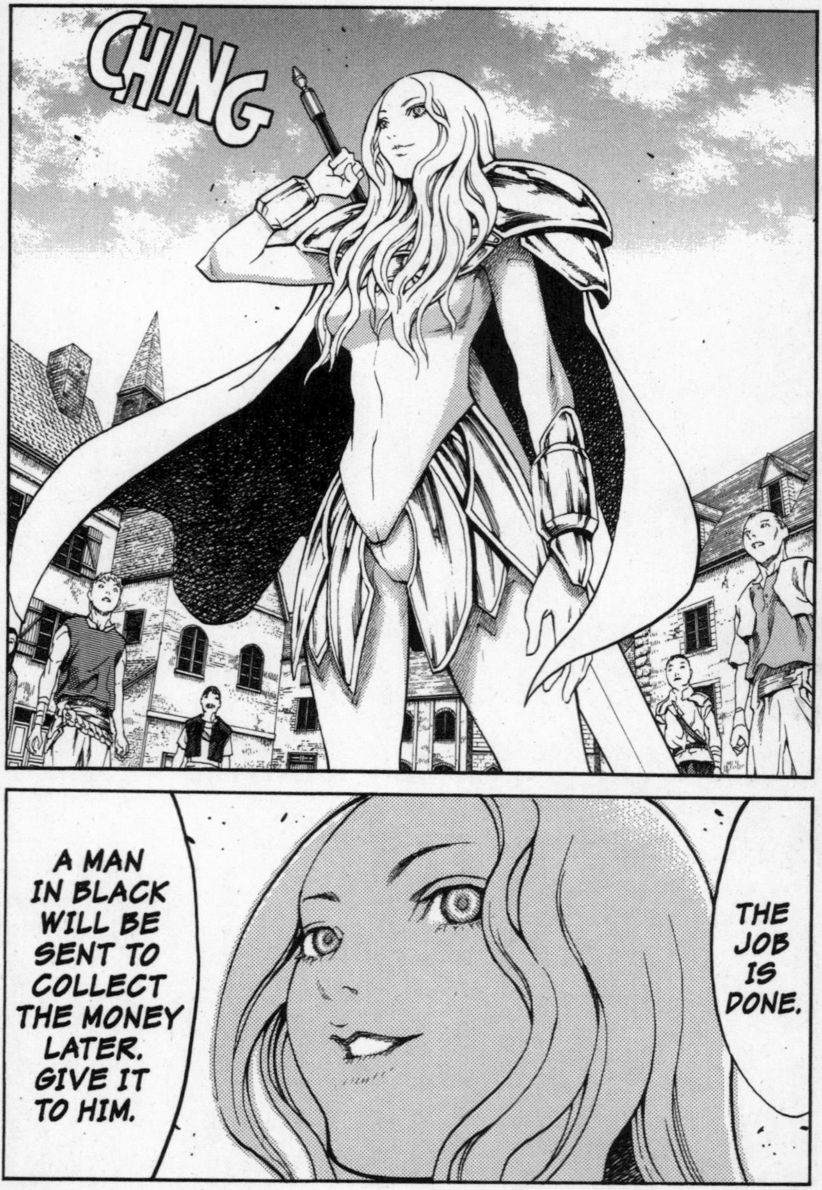
CHING
THE JOB IS DONE.
A MAN IN BLACK WILL BE SENT TO COLLECT THE MONEY LATER. GIVE IT TO HIM.

READ THIS WAY

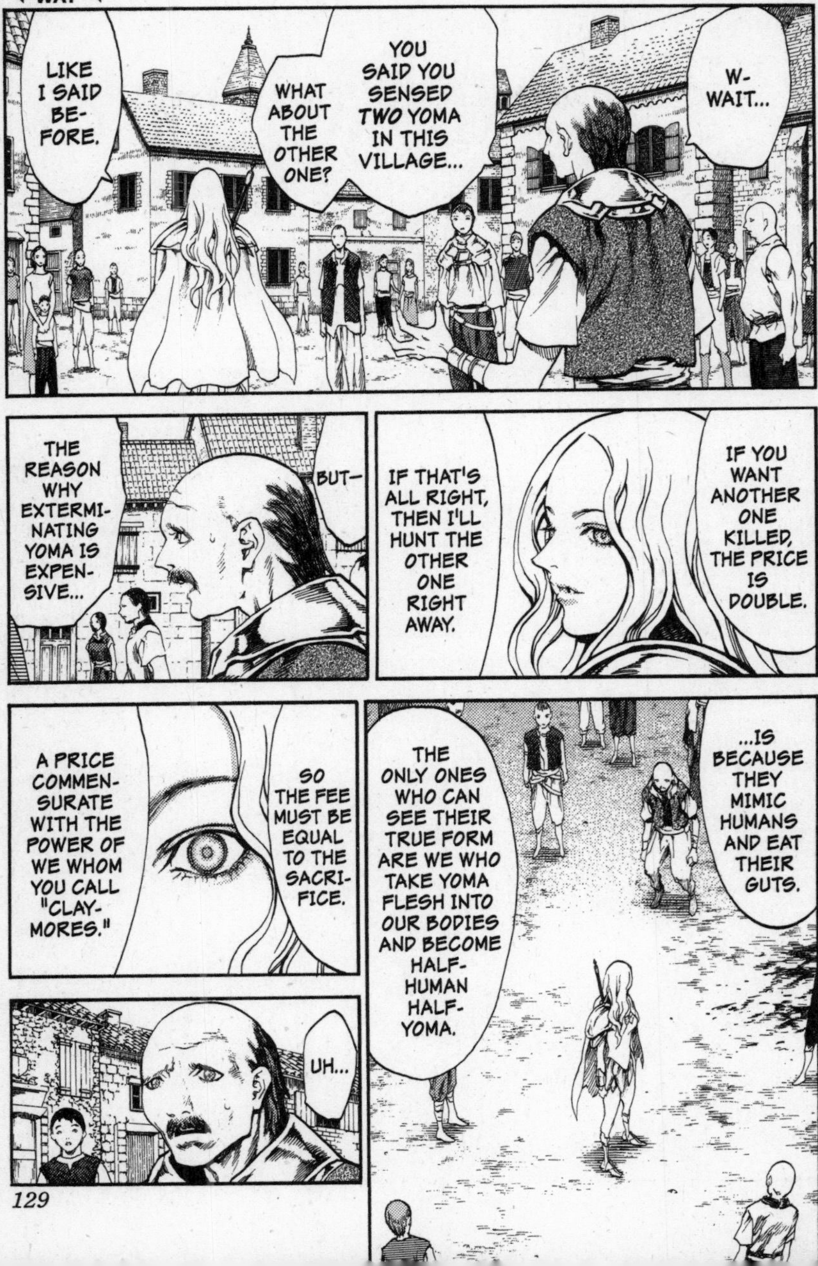
W-WAIT...
YOU SAID YOU SENSED *TWO* YOMA IN THIS VILLAGE...
WHAT ABOUT THE OTHER ONE?
LIKE I SAID BEFORE.
IF YOU WANT ANOTHER ONE KILLED, THE PRICE IS DOUBLE.
IF THAT'S ALL RIGHT, THEN I'LL HUNT THE OTHER ONE RIGHT AWAY.
BUT—
THE REASON WHY EXTERMINATING YOMA IS EXPENSIVE...
...IS BECAUSE THEY MIMIC HUMANS AND EAT THEIR GUTS.
THE ONLY ONES WHO CAN SEE THEIR TRUE FORM ARE WE WHO TAKE YOMA FLESH INTO OUR BODIES AND BECOME HALF-HUMAN HALF-YOMA.
SO THE FEE MUST BE EQUAL TO THE SACRIFICE.
A PRICE COMMENSURATE WITH THE POWER OF WE WHOM YOU CALL "CLAYMORES."
UH...

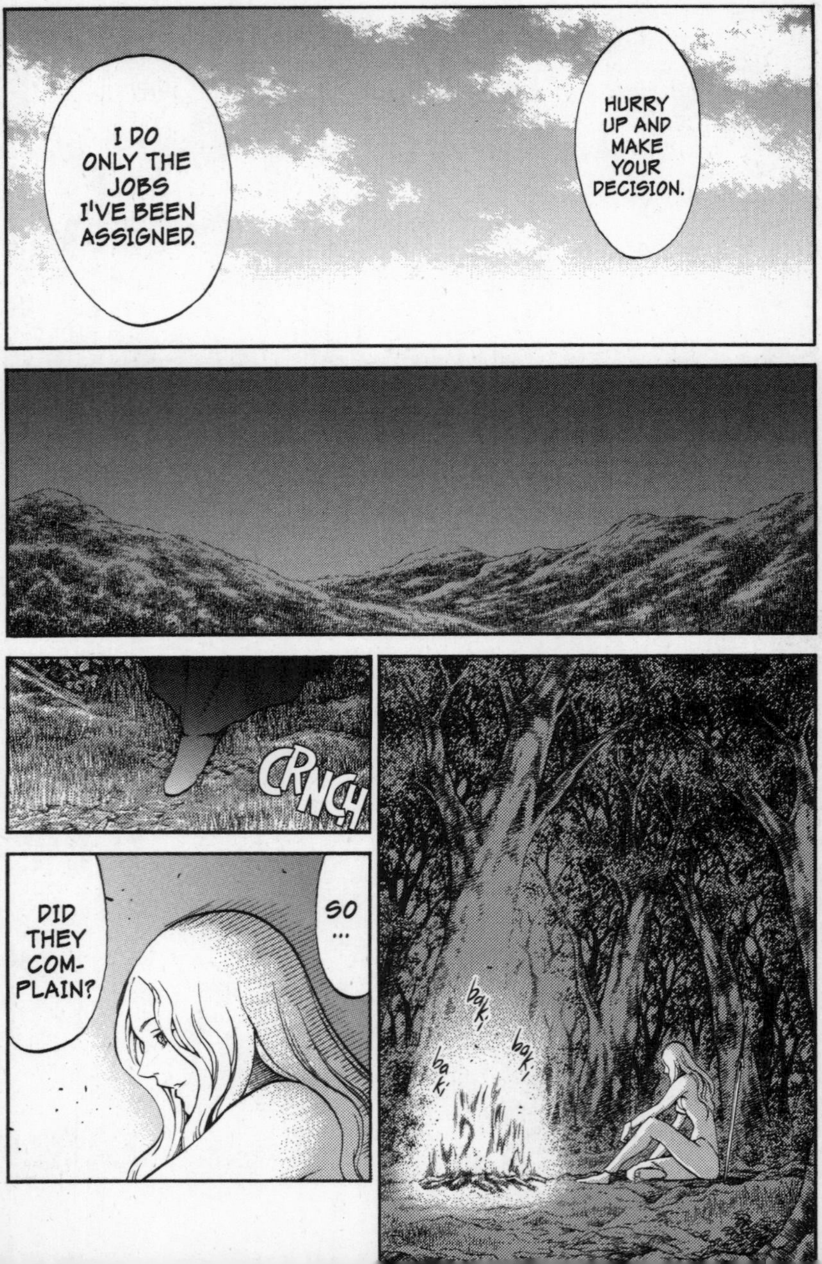
HURRY UP AND MAKE YOUR DECISION.
I DO ONLY THE JOBS I'VE BEEN ASSIGNED.
baki
baki
baki
CRNCH
SO...
DID THEY COM-PLAIN?

READ THIS WAY

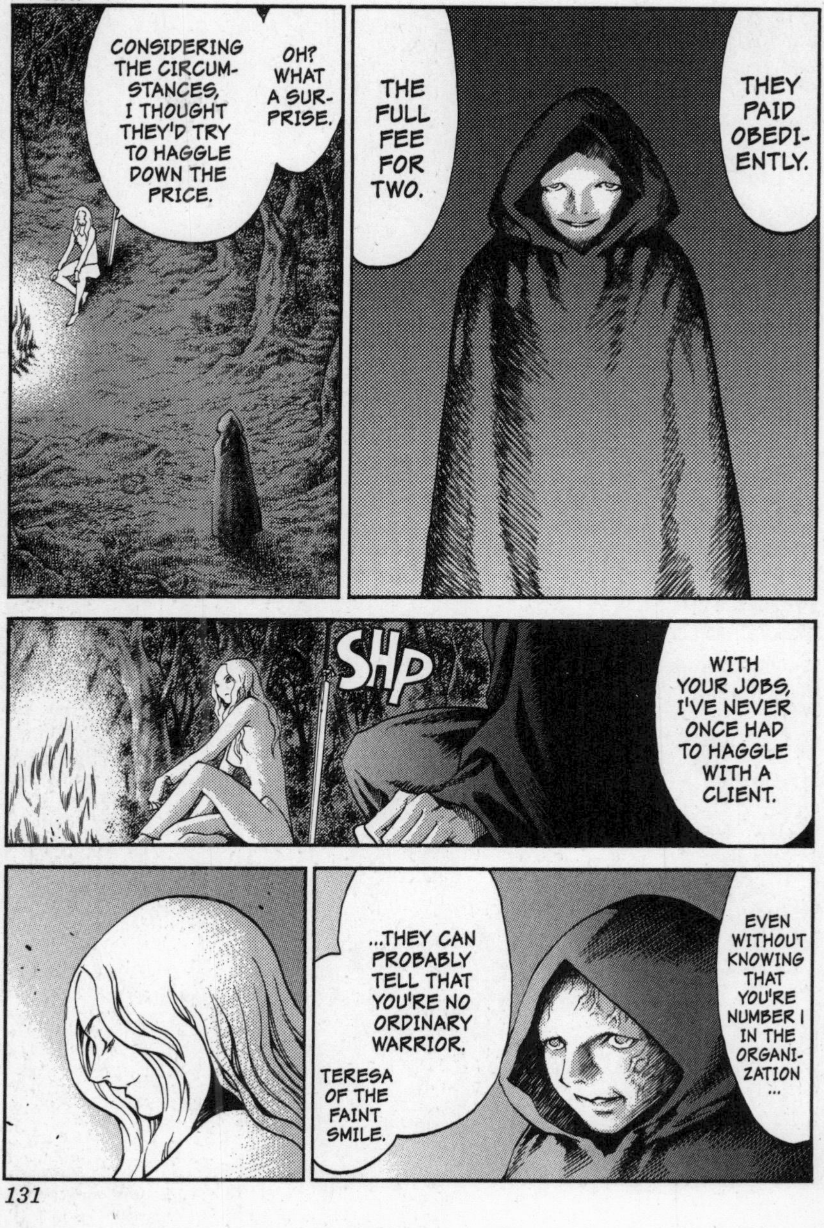
THEY PAID OBEDIENTLY.
THE FULL FEE FOR TWO.
OH? WHAT A SURPRISE.
CONSIDERING THE CIRCUMSTANCES, I THOUGHT THEY'D TRY TO HAGGLE DOWN THE PRICE.
WITH YOUR JOBS, I'VE NEVER ONCE HAD TO HAGGLE WITH A CLIENT.
SHP
EVEN WITHOUT KNOWING THAT YOU'RE NUMBER 1 IN THE ORGANIZATION...
...THEY CAN PROBABLY TELL THAT YOU'RE NO ORDINARY WARRIOR.
TERESA OF THE FAINT SMILE.

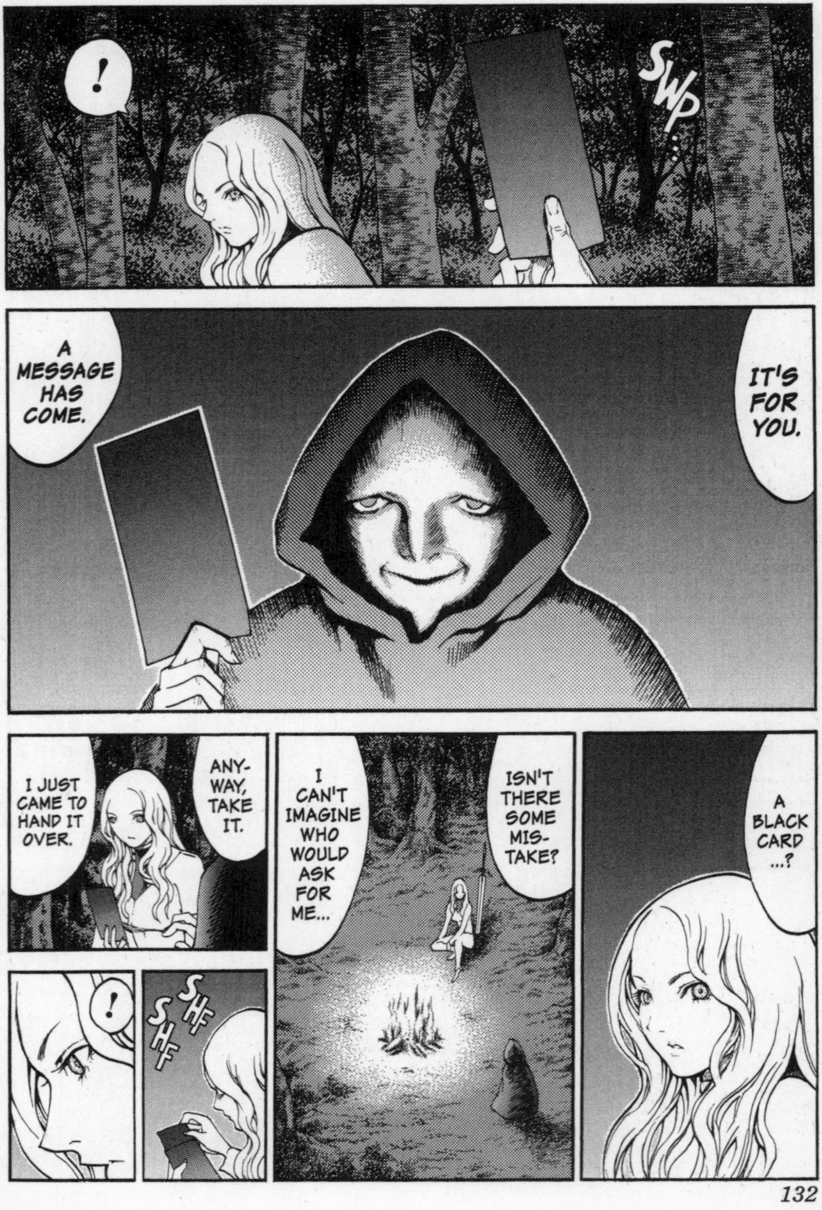
SWP...
!
IT'S FOR YOU.
A MESSAGE HAS COME.
A BLACK CARD ...?
ISN'T THERE SOME MIS-TAKE?
I CAN'T IMAGINE WHO WOULD ASK FOR ME...
ANY-WAY, TAKE IT.
I JUST CAME TO HAND IT OVER.
SHF SHF
!

READ THIS WAY

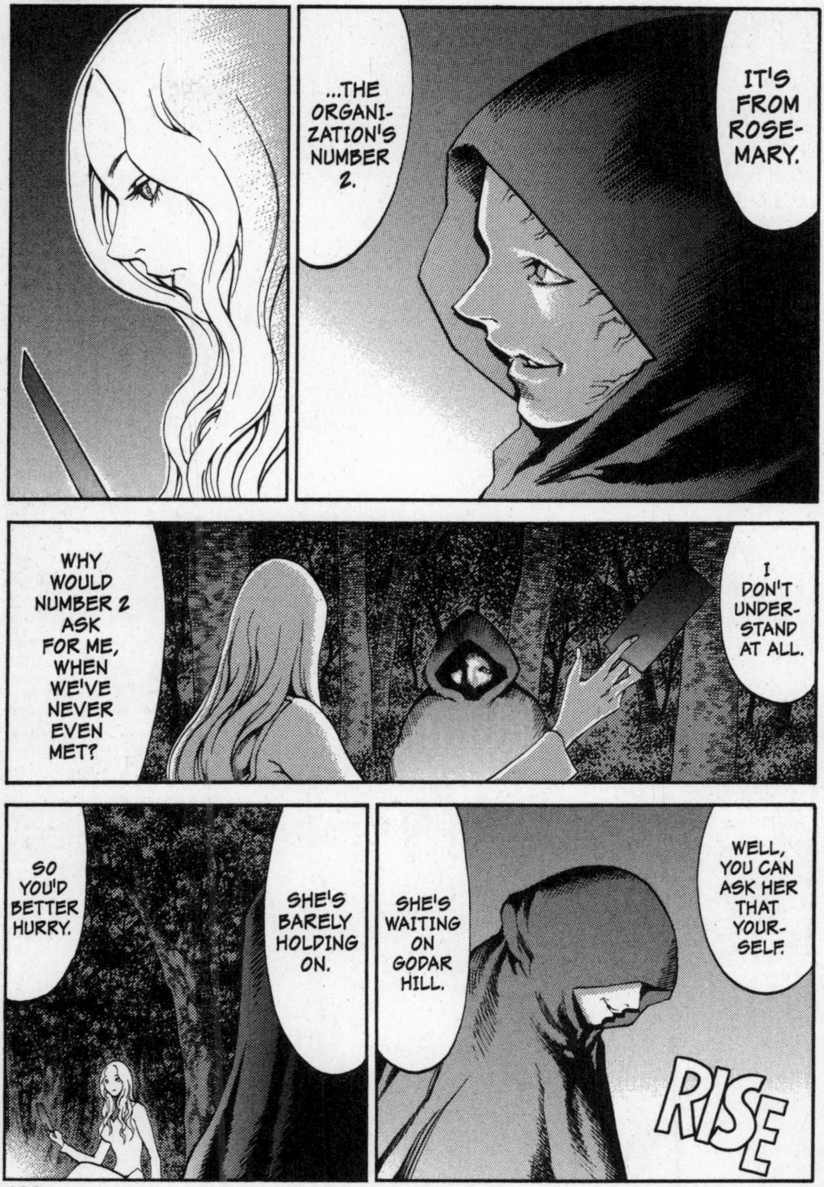
IT'S FROM ROSEMARY.
...THE ORGANIZATION'S NUMBER 2.
I DON'T UNDERSTAND AT ALL.
WHY WOULD NUMBER 2 ASK FOR ME, WHEN WE'VE NEVER EVEN MET?
WELL, YOU CAN ASK HER THAT YOURSELF.
RISE
SHE'S WAITING ON GODAR HILL.
SHE'S BARELY HOLDING ON.
SO YOU'D BETTER HURRY.

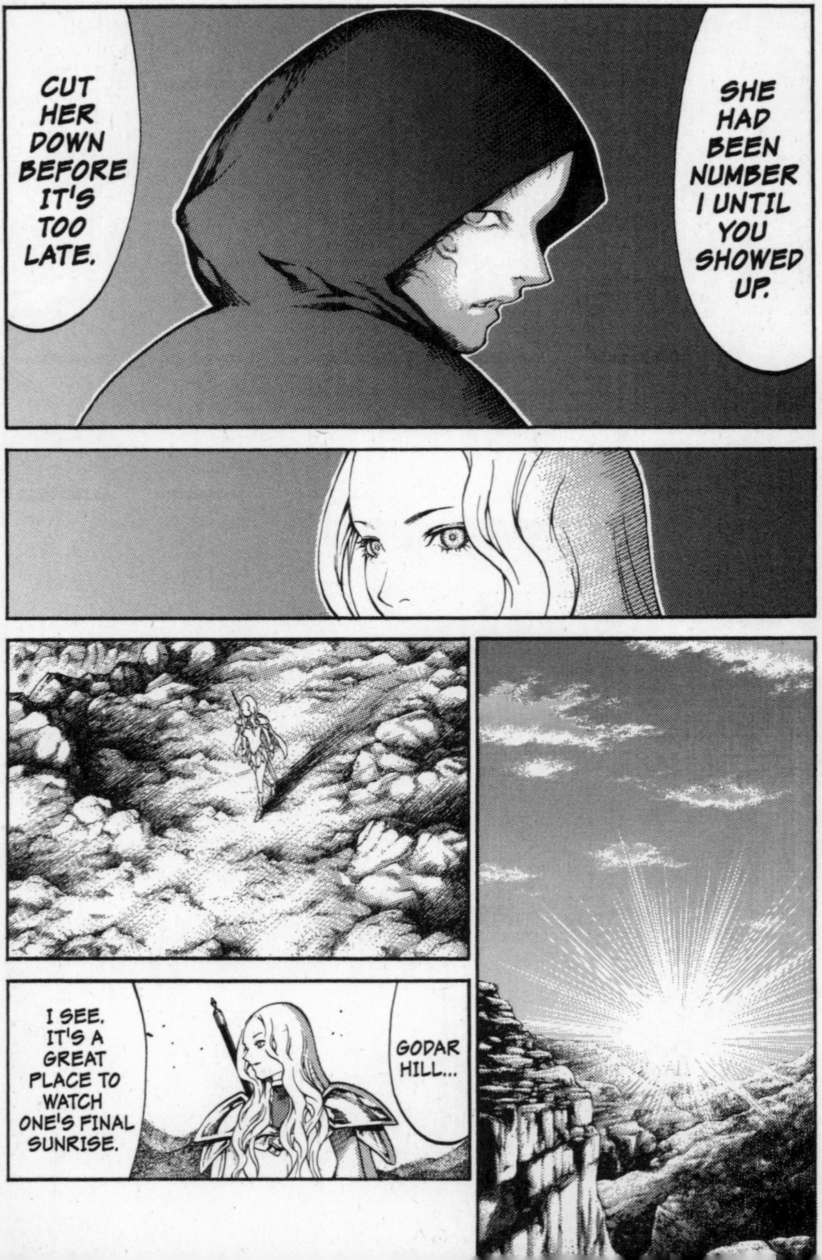
SHE HAD BEEN NUMBER I UNTIL YOU SHOWED UP.
CUT HER DOWN BEFORE IT'S TOO LATE.
GODAR HILL...
I SEE. IT'S A GREAT PLACE TO WATCH ONE'S FINAL SUNRISE.

READ THIS WAY

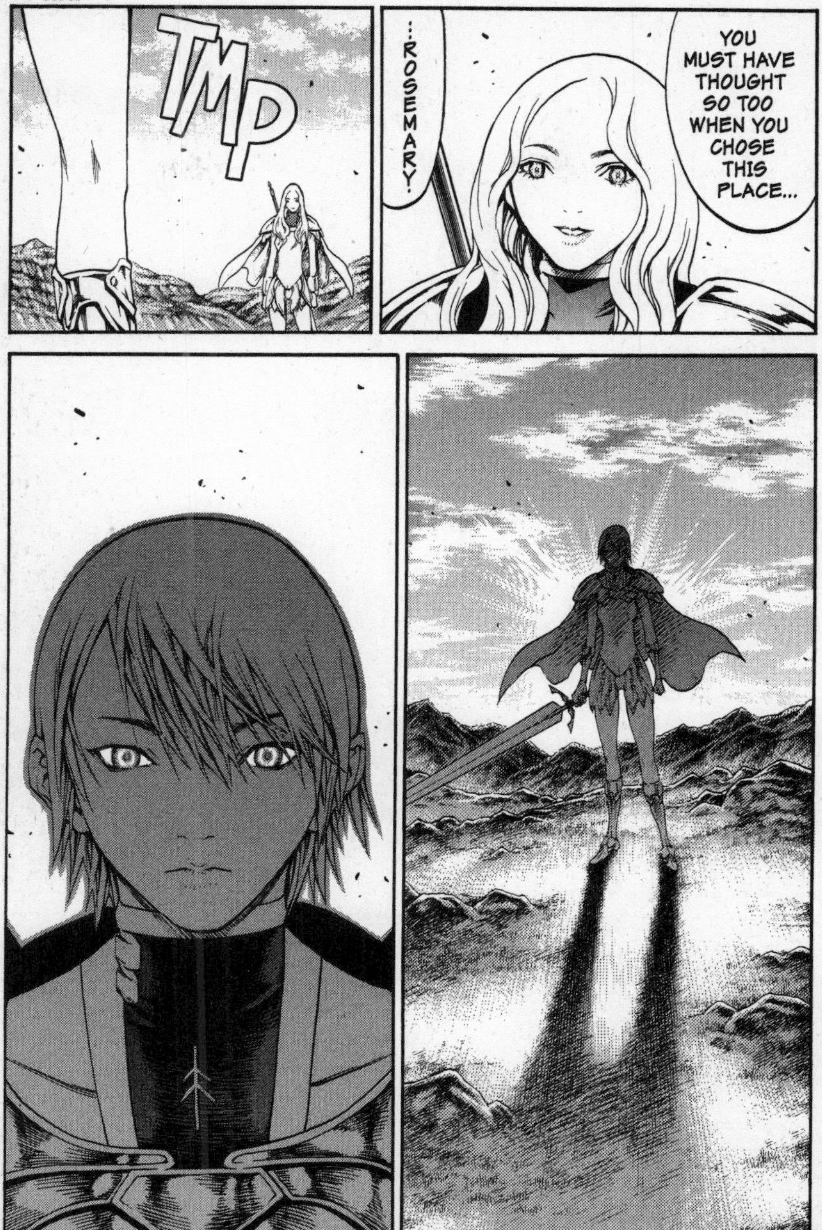
YOU MUST HAVE THOUGHT SO TOO WHEN YOU CHOSE THIS PLACE...
...ROSEMARY.
TMP

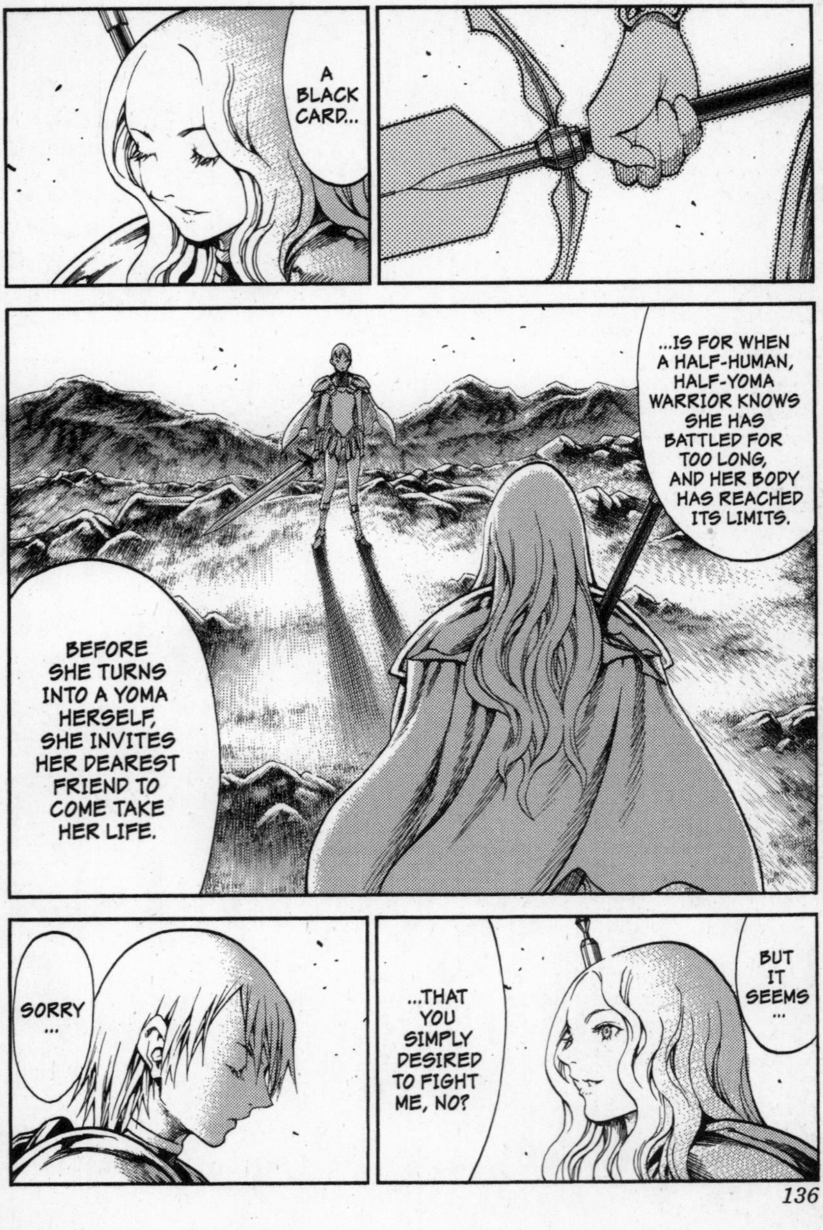
A BLACK CARD...
...IS FOR WHEN A HALF-HUMAN, HALF-YOMA WARRIOR KNOWS SHE HAS BATTLED FOR TOO LONG, AND HER BODY HAS REACHED ITS LIMITS.
BEFORE SHE TURNS INTO A YOMA HERSELF, SHE INVITES HER DEAREST FRIEND TO COME TAKE HER LIFE.
BUT IT SEEMS ...
...THAT YOU SIMPLY DESIRED TO FIGHT ME, NO?
SORRY ...

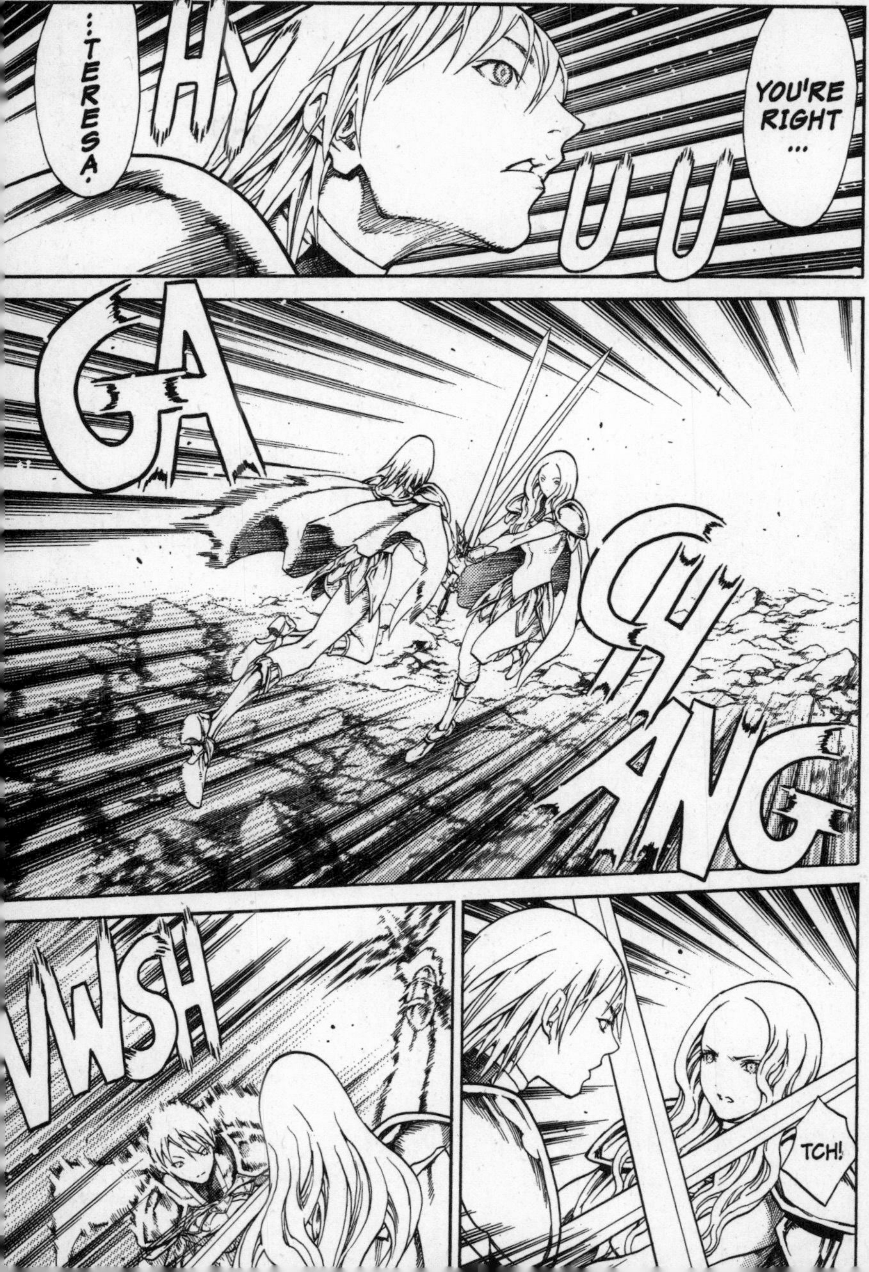
YOU'RE RIGHT ...
...TERESA.
HYUUU
GA
CHANG
TCH!
VWSH

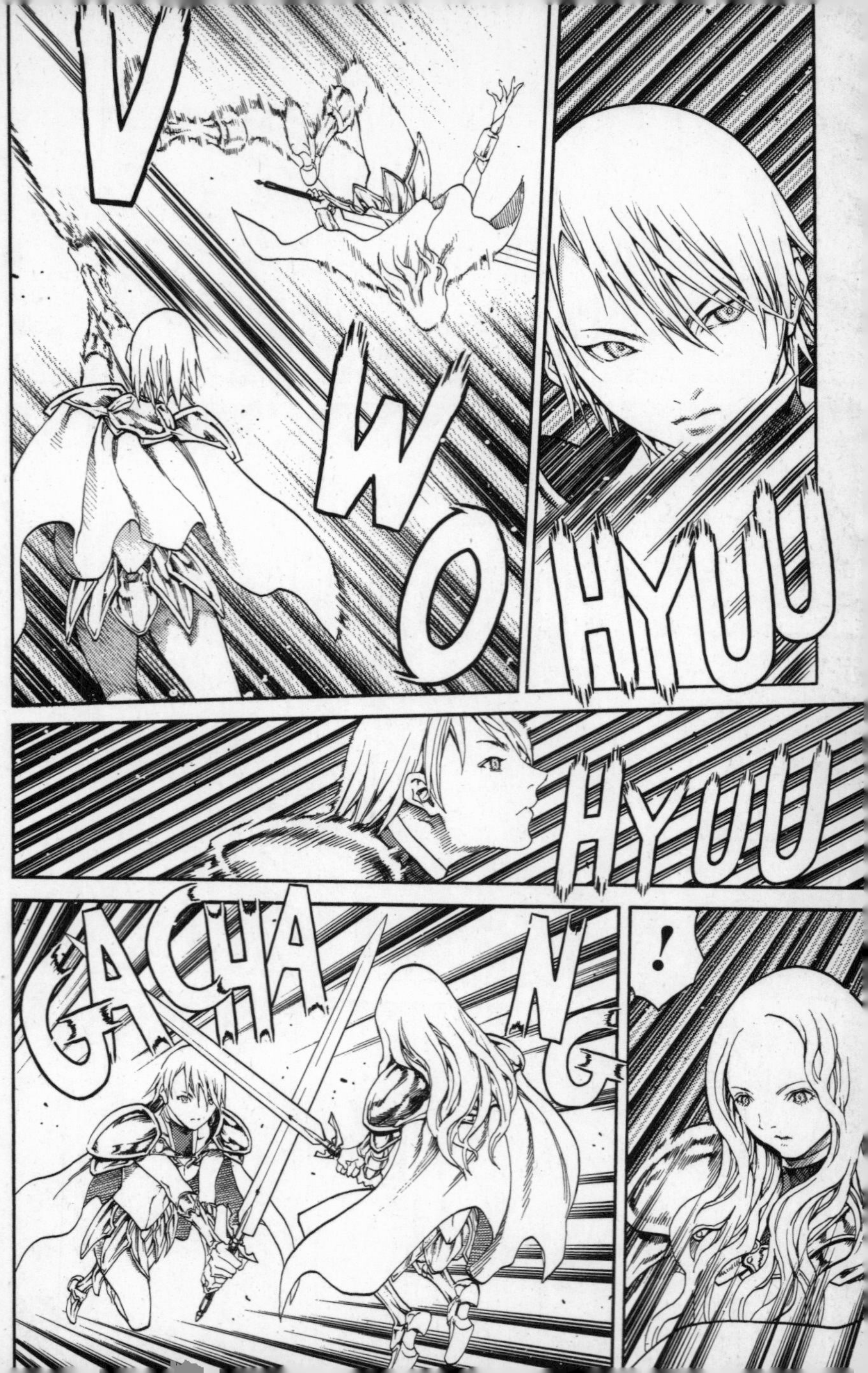
HYUU
VWO
HYUU
!
GACHANG

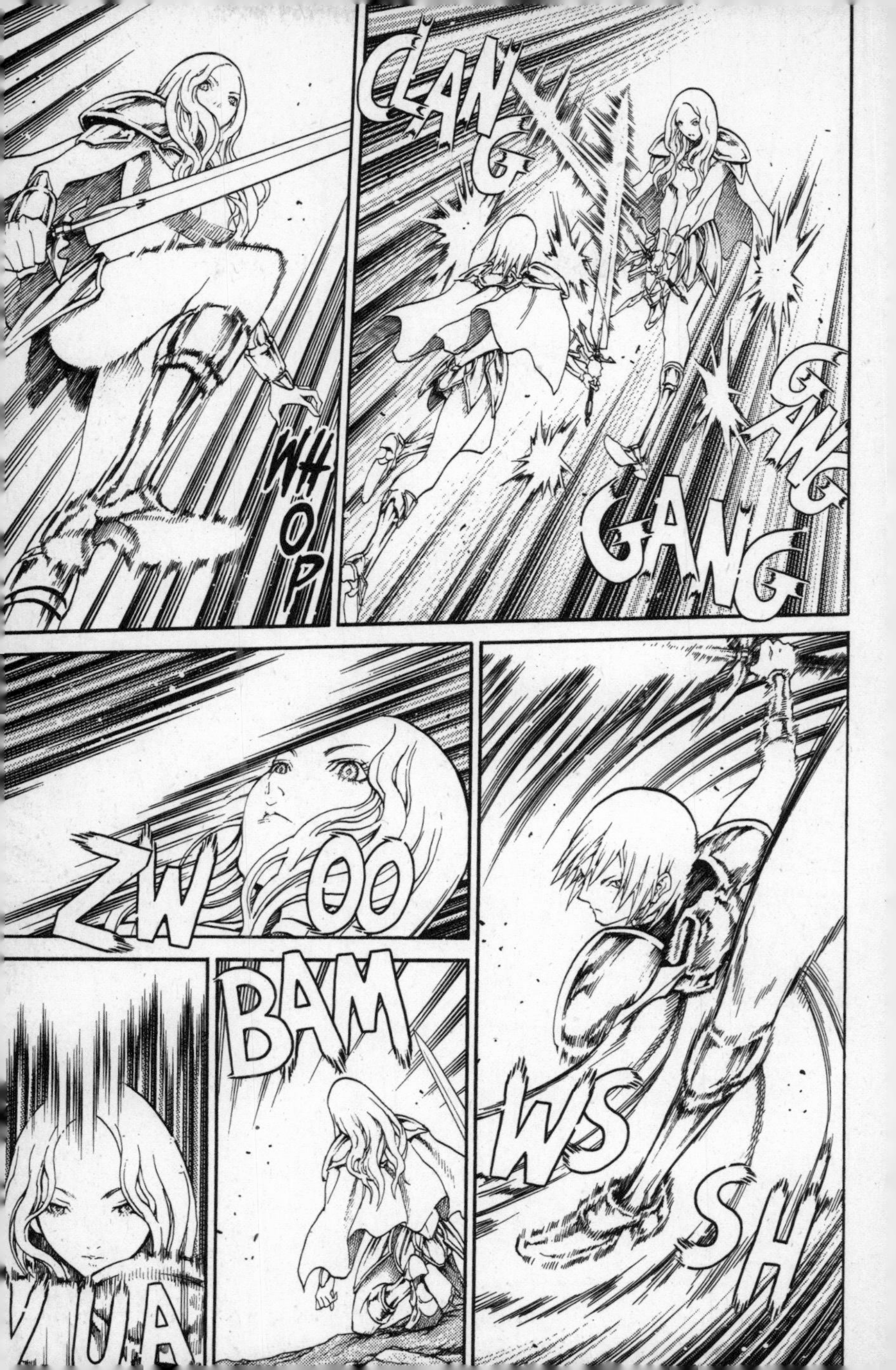
CLANG
GANG
GANG
WHOOP
WSSH
ZWOO
BAM
VUA

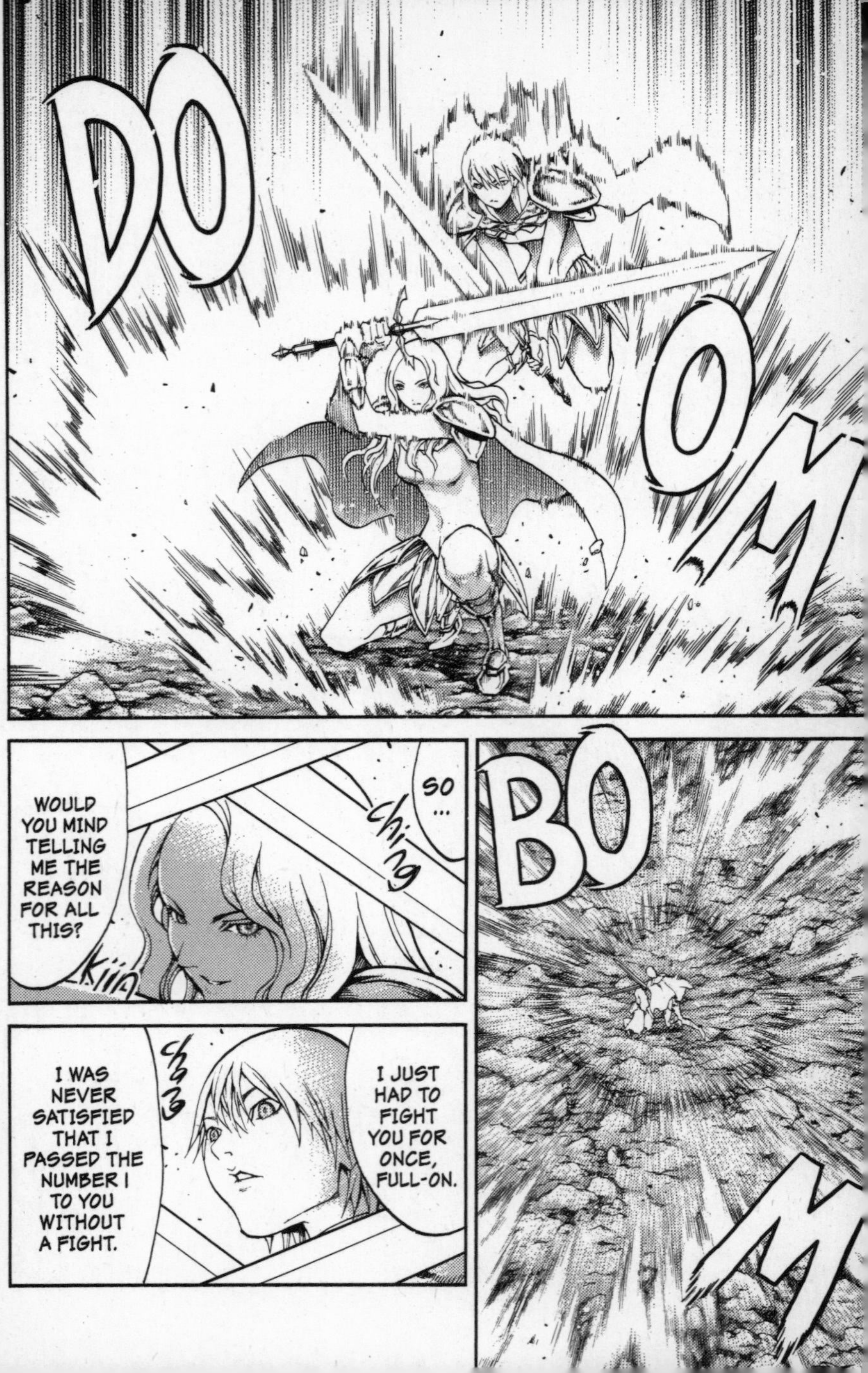

DO
OM
BO
M
SO ...
ching
WOULD YOU MIND TELLING ME THE REASON FOR ALL THIS?
kiin
I JUST HAD TO FIGHT YOU FOR ONCE, FULL-ON.
I WAS NEVER SATISFIED THAT I PASSED THE NUMBER I TO YOU WITHOUT A FIGHT.

READ THIS WAY

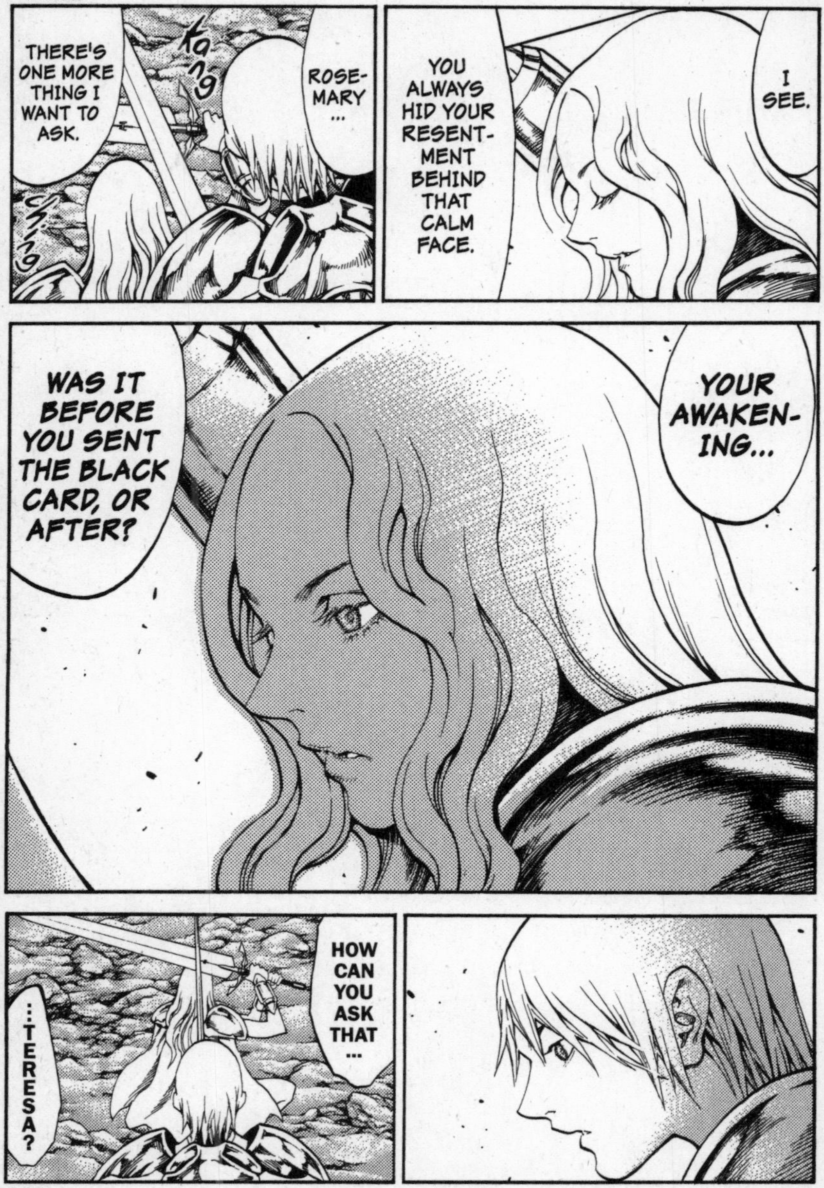
I SEE.
YOU ALWAYS HID YOUR RESENTMENT BEHIND THAT CALM FACE.
ROSEMARY...
kang
THERE'S ONE MORE THING I WANT TO ASK.
ching
YOUR AWAKENING...
WAS IT BEFORE YOU SENT THE BLACK CARD, OR AFTER?
HOW CAN YOU ASK THAT...
...TERESA?

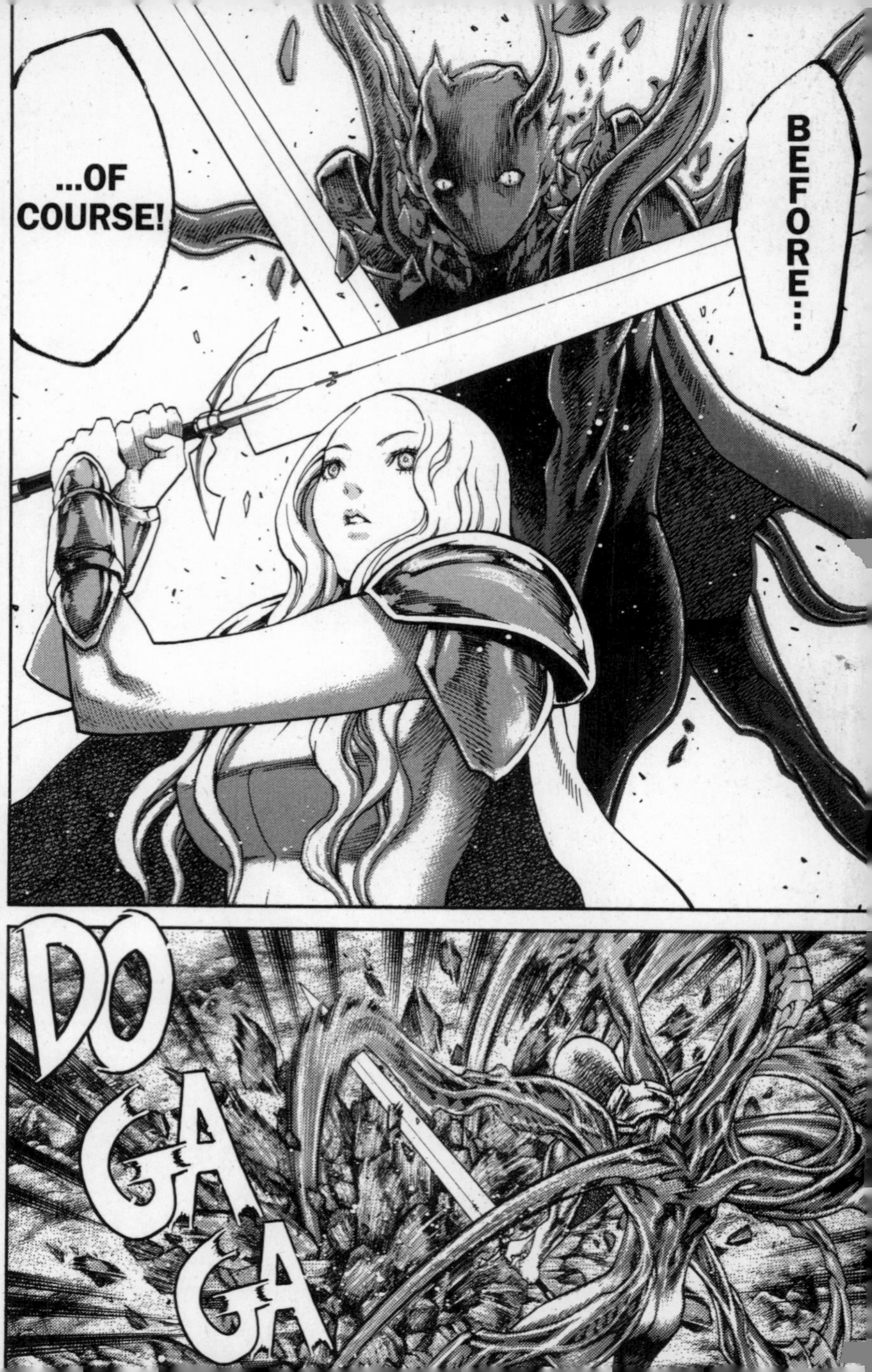
BEFORE...
...OF COURSE!
DO GA GA

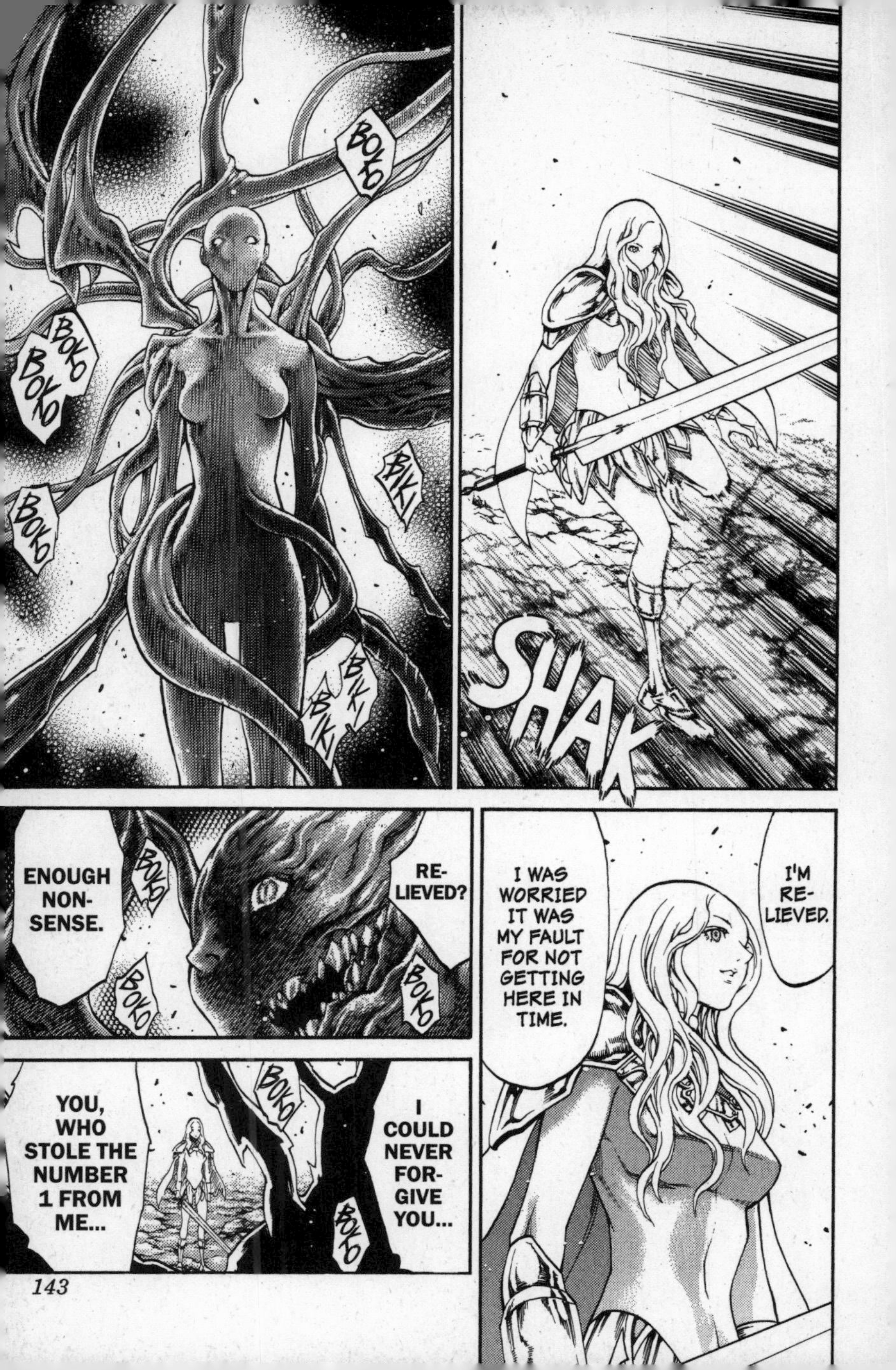
SHAK
BOKO
BOKO BOKO
BIKI
BOKO
BIKI BIKI
I'M RE-LIEVED.
I WAS WORRIED IT WAS MY FAULT FOR NOT GETTING HERE IN TIME.
RE-LIEVED?
BOKO
BOKO
ENOUGH NON-SENSE.
BOKO
BOKO
I COULD NEVER FOR-GIVE YOU...
BOKO
YOU, WHO STOLE THE NUMBER 1 FROM ME...

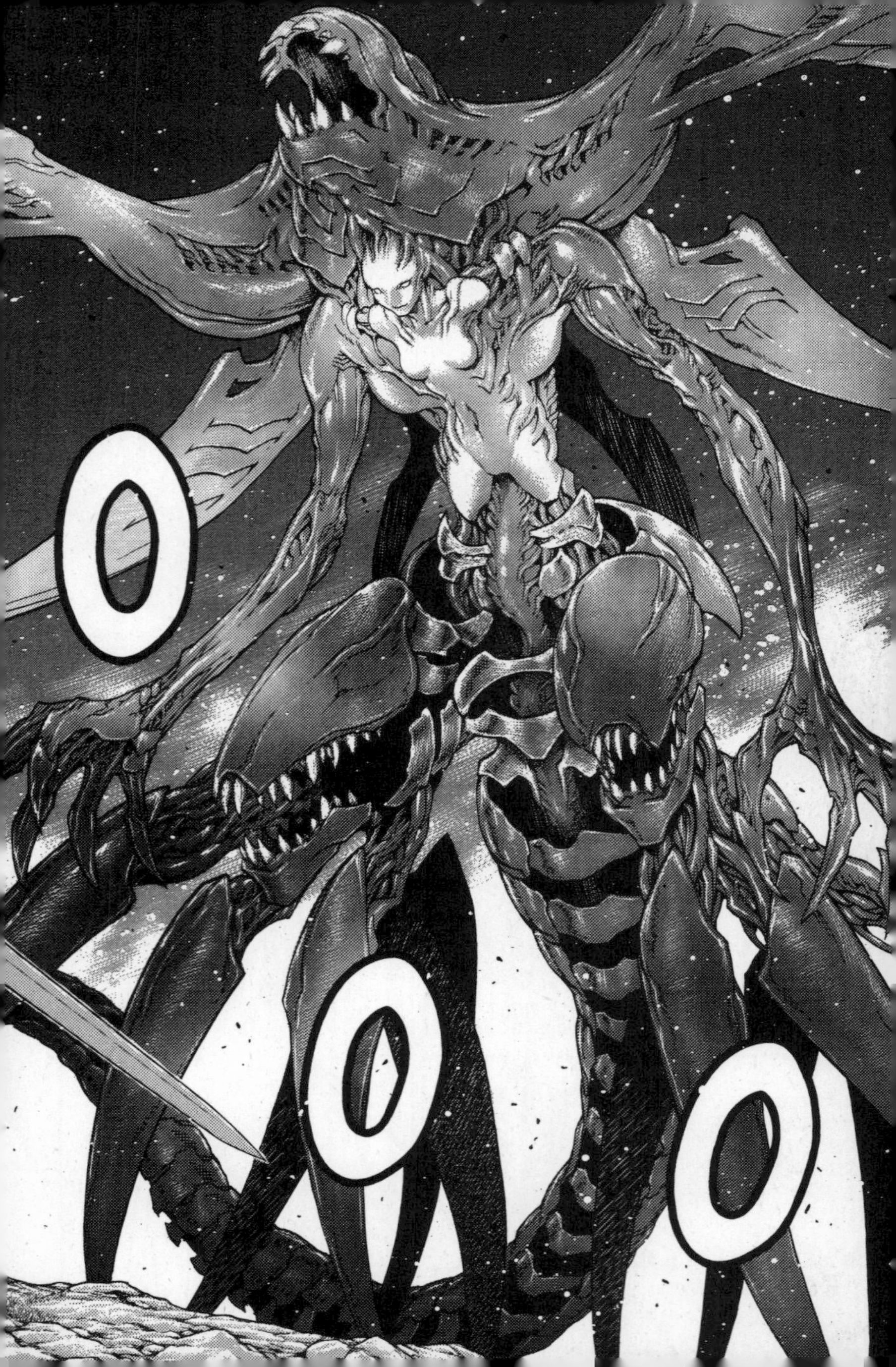
OOO

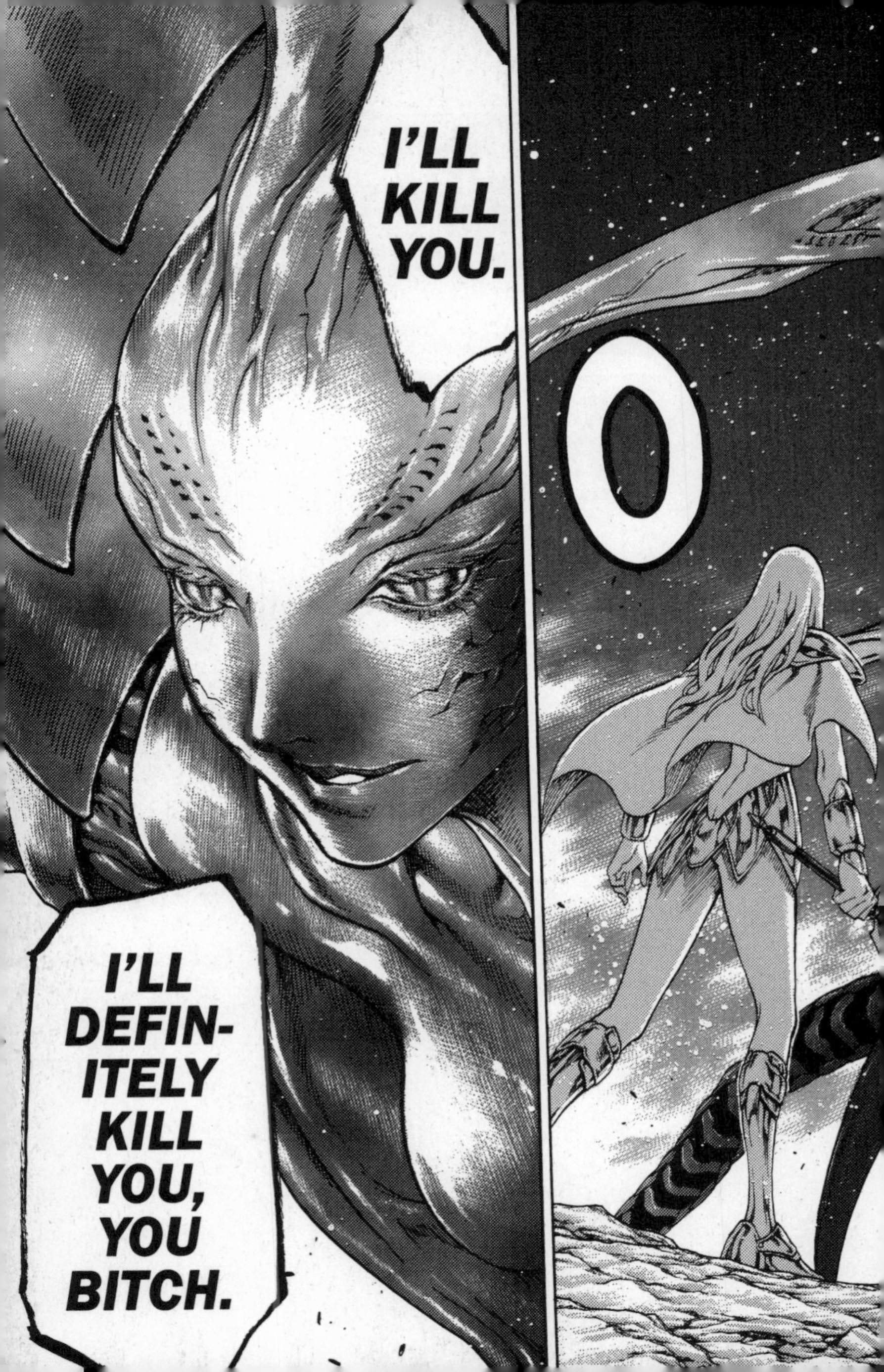
O
I'LL KILL YOU.
I'LL DEFIN-ITELY KILL YOU, YOU BITCH.

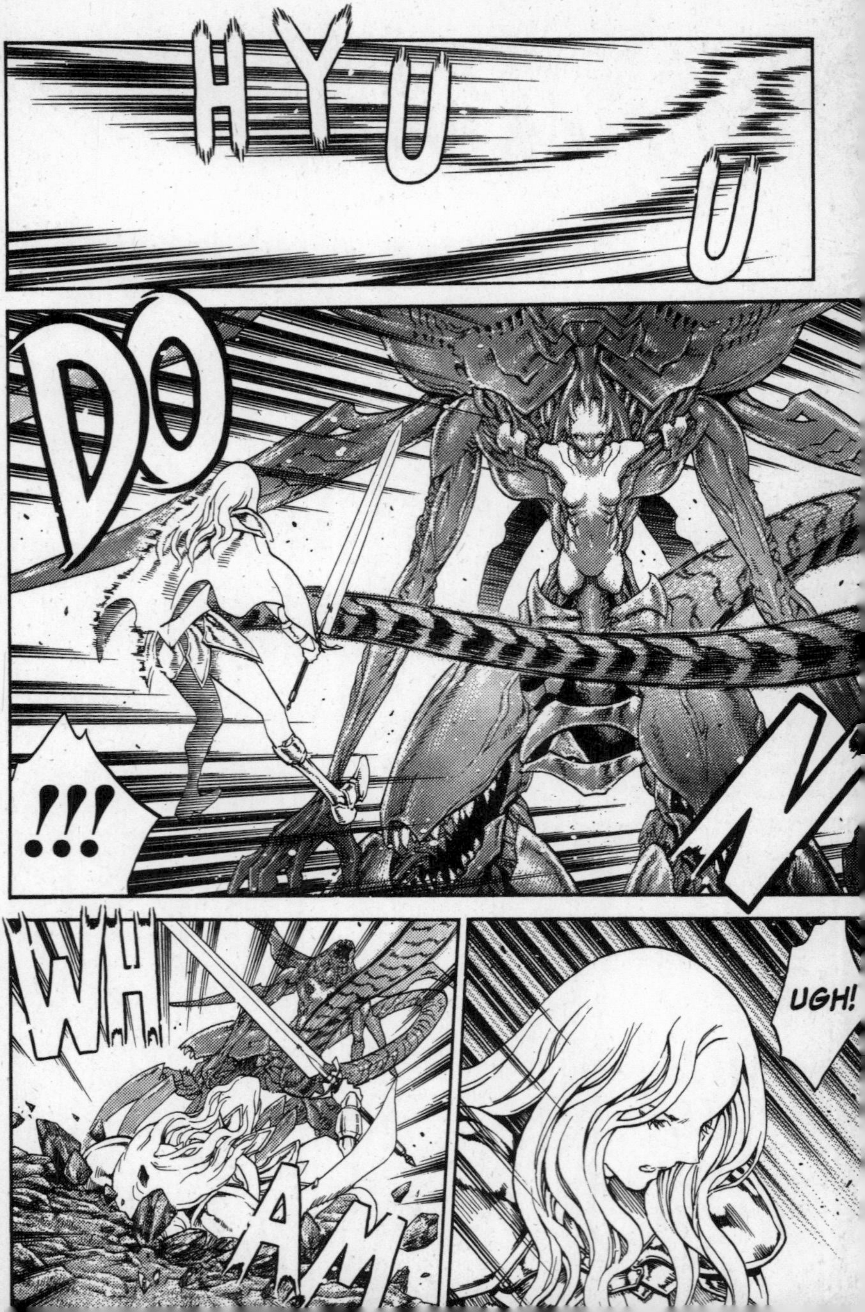
HYU
U
U
DO
N
!!!
UGH!
WH
AM

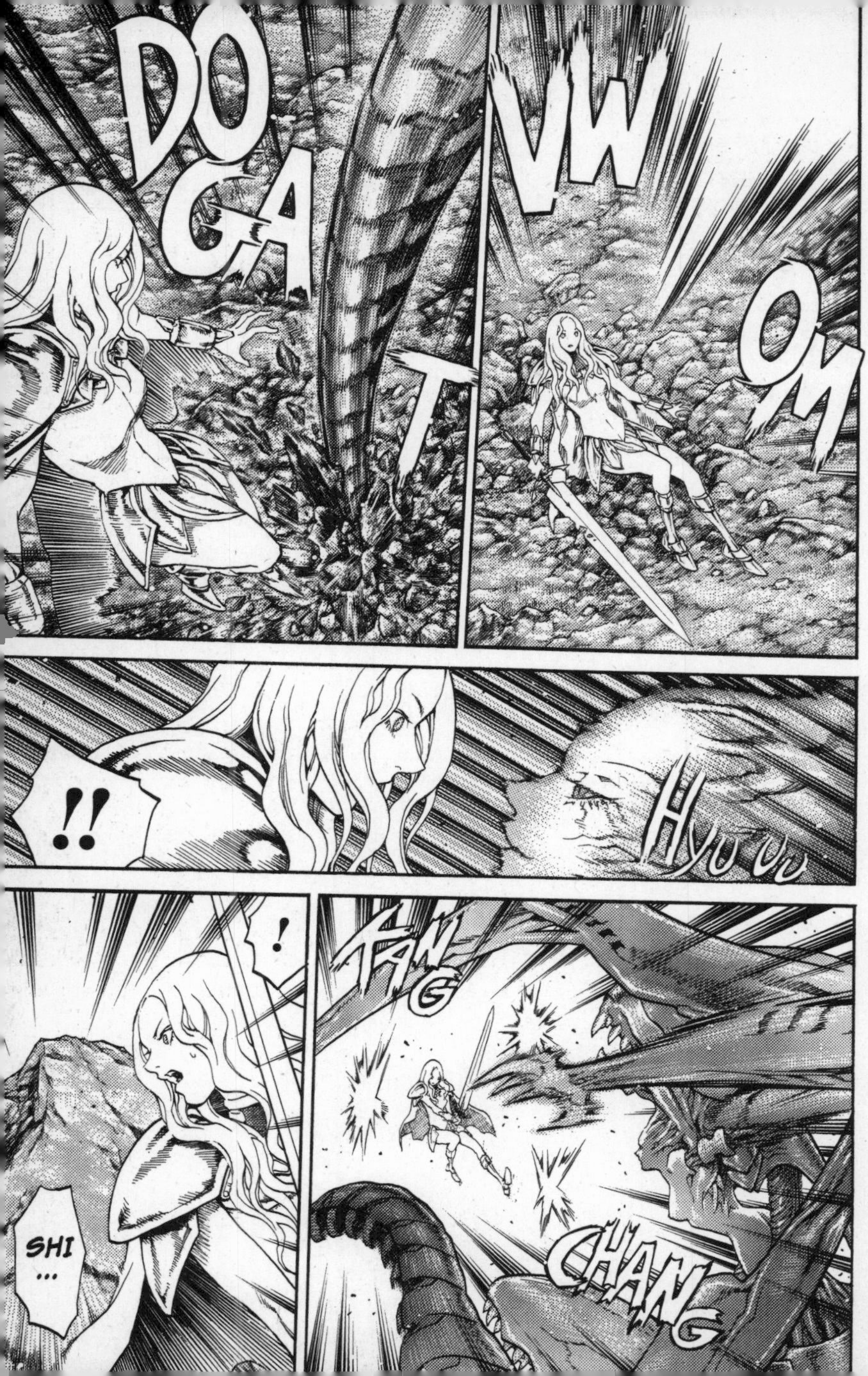
VWOM
DOGAT
Hyuuu
!!
TANG
CHANG
!
SHI ...

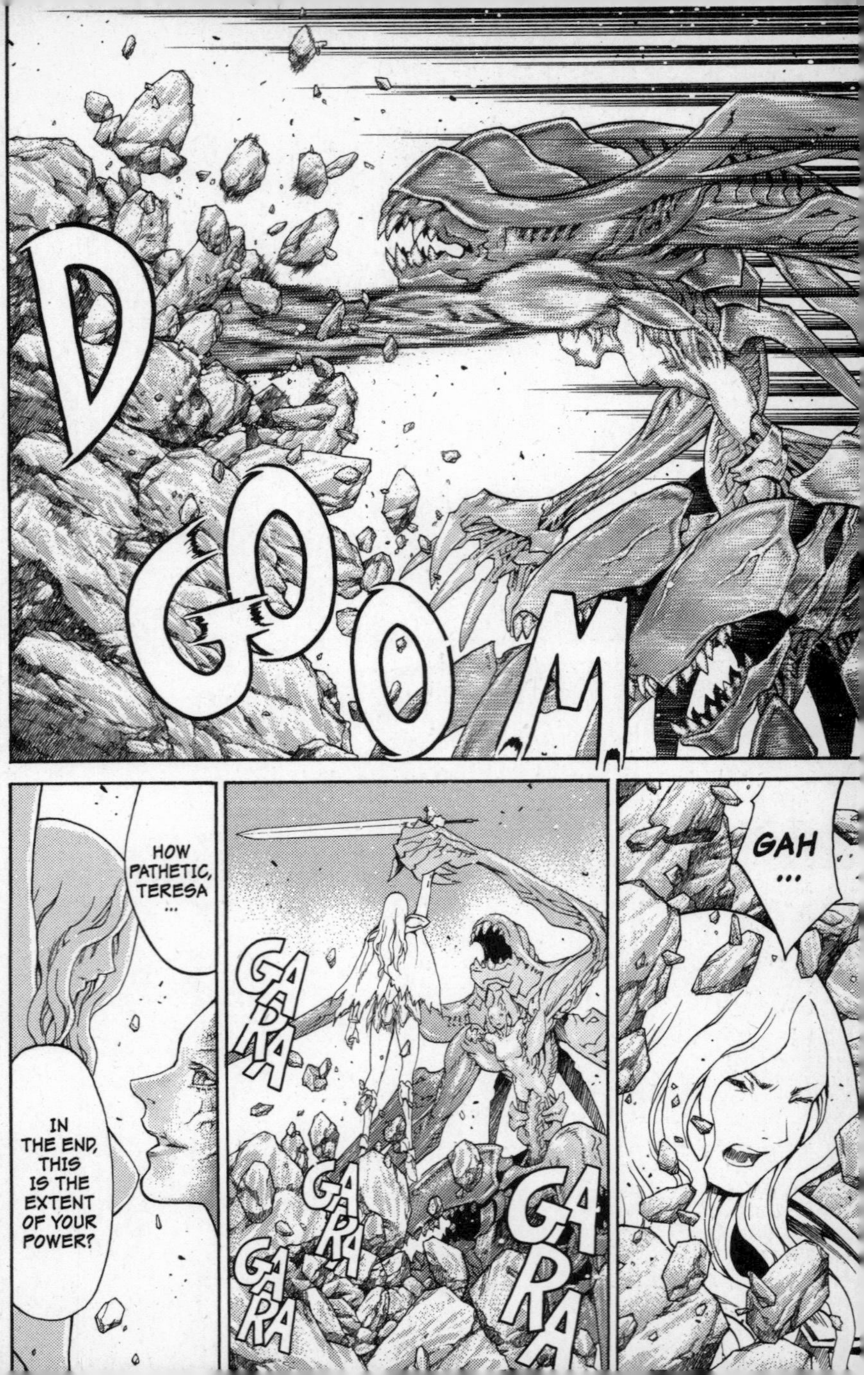
DGOOM
GAH ...
GARA
GARA
GARA
GARA
HOW PATHETIC, TERESA ...
IN THE END, THIS IS THE EXTENT OF YOUR POWER?

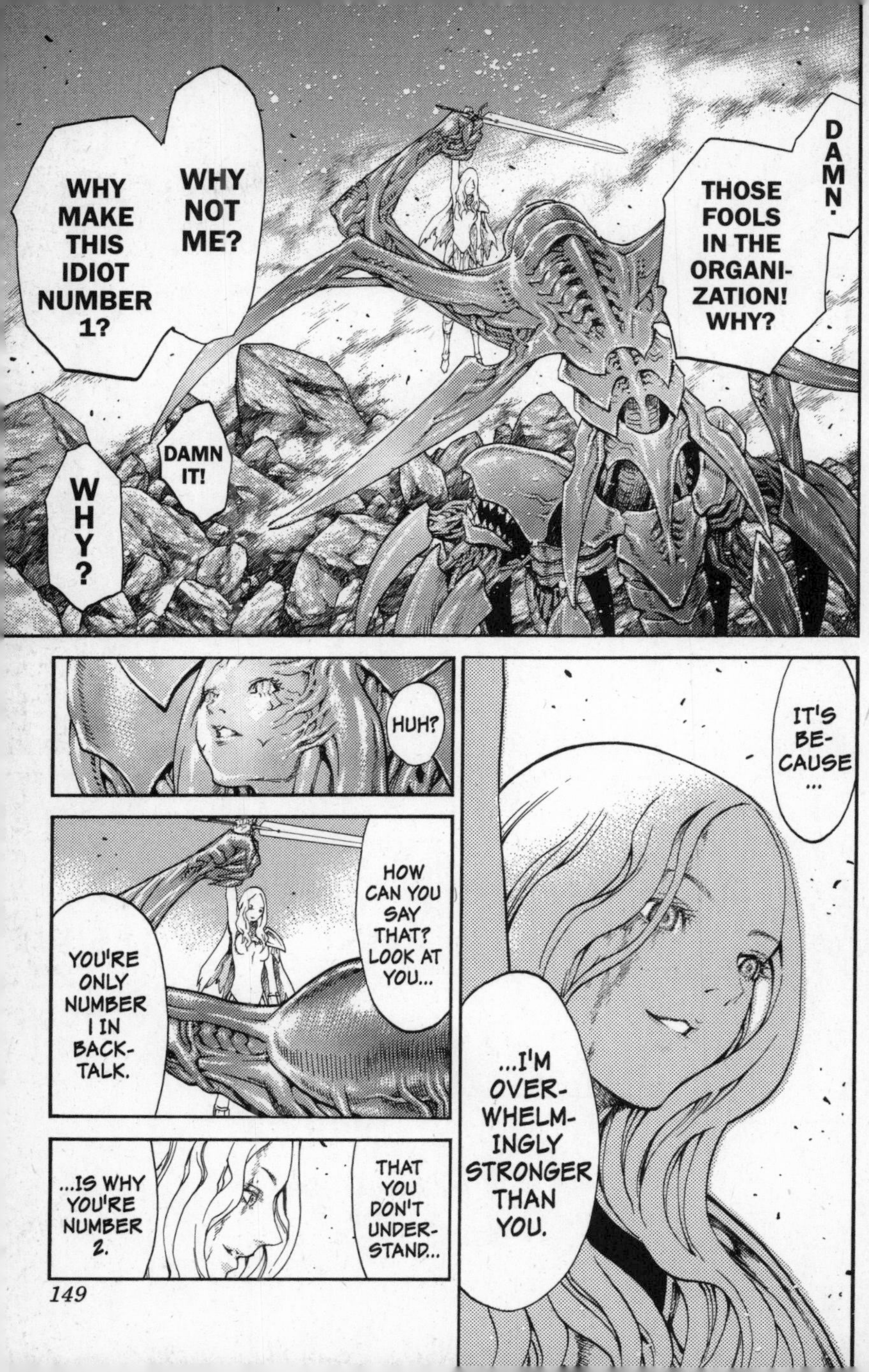
DAMN.
THOSE FOOLS IN THE ORGANIZATION! WHY?
WHY NOT ME?
WHY MAKE THIS IDIOT NUMBER 1?
DAMN IT!
WHY?
IT'S BECAUSE...
...I'M OVERWHELMINGLY STRONGER THAN YOU.
HUH?
HOW CAN YOU SAY THAT? LOOK AT YOU...
YOU'RE ONLY NUMBER I IN BACKTALK.
THAT YOU DON'T UNDERSTAND...
...IS WHY YOU'RE NUMBER 2.

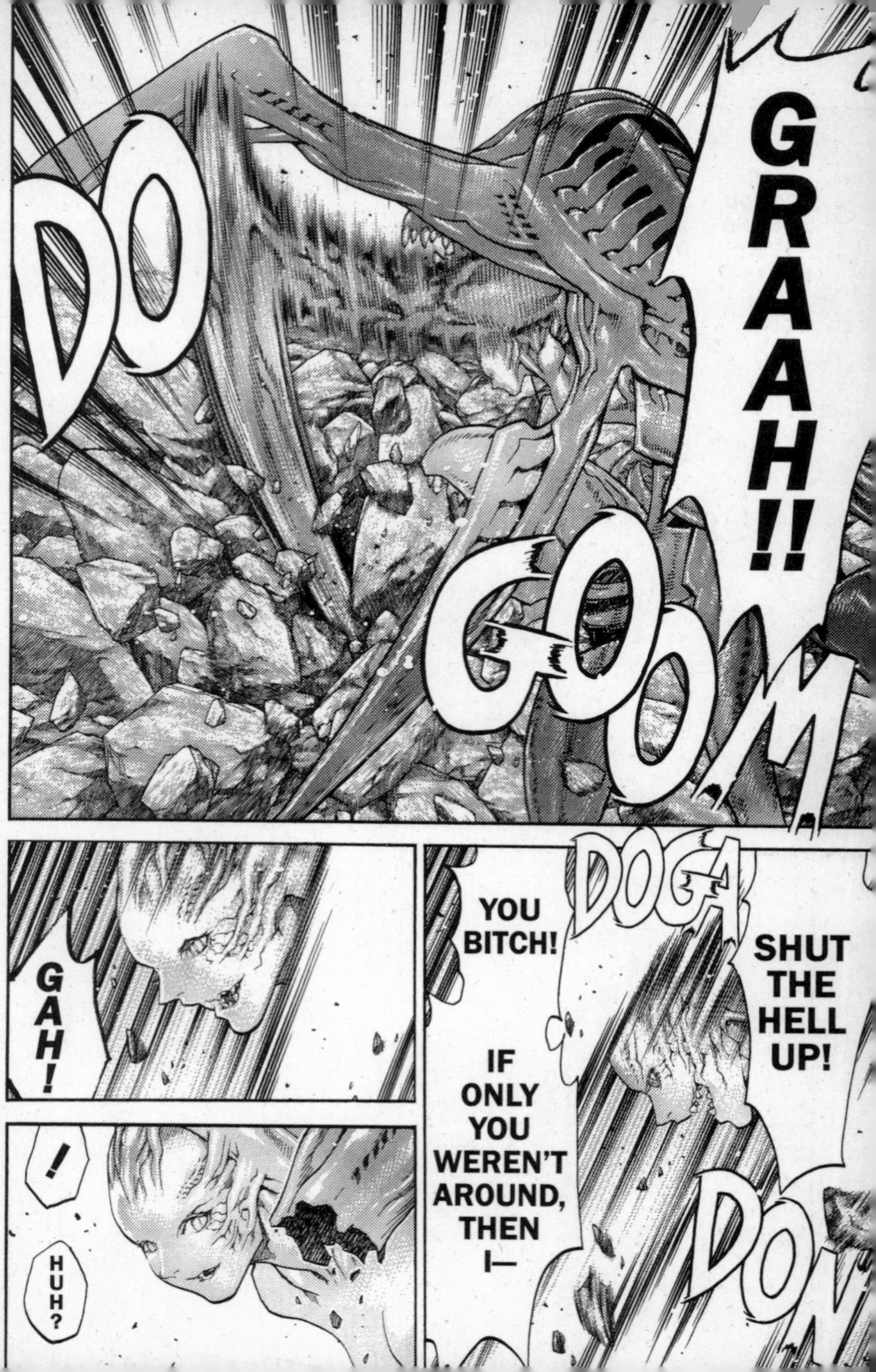
GRAAH!!
GOOM
DO
DOGA
SHUT THE HELL UP!
YOU BITCH!
IF ONLY YOU WEREN'T AROUND, THEN I—
DON
GAH!
!
HUH?

READ THIS WAY

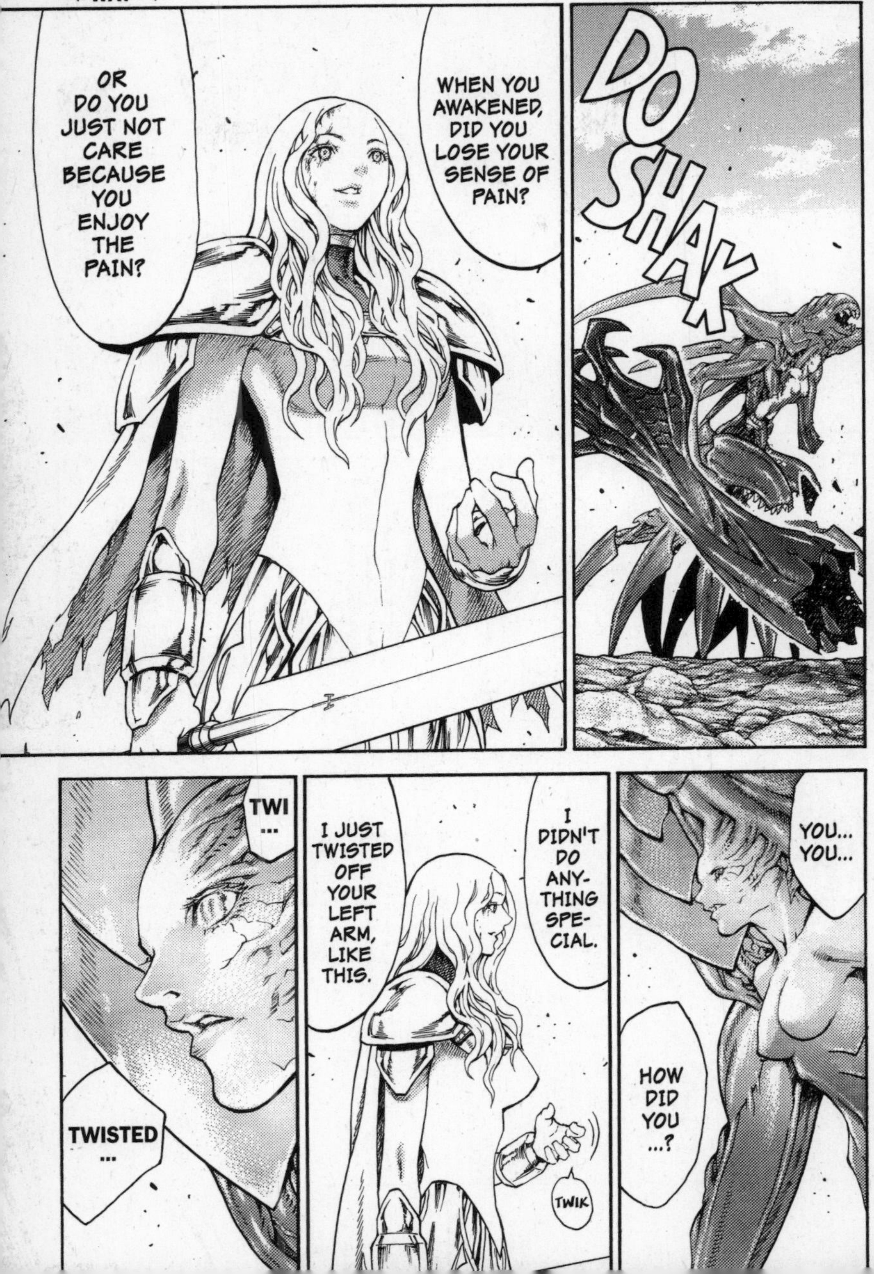
DO SHAK
WHEN YOU AWAKENED, DID YOU LOSE YOUR SENSE OF PAIN?
OR DO YOU JUST NOT CARE BECAUSE YOU ENJOY THE PAIN?
YOU... YOU...
HOW DID YOU ...?
I DIDN'T DO ANY-THING SPE-CIAL.
I JUST TWISTED OFF YOUR LEFT ARM, LIKE THIS.
TWIK
TWI ...
TWISTED ...

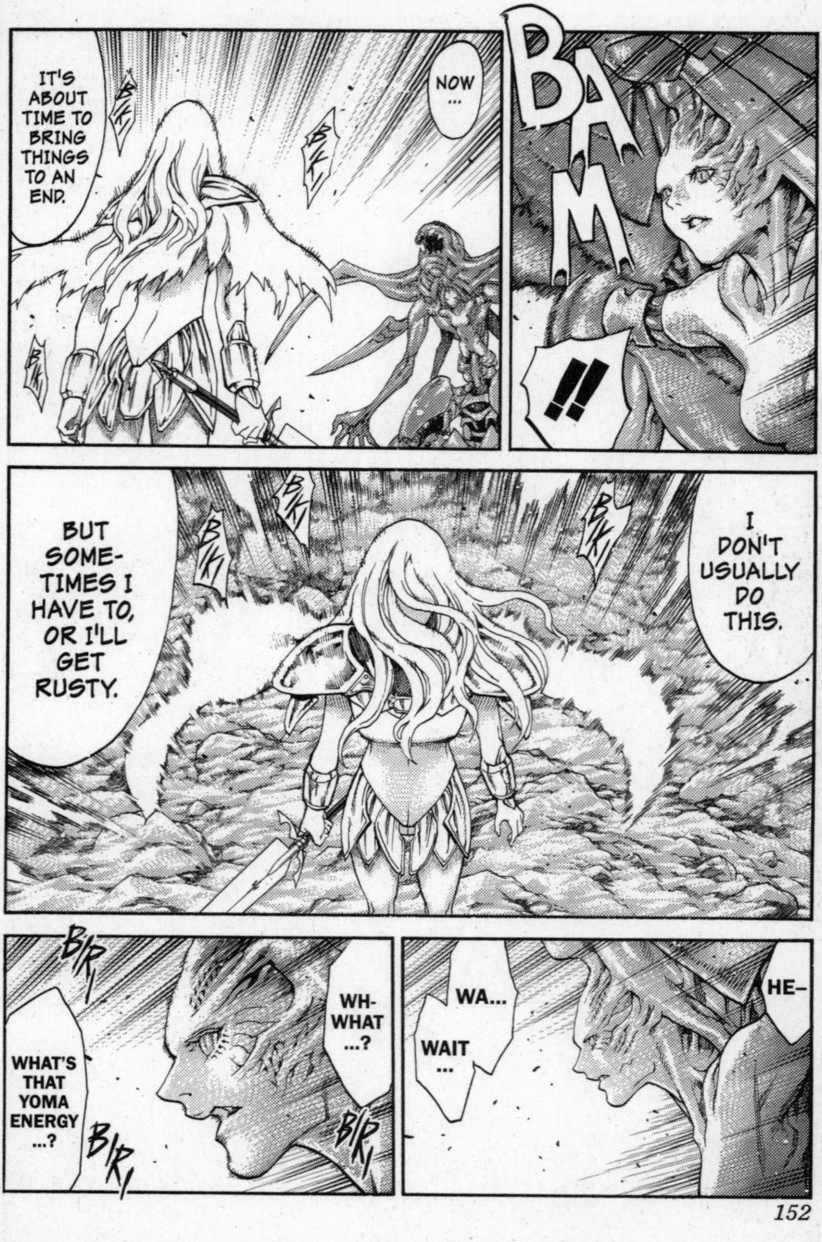
BAM
!!
BIKI
BIKI
NOW ...
BIKI
IT'S ABOUT TIME TO BRING THINGS TO AN END.
BIKI
I DON'T USUALLY DO THIS.
BIKI
BIKI
BUT SOMETIMES I HAVE TO, OR I'LL GET RUSTY.
HE–
WA... WAIT ...
WH- WHAT ...?
BIRI
BIRI
WHAT'S THAT YOMA ENERGY ...?
BIRI

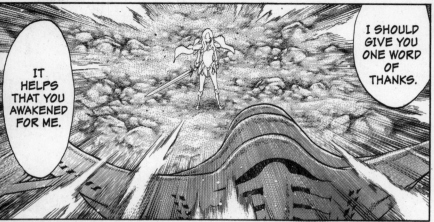

I SHOULD GIVE YOU ONE WORD OF THANKS.

IT HELPS THAT YOU AWAKENED FOR ME.

INSTEAD OF A COMRADE, I MUCH PREFER KILLING ...

...AN AWAK-ENED ONE.

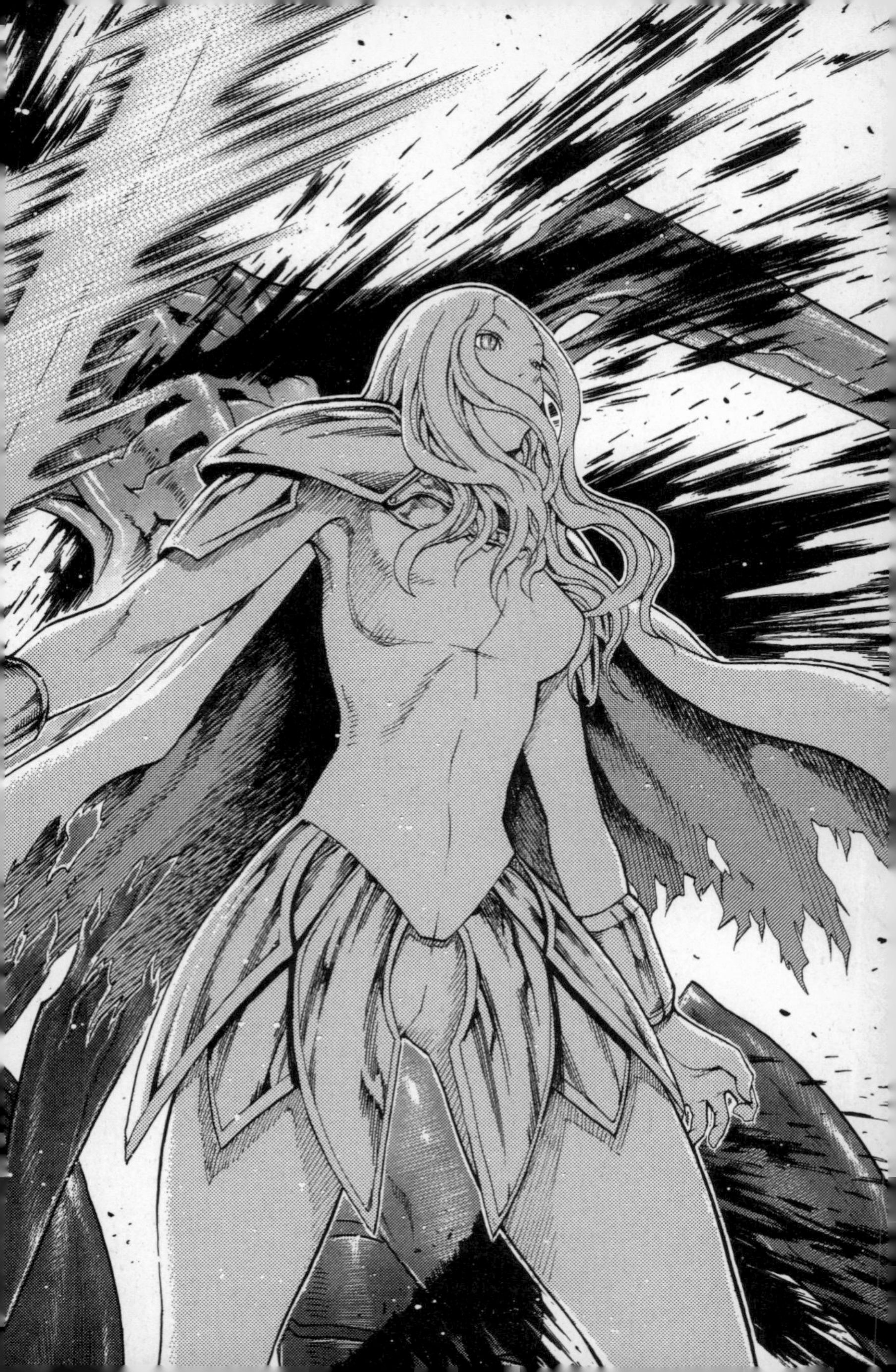

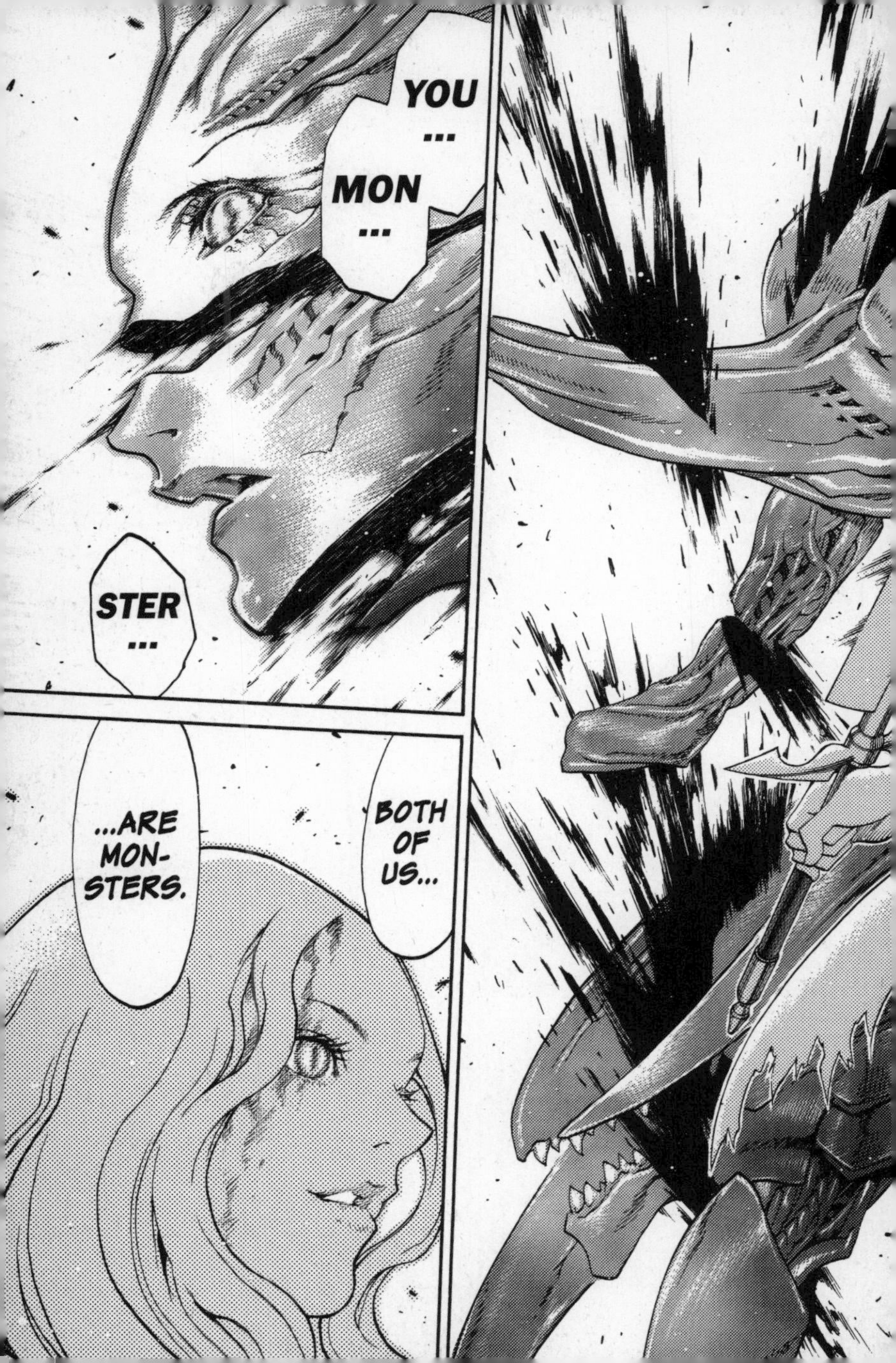
YOU ... MON ...
STER ...
BOTH OF US...
...ARE MON-STERS.

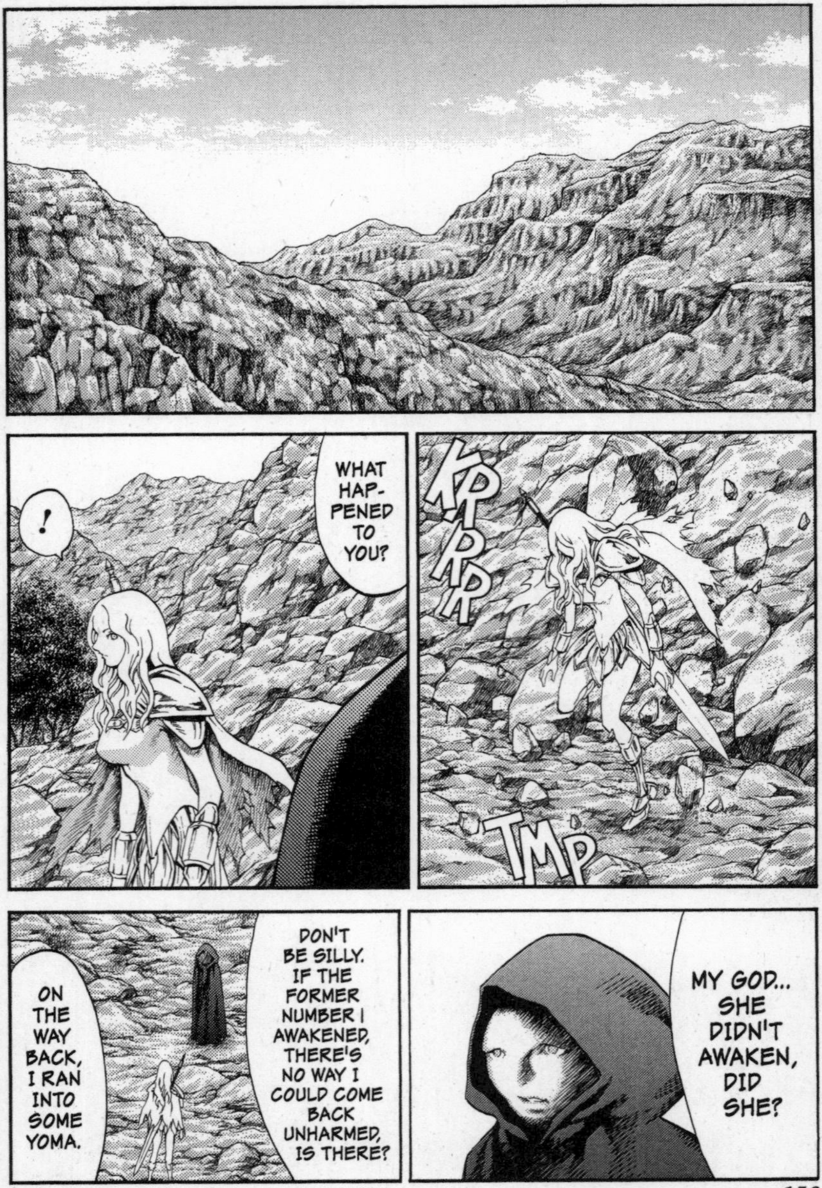
KRRR
TMP
WHAT HAP-PENED TO YOU?
!
MY GOD... SHE DIDN'T AWAKEN, DID SHE?
DON'T BE SILLY. IF THE FORMER NUMBER I AWAKENED, THERE'S NO WAY I COULD COME BACK UNHARMED, IS THERE?
ON THE WAY BACK, I RAN INTO SOME YOMA.

READ THIS WAY

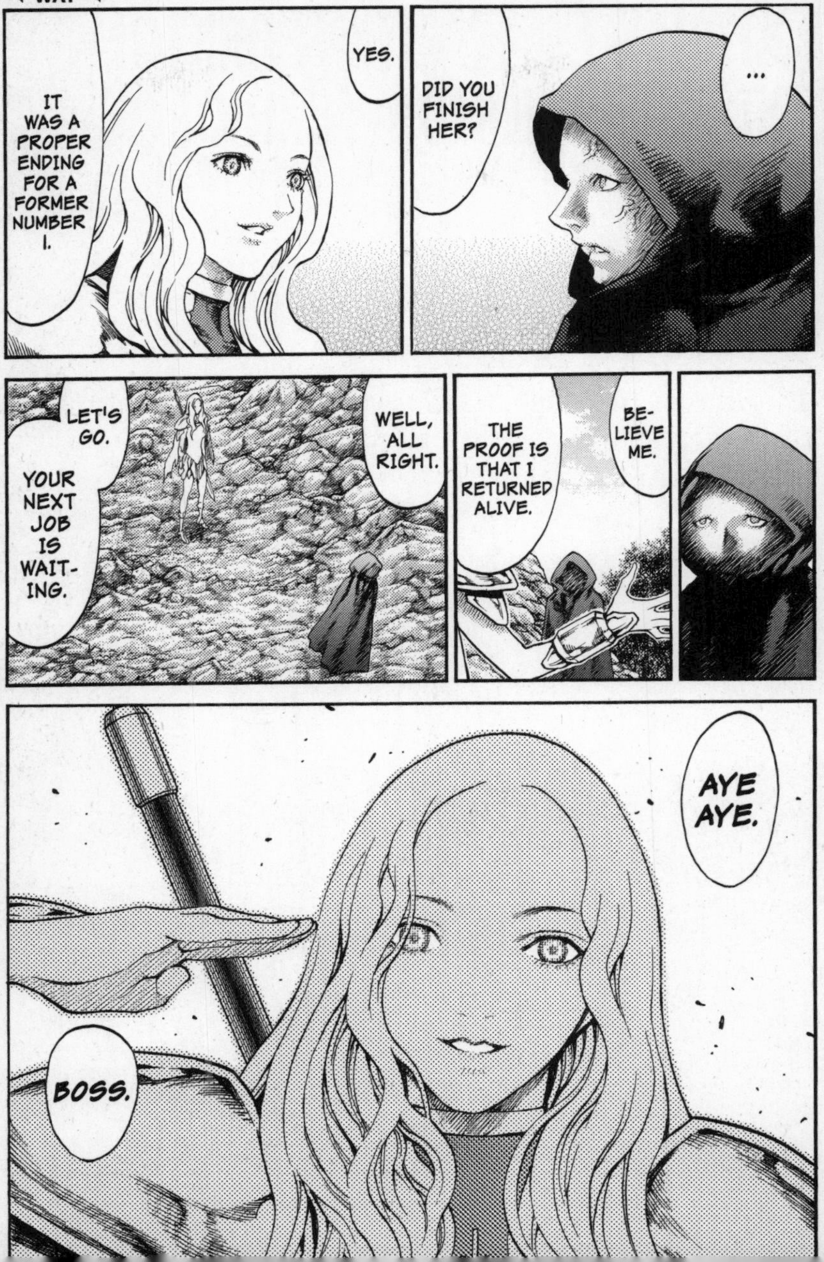
...
DID YOU FINISH HER?
YES.
IT WAS A PROPER ENDING FOR A FORMER NUMBER 1.
BE-LIEVE ME.
THE PROOF IS THAT I RETURNED ALIVE.
WELL, ALL RIGHT.
LET'S GO.
YOUR NEXT JOB IS WAITING.
AYE AYE.
BOSS.

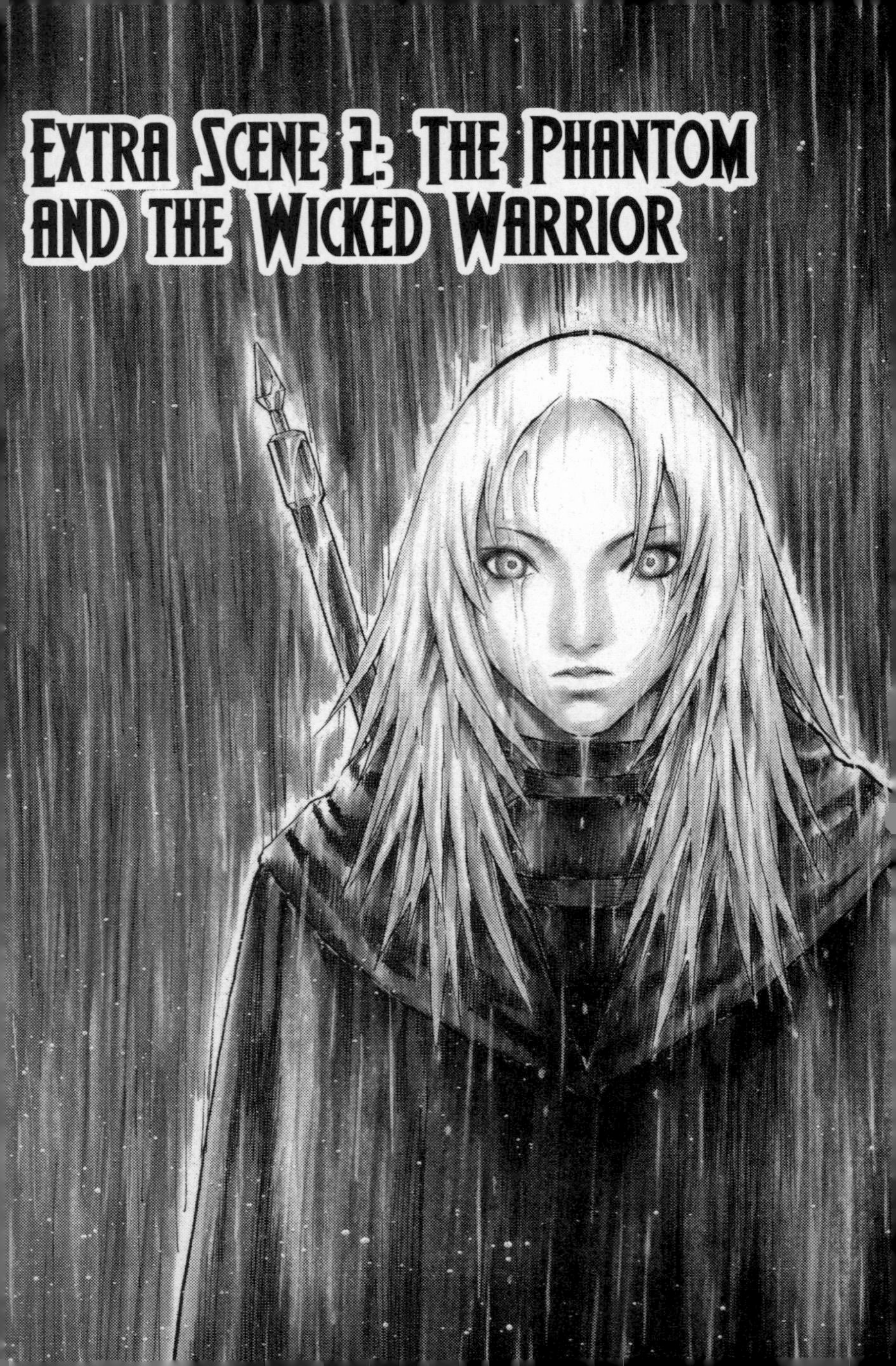
EXTRA SCENE 2: THE PHANTOM AND THE WICKED WARRIOR

READ THIS WAY

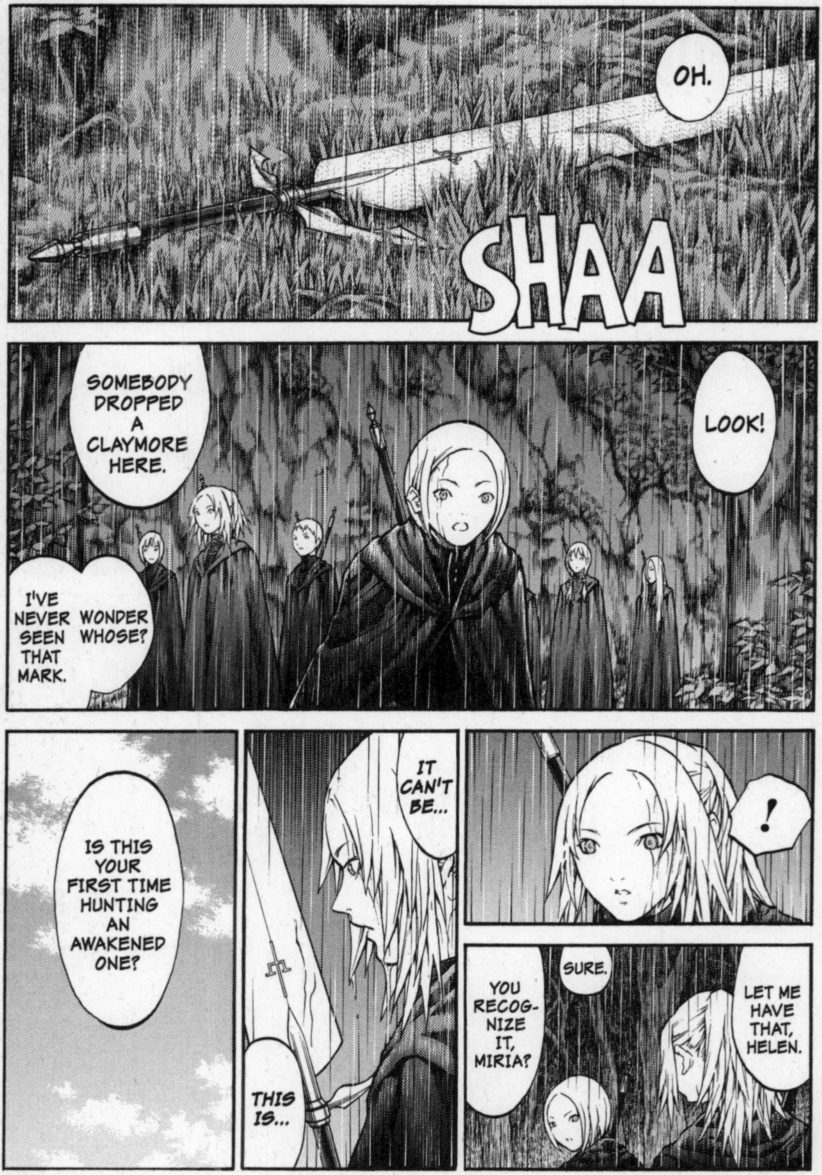

OH.
SHAA
LOOK!
SOMEBODY DROPPED A CLAYMORE HERE.
WONDER WHOSE?
I'VE NEVER SEEN THAT MARK.
!
LET ME HAVE THAT, HELEN.
SURE.
YOU RECOGNIZE IT, MIRIA?
IT CAN'T BE...
THIS IS...
IS THIS YOUR FIRST TIME HUNTING AN AWAKENED ONE?

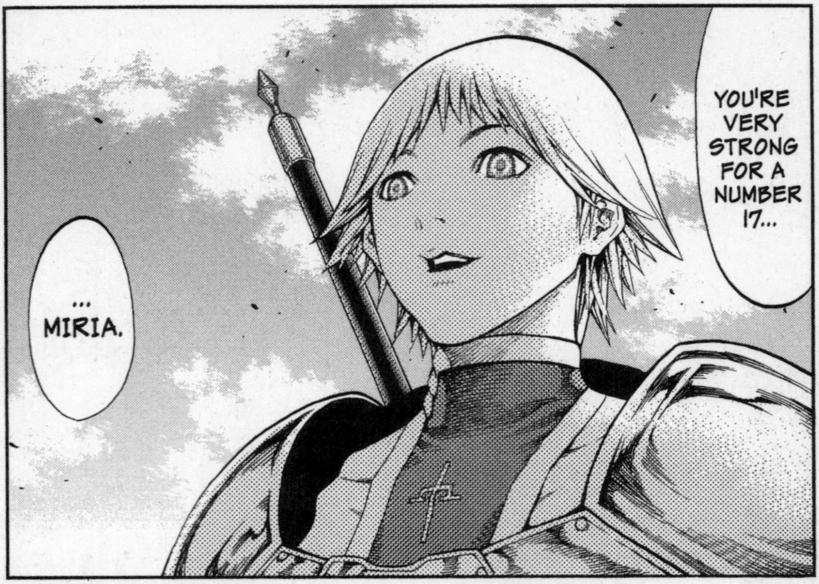
YOU'RE VERY STRONG FOR A NUMBER 17...
... MIRIA.
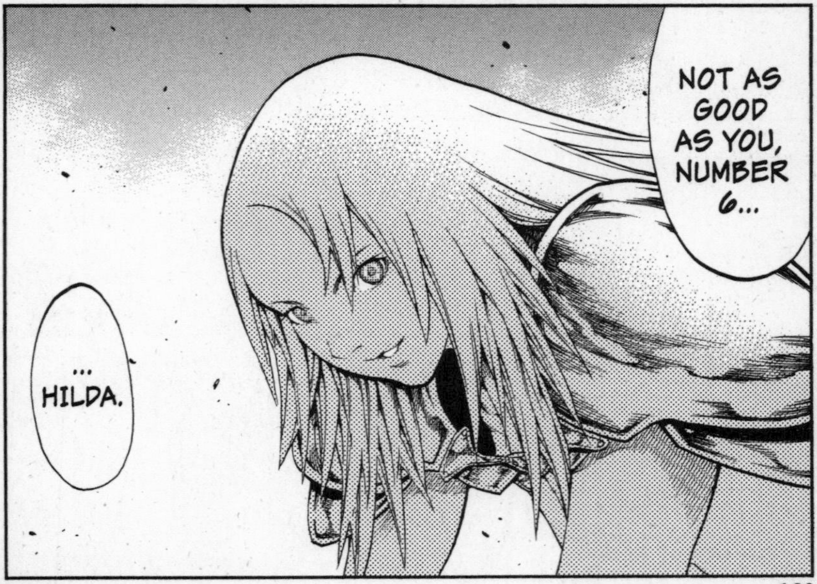
NOT AS GOOD AS YOU, NUMBER 6...
... HILDA.

READ THIS WAY

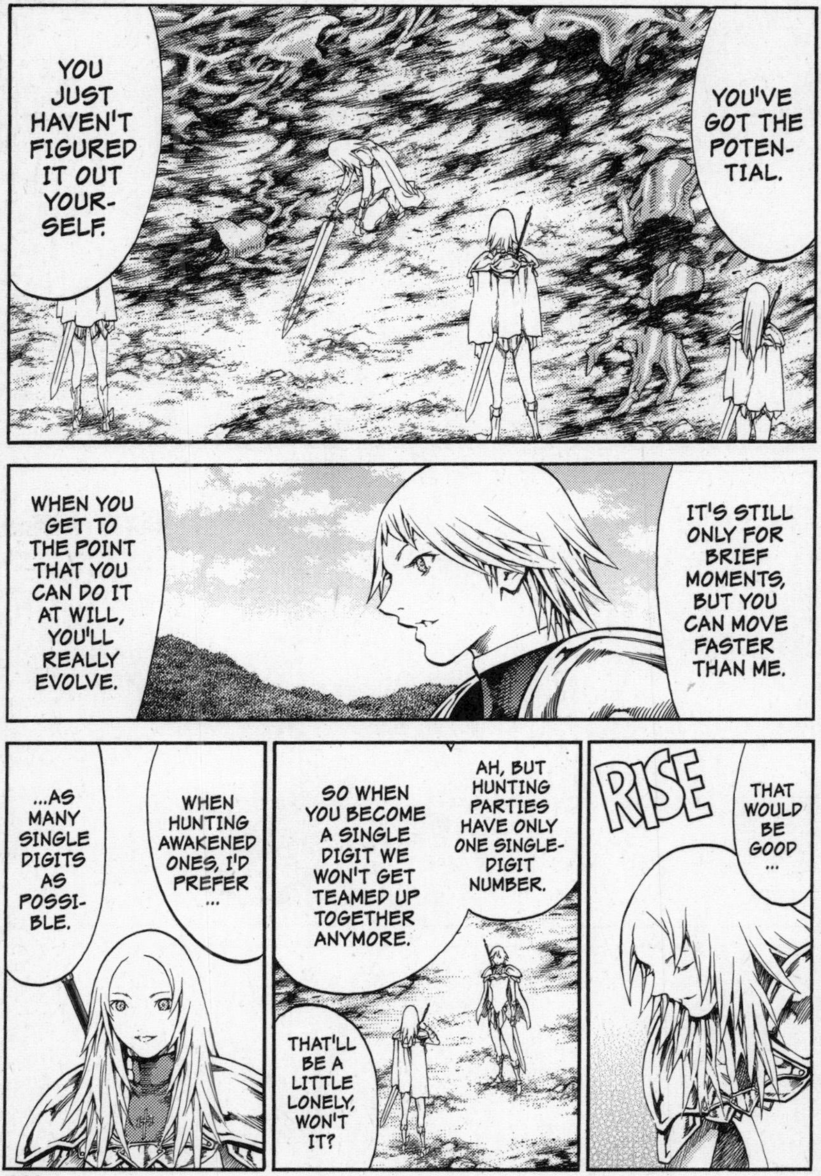

YOU'VE GOT THE POTENTIAL.
YOU JUST HAVEN'T FIGURED IT OUT YOURSELF.
IT'S STILL ONLY FOR BRIEF MOMENTS, BUT YOU CAN MOVE FASTER THAN ME.
WHEN YOU GET TO THE POINT THAT YOU CAN DO IT AT WILL, YOU'LL REALLY EVOLVE.
RISE
THAT WOULD BE GOOD ...
AH, BUT HUNTING PARTIES HAVE ONLY ONE SINGLE-DIGIT NUMBER.
SO WHEN YOU BECOME A SINGLE DIGIT WE WON'T GET TEAMED UP TOGETHER ANYMORE.
THAT'LL BE A LITTLE LONELY, WON'T IT?
WHEN HUNTING AWAKENED ONES, I'D PREFER ...
...AS MANY SINGLE DIGITS AS POSSIBLE.

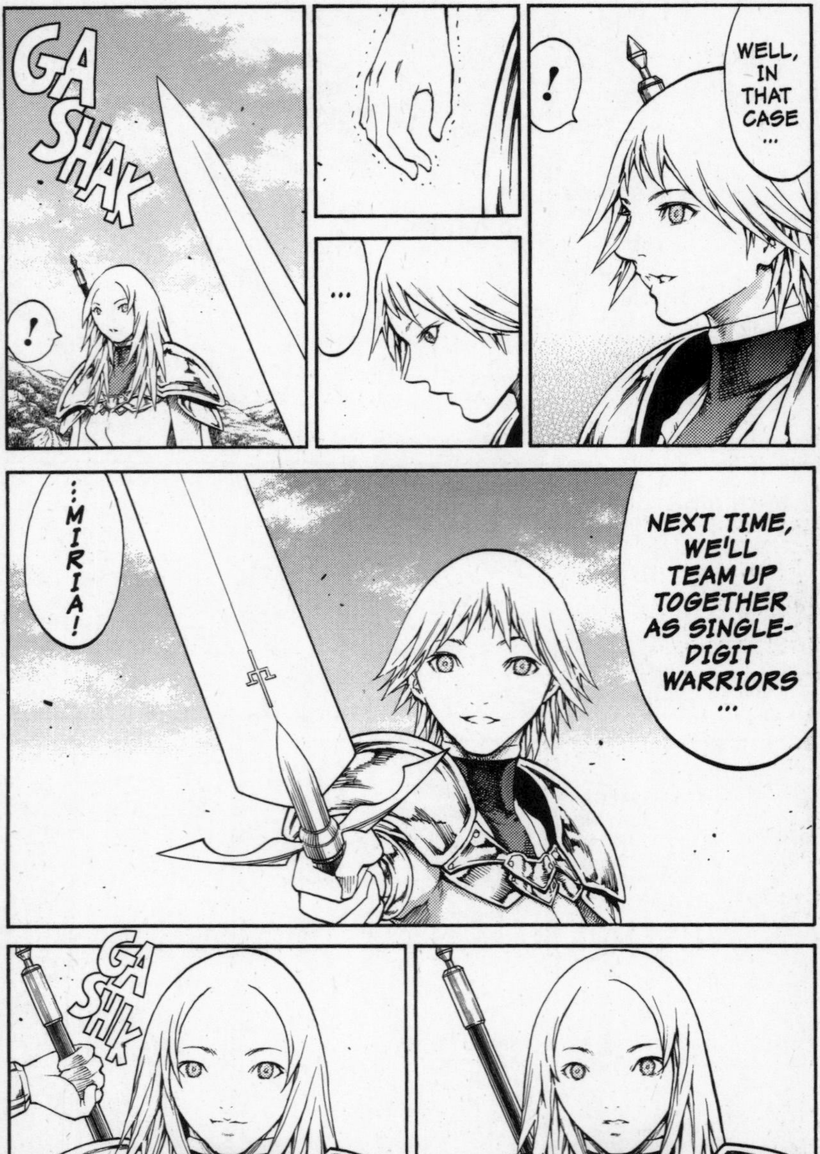
WELL, IN THAT CASE ...
!
...
GA SHAK
!
NEXT TIME, WE'LL TEAM UP TOGETHER AS SINGLE-DIGIT WARRIORS ...
...MIRIA!
GA SHIK

READ THIS WAY

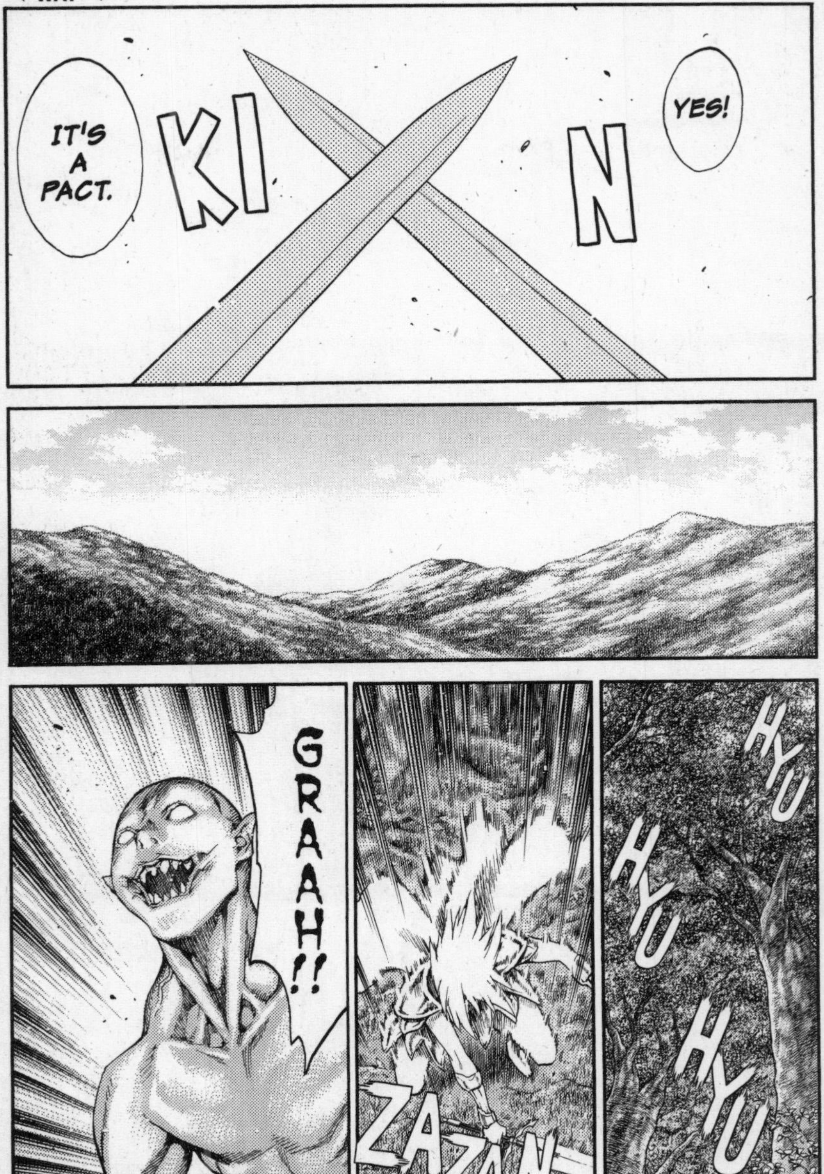
YES!
KI N
IT'S A PACT.
HYU HYU HYU HYU HYU
ZAZAN
GRAAAH!!

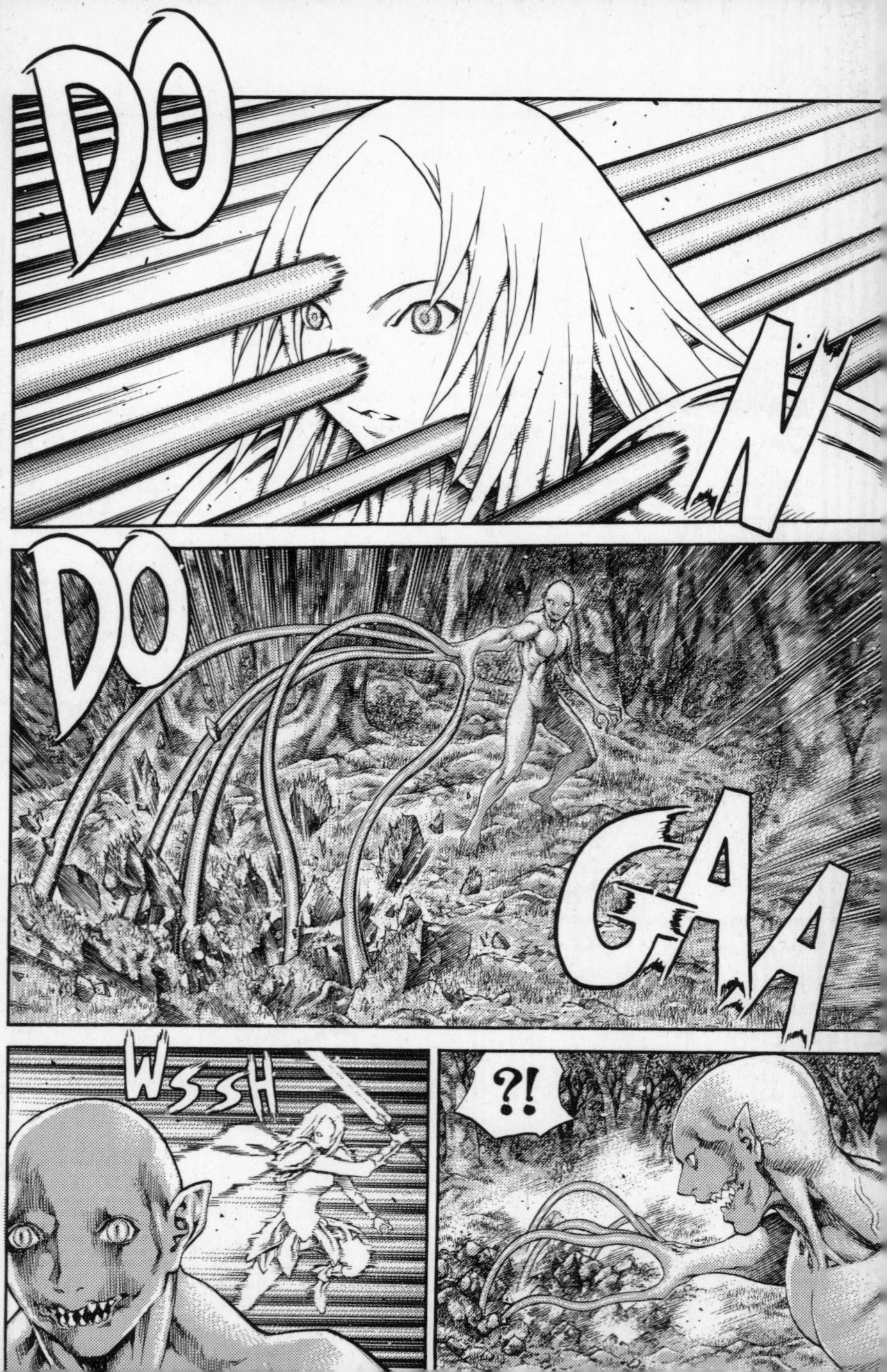
DO
N
DO
GAA
?!
WSSH

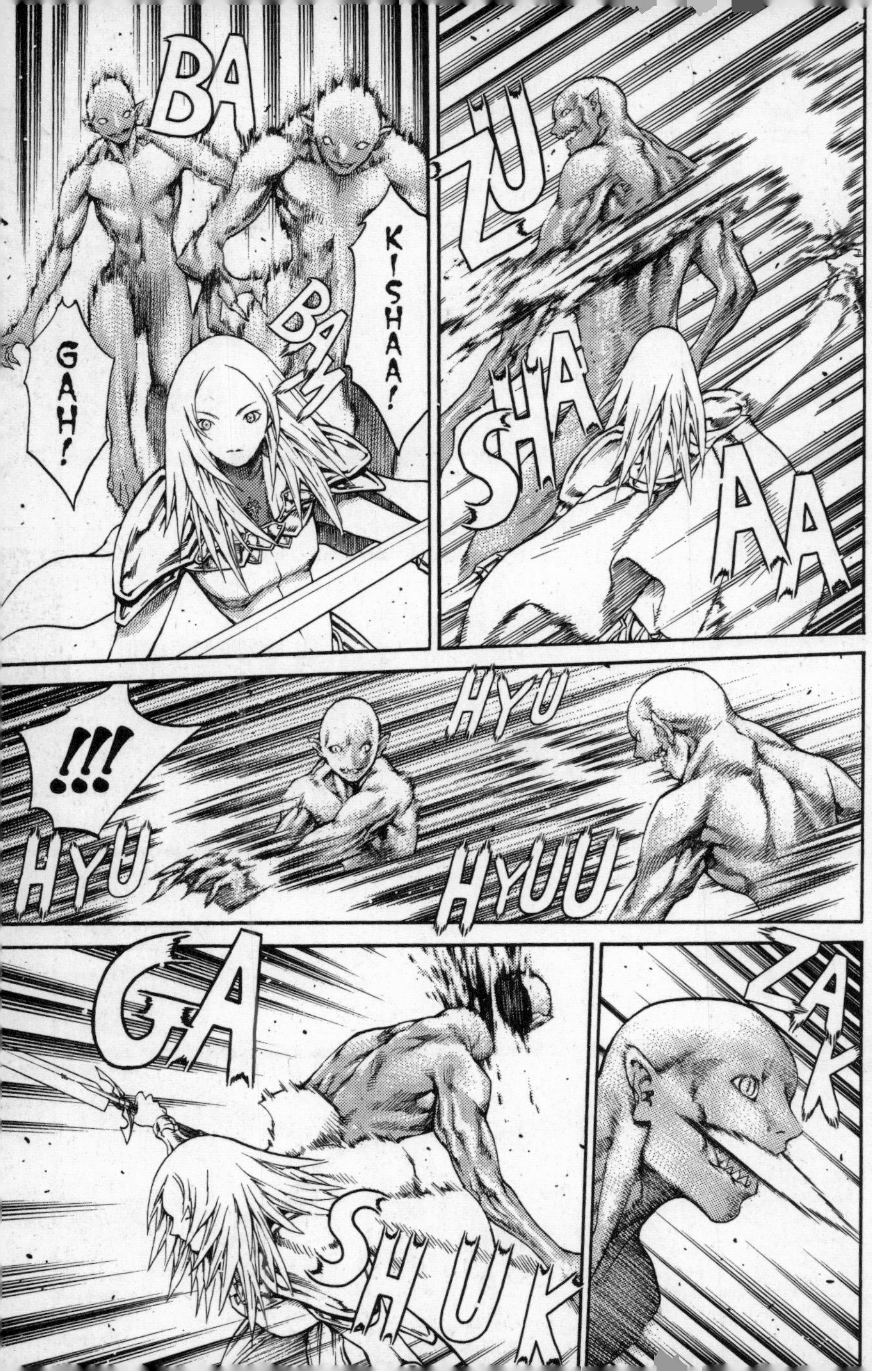

ZU
SHA
AA
BA
BAM
KISHAA!
GAH!
HYU
!!!
HYUU
HYU
ZAK
GA
SHUK

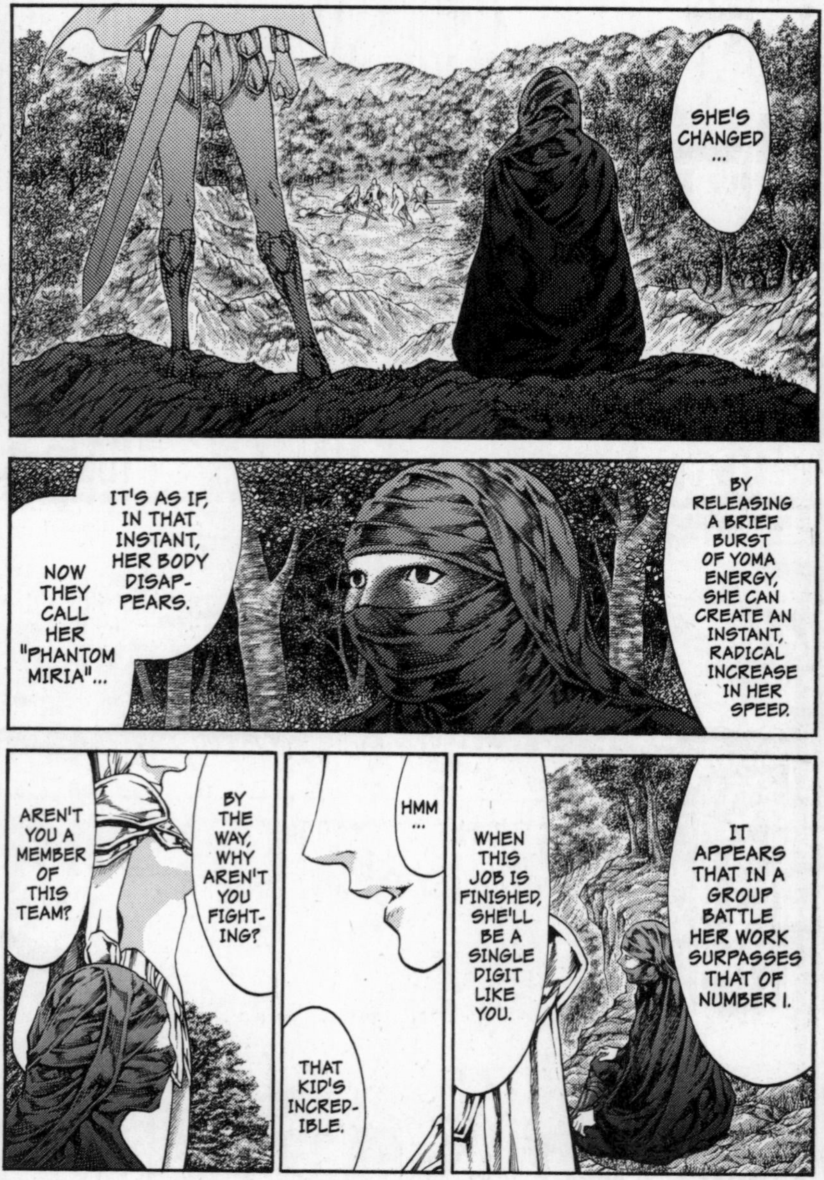
SHE'S CHANGED ...
BY RELEASING A BRIEF BURST OF YOMA ENERGY, SHE CAN CREATE AN INSTANT, RADICAL INCREASE IN HER SPEED.
IT'S AS IF, IN THAT INSTANT, HER BODY DISAPPEARS.
NOW THEY CALL HER "PHANTOM MIRIA"...
IT APPEARS THAT IN A GROUP BATTLE HER WORK SURPASSES THAT OF NUMBER 1.
WHEN THIS JOB IS FINISHED, SHE'LL BE A SINGLE DIGIT LIKE YOU.
HMM ...
THAT KID'S INCREDIBLE.
BY THE WAY, WHY AREN'T YOU FIGHTING?
AREN'T YOU A MEMBER OF THIS TEAM?

READ THIS WAY

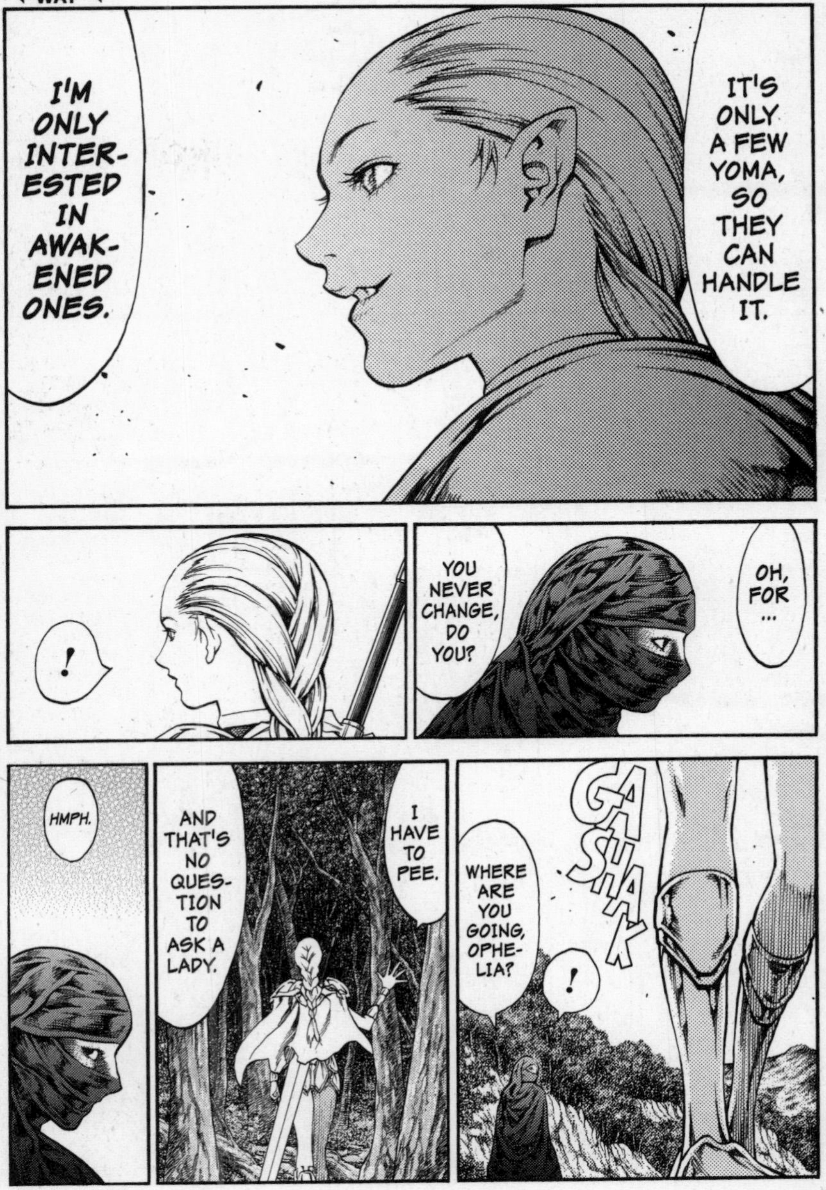

IT'S ONLY A FEW YOMA, SO THEY CAN HANDLE IT.
I'M ONLY INTER-ESTED IN AWAK-ENED ONES.
OH, FOR ...
YOU NEVER CHANGE, DO YOU?
!
GASHAK
WHERE ARE YOU GOING, OPHE-LIA?
!
I HAVE TO PEE.
AND THAT'S NO QUES-TION TO ASK A LADY.
HMPH.

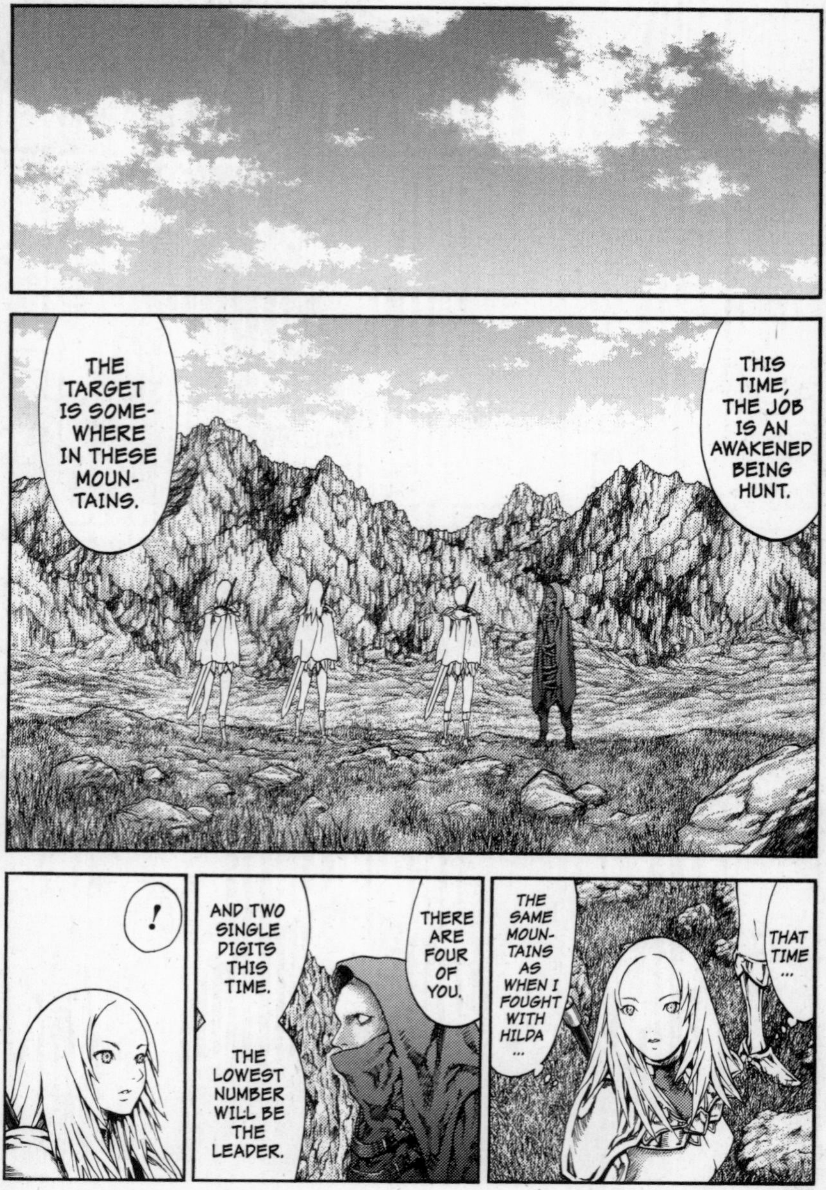
THIS TIME, THE JOB IS AN AWAKENED BEING HUNT.
THE TARGET IS SOME-WHERE IN THESE MOUN-TAINS.
THAT TIME ...
THE SAME MOUN-TAINS AS WHEN I FOUGHT WITH HILDA ...
THERE ARE FOUR OF YOU.
AND TWO SINGLE DIGITS THIS TIME.
THE LOWEST NUMBER WILL BE THE LEADER.
!

READ THIS WAY

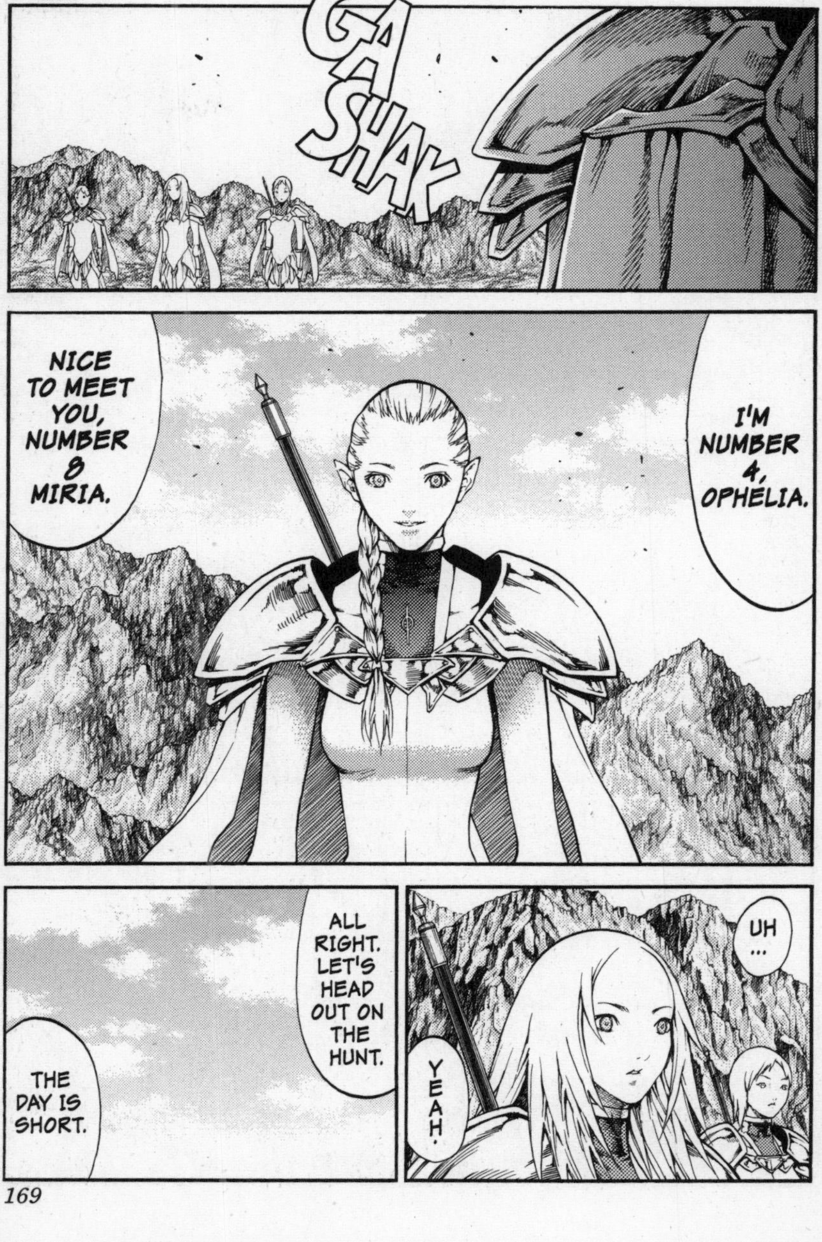
GASHAK
I'M NUMBER 4, OPHELIA.
NICE TO MEET YOU, NUMBER 8 MIRIA.
UH ...
YEAH.
ALL RIGHT. LET'S HEAD OUT ON THE HUNT.
THE DAY IS SHORT.

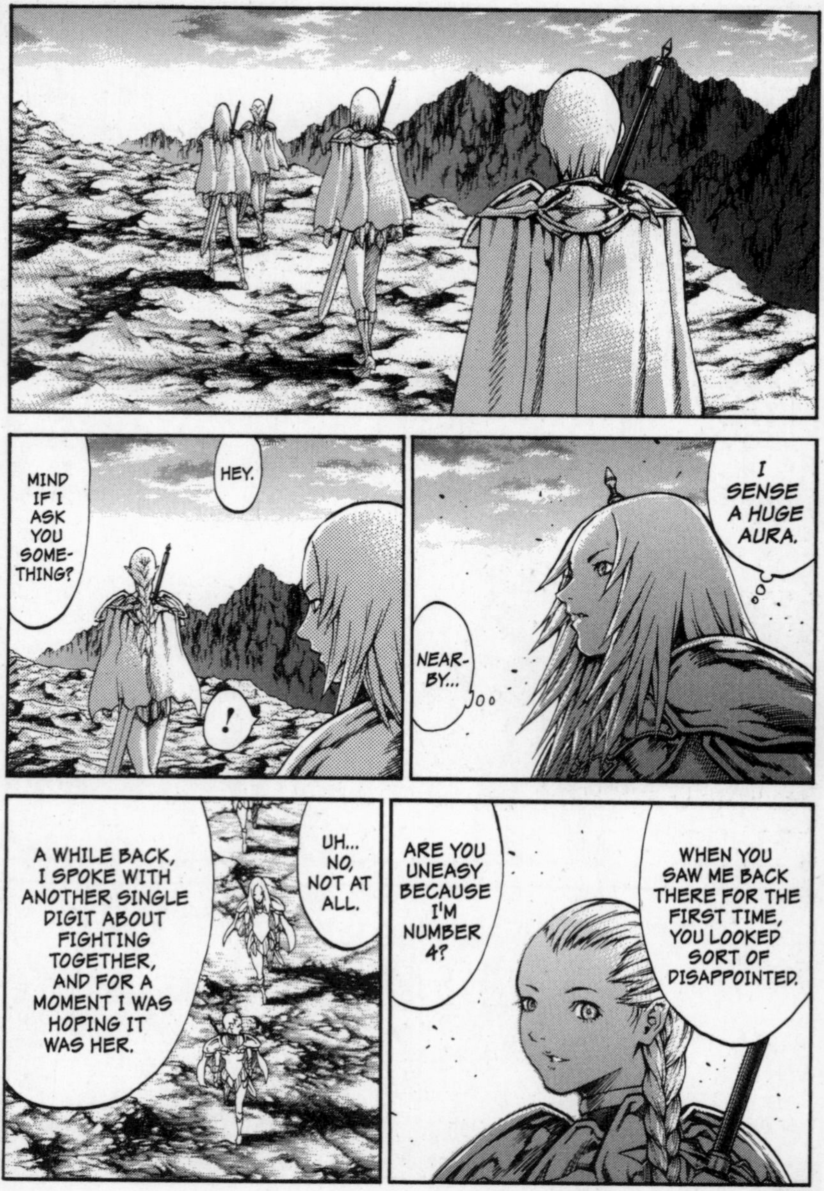
I SENSE A HUGE AURA.
NEARBY...
HEY.
MIND IF I ASK YOU SOMETHING?
!
WHEN YOU SAW ME BACK THERE FOR THE FIRST TIME, YOU LOOKED SORT OF DISAPPOINTED.
ARE YOU UNEASY BECAUSE I'M NUMBER 4?
UH... NO, NOT AT ALL.
A WHILE BACK, I SPOKE WITH ANOTHER SINGLE DIGIT ABOUT FIGHTING TOGETHER, AND FOR A MOMENT I WAS HOPING IT WAS HER.

READ THIS WAY

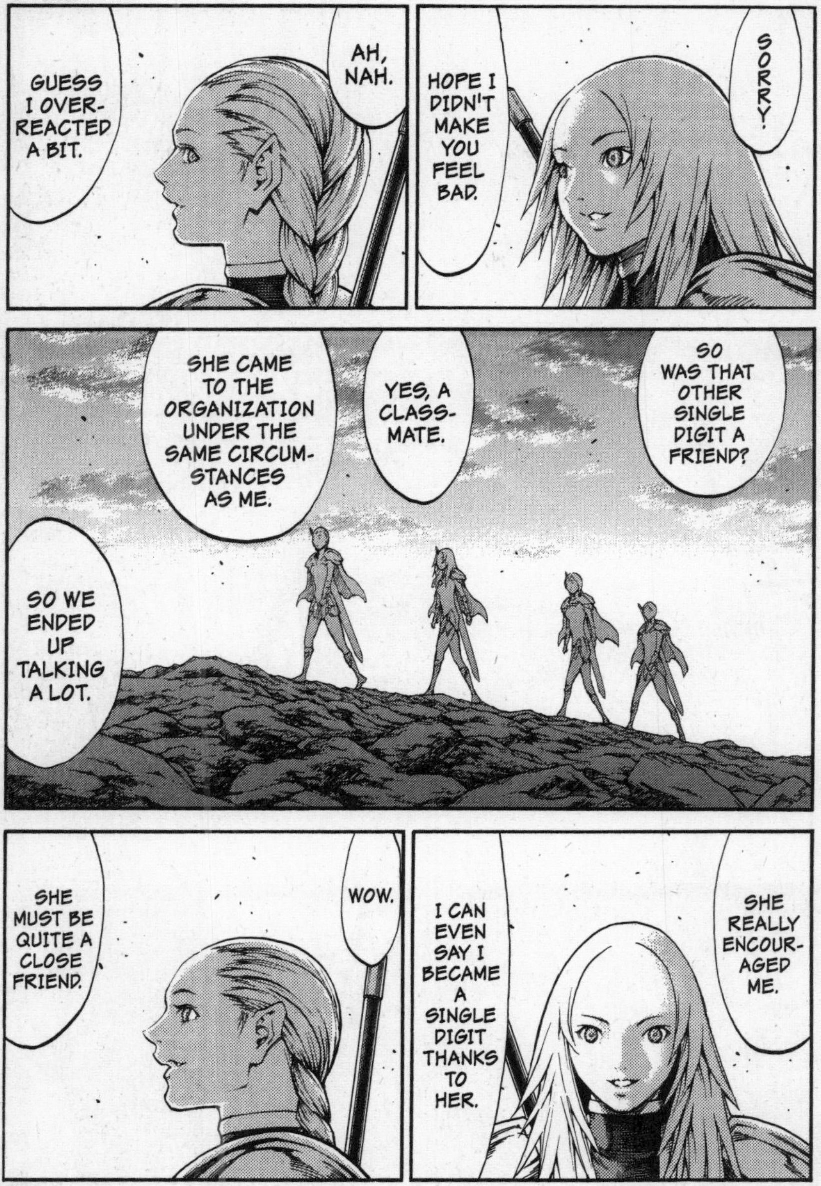
SORRY.
HOPE I DIDN'T MAKE YOU FEEL BAD.
AH, NAH.
GUESS I OVER-REACTED A BIT.
SO WAS THAT OTHER SINGLE DIGIT A FRIEND?
YES, A CLASS-MATE.
SHE CAME TO THE ORGANIZATION UNDER THE SAME CIRCUM-STANCES AS ME.
SO WE ENDED UP TALKING A LOT.
SHE REALLY ENCOUR-AGED ME.
I CAN EVEN SAY I BECAME A SINGLE DIGIT THANKS TO HER.
WOW.
SHE MUST BE QUITE A CLOSE FRIEND.

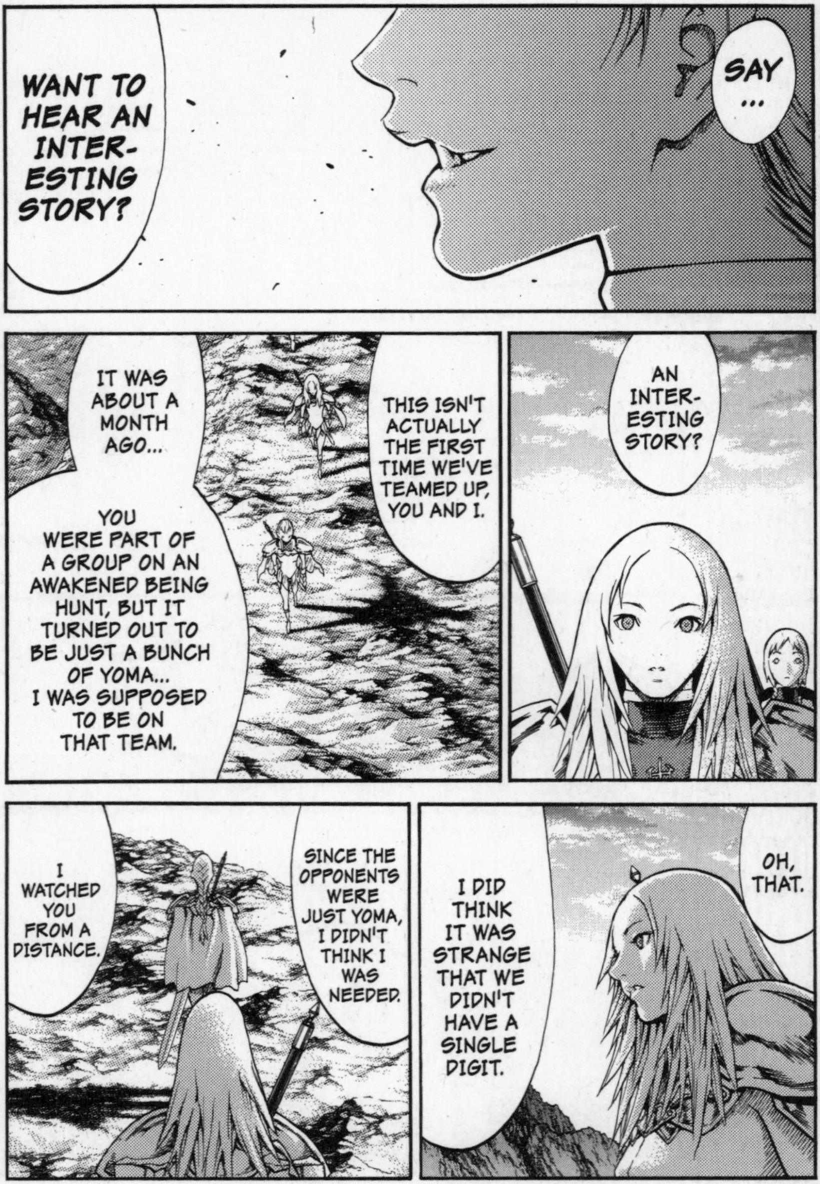
SAY...
WANT TO HEAR AN INTERESTING STORY?
AN INTERESTING STORY?
THIS ISN'T ACTUALLY THE FIRST TIME WE'VE TEAMED UP, YOU AND I.
IT WAS ABOUT A MONTH AGO...
YOU WERE PART OF A GROUP ON AN AWAKENED BEING HUNT, BUT IT TURNED OUT TO BE JUST A BUNCH OF YOMA... I WAS SUPPOSED TO BE ON THAT TEAM.
OH, THAT.
I DID THINK IT WAS STRANGE THAT WE DIDN'T HAVE A SINGLE DIGIT.
SINCE THE OPPONENTS WERE JUST YOMA, I DIDN'T THINK I WAS NEEDED.
I WATCHED YOU FROM A DISTANCE.

READ THIS WAY

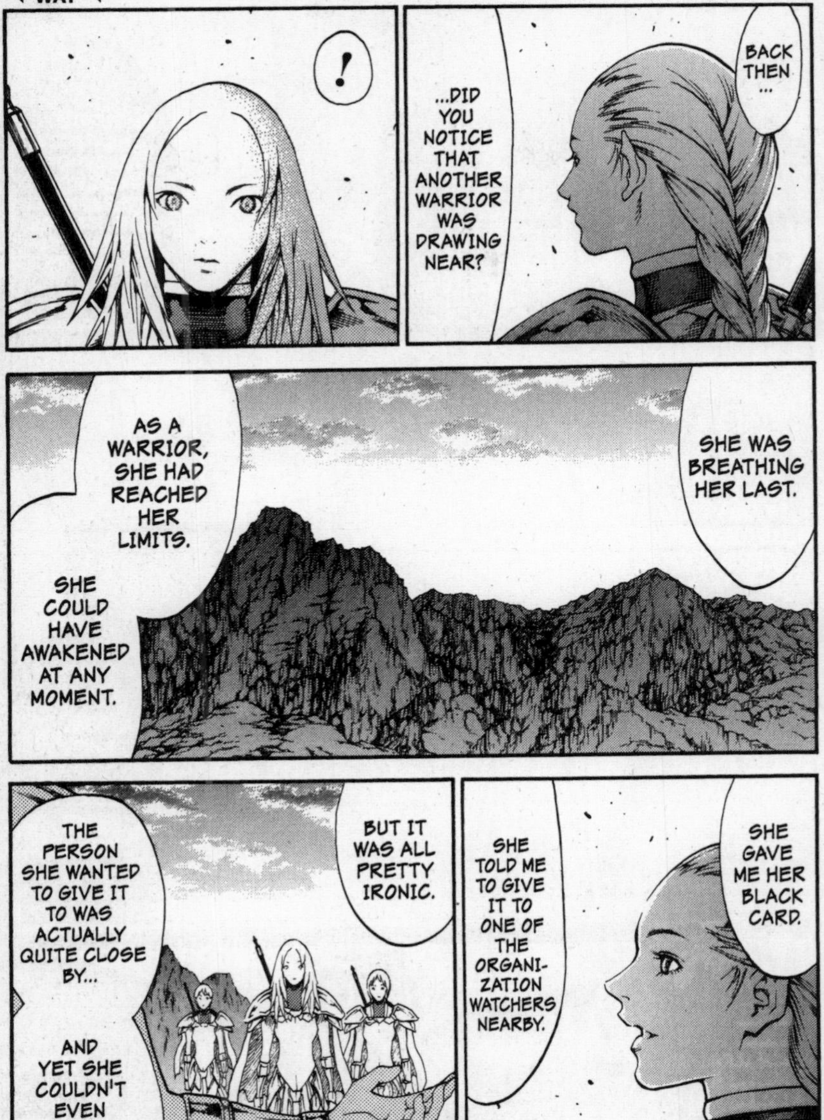
BACK THEN...
...DID YOU NOTICE THAT ANOTHER WARRIOR WAS DRAWING NEAR?
!
SHE WAS BREATHING HER LAST.
AS A WARRIOR, SHE HAD REACHED HER LIMITS.
SHE COULD HAVE AWAKENED AT ANY MOMENT.
SHE GAVE ME HER BLACK CARD.
SHE TOLD ME TO GIVE IT TO ONE OF THE ORGANI-ZATION WATCHERS NEARBY.
BUT IT WAS ALL PRETTY IRONIC.
THE PERSON SHE WANTED TO GIVE IT TO WAS ACTUALLY QUITE CLOSE BY...
AND YET SHE COULDN'T EVEN SENSE HER AURA.

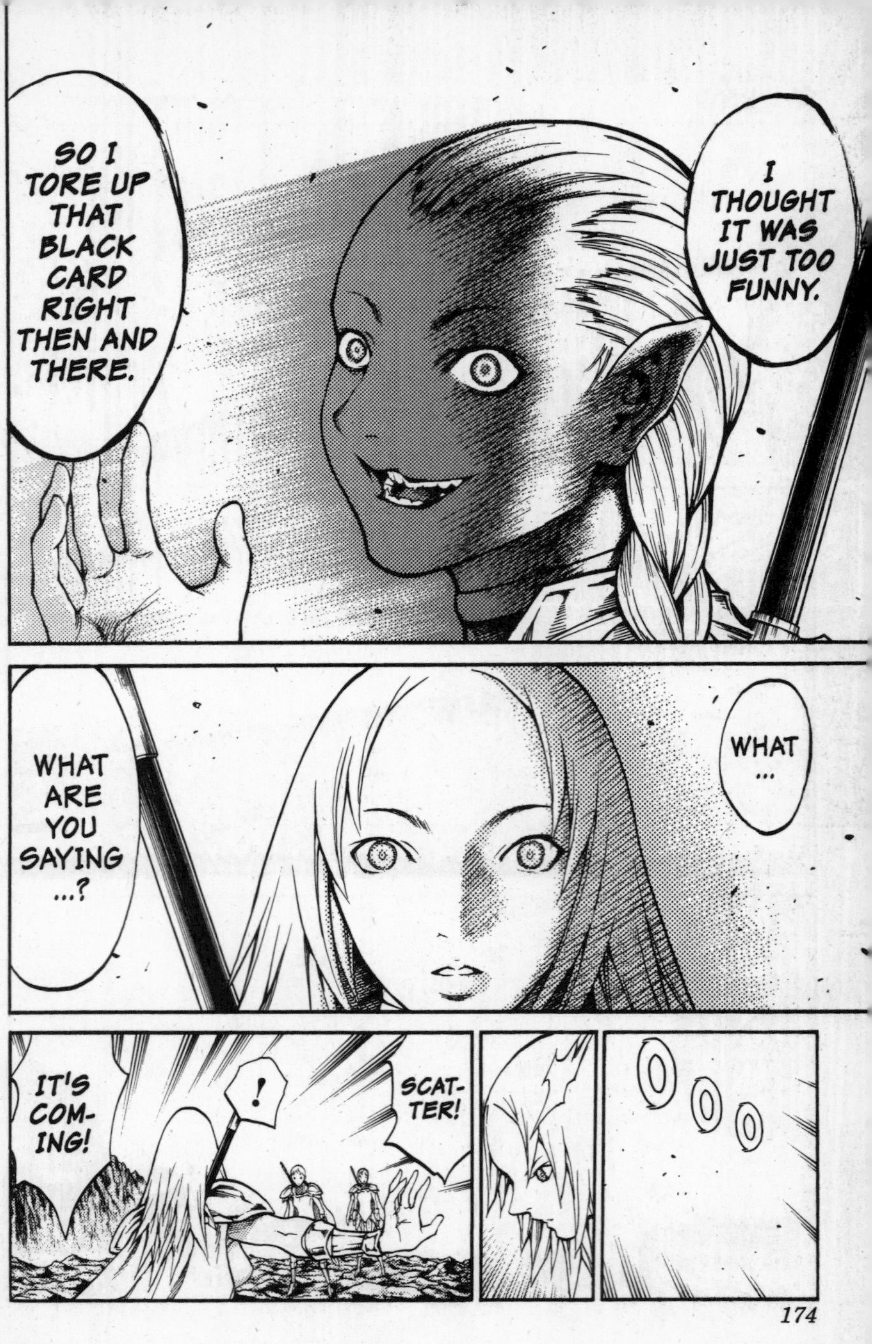
I THOUGHT IT WAS JUST TOO FUNNY.
SO I TORE UP THAT BLACK CARD RIGHT THEN AND THERE.
WHAT ...
WHAT ARE YOU SAYING ...?
SCAT-TER!
!
IT'S COM-ING!

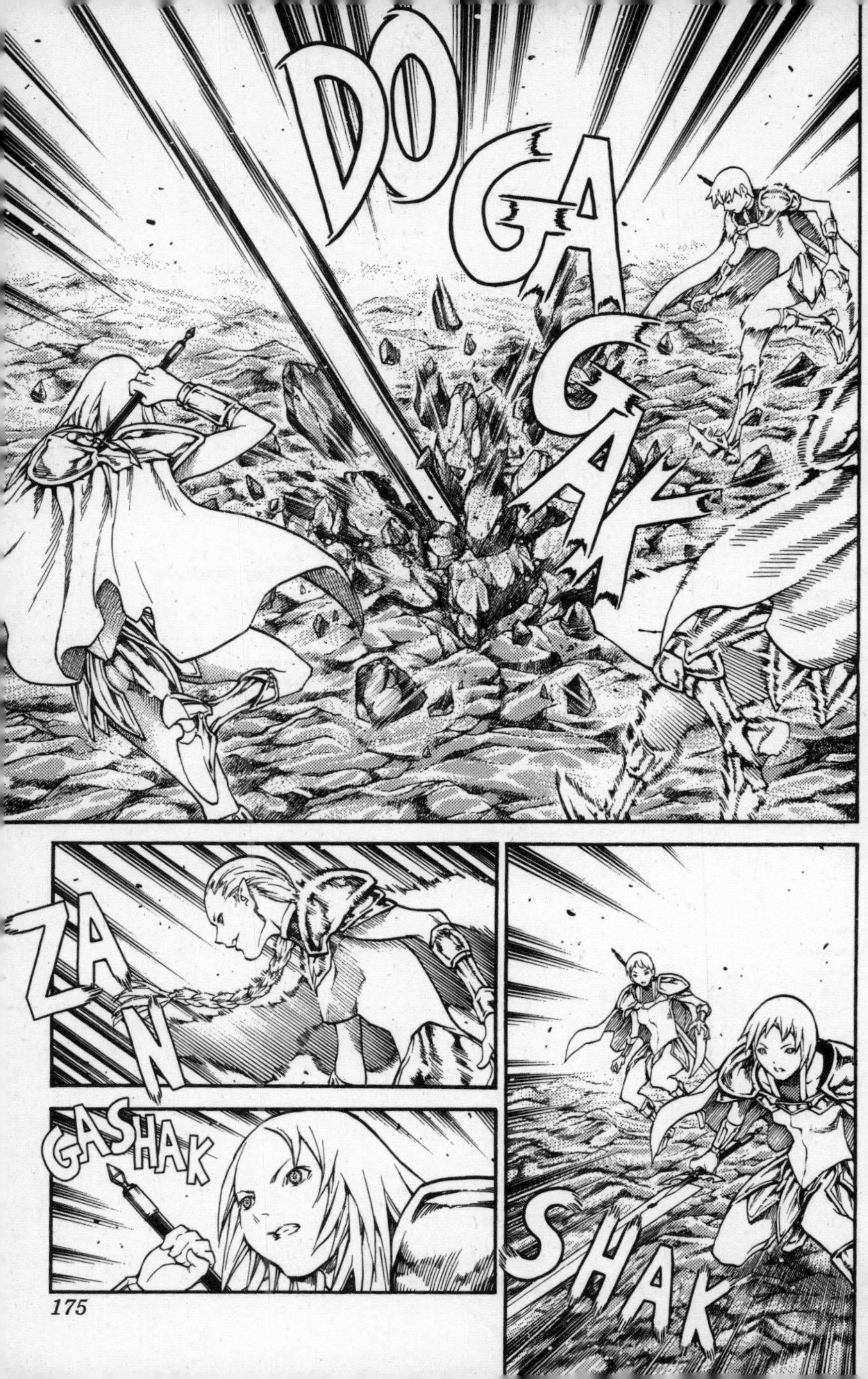
DOGAGAK
SHAK
ZAN
GASHAK

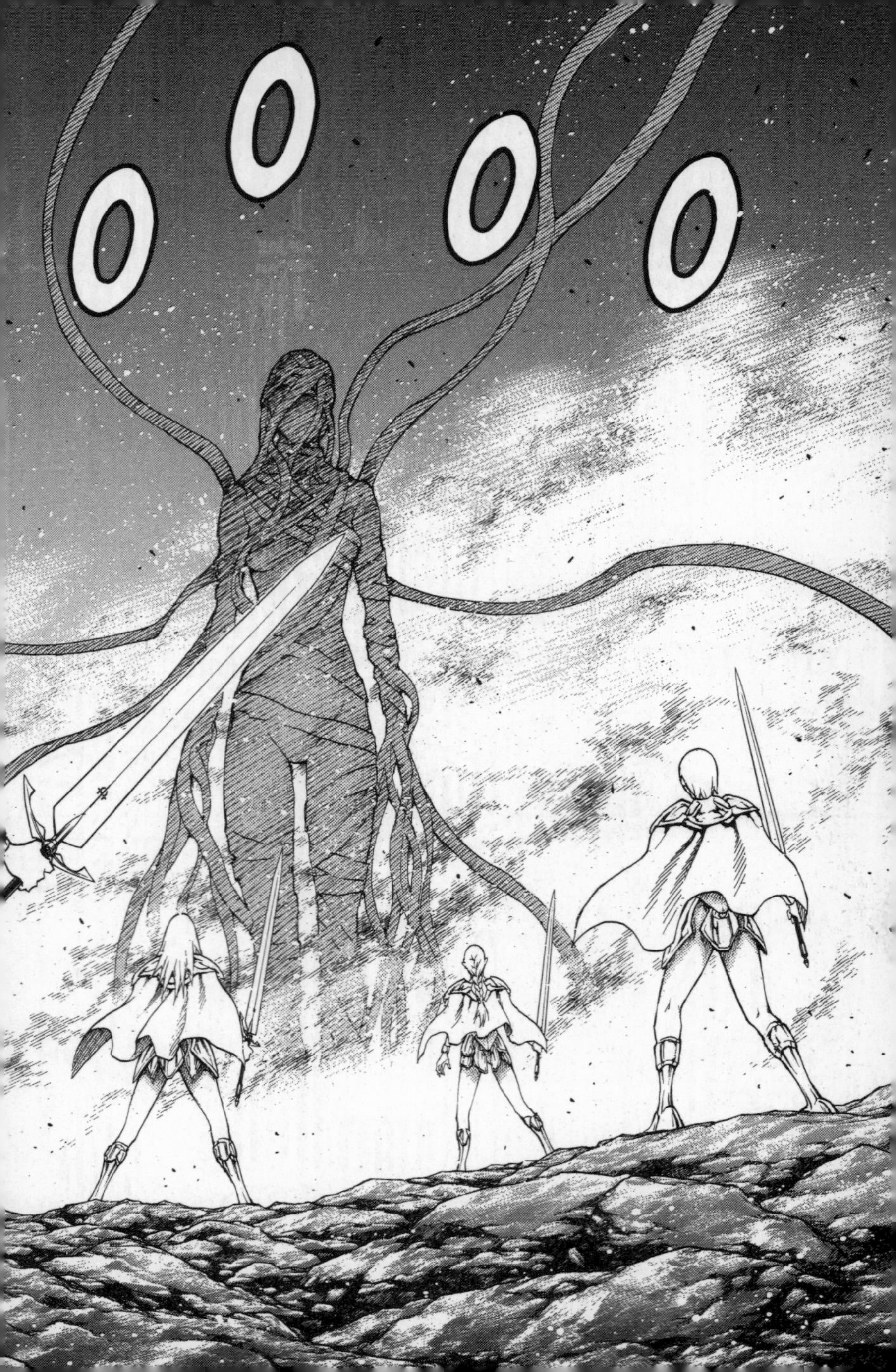

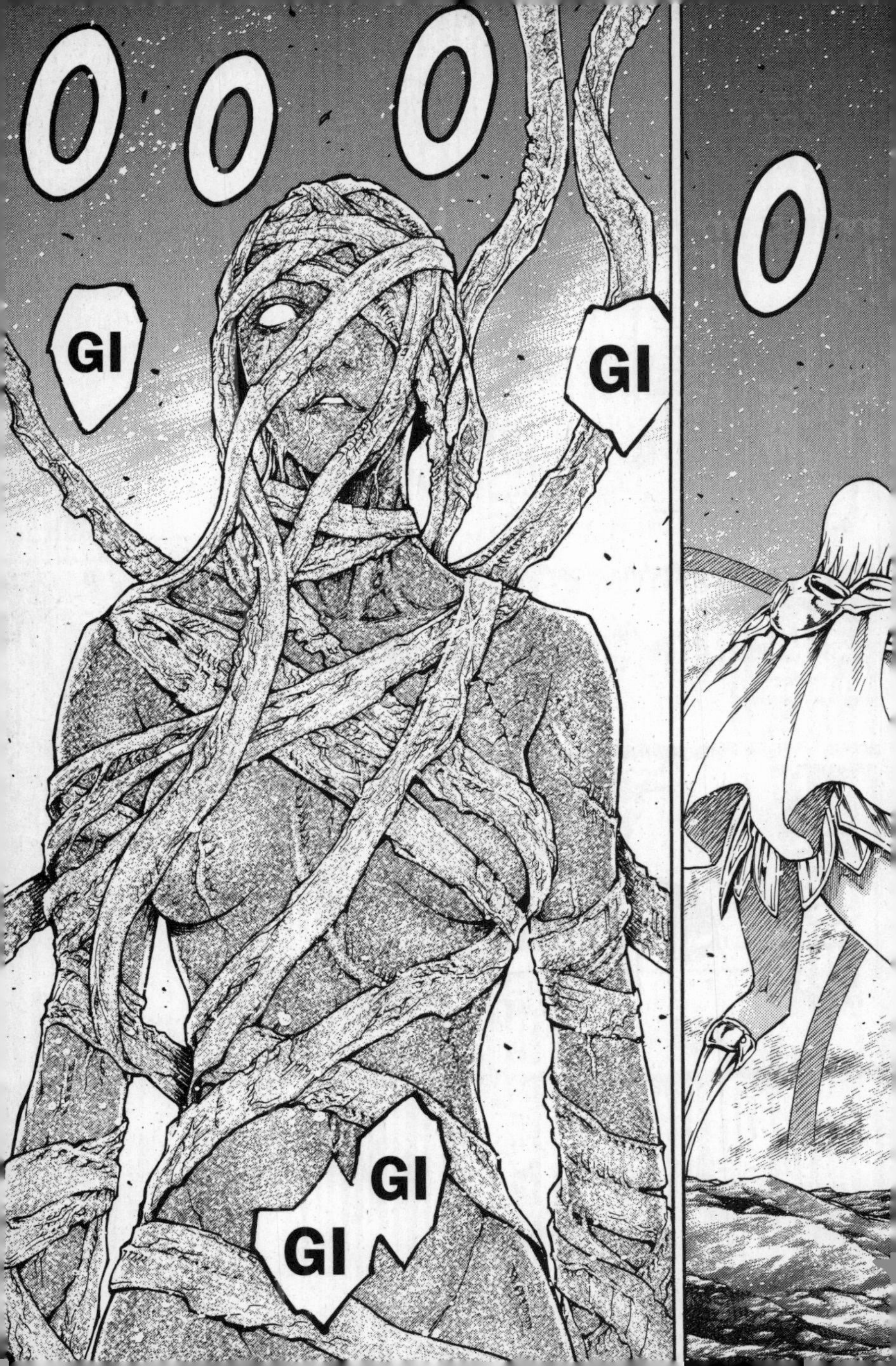
O
OOO
GI
GI
GI
GI

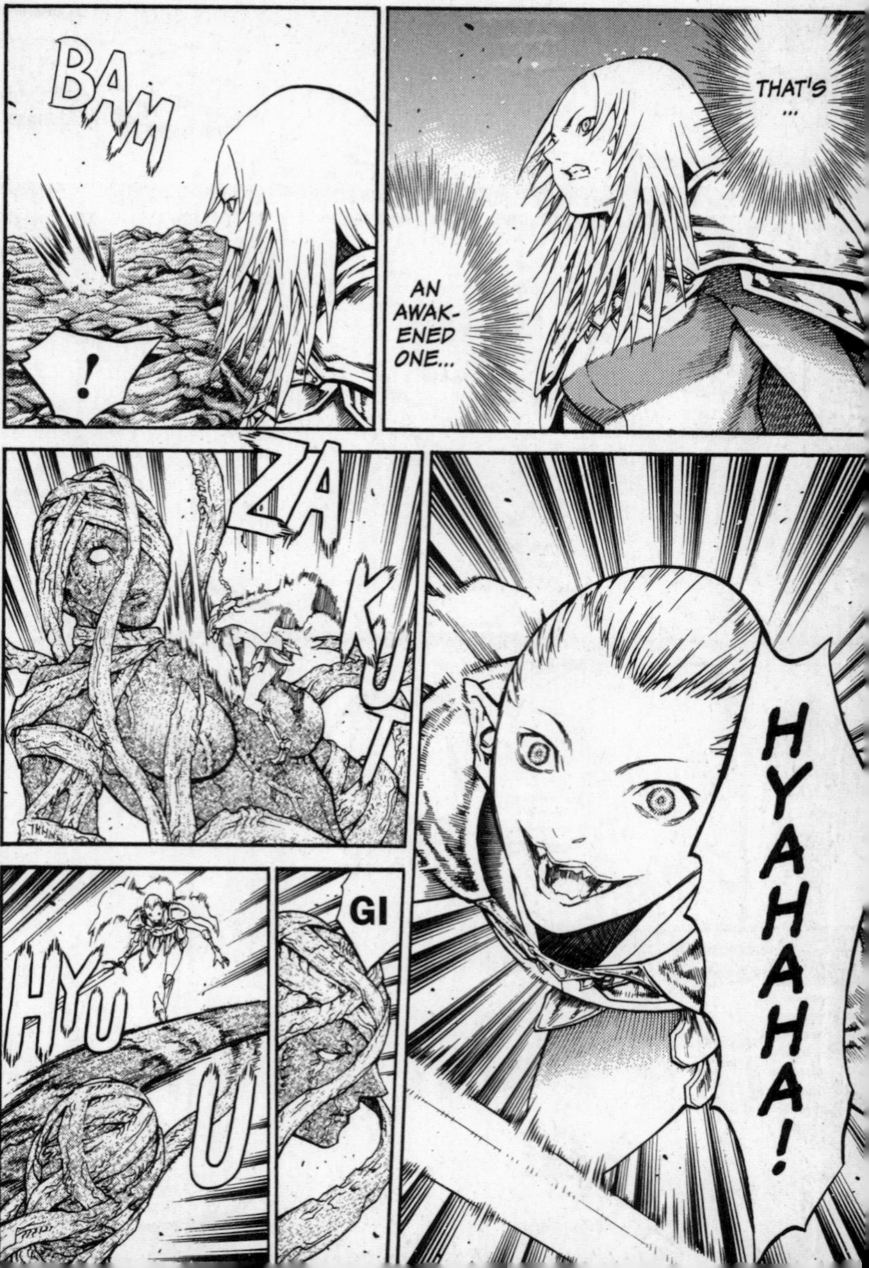
THAT'S ...
AN AWAK-ENED ONE...
BAM
!
HYAHAHA!
ZAKUT
GI
HYUU

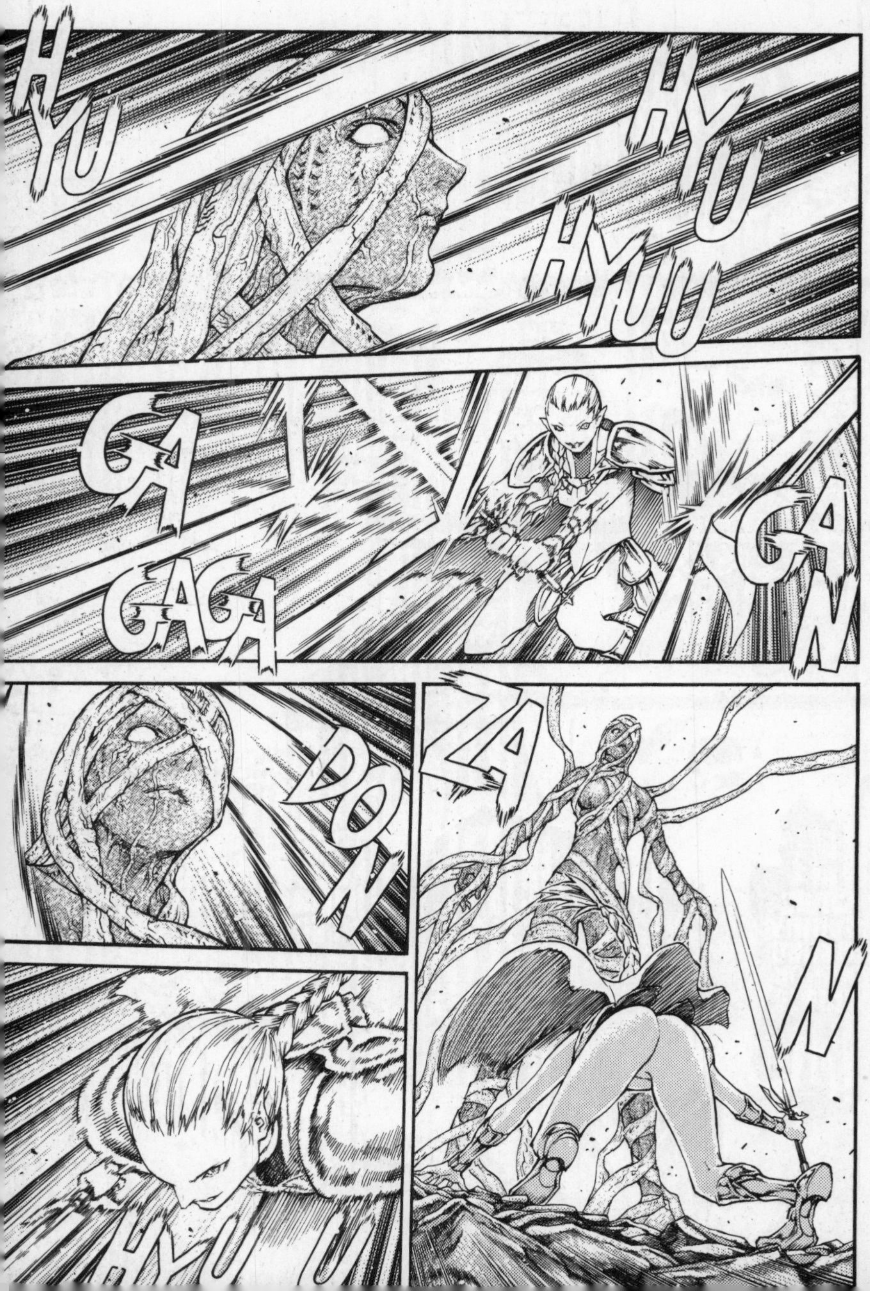
HYU
HYU
HYUU
HYU
GAN
GA
GAGA
ZA
N
DO
DON

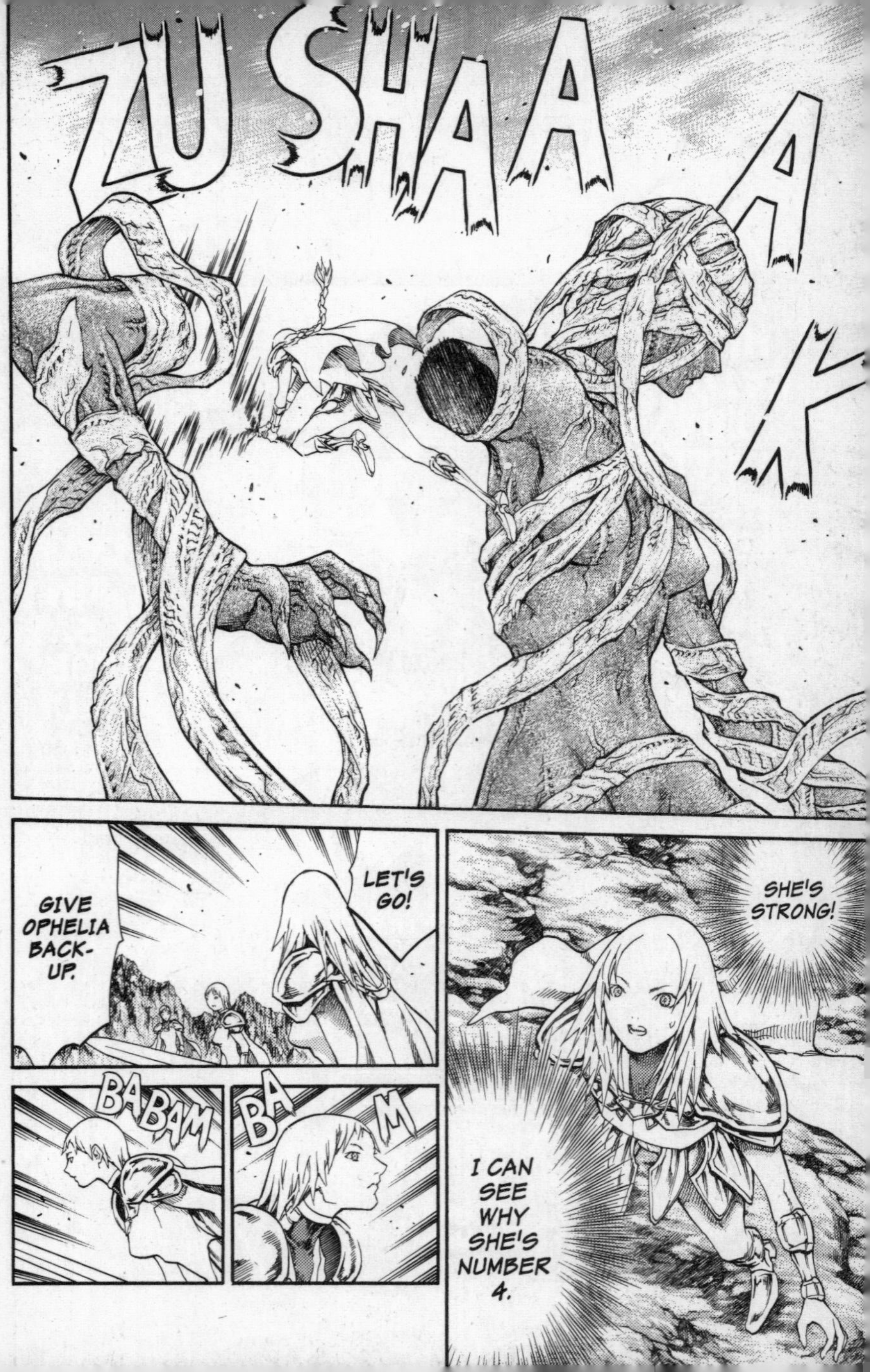
ZUSHAAAK
SHE'S STRONG!
I CAN SEE WHY SHE'S NUMBER 4.
LET'S GO!
GIVE OPHELIA BACK-UP.
BAM
BABAM

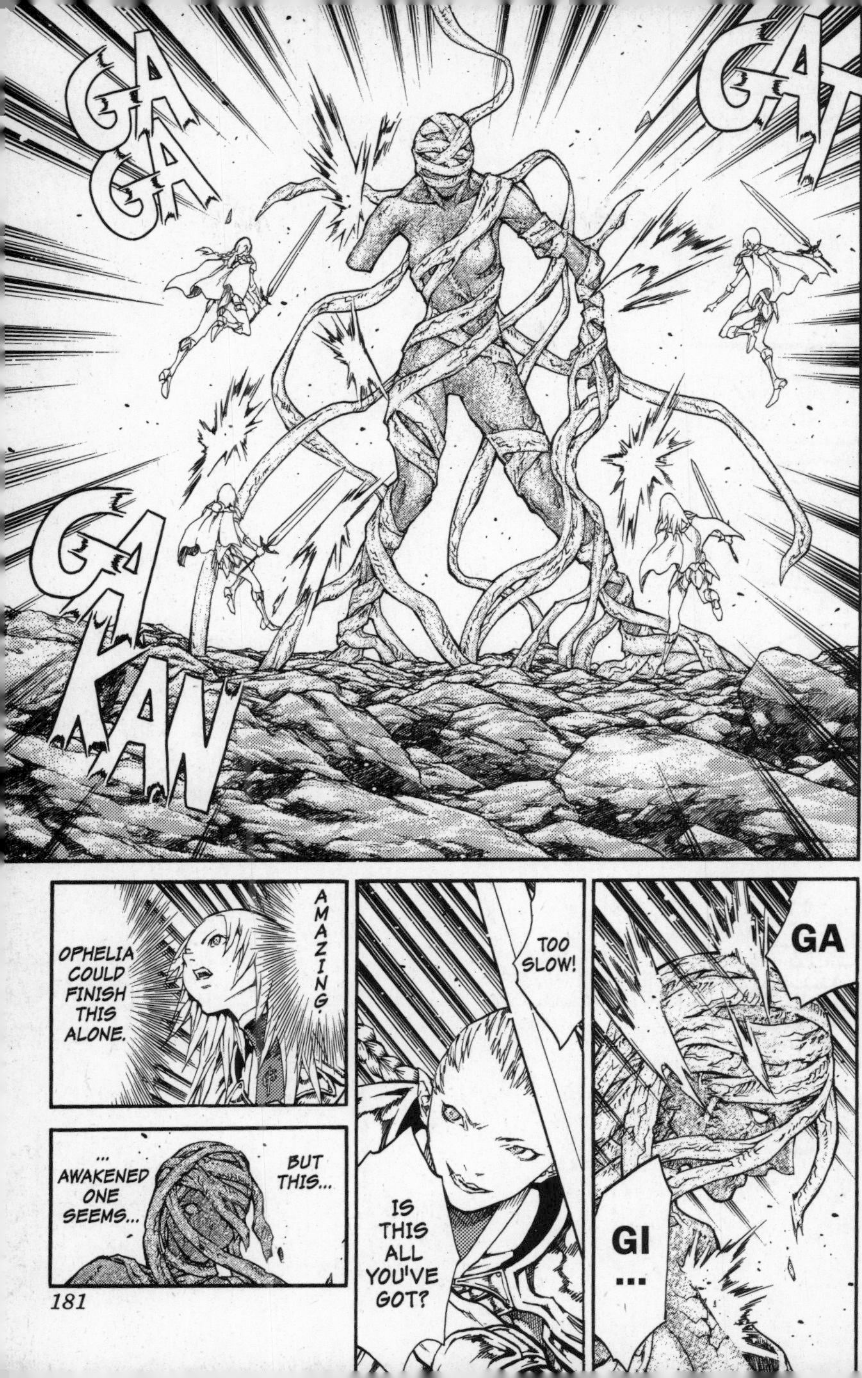
GAT
GAGAGA
GAKAN
GA
GI...
TOO SLOW!
IS THIS ALL YOU'VE GOT?
AMAZING.
OPHELIA COULD FINISH THIS ALONE.
BUT THIS...
...AWAKENED ONE SEEMS...

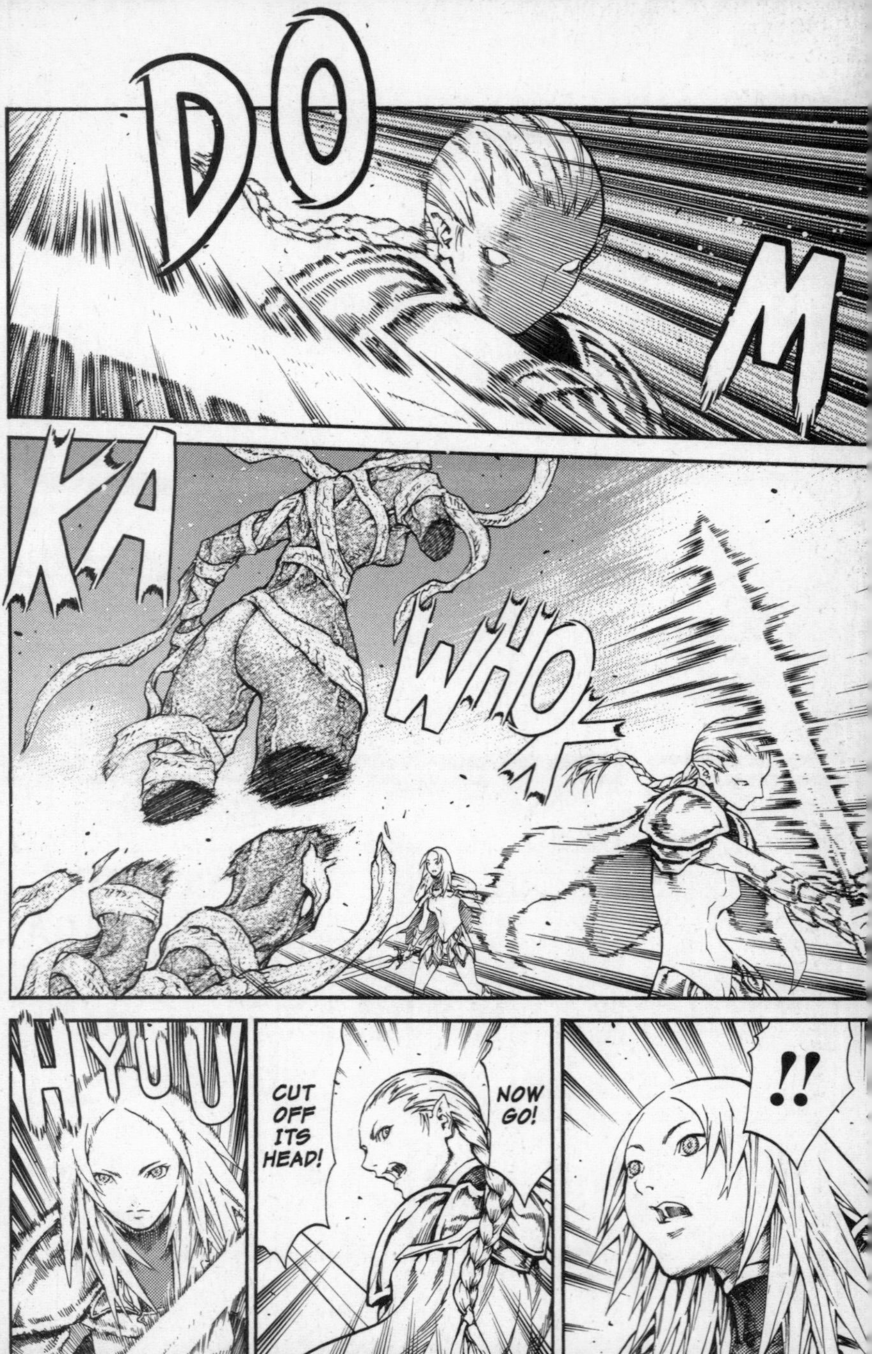
DO
M
WHOK
KA
!!
NOW GO!
CUT OFF ITS HEAD!
HYUU

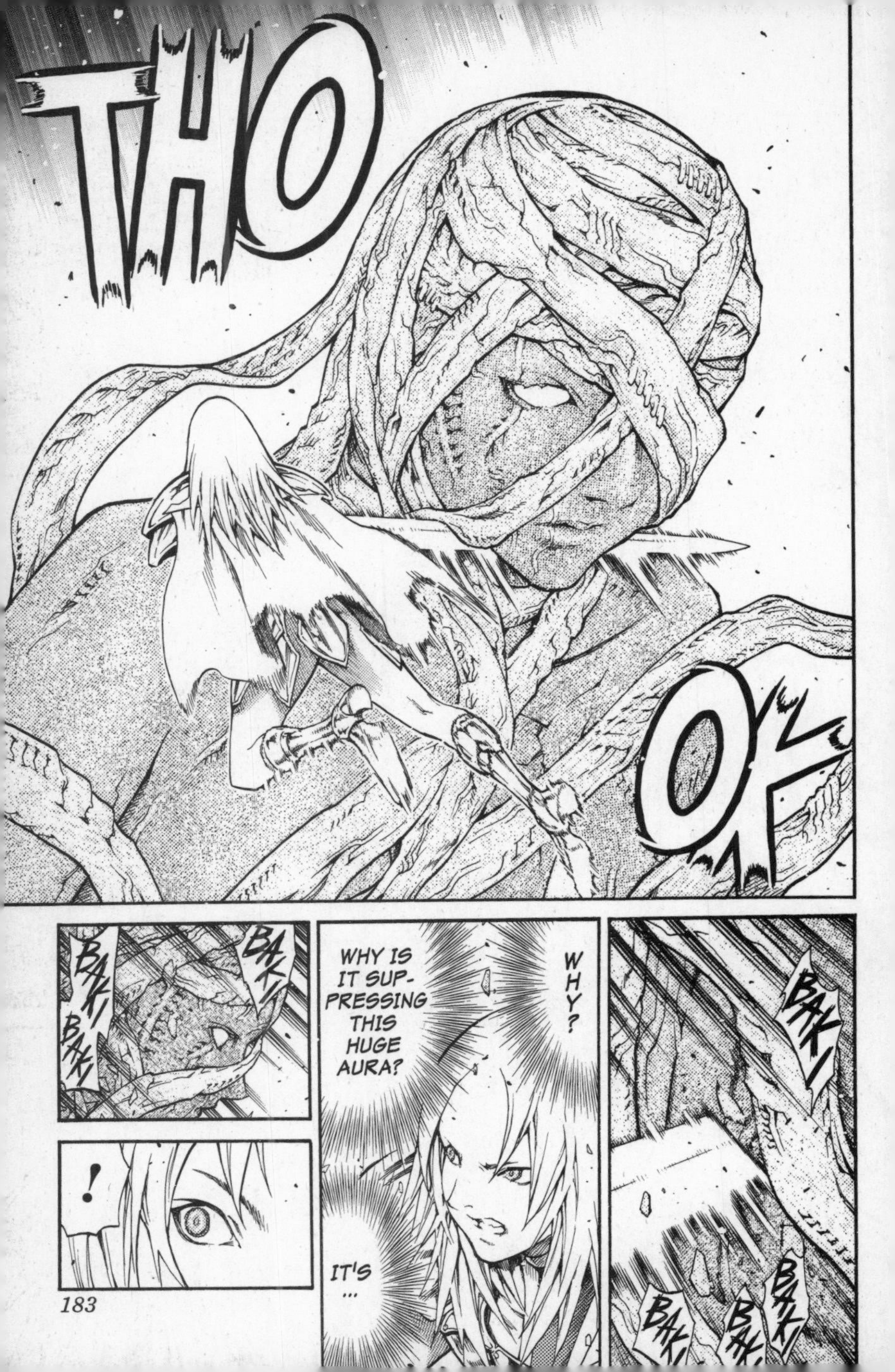
THO
O
BAKI
BAKI
BAKI
BAKI
WHY?
WHY IS IT SUP-PRESSING THIS HUGE AURA?
IT'S ...
BAKI
BAKI
BAKI
!

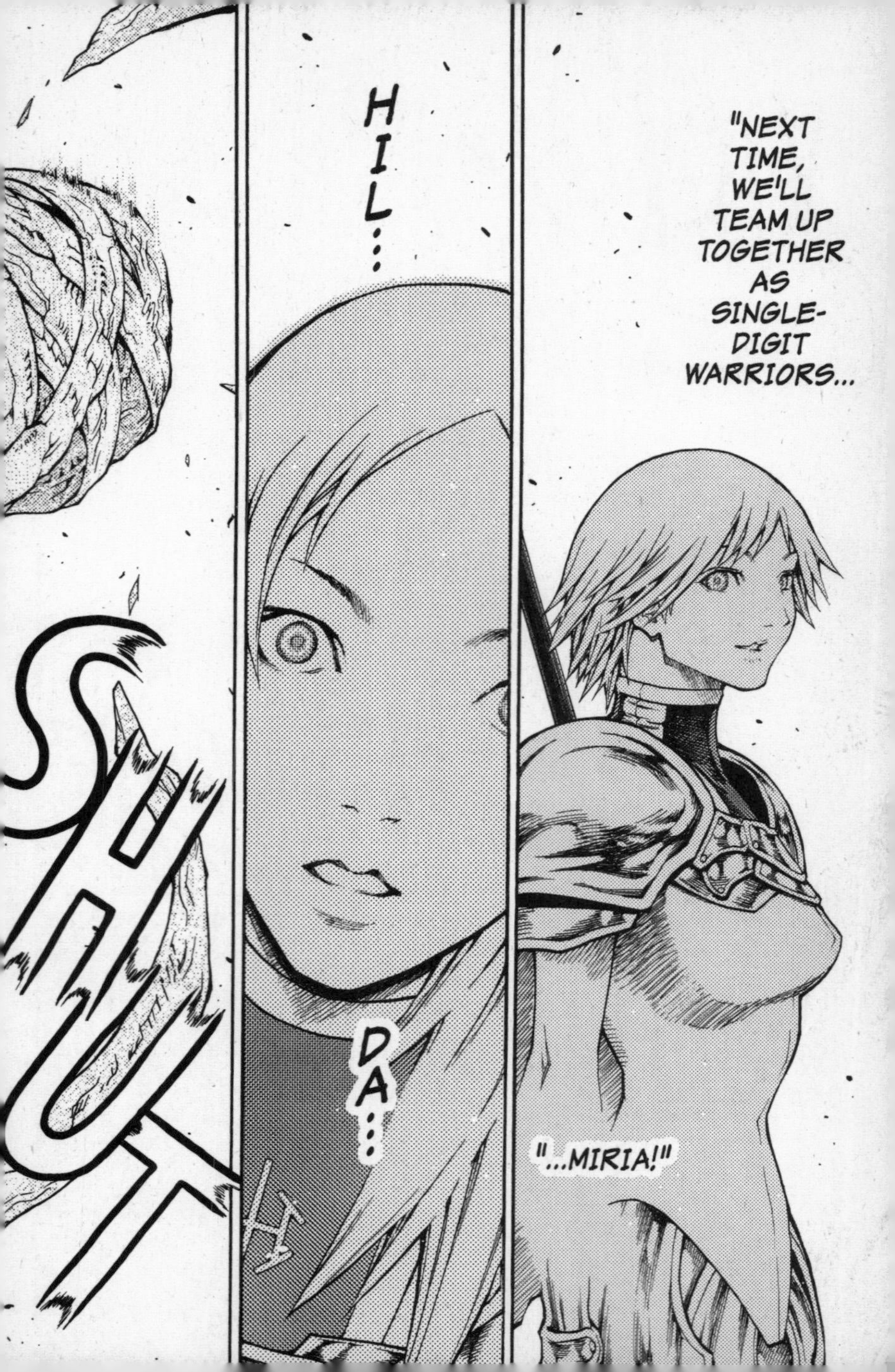
"NEXT TIME, WE'LL TEAM UP TOGETHER AS SINGLE-DIGIT WARRIORS...
"...MIRIA!"
HIL...
DA...
SHUT

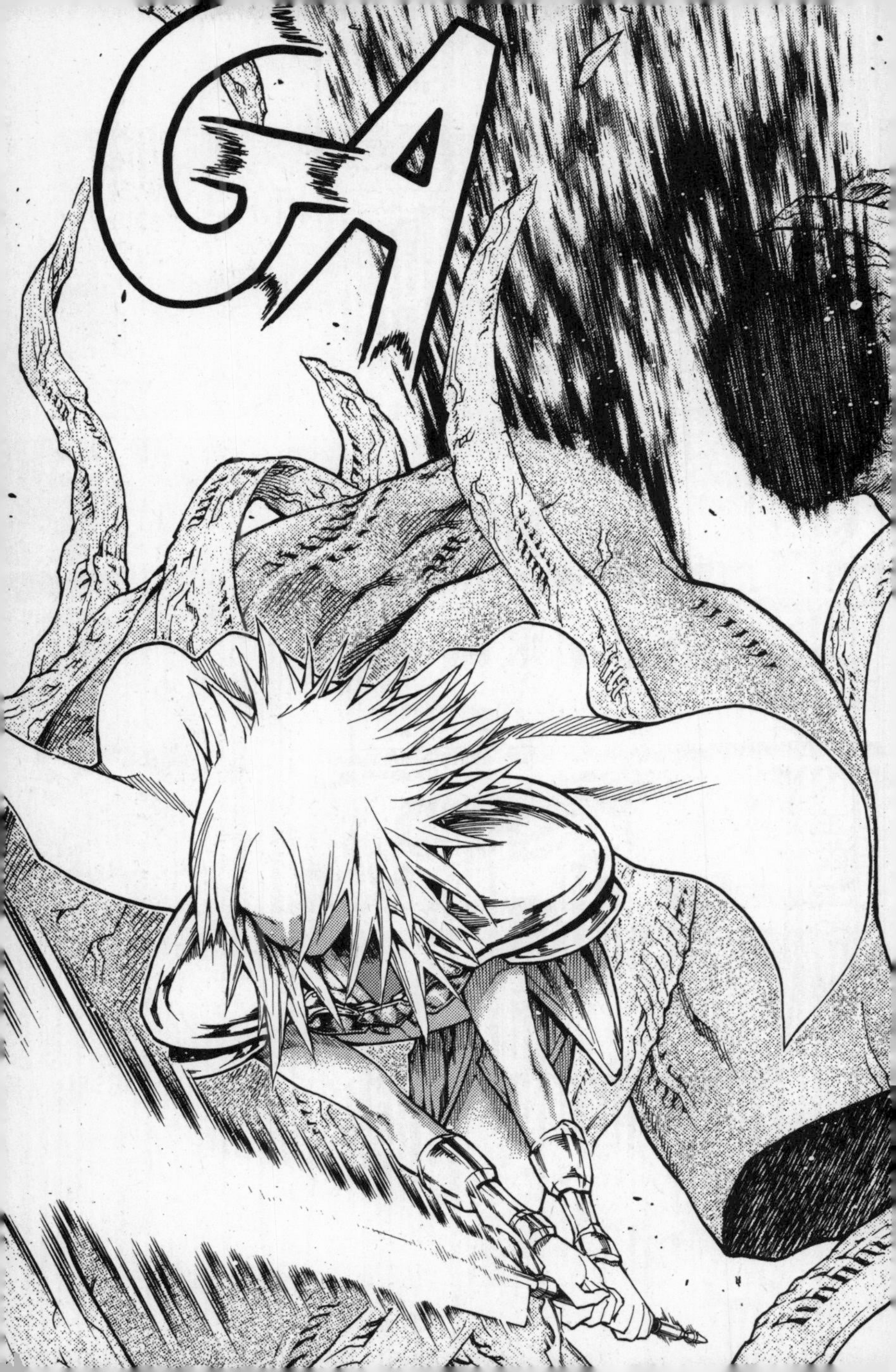
GA

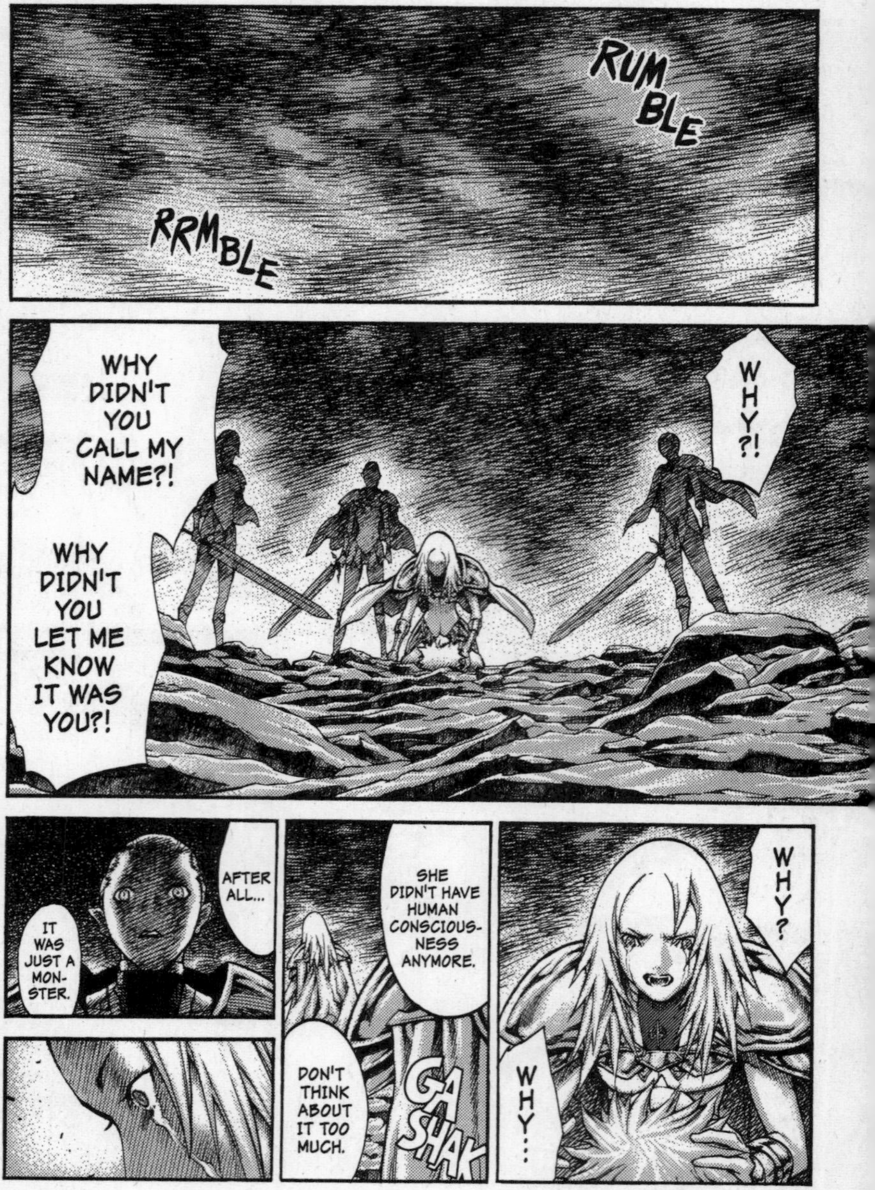
RUMBLE
RRMBLE
WHY?!
WHY DIDN'T YOU CALL MY NAME?!
WHY DIDN'T YOU LET ME KNOW IT WAS YOU?!
WHY?
WHY...
SHE DIDN'T HAVE HUMAN CONSCIOUS-NESS ANYMORE.
GASHAK
DON'T THINK ABOUT IT TOO MUCH.
AFTER ALL...
IT WAS JUST A MON-STER.

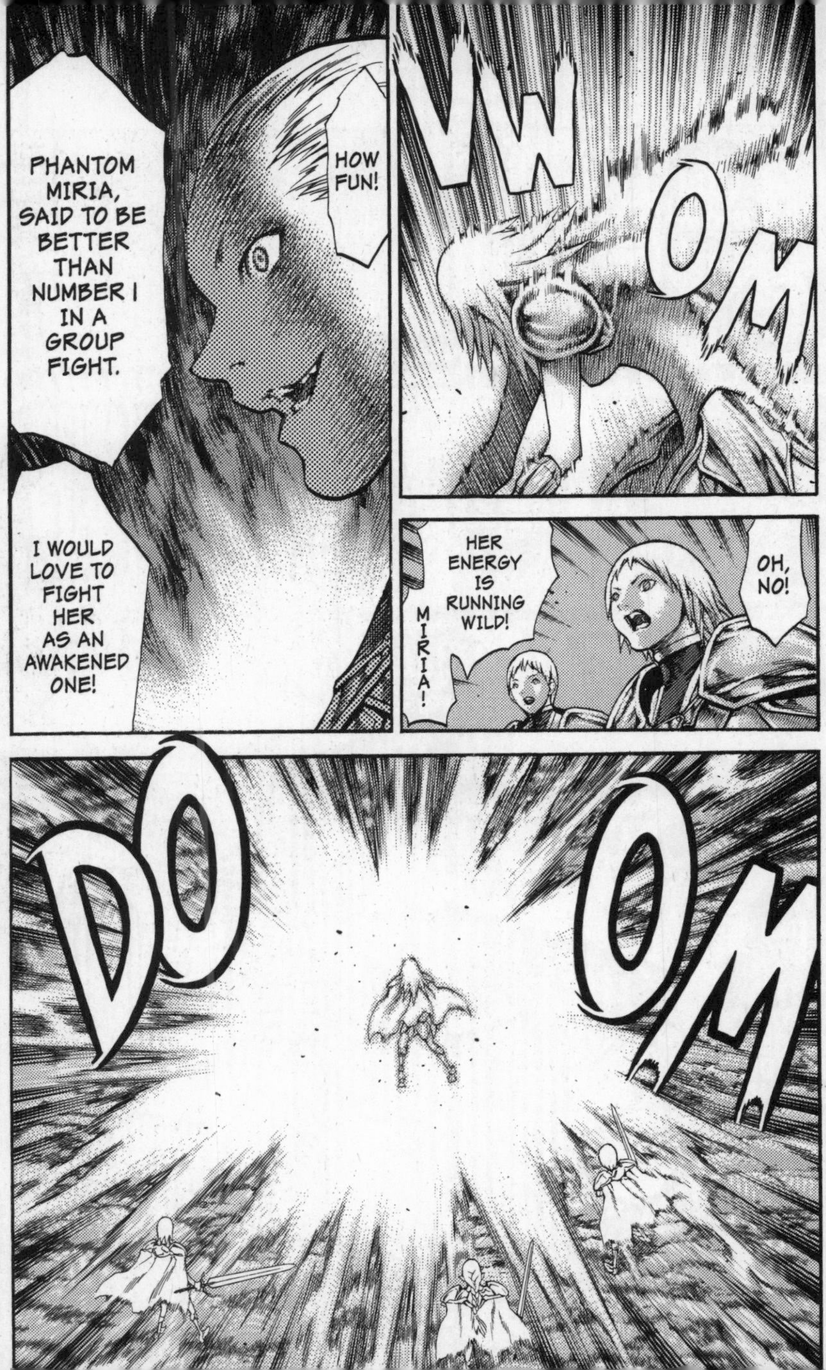
VWOOM
OH, NO!
HER ENERGY IS RUNNING WILD!
MIRIA!
HOW FUN!
PHANTOM MIRIA, SAID TO BE BETTER THAN NUMBER 1 IN A GROUP FIGHT.
I WOULD LOVE TO FIGHT HER AS AN AWAKENED ONE!
DOOM

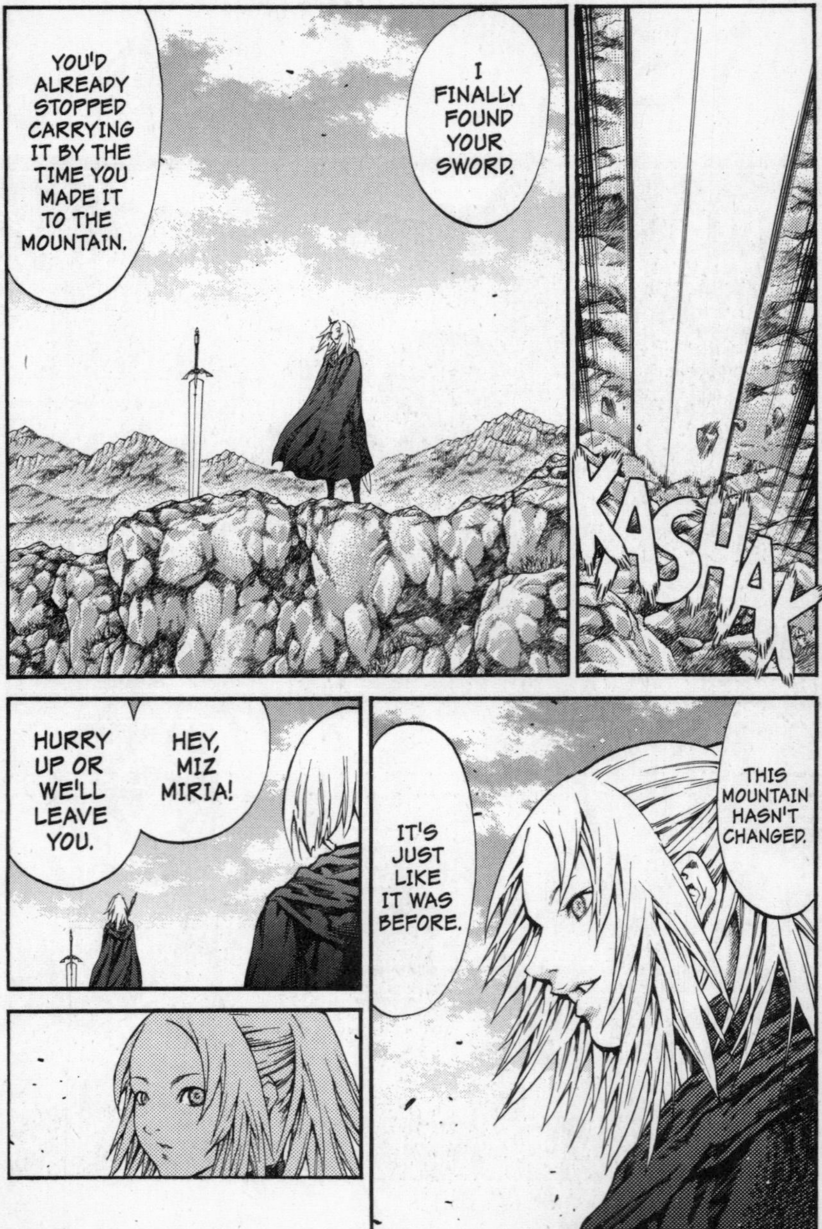
KASHAK
I FINALLY FOUND YOUR SWORD.
YOU'D ALREADY STOPPED CARRYING IT BY THE TIME YOU MADE IT TO THE MOUNTAIN.
THIS MOUNTAIN HASN'T CHANGED.
IT'S JUST LIKE IT WAS BEFORE.
HEY, MIZ MIRIA!
HURRY UP OR WE'LL LEAVE YOU.

READ THIS WAY

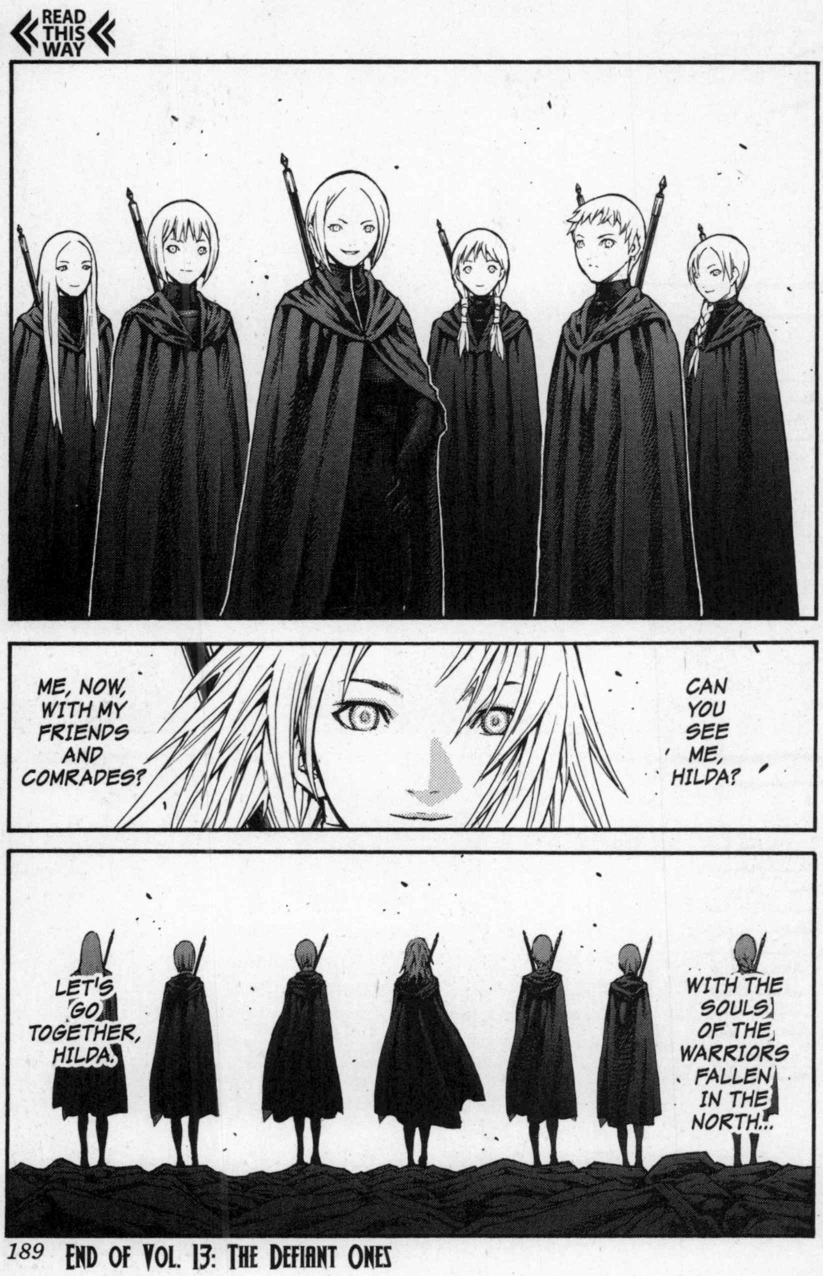
CAN YOU SEE ME, HILDA?
ME, NOW, WITH MY FRIENDS AND COMRADES?
WITH THE SOULS OF THE WARRIORS FALLEN IN THE NORTH...
LET'S GO TOGETHER, HILDA.

 End of Vol. 13: The Defiant Ones

IN THE NEXT VOLUME

Continuing their hunt for Galatea, the Organization's former number 3, Clarice and Miata enter the Holy City of Rabona. However, what they encounter there is something far beyond what they anticipated. Also included are bonus stories of Priscilla and Isley's first meeting, and of Clare's training at the Organization.

Available in March 2009